PROFILES IN CORRUPTION

ALSO BY PETER SCHWEIZER

Secret Empires: How the American Political Class Hides Corruption and Enriches Family and Friends

Clinton Cash: The Untold Story of How and Why Foreign Governments and Businesses Helped Make Bill and Hillary Rich

Extortion: How Politicians Extract Your Money, Buy Votes, and Line Their Own Pockets

Throw Them All Out: How Politicians and Their Friends Get Rich off Insider Stock Tips, Land Deals, and Cronyism That Would Send the Rest of Us to Prison

Architects of Ruin: How Big Government Liberals Wrecked the Global Economy— and How They Will Do It Again If No One Stops Them

Landmark Speeches of the American Conservative Movement (with Wynton Hall)

The Reagan Presidency: Assessing the Man and His Legacy (with Paul Kengor)

Do as I Say (Not as I Do): Profiles in Liberal Hypocrisy

The Bushes: Portrait of a Dynasty (with Rochelle Schweizer)

Reagan's War: The Epic Story of His Forty-Year Struggle and Final Triumph over Communism

Disney: The Mouse Betrayed (with Rochelle Schweizer)

Victory: The Reagan Administration's Secret Strategy that Hastened the Collapse of the Soviet Union

PROFILES IN CORRUPTION

Abuse of Power by America's
Progressive Elite

PETER SCHWEIZER

HARPER

NEW YORK · LONDON · TORONTO · SYDNEY

HARPER

FIRST HARPER PAPERBACKS EDITION PUBLISHED 2021.

Library of Congress Cataloging-in-Publication Data has been applied for.

ISBN 978-0-06-289793-0 (pbk.)

21 22 23 24 25 LSC   10 9 8 7 6 5 4 3 2 1

For my mom, Kerstin Schweizer

CONTENTS

PROFILES IN CORRUPTION

THE CRANNIED WALL

I t is often the small acts of corruption that herald the giant ones to follow.

Taken on their own, Bill and Hillary Clinton's little corruptions while he was Arkansas attorney general and governor might have seemed like no big deal. Hillary got favorable treatment from commodity traders and she made almost $100,000 trading cattle futures.[1] Leveraged power also got them cut in on a little real estate deal called Whitewater.[2] Yet, now we can see how these small liberties fit a pattern of using public power for personal gain, the scope of which has been limited only by the influence of the public office they held.

By the time they achieved national power in Washington, the size and scope of their corruptions began to snowball. In the waning days of his White House tenure, Bill Clinton infamously pardoned billionaire fugitive Marc Rich, who had donated to his campaign.[3] As Hillary Clinton joined the U.S. Senate and then served as secretary of state in the Obama administration, they cranked up the pay-to-play operation known as the Clinton Foundation. For those who still doubt the corrupt nature of the Clinton Foundation, they should examine the internal review done of the foundation at the request of Chelsea Clinton by the law firm Simpson Thacher, publicly available courtesy of the leaked emails of Clinton campaign chairman, John Podesta.

The review discovered that high-dollar donors to the foundation "may have an expectation of quid pro quo benefits in return for gifts," and that the charity ignored conflict of interest guidelines.[4] There is also the stunning change in the fortunes of the Clinton Foundation following Hillary Clinton's loss in the 2016 election. While the Clintons now had more time than ever to raise money from foreign and domestic sources for their foundation, donations plummeted dramatically. Hillary Clinton's first year as secretary of state coincided with the foundation raising $249 million; in 2017, the year after her loss, it managed to raise only $38.4 million. Anyone who does not see the connection between the Clintons' official government power and their ability to raise money overseas is clearly not paying attention.[5]

Then of course, there was the moving of her entire email communication system onto a private server to avoid compliance with the Freedom of Information Act (FOIA) and other federal laws.[6]

As the old saying goes, if you cannot trust someone with a little power, you had better not trust them with a lot. With the Clintons, there were early warning signs that often went unheeded. Today the Clintons are part of American political history, but others are emerging to take their place in the progressive pantheon with their own nascent models of corruption. The challenge now is bringing the latest warning signs to light—and taking them seriously.

Arguably the greatest American political novel, Robert Penn Warren's *All the Kings Men* is set in the Depression-era Deep South. It tells the story of Jack Burden, the scion of a wealthy and influential family with a penchant for history, who becomes the right-hand man to Governor Willie Stark, a charismatic populist. Stark grew up hardscrabble poor and rides into office promising to be a reformer who will make everything right.

But he's also a corrupt blackmailer who leverages his power for his own personal ends.

Burden refers to Stark as "the Boss," an allusion to the fact that Stark has built his political empire through cronyism, corruption, patronage, and intimidation. The Boss wants Burden to investigate one of his fiercest critics, Judge Irwin. The Boss wants dirt on the judge, and he expects Burden to "make it stick." The problem: venerable Judge Irwin is a father figure to Burden; they were very close during his childhood, and Burden is confident that there is no dirt to be found. The Boss disagrees: "Man is conceived in sin and born in corruption, and he passeth from the stink of the didie to the stench of the shroud. *There's always something.*"

Burden does what Stark asks and starts to dig into Judge Irwin's finances. Much to his profound disappointment, he discovers that the Boss is correct: his old family friend is corrupt. He took a bribe. Burden also learns that Judge Irwin is actually his father.

Burden traces the serpentine flow of corporate money to the judge himself, observing what he calls "the flower-in-the-crannied-wall theory."

So I plucked the flower out of its cranny and discovered an astonishing botanical fact. I discovered that its delicate little root, with many loops and kinks, ran all the way to New York City, where it tapped the lush dung heap called Madison Corporation. The flower in the cranny was the Southern Belle Fuel Company. So I plucked another little flower called the American Electric Power Company, and discovered that its delicate little root tapped the same dung heap.[7]

The corrupt facts are exposed. Dishonored and distraught, Judge Irwin commits suicide.

Warren's analogy, a study in contrast between the attractive flower and its dark roots, winding their way in the muck, sustaining the surface beauty, succinctly describes the labyrinthine set of deep relationships enjoyed by some prominent American politicians today. Hidden self- and family-enriching relationships lie beneath the charismatic exterior. While few today would follow the outdated pattern of 1930s bribery, current political figures often benefit from financial ties with special-interest parties that are hard to trace, obscured behind what seems like a rock wall. Tracing those money roots may take much digging, but understanding the flower's, or politician's, ecosystem within "the crannied wall" reveals how they use (or would use) whatever public power is vested in them.

Part of the challenge is first identifying the tie between political power and those with whom they leverage their position. These are the roots behind the crannied wall. Jack Burden calls these "a relationship in time."[8]

Those complex rooted relationships provide the background for how politicians wield power—leverage their position—for their own benefit, or for the benefit of those close to them.

All the King's Men is a study in how politicians can wrap their public acts in the glory of the "public good," while actually leveraging power for themselves. The Boss is the perfect example of the crusading politician who says he wants to change the system—and perhaps even does—but ultimately crusades for his own advancement and that of those close to him.

While many today want to talk about income inequality in America, the larger divide is one of *power inequality*. What makes so many people angry at Washington is the fact that those with political power get to operate by a different set of rules than the rest of us. They use their own levers of power to protect their family and friends from the scales of justice; bail out their failing businesses; steer taxpayer money to them. When they misstep, they are excused or it is covered up. While those with little or no power have to pay for the consequences of their actions, the political class often does not. The power elite—the people who grease the wheels for themselves—are the most disconcerting and dangerous ones.

In my experience, Willie Stark, whom Warren modeled after Louisiana governor Huey P. Long, is often imitated in American politics today, although in a far less crude manner. The Willie Starks of today talk about lifting others up but in fact they use their positions to advance and enrich themselves, their family, and their friends, and do so using methods and deceptions that we generally call corrupt, whether or not the evidence allows legal prosecution.

Let me be clear: there are also true public servants, on both sides of the aisle, who navigate the challenging world of politics with integrity, and for the good of the country. But they appear to be a dying group.

Willie Stark articulates perfectly that corruption is a profound human problem. Public power, and thus influence, makes it tempting to leverage your position for the direct benefit of yourself, family, friends, and those who will keep you there. The greater the public power, the longer the lever arm a politician has to tip the scales.

This book focuses on progressive politicians—not because they alone are vulnerable to corruption—far from it. Clearly, the abuse of political power is a human problem across the full spectrum of political beliefs. But I focus on progressives here because they are unique in one respect from all others on the contemporary American political scene: they all favor the rapid and radical expansion of federal political power in the United States. Whether their goal is to pursue an abstract idea such as economic equality, transform the health care system, or use the judicial system to right social wrongs, progressives are unique in asking citizens to trust government officials with even more power than they currently possess.

In short, progressives are asking us to give them more leverage over our lives. Their policy ideas would dramatically *increase* power inequality in America between the political class and the rest of America.

In contrast to classical liberals, who for centuries have been concerned about the concentration of and abuse of power, progressives have positioned themselves as more concerned with pursuing their goals than exploring the problems that come with misuse of that power. It is one of the great ironies that while modern progressives speak often about the abuse of power by others, they rarely are willing to address the blunt realities that their desire for greater power creates new opportunities for leverage and corruption. Millennial American big government as we know it is already a result of early-twentieth-century progressive reasoning that arose in response to machine politics and corruption in America's major cities and small towns. Progressives, so called for their goal of "progress" out of the dark age of such corruption, theorized that the solution was to increase federal government proportionally to fight existing corruption. For the People, the government would bring Light to such Darkness. And while some corporate darkness was expelled by this theory in action, more was created as the increase in government meant more crannies in which it could hide. More money roots to take hold.

This generation of American progressives again posits Corporate America and its corruptions as the source of American problems, from health care and education, to roads and economic inequalities. They variously claim again that they will fight the darkness of such corporate power with the light of greater power for themselves in Washington.

It therefore seems fair to ask: How have they individually exercised whatever public power they have held so far? Have they been good stewards of their vested power, or have they wielded that saber for personal benefit, including benefits extending to family and friends? What secret entanglements do they hold?

Good stewardship of power is an ethical, not just a legal, standard. Do these progressives honor that standard, or do they operate on the principle of avoiding jail? Good stewardship of power speaks of a commitment to a level playing field, equal opportunities, and equal legal standards—liberty and justice for all—better than any stump speech.

Some of those profiled here have run urban political machines; others have been legislators most of their lives. Some of those profiled here have been in politics less than a decade but have managed to leverage their position with dramatic effect to their own benefit. Others have been on the national stage for decades and have slowly built the capacity to leverage for their family. What follows are not personal biographies. You will not see a discussion of personal matters, their positions on issues, or their votes on bills, except as they relate to their manipulation of the system for their benefit.

Much of what you read in the chapters to follow will be strikingly new. Even those who follow the news are likely to be startled by the fact that the revelations about these figures long in the national spotlight have rarely been mentioned before. How does that happen?

Part of the problem is that political figures have become increasingly masterful at "appearing to be scrutinized without revealing anything significant."[9] We are fed tantalizing trivial matters, but little of investigative substance.

With the growing obsession with the horse race aspect of politics, the media, our so-called Fourth Estate, is also a major culprit. News has become a sporting event, with breathless accounts of who is ahead, who is behind, and what the polls say. "We know from decades of research that the mainstream media tend to see elections through the prism of competition," as one scholar puts it.[10] Horse race political journalism is easier to produce than investigative reporting. You simply interview PR-happy insiders, attend some campaign events and assess crowd size, and check the polls.

As Professor Thomas E. Patterson of the Shorenstein Center notes, "Journalists' focus on the Washington power game—who's up and who's down, who's getting the better of whom—can be a fascinating story but at the end of the day, it's food for political junkies. It's remote enough from the lives of most Americans to convince them that the political system doesn't speak for them, or to them."[11]

Then there is what you might call the Trump Vortex. The media has increasingly become fixated on one political figure: President Donald Trump. Some of the reporting on Trump has been terrific; some of it has been terrible. Either way, the singular focus on Trump creates the false impression that no other prominent politicians have done anything remotely ethically suspect or relevant to the discussion, and thus deserving the light of news coverage.[12]

Make no mistake, Trump, as one of the most powerful people in the world, should be scrutinized by journalists—just not at the expense of failing to investigate other politicians, especially those aspiring to the same job and level of power.

The *Washington Post* reportedly added sixty jobs to its newsroom to cover a variety of beats—but primarily focused on Trump. "The new Trump administration promises great upheaval, conflict and, I'd expect, an unprecedented volume of high-level leaks, some of which will produce eye-opening stories and series," noted Fred Ryan, *Washington Post* CEO and publisher. *Washington Post* associate editor and journalistic legend Bob Woodward explains further, "We have twenty people working on Trump, we're going to do a book, we're doing articles about every phase of his life." [13]

The *New York Times* has likewise committed vast resources to investigating Trump. The *Times*, for example, had three reporters spend more than a year digging through more than 100,000 pages of documents relating to Trump family finances. [14]

What these journalists have not been focusing on is how some of today's best-known political figures have leveraged their connections to benefit themselves, their friends, or their families.

What follows is a series of narratives exploring how America's leading progressives have exercised power during their rise to prominence. It also lays out for the first time many of the entangling alliances that these progressives have with financiers, or even foreign governments. Readers will be surprised to learn, for example, that Elizabeth Warren's son-in-law appears to have financial ties to the Iranian government.

The pathways of these progressives are different, so likewise the conduct exposed in each story is different. Each has a "business model" for leveraging their position and power for personal benefit.

Who benefits from the corruption that follows in the chapters you are about to read? The politicians themselves are often indirect beneficiaries when the benefits go to a family member, close friend, or associate to obscure the corrupt act. Essentially, it boils down to four groups of people: family, friends, donors, and machine patrons.

The methods used also often fall into specific categories. There are the *sweetheart deals* involving family members and friends. The family has long been the pathway that political figures use to route power and benefits for their own self-enrichment. Technically, it is not self-enrichment, but practically speaking, money flow to family increases the wealth of the family estate. International bribery standards are quite clear: money or deals given to a politician's family or close friend in return for a favor is as much a bribe as if the money went straight to the politician. The same must be said for leveraging their position: the politician whose family is given deals is no different from the politician who receives those deals himself. In the chapters that follow, Joe Biden emerges as the king of the sweetheart deal, with no less than five family members benefiting from his largesse, favorable access, and powerful position for commercial gain. In Biden's case, these deals include foreign partners and in some cases even U.S. taxpayer dollars.

Another method is *income generation*, whereby political power translates into a direct revenue stream for political figures or their family members. Elizabeth Warren benefited enormously from the government power she wielded early in her government career to the tune of millions of dollars. And her daughter benefits financially from her proximity to her mother as a powerful U.S. senator. Some of the politicians studied here appear to have family cultures that feel entitled to use political status and power for their own benefit, and relish in the opportunities presented. Sherrod Brown has used his legislative authority to the benefit of his class-action attorney brother, pushing a strange health care agenda that dovetails with his brother's litigation. Los Angeles mayor Eric Garcetti's family has benefited from his ability to approve major real estate projects.

Another powerful form of political corruption involves *bending the law.* Does it seem as if some people get away with everything? Political power can be wielded to create "unequal protection under the law." Some of those profiled here have held elected positions as prosecutors and they have leveraged their power to advance the interests or protect the interests of their powerful friends. Guilty parties, even of serious crimes, go free because of their connections to the politician. This is the *cover-up,* a powerful subset of bending the law.

Other times, the innocent face legal threats because the politician is leveraging their position to extract benefits for themselves. Corruption involving legislation is bad, but the goal of a proposed law might be efficiency, fairness, or some policy goal; it typically involves a group decision. Corruption involving the criminal justice system is potentially far worse. The criminal justice system is supposed to be about equal justice under the law, yet one person can decide the fate of justice by deciding to pursue or ignore a case, or by dropping charges against someone. Prosecutors are given the power to charge or not charge individuals with criminal offenses. Justice that is not blind to a suspect's political connections, financial ties, or other alliances is abuse of power. These charges can include incredibly troubling cases. Kamala Harris, for example, has taken what by many accounts are politically motivated actions that silenced major criminal investigations into child abuse. She also dropped charges against a politically connected contractor whose fraud potentially endangered thousands of people. Under Harris, the corporate clients of her husband's law firm avoid legal scrutiny. To a lesser extent, Amy Klobuchar also has been accused of using her position in office to protect political patrons and legally extract money from corporations.

Another avenue for corruption is *legislation*. This is all about shaking down donors with the threat of punitive laws, or passing new rules or laws that benefit those closest to you. Often this involves powerful corporations. Progressives speak of the dangers of corporate power, but they can and often do the bidding of those who happen to be financially backing them. Senator Amy Klobuchar has mastered the art of soliciting large campaign contributions from corporations in exchange for sponsoring legislation that they favor. The pattern and timing of contributions—as it relates to legislation she has introduced—make it hard not to conclude that it is a sophisticated form of extraction. Even Senator Bernie Sanders has staked out positions that benefit the corporate interests of his backers and wealthy friends. Often crony corporatism does not involve a broad-based policy issue such as lower corporate taxes that would benefit all corporations, but rather niche projects that involve special benefits specifically for them or their narrow industry. Cory Booker has used his political power for the benefit of patrons, friends, and political aides.

Finally, there is *publicity*, the use of your power and office to promote the commercial interests of your family. Joe Biden has mastered this technique, touting businesses that are owned by family members without revealing that fact to the public. And Elizabeth Warren has seen her political rise intertwined with the commercial and corporate activities of her daughter.

So let us begin first by exploring the immense power and opportunities for abuse present when a prosecutor is prepared to distort their responsibilities to uphold the law for their own political benefit.

2

KAMALA HARRIS

President Barack Obama stood in front of an array of well-heeled donors in a private home in super-rich Atherton, California. Having just been reelected five months earlier, he was touting his White House accomplishments. After a few comments, he praised California attorney general Kamala Harris, who was also in the room, and highlighted her "dedication and brilliance." He added: "She also happens to be by far the best-looking attorney general in the country."[1]

While the comments struck some observers as inappropriately personal and unprofessional, they revealed the close and long history that Obama and Harris shared. Harris had first supported Obama while he was running for the Senate in Illinois back in 2004. After he was elected, Obama flew out to San Francisco and held a fund-raiser for Harris. She had just been elected San Francisco district attorney and needed to retire some campaign debt. The newly minted senator from Illinois showed up at San Francisco's famed Bimbo's on Broadway to help. In 2007, when Obama announced his plans to run for president in Springfield, Illinois, she was again by his side. Harris and several members of her family joined the campaign. Harris, her sister Maya, and brother-in-law Tony West would labor over the next year to help Obama's ambition become a reality. Kamala walked the snowbound precincts of Iowa, visited New Hampshire, and traveled to Nevada and Pennsylvania to campaign for him. Harris took the helm of his California campaign, serving as cochair. When Obama won, she was with him in Chicago's Grant Park to celebrate the victory.[2]

Harris is widely admired in progressive circles as the "female Obama."[3] Smooth, polished, and confident, she has worked hard to "cultivate a celebrity mystique while fiercely guarding her privacy."[4] This rising star in the Democratic Party also has a taste for expensive Manolo Blahnik shoes and Chanel handbags.[5]

Harris paints herself as a gritty lawyer who is climbing the ladder of power by her own strength and determination. She has also positioned herself as "smart on crime," even publishing a book by that same title.[6]

The reality of her rise to prominence is far more complicated—and how she has leveraged her power along the way is troubling. Harris's elevation to national politics is closely tied to one of California's most allegedly corrupt political machines and investigations into her tenure as a prosecutor raise disturbing questions about her use of criminal statutes in a highly selective manner, presumably to protect her friends, financial partners, and supporters.

Most disturbing, she has covered up information concerning major allegations of criminal conduct, including some involving child molestation.

Kamala Devi Harris was born to Donald Harris, her Jamaican-born father and Dr. Shyamala Gopalan, her Tamil Brahmin mother from India. Her father is a Marxist economist who taught at Stanford University; at one point, he advised the Jamaican government. Her mother was a highly regarded research scientist who worked in the field of breast cancer.[7] Her parents were divorced when Kamala was five, and her mother's family had a defining influence on her childhood. "One of the most influential people in my life, in addition to my mother, was my grandfather

T. V. Gopalan, who actually held a post in India that was like the Secretary of State position in this country," Harris recalled. "My grandfather was one of the original Independence fighters in India, and some of my fondest memories from childhood were walking along the beach with him after he retired and lived in Besant Nagar, in what was then called Madras." Harris draws on those Indian roots to define herself. "When we think about it, India is the oldest democracy in the world—so that is part of my background, and without question has had a great deal of influence on what I do today and who I am."[8]

Harris recounts regular visits as a child to her mother's homeland. After she was elected district attorney of San Francisco in 2003, she traveled to India and found that her grandmother had organized a party and press conference for her. Her grandfather was still a government official in Chennai. "One by one people came to pay homage. 'It was like a scene out of *The Godfather*,' " Kamala said.[9] Harris was close to her grandfather, who was "a joint secretary in the central government," and "instilled in her a thirst for service."[10]

While Harris attended Howard University, a traditionally black college, and served as president of the Black Law Students Association at Hastings College of Law in San Francisco, many saw her leaning more toward her mother's culture than her father's. According to her mother Shyamala, Kamala knows "all the Hindu mythology and traditions," and that "Kamala will be equally at ease in a temple or a church." Harris was born during Dusshera, a major Hindu celebration. "So I gave her the name thinking of Goddess Lakshmi."[11] Shyamala insisted that giving her daughters names derived from the Indian pantheon was important to her children's development. "A culture that worships goddesses produces strong women," she says.[12] Adds her mother,

"Kamala is a frequent visitor to the Shiva Vishnu temple in Livermore [California]. She performs all rituals and says all prayers at the temple. My family always wanted the children to learn the traditions, irrespective of their place of birth." [13]

───────────

Kamala Harris's entrée into the corridors of political power largely began with a date. In 1994, she met Willie Brown, who at the time was the second-most-powerful man in California politics. As Speaker of the State Assembly, Brown was a legend in Sacramento and around the state. He represented a district in the Bay Area and was well known in San Francisco social circles. In addition to running the California Assembly, Brown ran a legal practice on the side, which meant taking fees from lobbyists and industries that may have wanted favorable treatment in Sacramento. Brown was under investigation several times, by the State Bar of California, the Fair Political Practices Commission, and the Federal Bureau of Investigation.[14] In 1986, for example, as California Assembly Speaker, he "received at least $124,000 in income and gifts . . . from special interests that had business before the Legislature." [15]

Despite a lifetime in politics and public service, Brown was known for his expensive Brioni suits, Borsalino hats, Ferraris, and Porsches.[16] Later he downgraded to a Jaguar. "My body would reject a Plymouth," he said.[17] Along the way he played a version of himself in *The Godfather Part III*. Brown finally retired from political office in 2004. He purchased a $1.8 million condo in the St. Regis in San Francisco two years later.[18]

Willie Brown was married in 1958 (and remains so today) but that did not matter: Brown was sixty at the time he began dating Kamala, who was twenty-nine. Brown was actually two years older than her father. Their affair was the talk of San Francisco in 1994.[19] Kamala's mother defends her daughter's decision—and offered choice comments about Brown. "Why shouldn't she have gone out with Willie Brown? He was a player. And what could Willie Brown expect from her in the future? He has not much life left."[20]

Brown began pulling levers for Harris that both boosted her career and put money in her pocket, rewarding Kamala with appointments to state commissions that paid handsomely and did not require confirmation by the legislature. He put Kamala on the State Unemployment Insurance Appeals Board and later the California Medical Assistance Commission. The Medical Assistance Commission paid $99,000 a year in 2002.[21] The Unemployment Insurance Appeals Board paid around $114,000 a year. Both posts were part-time. At the time, she was working as a county employee making around $100,000.[22]

Along the way, Brown also bought young Kamala a new BMW.[23]

Perhaps the most important thing Brown gave Harris was access to his vast network of political supporters, donors, and sponsors. Soon she was publicly arm in arm with Brown in the most elite circles of San Francisco, including lavish parties and celebrity galas.[24]

By 1995, Willie Brown was running for mayor of San Francisco and Harris was regularly by his side. On election night, Willie Brown stood before his guests at the Longshoremen's Union Hall. He was all smiles as the election results rolled in. Harris was in front of the crowd with him, smiling, and handed him a blue baseball cap emblazoned with "Da Mayor." Brown placed the cap on his head and then Rev. Cecil Williams, a local fixture and longtime Brown friend, handed him a piece of paper.[25]

"It's over!" he proclaimed.[26]

The election wasn't the only thing that was over that night.

Many had speculated that Brown would divorce his wife and marry Harris, but that didn't happen. Shortly after Brown's electoral victory, he and Harris split up. There are conflicting reports as to who actually left whom. Most accounts report that Brown broke up with Harris.[27]

After the split, Kamala Harris started dating another prominent man: television talk-show host Montel Williams.[28]

The romance with Brown might have been over, but Harris had political ambitions of her own, and the two remained allies. Brown, as mayor, would prove to be enormously helpful in her rise to political power.

Willie Brown possessed the most powerful political machine in Northern California. As mayor, he leveraged that power to enrich his friends and allies. During his tenure, Brown came under FBI investigation twice for corruption involving lucrative contracts flowing from the city to his political friends. His operation was soon dubbed "Willie Brown Inc." Even local Democrats who might agree with Brown's political views were turned off by the cronyism and corruption that was rampant under "Da Mayor." "I thought it was only in Third World countries that people were forced to pay bribes to get services they're entitled to from their government," said U.S. district judge Charles Legge about the rampant corruption under Brown. "But we find it right here in San Francisco."[29]

Three years or so after Brown's election, San Francisco district attorney Terence Hallinan hired Kamala Harris to head up his office's Career Criminal Unit.[30] Hallinan, nicknamed "K.O." for his boxing skills, was a tough progressive who had little problem taking on the most powerful forces in San Francisco, whether it be the police or the new mayor.[31] Hallinan insisted that Harris's connection to Willie Brown had nothing to do with the hiring. Whether it did or not, Hallinan would soon regret his decision.

Shortly after she joined Hallinan's office, the number two slot in the prosecutor's office opened up. Harris wanted the job, but Hallinan chose someone else.[32] Brown seemed furious at Hallinan, ostensibly for other matters. The mayor was publicly attacking Hallinan for failing to do his job. An insider had a different take. "This whole thing is about Kamala Harris," one Brown friend told the San Francisco Chronicle. "Cross one of Willie's friends and there will be hell to pay."[33]

The relationship between Willie Brown and Terence Hallinan had always been a complicated one. Hallinan had publicly embraced one of Brown's rivals, Tom Ammiano. Hallinan had also been investigating Brown allies for corruption.[34]

Passed over by Hallinan, Harris abruptly left the district attorney's office and went to work at the city attorney's office, which was run by a close Brown ally. Soon the Brown machine was cranking up to help Kamala Harris run against Hallinan.[35]

By 2003, Harris threw her hat in the ring and announced her decision to challenge Hallinan for his position as San Francisco district attorney. Less known in San Francisco than her opposition, she regularly came a distant third in opinion polls, often registering in the single digits.[36] But she could count on the Willie Brown Machine, which at the time ran so much of San Francisco. Rebecca Prozan, a former Willie Brown aide, was brought on as Harris's campaign manager to give her a boost.[37] Harris's finance chair was Mark Buell, a major Democratic Party fund-raiser. A political consultant named Philip Muller set up an independent expenditure committee called the California Voter Project. Armed with a letter from Brown, he raised money to help boost her campaign. Muller had worked on both of Brown's mayoral races.[38] Beyond Muller's independent efforts, the flow of money directly into her campaign was unlike anything the district attorney's race had ever seen. "She's hauling in campaign cash like there's no tomorrow," said the *San Francisco Weekly*.[39]

Much of the money came from the super-wealthy of San Francisco who were close to Brown. The mayor himself gave the maximum contribution—$500—and penned a letter that Philip Muller, his close aide, took around to wealthy donors to raise cash. The letter asked the San Francisco elite to cough up five hundred dollars each to "help Kamala win."[40]

While Kamala Harris would later cast the campaign as a grass-roots operation, it was a much more exclusive affair. The San Francisco elite embraced her, which meant all-white fund-raisers in Pacific Heights. Frances Bowes, heir to the fortune made from Hula-Hoops and Frisbees, hosted an event and brought friends like romance novelist Danielle Steel to write large checks. Bowes had originally met Harris through a "longtime Willie Brown crony" while Brown and Harris were still dating. The Brown endorsement of her campaign also opened doors—and wallets. "Why, Willie Brown just wrote us a letter on her behalf," Bowes said.[41]

Friends and alliances with the San Francisco elite she had formed while dating Willie Brown also came to her aid. The Getty clan, heirs to the vast J. Paul Getty fortune, were "strongly behind Harris," and Vanessa and Billy Getty became "good friends."[42]

Harris denied that there was an effort by Brown to help her, but as the *San Francisco Chronicle* noted, "a large number of her contributors also have been donors to Harris' onetime boyfriend and political sponsor, Mayor Willie Brown." Darolyn Davis, who worked as Brown's communications director during his days in Sacramento as the Assembly Speaker, threw a fund-raiser that netted nearly $15,000.[43]

Very quickly, the upstart challenger was dramatically outraising the incumbent. Indeed, Harris raised double what Hallinan did. The money flow was so great that it led Hallinan to allege that Harris broke a law by surpassing a voluntary spending cap that she had pledged in writing to honor. In January 2003, shortly after announcing her campaign, Harris had signed a form saying that she would stick to the city's $211,000 voluntary spending cap for the campaign. An official handbook put out by the city's Department of Elections identified candidates that had signed the pledge.[44] The voter's guide is designed to let voters know which candidates agreed to abide by the law.

Harris signed the pledge—and then blew right past the spending limit. By the end of November, she had raised $621,000—almost three times more than the cap she had pledged to honor.[45] The San Francisco Ethics Commission vote to fine Harris was unanimous. Her campaign had to pay a $34,000 fine, a record in city elections.[46]

Blowing past the financial cap was not the only ethical issue raised about her campaign. Critics questioned the donations she accepted from individuals with matters sitting before her at her office in the city attorney's office. In particular, she was taking "campaign contributions from slumlords with cases before" her office.[47] According to Harris's campaign donor filings, more than 10 percent of her donors were owners or operators of single-room-occupancy hotels identified as "problematic" by city officials. Donors included hotel owners cited by city officials as a "city nuisance" because of numerous arrests for "drug activity, assault, rape, robbery and burglary." Another donor was the son of a hotel owner who verbally harassed a deputy city attorney and at one point threatened to shoot the attorney over code enforcement.

Carol Langford, a legal ethics expert who headed the American Bar Association ethics committee, saw the money flow as a major problem. "Of course, there's a conflict there. If your office sues someone and you take money from the defendant, that's a conflict." She added, "Consider the tenants of these flea-bag hotels who are worried about bugs and rats—and then they see someone who is supposed to be protecting them taking money from the landlord. What are they going to think?"[48] Hallinan, who was being vastly outspent in the campaign, claimed that "many of the contributors are connected with city government." He argued that they were not giving that money for nothing; she would have trouble dealing with "corruption in city agencies" because of the conflict of interest.[49]

The ethical problems with Harris's campaign went beyond the financial questions. Shortly after the election, complaints emerged from city cleaning crews who said they were forced during the campaign to attend political events for mayoral candidate Gavin Newsom and Kamala Harris.[50] Willie Brown had a history of deploying a "patronage army"—a cadre of city employees who performed political work because they owed him their jobs—to help favored candidates win elections.[51]

In this particular case, workers assigned to street cleaning crews complained that they were asked to do political work including during Kamala Harris's run for district attorney. Mohammed Nuru, a Brown protégé hired in 2000, was the deputy director of operations in the City's Department of Public Works. He ran among other things a project called San Francisco League of Urban Gardeners (popularly known as SLUG). The organization was supposedly hired by the city to provide cleanup and gardening work around the Bay Area. But they also served another purpose: as a resource to be deployed as part of the Willie Brown machine. In the 2003 election, they were deployed to help, among others, Kamala Harris in her bid for district attorney.[52]

According to internal records, SLUG employees were told by their bosses to "attend campaign events for" Kamala Harris.[53] Campaign manager Rebecca Prozan admitted that she had conversations with the head of SLUG, Nuru, throughout the campaign, although she denies asking him to bring workers to the rallies. The results were undeniable. In one instance, Prozan admitted that the Harris campaign had mailed out 9,000 flyers for a public event, but only 50–75 people actually showed up. An investigator said, "Prozan concluded that all or most of the attendees were in fact SLUG workers." Reportedly, Ron Vinson, a former Willie Brown deputy press secretary, led the workers into events.[54]

In the November 2003 elections, Harris came in second behind Hallinan in a three-person race. Because neither candidate received a majority of the vote, there was a runoff.[55] Winning the upset runoff victory, in early January 2004, Kamala Harris was sworn in as San Francisco district attorney. She decided to take the oath on a copy of the Bill of Rights rather than the Bible. There were two benedictions—one from a Hindu priest in Sanskrit, the other from an African American minister. The national anthem was played—as well as the National Black Anthem. After the swearing in, there was sitar music, and soul and Indian food were provided.[56]

One week after she was sworn in as district attorney, the city opened an investigation into the allegations that city workers were pressured to campaign for Harris and newly elected Mayor Gavin Newsom. But no charges were ever brought.[57]

As San Francisco district attorney, Kamala Harris enjoyed enormous discretion in the handling of legal cases. She would often determine which cases to prosecute and which not to. This was particularly true in highly public and politically sensitive cases. Over the course of her tenure, a consistent pattern emerged of favoring individuals and institutions that were either her political supporters, or those closely aligned with Willie Brown, or both. Some of these cases involved all-too-common instances of big-city cronyism and corruption involving city contracts, but other cases would involve disturbing crimes that were covered up.

Perhaps the deepest and most troubling mystery of Kamala Harris's tenure as a prosecutor centers on the disturbing issue of sexual abuse of children by priests. Harris often recounts her background as a sex crimes prosecutor earlier in her career to attack others for their legal failings in this area. In July 2019, for example, she rightly criticized the lax penalties that pedophile Jeffrey Epstein faced in his plea agreement with prosecutors. Harris attacked the prosecutor in the case, Alex Acosta, who was now labor secretary in the Trump administration, for "protecting predators." Harris even went after the law firm that represented Epstein in those criminal proceedings, arguing that their representation of him "calls into question the integrity of the entire legal system." Critics noted that she gladly took campaign donations from the same firm.[58]

But Harris's handling of the widespread priest abuse scandal in San Francisco, and later in the entire state of California, raises far more questions. During her decade-and-a-half tenure as a chief prosecutor, Harris would *fail to prosecute a single case* of priest abuse and her office would strangely hide vital records on abuses that had occurred despite the protests of victims groups.

Harris's predecessor as San Francisco district attorney, Terence

Hallinan, was aware of and had prosecuted numerous Catholic priests on sexual misconduct involving children. And he had been gathering case files for even more.[59] In the spring of 2002, Pope John Paul II convened a meeting in Rome to discuss how to deal with the spreading news of abuse.[60] By 2003, with a rising national tide of complaints, the scandals would soon reach cities and towns across America. The *Boston Globe* produced a Pulitzer Prize–winning series on priest abuse and efforts to cover it up. The scandal had now most definitely engulfed San Francisco. Hallinan's office had launched an investigation and quickly discovered that the San Francisco Archdiocese had extensive internal records concerning complaints going back some seventy-five years. In spring of 2002, Hallinan demanded the church turn them over to his office. A month later, the archdiocese reluctantly complied.[61]

The secret documents were explosive and reportedly contained the names of about forty current and former priests in the San Francisco area who had been identified in sexual abuse complaints. Hallinan used the information from the files to begin pursuing legal cases against them. In nearby San Mateo and Marin County, prosecutors obtained the same church records and those in Marin charged Father Gregory Ingels in 2003.[62] But by June 2003, Hallinan and other prosecutors had hit a roadblock: the U.S. Supreme Court ruled that California's law extending the statute of limitations for priest abuse cases was unconstitutional.[63]

Nevertheless, Hallinan was determined to pursue the cases. Discussions began among California district attorneys about how diocese abuse documents might be released to the public.[64] Victim advocates were in favor of releasing them, arguing that redacting the names of victims and other sensitive information could protect their privacy.[65] Hallinan's aggressive pursuit of these issues was of major concern to the Catholic Church and related institutions, which were facing mounting legal bills and settlements dealing with cases going back decades. Several priests were dismissed due to the anticipated release of the documents.[66]

The records that Hallinan had in his possession touched on well-connected institutions at the heart of California's power structure. St. Ignatius College Preparatory School, in the Archdiocese of San Francisco, counted California governor Jerry Brown and the powerful Getty family as alumni.[67] The school faced enormous vulnerabilities because of abuse problems there. Based on documents later released by the Jesuits who ran St. Ignatius, in the nearly sixty-year span from 1923 to 1982, in forty-three of those years the school employed at least one priest on the faculty who was later accused of abuse.[68]

Hallinan's investigation threatened to bring dozens of additional cases to light.

The Catholic Archdiocese in San Francisco had reason to be extremely nervous.

According to San Francisco election financial disclosures, high-dollar donations to Harris's campaign began to roll in from those connected to the Catholic Church institutional hierarchy. Harris had no particular ties to the Catholic Church or Catholic organizations, but the money still came in large, unprecedented sums. Lawyer Joseph Russoniello represented the church on a wide variety of issues, including the handling of the church abuse scandal.[69] He served on the Catholic Church's National Review Board (NRB) of the U.S. Conference of Catholic Bishops. The purpose of the NRB was to review Catholic Church abuse cases.[70] Russoniello was also a partner in the San Francisco law firm Cooley Godward. Russoniello donated the maximum amount by law to her campaign, $1,250, and his law firm added another $2,250. He also sat on Harris's advisory council when she was San Francisco district attorney. Another law firm, Bingham McCutcheon, which handled legal matters for the archdiocese concerning Catholic Charities, donated $2,825, the maximum allowed. Curiously, Bingham McCutcheon had only donated to two other candidates running for office in San Francisco before, for a total of $650. As with Russoniello, their support was unusual.[71]

Another law firm, Arguedas, Cassman & Headley, was defending a San Francisco priest against abuse claims at the time. They donated $4,550 to Harris. The lawyer in the case, Cristina Arguedas, also served on Kamala Harris's advisory council.[72]

Beyond these law firms, board members of San Francisco Catholic archdiocese–related organizations and their family members donated another $50,950 to Harris's campaign.[73]

Harris also had ties to those who were working to prevent the Catholic Church documents from coming to light. Harris counts among her mentors Louise Renne, who as a city attorney for San Francisco recruited Harris to come work with her as a city attorney after her falling-out with Hallinan.[74] Louise Renne's husband, Paul, was an attorney at the law firm Cooley Godward, where Russoniello worked.[75] Russoniello negotiated the agreement to bury the abuse records from public view.[76]

Hallinan's loss to Harris changed more than the nameplate down at the San Francisco district attorney's office. With the changing of the guard, the fate of the investigation into Catholic priest abuse would dramatically change—and not for the better.

Harris, who had been a sexual crimes prosecutor early in her career, moved in the opposite direction of Hallinan and worked to cover-up the records. Hallinan's office had used the archdiocese files to guide its investigations and talked publicly about releasing the documents after removing victims' names and identifiers. Harris, on the other hand, abruptly decided to bury the records. For some reason, she did not want the documents released in any form.[77] Harris's office claimed that the cover-up was about protecting the victims of abuse. "District Attorney Harris focuses her efforts on putting child molesters in prison," her office claimed. "We're not interested in selling out our victims to look good in the paper."[78]

This was a bold claim coming from Harris. During the 2003 campaign, a woman who was allegedly tortured by a boyfriend with a hot iron "blasted" Harris for citing her story during a campaign debate. "I am appalled by Kamala Harris referring to my case," she said. "Harris is supposedly for victims, but she never consulted me before using my case." In short, she had publicly talked about a case the victim did not want mentioned.[79]

When it came to the priest abuse scandal, the opposite was true. Victims' groups wanted the documents released and Harris was stopping it. They were outraged by her actions. Far from protecting victims, they argued, the cover-up was actually protecting the abusers by keeping their alleged crimes secret.

"They're full of shit," said Joey Piscitelli, the northwest regional director of Survivors Network of Those Abused by Priests (SNAP), the largest and most active victims' group. "You can quote me on that. They're not protecting the victims."[80]

Rick Simons, an attorney who represented multiple victims of clergy abuse, also attacked Harris's actions. Hiding the records "shows a pattern and practice and policy of ignoring the rights of children by one of the largest institutions of the city and county of San Francisco, and in the Bay Area."[81]

Kam Kuwata, a consultant to Los Angeles district attorney

Rocky Delgadillo, said there was "no reason why transparency and protecting the victim cannot work hand in hand."[82]

With the outcry of victims groups, Harris's office then attempted to shift blame, claiming that the idea of burying the evidence had been first suggested by her predecessor, Hallinan.[83] But he responded angrily to her claims. "I told Jack Hammel [the archdiocese's legal counsel] in no uncertain terms that I wouldn't go along with anything like that." He went on to point out that the documents contained information about a "potential target of a criminal investigation" and asserted he "wouldn't do a deal like that for [the archdiocese] any more than I would if it were an Elks Club with a bunch of pedophiles. Those are the kinds of deals that have allowed the church sex scandal to go on as long as it has."[84]

Harris's actions were strange because they ran contrary to her public image as a fighter for victims—particularly children. Her decision regarding the diocese abuse records set off a chain reaction among those trying to bring to light the widespread abuse that was taking place. James Jenkins, a psychologist who was the founding chairman of the archdiocese's Independent Review Board, which was offering oversight on how to handle abuse claims, abruptly resigned from the board. He accused the church of "deception, manipulation and control" for blocking the release of the board's findings. Jenkins argued that Harris's deal with the archdiocese not only denied the rights of known victims, it also prevented other possible cases from coming forward. If the names of the priests who had faced credible charges were released, he said, it "would encourage other victims to come forward with their stories. . . . Usually, people who do these things have multiple offenses, usually with multiple victims. The rule of thumb is there are seven more victims for every one who comes forward."[85]

Transparency tends to embolden victims. Statistical evidence from the archdiocese confirms the view that releasing the names of accused priests led to an increase in the number of victims bringing charges. A good example of this is in Los Angeles, where District Attorney Steve Cooley ignored the church's cry to hide the report and did the opposite of Kamala Harris: he released the records. According to SNAP, this led to more than 211 self-reported or litigation-revealed abusers being named in the Los Angeles Archdiocese.[86] In San Francisco, there were only thirty-six, according to a lawsuit filed in 2012.[87]

So, what has happened to these abuse records? It is unclear. In April 2010, a journalist with the *San Francisco Weekly* asked for the records through California's Public Records Act. Harris's office denied the request, offering conflicting explanations as to why they could not provide them.[88] In 2019, I requested those records through a California attorney. The San Francisco district attorney's office responded that they no longer had them in their possession. Were they destroyed? Were they moved somewhere else? It remains a disturbing mystery.

Beyond the handling of these abuse records, Harris also had an abysmal record in prosecuting priest cases.

She somehow served as San Francisco district attorney from 2004 to 2011, and then as California attorney general from 2011 to 2017, and *never brought a single documented case* forward against an abusive priest.[89] It is an astonishing display of inaction, given the number of cases brought in other parts of the country. To put this lack of action in perspective, at least fifty other cities charged priests in sexual abuse cases during her tenure as San Francisco district attorney. San Francisco is conspicuous by its absence.[90]

The blind eye to priest sexual abuse was just part of a pattern of favoritism that has permeated Harris's career as a prosecutor.

Though not as dramatic as the sexual crimes, there were numerous instances where she was apparently prepared to look the other way to protect politically connected insiders.

Her actions represent the ultimate form of leveraging power in the criminal justice realm—deciding not to pursue criminal charges.

It was the sort of thing that vice cops are supposed to do. At San Francisco's adult entertainment clubs, dancers were taking customers behind closed doors and having sex for money. After repeated complaints that strip clubs in San Francisco were often really serving as prostitution clubs, the San Francisco Police Department decided to take action. They sent out letters to a couple dozen strip clubs and warned them that the police would be looking into their activities. They would be checking their business licenses and making sure that their permits were up to date. The police action caught the attention of newly installed district attorney Kamala Harris, and her staff sent the message to hold off on the enforcement. Meanwhile, in response to continued complaints, the police conducted a pair of sting operations. Three undercover officers went into each of the two clubs and were quickly solicited by female employees for paid sex. At both the Market Street Theater and the New Century Theater, it happened "within minutes." When the operations were done, nine women were arrested, as was the general manager of the New Century. The cops claimed that they were "slam-dunk cases."[91]

But Kamala Harris dropped the cases.

"It just leaves me in amazement," said San Francisco Police Department vice captain Tim Hettrich. It was "almost legalizing prostitution."[92]

Publicly, Harris claimed that the problem was that the police should be focused on arresting "street-level pimps and johns." In a statement, Harris claimed that there had been "no arrests" of either. The San Francisco Police Department was incredulous. "That's an outright lie," said police investigator Joe Dutto. There were fifty to seventy johns arrested every month.[93]

Harris then argued that the problem was that the doors for the private booths at the clubs were not legal and that the Department of Building Inspection should deal with them. Ken Harrington, a top building inspector, fired off a snarky memo requesting the very precise parameters of the "job" they were to do to satisfy the DA. Apparently flabbergasted that his office was responsible (not the cops), he stated, "The next thing, she'll be blaming the gunshot homicide rate on us for not enforcing the city's lead abatement ordinance."[94]

Harris's strange objections to prosecuting prostitution cases connected to these raids have a possible explanation. The owner of both the Market Street and New Century theaters was a company called Déjà Vu. An owner of Déjà Vu, Sam Conti, had a long history with Willie Brown. Conti had first hired Brown as his defense attorney back in 1977. They remained friends. At Conti's 2009 funeral, Brown delivered a videotaped eulogy.[95]

Harris's handling of this simple vice matter would set up questions about her prosecutorial conduct as it related to powerful political allies and friends. While she was prepared to throw the book at those with no connections to her, those with links to her or her powerful allies would often get charges dropped. It was selective enforcement of the law, hardly what one could call "blind justice."

Kamala Harris entered the San Francisco attorney general's office facing a whole host of issues beyond priest sexual abuse and strip clubs; among them was the rampant corruption that had become so common under her ex-boyfriend and political sponsor, Willie Brown. During the bitter campaign, Terence Hallinan had publicly stated that Harris would be unwilling to bring corruption charges against allies and friends of Willie Brown because they were still too close.[96] Her record as a prosecutor would prove him correct.

Willie Brown appointed Hector Chinchilla, a real estate lawyer, as head of the San Francisco Planning Commission shortly after he became mayor. The planning commission has enormous power in San Francisco in determining which projects proceed and which do not. Chinchilla, sensing an opportunity, hired himself out as a consultant to developers who were seeking city planning permits from his commission. Over the course of the next several years, he took in $181,000 from developers.[97] The corruption case seemed clear. Developers told city officials that they had been told that if they hired Chinchilla he would "run interference" regarding opposition to their development. Reportedly, "Chinchilla performed anything needed on the project."[98]

In 2002, then-prosecutor Terence Hallinan had charged Chinchilla with seven misdemeanor ethics laws violations. "We do regard it as a major corruption case and indicative of what is going on in San Francisco," he said at the time. "It is very disturbing that that kind of atmosphere is pervading in San Francisco."[99]

Given how close Chinchilla was to Willie Brown, the case "roiled City Hall." Barely eight months in office, after a judge dismissed some charges, Harris dropped all remaining charges against Chinchilla.[100]

It would not be the only case of Harris dropping the criminal charges of a Willie Brown ally. Even in instances where fraud directly threatened public safety, Harris struck legal deals with the friends and allies of Willie Brown. Consider the case of Ricardo Ramirez. Ramirez ran a cement and concrete company called Pacific Cement. As of 2003, a full one-third of the public works projects in San Francisco used Pacific.[101]

Ramirez was a colorful but ruthless player in the construction business. He liked to wear $500 cowboy boots and roamed around the city in a $100,000 Mercedes-Benz. He threw lavish parties with Mariachi bands and tossed around a lot of campaign cash. Having given almost $100,000 to politicians over the previous eight years made him a "well-connected political player" in San Francisco. Those contributions often went to the Willie Brown machine and were not always legal. In 1997, state officials found that Ramirez had illegally contributed $2,000 to Brown's 1995 mayoral campaign.[102] His ties to Brown went beyond financial contributions. Ramirez was reportedly friends with Brown, but he also hired connected officials like Jim Gonzalez, who worked as a lobbyist for Ramirez. Longtime Willie Brown buddy Charlie Walker was also a close friend.

Ramirez might have gone down in the annals of San Francisco political history only as a contractor greasing palms to get city contracts, but he also cut dangerous corners threatening San Francisco public safety. Ramirez was using inferior and cheaper recycled concrete on major projects like the Golden Gate Bridge, parking garages, and light-rail projects. These were massive projects where structural integrity was key: the half-mile stretch of the Bay Bridge's western approach; the parking garage at Golden Gate Park; a wastewater treatment plant in nearby Burlingame; and the Municipal Railway's Third Street light-rail project. The projects required solid concrete, but Ramirez was actually using inferior recycled concrete, which contains recycled debris rather than hard rock. Prone to water penetration, recycled concrete is more likely to crack and to wear quickly. Recycled concrete is acceptable for decorative work, but for major load-bearing projects like roads or bridges, it is considered unsafe.[103]

Ramirez's company was able to keep up the scam for a while, but it eventually caught up with him. Public works agency officials went public with the fact that Ramirez's company had defrauded them. Strangely, Ramirez never faced charges for delivering substandard concrete. Instead, Harris's office settled for a plea deal involving a single environmental count, illegally storing waste oil at one of his production facilities. To avoid jail time, he agreed to a year in home detention and payment of $427,000 in fines and restitution.[104]

City officials were mystified. Tony Anziano, an official with the state agency Caltrans who was in charge of the Bay Bridge approach project, said the agency had been defrauded by Ramirez and his company. According to the *San Francisco Chronicle,* Anziano "said that Caltrans had always cooperated with prosecutors and that he couldn't explain why they hadn't pursued charges."[105]

Harris and her office refused to offer an explanation as to why they were going so light on Willie Brown's friend and donor. "Harris' office had no explanation for why it dropped the concrete case," noted the *Chronicle.*[106]

———

Kamala Harris's signature program as San Francisco district attorney was called Back on Track—a program designed to give first-time drug offenders an opportunity to avoid a criminal record. If they participated in and successfully passed through the program, their drug record was wiped clean.[107]

Harris would tout the program as enormously successful. "Back on Track is an innovative initiative that has achieved remarkable results," she said in 2009 as she prepared her run for California attorney general. "It has dramatically reduced recidivism—the re-offense rate—among its targeted population (nonviolent, first-time, low-level drug offenders)." She boasted that fewer than 10 percent of Back on Track graduates in San Francisco had re-offended, but those numbers were highly deceptive in that they only reflected those who graduated. During the first four years of her program, for example, they kicked out almost half of those chosen for the program. The real recidivism rate was likely much higher.[108]

The program was also fraught with other problems that Harris was hoping the public would ignore. Those included were not just nonviolent, first-time offenders who had committed a single drug offense. Some were illegal immigrants and violent criminals such as Alexander Izaguirre. Izaguirre had gone through the program even though he had two arrests (instead of just one) within eight months. One for selling cocaine, the other for a purse snatching. Given those facts, it is unclear how Izaguirre even got enrolled. More, Izaguirre was one of at least seven illegal immigrants who were signed up. The problem was that the job-training program that Harris had enrolled him in was training him for jobs that he could not legally hold given his immigration status.[109]

One night, while he was still in the program, Izaguirre went to San Francisco's exclusive Pacific Heights neighborhood and committed a particularly brutal crime. Amanda Kiefer was walking down the street when Izaguirre snatched her purse and jumped into a waiting SUV. Rather than drive off, the SUV sped toward Kiefer to run her down. Kiefer jumped on the hood and saw Izaguirre and the driver laughing. The driver slammed on the brakes throwing Kiefer to the ground. The impact fractured her skull. Blood was oozing from her ear.[110]

Kiefer would later ask why he was even in the program. "If they've committed crimes and they're not citizens, then why are they here? Why haven't they been deported?"[111]

Harris did not offer an explanation. Instead, she simply explained that enforcing federal immigration law was not her job.[112] Never mind that her oath of office required her to enforce the laws of the state of California and to protect and defend the Constitution of the United States.

Harris has a habit of dealing with problems by covering them up.

In 2009, Harris set her ambitions higher and announced her bid for California attorney general. She enjoyed the backing of the San Francisco establishment, Willie Brown, and won a very tight 2010 race against Republican Steve Cooley, who was the Los Angeles County district attorney at the time. In the end, Harris won by fewer than 75,000 votes, or less than 1 percent, out of more than 9.6 million votes cast in the election.[113]

The pattern of selective enforcement of laws continued during her tenure as attorney general. Beyond the move to Sacramento and the new job, Harris also became romantically involved with Los Angeles attorney Douglas Emhoff. The two met on a blind date set up by a close friend of Harris. They were engaged in March 2014. By August, they were married. It was a private ceremony presided over by her sister, Maya. Guests were sworn to secrecy.[114]

Emhoff has practiced corporate law most of his career and specializes in defending corporations facing charges of unfair business practices and entertainment and intellectual property law matters.[115] He established his own boutique firm in Los Angeles, but was later tapped to become the partner-in-charge at the Los Angeles office of Venable LLP, an international law firm with offices around the country.[116] As partner-in-charge, Emhoff was involved in all cases coming out of the office. Venable's clients included a parade of corporations who had matters sitting on Kamala Harris's desk. The fate of many of those cases is further evidence of the selective nature of the way she has exercised power, often for the benefit of friends, family, and those with whom they have financial ties.

Nutritional supplement companies have faced a myriad of legal actions over the years about what critics claim are exaggerated statements about the effectiveness of their products. This would seem to be a natural area for Harris to use her powers as attorney general and as a self-professed consumer advocate.

Indeed, in 2015 the attorneys general from fourteen other states, including New York, launched an effort to investigate nutrition companies on the grounds of false advertising and mislabeling. They claimed, "Many products contained ingredients that were not listed on their labels and that could pose serious health risks." Harris, who had a history of working with these AGs on other issues, did not participate.[117]

At the same time that these states were pursuing the nutritional supplement issue, the Obama administration's Department of Justice (DOJ) was also going after dietary supplement producers, charging them with exaggerated claims about their products "that are unsupported by adequate scientific evidence."[118] Their targets included General Nutrition Corporation (GNC), Herbalife, AdvoCare International, Vitamin Shoppe, Walgreens, and others.

The Federal Trade Commission (FTC) opened an investigation into Herbalife in March 2014.[119] In California, Harris's attorney general's office had received more than seven hundred complaints about Herbalife.[120] In July 2016, the FTC won a $200 million settlement against Herbalife.[121] But Harris never even investigated the company.

Something very strange occurred in this instance when it came to Harris's handling of the matter. The *Los Angeles Times* noted her conspicuous failure to participate in the action.[122]

It is worth noting that those corporations in question all happened to be clients of her husband's law firm, Venable LLP. GNC, Herbalife, AdvoCare International, Vitamin Shoppe, and others were represented by Venable.[123] Indeed, her husband's office had only months earlier, in January, represented Walgreens in a case involving false advertising claims. Though the lawsuit was dismissed, the possibility of another class action case remained.[124]

Herbalife was one of Venable's large clients, paying the firm for thousands of hours of legal work.[125] Herbalife had been the subject of a standing court order since 1986 concerning its advertising claims and practices.[126] Critics point out that Harris declined to enforce those standing court orders.[127]

As Harris was deciding on how to deal with the Herbalife matter, the company's lobbying firm threw her a fund-raiser. On February 26, 2015, the Podesta Group, which specifically represented Herbalife, held a luncheon fund-raiser for Harris in Washington, D.C.[128]

In 2015, prosecutors from Harris's own attorney general's office based out of San Diego sent her a long memorandum arguing that Herbalife needed to be investigated. They also requested additional resources to probe further into the company and its practices. Harris declined to investigate or provide the resources—and never offered a reason.[129]

By August 2015, Venable LLP promoted Emhoff to managing director of the West Coast operations.[130]

This was not the only case in which Harris exercised her prosecutorial powers selectively. Those with the right connections avoided legal scrutiny even in generally clear-cut cases. Governor Jerry Brown was a Harris political ally and endorsed her candidacy for the U.S. Senate.[131] Brown's sister, Kathleen, joined the board of Sempra Energy in June 2013. In 2015 and 2016, the company suffered "the biggest methane gas leak from a well blowout in US history." For more than one hundred days gas streamed out of the company's well. The culprit was a corroded metal lining that had ruptured after long-term exposure to groundwater.[132] It was a major environmental failure by the company. As attorney general, Harris often took on environmental cases with gusto. In this case, Harris's office refused to investigate the matter.[133]

Political power creates leverage opportunities when a politician wants something from someone.

The Daughters of Charity owned several hospitals in California that were struggling and at risk of being shut down. The charity wanted to sell those hospitals to another nonprofit chain in the hopes of preserving them to serve the local communities in which they were based. The matter required a simple approval by California attorney general Kamala Harris as required by state regulations. A powerful union, United Healthcare Workers West (UHW), threatened to "blow up the deal" by offering to support her bid for the U.S. Senate if she would stymie the sale, and further, threatened to spend it on an opponent if she would not.[134]

Founded in Paris in 1633, the Daughters of Charity is dedicated to serving the poor. By the nineteenth century, the order was in the United States and eventually began opening hospitals. As of 2002, the Daughters of Charity Health System (DCHS) consisted of six California hospitals. The system found itself in difficult financial conditions in 2014.[135] The charity was facing serious economic challenges in the changing world of health care. The nonprofit hospital chain had suffered an operating loss of $146 million, so they opened up the sale of the hospitals for a competitive bidding process that lasted thirteen months and brought in more than two hundred bids. Daughters of Charity selected a bid from Prime Healthcare Services for $843 million. The choice was simple, as Prime Healthcare's was the only bid that promised to honor a $250 million unfunded pension for 17,000 current and former employees; maintain the facilities for at least five years, ensuring that communities would not immediately close money-losing hospitals; commit $250 million in capital expenditures; and maintain the existing union contracts with employees. Prime Healthcare had a history of good performance in these circumstances. Over the previous fifteen years, they had acquired thirty-five hospitals around the United States that were either bankrupt or in deep financial trouble and had managed to save every one of them.[136]

As California attorney general, Harris spent lots of time deciding which legal cases to bring and how to defend the state in court. She also had a role in providing regulatory approval. Which meant, of course, leverage over companies.

One of her regulatory responsibilities was the Non-Profit Hospital Transfer Statute, which meant she needed to approve such transactions as the Prime Healthcare acquisition of Daughters of Charity. Not only had the Daughters of Charity Hospital voted in favor of Prime's bid as the "best and only" option to keep the hospitals open, but also a broad coalition of groups supported Prime Healthcare's proposal. The California National Organization for Women and the California State Conference of the National Association for the Advancement of Colored People (NAACP) supported the bid. So, too, did newspapers like the *San Francisco Chronicle* and the *Los Angeles Times*. Indeed, the California Nursing Association (CNA), which represented 90,000 registered nurses in California, came out in support.[137]

But powerful political allies of Harris's did not like the deal. In particular, the Service Employees International Union (SEIU), UHW's parent union, was strongly opposed. The union was a longtime backer of Harris and she coveted their support as she looked to run for the U.S. Senate in 2016. During her 2010 and 2014 elections for attorney general, SEIU and UHW had donated more than $204,000. (In 2014, they were her leading campaign contributor.) They also provided millions more through political action committees. Executives involved in the deal heard that the SEIU was promising Harris $25 million through SEIU COPE, the national political action committee, if she squelched the deal.[138]

SEIU leaders hated Prime Healthcare. The nonprofit chain had a good working relationship with many unions, including the California Nurses Association, but SEIU was not among them. SEIU wanted full unionization of all of Prime's California hospitals. They also wanted to unionize the nurses under their UHW, but the CNA already represented the nurses at Prime.[139]

Public hearings were held in the affected communities by Daughters of Charity, and there was "overwhelming support" for the sale of DCHS to Prime.[140]

But the nonprofit chain refused SEIU's demands.[141]

According to a lawsuit file by Prime Healthcare, SEIU officials boldly told the head of Prime Healthcare that unless they allowed their union to take over representation of the nurses, Harris would not approve the deal. If true, it was an extraordinary statement from union officials: they would dictate the regulatory approval of the transaction.[142]

Prime Healthcare also alleged that Harris's office informed advisors for DCHS that the attorney general would approve the deal only if Prime allowed SEIU-UHW to unionize the chain.[143] The Daughters of Charity ended up filing a lawsuit against the SEIU-UHW accusing the union of extortion.[144]

The Prime Healthcare complaint against Harris claimed that on February 20, 2015, Harris publicly "approved" the transaction, but put impossible conditions on the deal. These were essentially "poison pill" requirements that her office knew would not be approved by Prime Healthcare. Indeed, the list of three hundred conditions was seventy-seven pages long. Furthermore, those conditions were nonnegotiable. The attorney general of California had never imposed such conditions on a hospital sale before. The consultant that Harris had brought in to review the deal had not suggested these conditions, according to the complaint. Indeed, senior executives from Harris's office allegedly informed Prime Healthcare that the conditions "were from the Attorney General, herself."[145]

This was not the first time Harris had allegedly blocked a deal involving Prime Healthcare, which claimed that back in 2011, SEIU officials took credit for getting Harris to block Prime Healthcare's acquisition of Victor Valley Community Hospital (VVCH). Although the independent consultant hired by Harris's office had allegedly recommended approving the deal, the attorney general said no.[146]

Instead, the complaint alleged that Harris wanted Victor Valley Community Hospital to support a bid by a competitor, KPC Global. She placed no conditions on the KPC Global purchase—even on fees or reimbursements—even though VVCH was a nonprofit hospital. When Victor Valley Hospital board members protested the decision, Harris allegedly threatened them with criminal investigations from her office and possible termination from the hospital board.[147]

SEIU leaders bragged to hospital executives about their power. On July 24, 2014, union boss Dave Regan told Dr. Prem Reddy, head of Prime Healthcare, that as long as the nonprofit resisted his efforts to unionize the hospitals, there would be no Prime Healthcare deals in California. He allegedly told Reddy that Harris was "his politician" and she "would do what [he] told her to." [148]

For the Daughters of Charity deal, SEIU favored a strange alternative, which, as alleged by Prime Healthcare, demonstrates where their interest actually stood. They did not push for a nonprofit chain like Prime Healthcare to take over the Charity hospitals; instead, they pushed for a New York City–based investment fund called Blue Wolf Capital Partners. The private equity firm had zero experience in operating hospitals. What they did have was close ties to organized labor and the Democratic Party.[149]

The Blue Wolf deal never materialized, but Harris had other ideas.

Having squelched the purchase of a nonprofit hospital chain by another nonprofit chain, Harris then jumped and offered conditional approval for Blue Mountain Capital to manage the hospital through one of its subsidiaries.[150] The deal was quite extraordinary and frankly bizarre, even though, unlike what Prime Healthcare had proposed, it would maintain the hospitals as nonprofit entities. Blue Mountain Capital had a hard-charging reputation in financial circles and had been neck-deep in the credit swap debacle back in 2008.[151] And in this particular case, Harris was approving a deal that was far worse for patients, according to Prime Healthcare's complaint. She allowed Blue Mountain to cut services that Prime Healthcare had promised to keep open. For Prime Healthcare, she had said that women's health services were required to remain open, for example, something that Prime Healthcare said it would do. Harris was allegedly allowing Blue Mountain Capital to close such services.[152]

Harris's approval of the purchase was remarkable. "I cannot recall a hedge fund incursion of any scale, let alone on this scale," said Richard B. Spohn, a partner in the law firm Nossaman LLP's health care practice. "It's anomalous and it's portentous in sort of an ominous way. The monetization of nonprofit assets in this fashion is worrisome." [153]

Blue Mountain Capital is headed by Andrew Feldstein, who has donated hundreds of thousands of dollars to the Democratic Party. His wife, Jane Veron, is also a major donor to the party, contributing tens of thousands of dollars.[154]

Harris has used her powers as a prosecutor to leverage her rise to power, and protect corrupt allies and friends. But sometimes leverage is exercised through the proxy of family.

JOE BIDEN

Gritty Joe Biden from Scranton, Pennsylvania, has been part of America's political life since 1972, when at just age twenty-nine he was elected to the U.S. Senate. America watched Joe Biden bury his first wife and daughter following a tragic automobile accident right after his election and shortly before Christmas.[1] America's heart went out to him again as Vice President Biden buried another child, son Beau Biden, when he died from brain cancer in 2015.[2]

Joe Biden has been on the stage—sometimes in a lead role—in every major national political drama since Watergate. As he recounts in his memoir: "As a United States senator I've watched (and played some small part in) history: the Vietnam War, Watergate, the Iran hostage crisis, the Bork nomination, the fall of the Berlin Wall, the reunification of Germany, the disintegration of the Soviet Union, 9/11, two wars in Iraq, a presidential impeachment, a presidential resignation, and a presidential election decided by the Supreme Court."[3]Although not as ideological as some, he has largely remained "a progressive Democrat to his core."[4]

To any American paying attention to politics, Biden was a familiar figure even before becoming Barack Obama's choice for vice president in 2008. In part this was because he had served as the longtime chairman of two powerful Senate committees—

Foreign Relations and Judiciary—so as Salena Zito notes, "We really have seen Biden's career unfold on television."[5]

At least we have seen the television-friendly portions of Joe Biden's political career unfold. Other aspects involving his family's complex and obscured international deals, leveraged on Joe's political status and power, have rarely been explored. The Biden family partners are often foreign governments, where the deals occur in the dark corners of international finance like Kazakhstan, China, Costa Rica, Jamaica, Ukraine, and Russia. Some deals have even involved U.S. taxpayer money. The cast of characters includes sketchy companies, violent convicted felons, foreign oligarchs, and other people who typically expect favors in return. Joe's public power positions Biden family members for highly lucrative deals they likely would not otherwise get. These deals also often occur with the appearance that Joe Biden has done favors for the partners who welcome such family members. These are not a few disparate enterprises, but rather moneymaking ventures that appear to be part of a well-organized family business.

Joe Biden has insisted in absolute terms that he never discusses family members' business activities.

The Biden family's apparent self-enrichment depends on Joe Biden's political influence and involves no less than five family members: Joe's son Hunter, daughter Ashley, brothers James and Frank, and sister Valerie.

When this subject came up in 2019 he declared, "I never talked with my son or my brother or anyone else—even distant family—about their business interests. Period."[6] As we will see, this is an impossibility.

Biden's political identity rests on his hardscrabble and humble roots, which create the impression that both he and his family are not interested in money. As one admiring newspaperman puts it:

"Biden sweats humanity."[7] Still, he does not necessarily like pedestrian labels. "I am always labeled as the 'middle class Joe,' " he groused in 2014. "In this town, that is not a compliment. It means you are not sophisticated."[8]

The Bidens started out in blue-collar Scranton, Pennsylvania, but in the face of financial hardship, moved to Delaware when he was still young. After first attending the University of Delaware and then law school at Syracuse University, he jumped almost immediately into politics. By the age of twenty-seven, Joe was running for New Castle County Council in Delaware.[9] From that beginning, Joe's political career was a family affair. His younger brothers James and Frank "organized a volunteer army of young people who worked the strong Democratic precincts."[10] When he ran for the U.S. Senate just two years later, James, then just twenty-two years old, was his finance chairman.[11] His sister Valerie was his campaign manager. She would go on to lead every one of his political campaigns over the next three decades until his vice presidential run with Barack Obama.[12]

From his earliest foray into politics to the present day, Biden's political life has been fused with his family. From the beginning, the Biden family, as one admiring biographer puts it, "formed the nucleus for [Joe Biden's] political operations."[13]

The notion of family was deeply embedded in the Biden psyche at an early age. "The single best thing [I learned from my father] is," Joe's son Hunter once said, "family comes first. Over everything."[14] This otherwise admirable character quality crosses the line into corruption when political position and vested power become the locomotive of the family money train. Love of family is not a legitimate excuse for the abuse of power.

The 1972 run for the U.S. Senate was pivotal. Young and little known, Joe was elected to the New Castle County Council just two years earlier. That made him an unusual commodity. In a 1974 interview he described his situation in terms that he now probably regrets. "I'm like the token black or the token woman," he explained on the PBS program *The Advocates*. "I was the token young person. I'm a 29-year-old oddball. The only reason I was able to raise the money is that I was able to have a national constituency to run for office, because I was 29." [15]

Biden was remarkably candid in that interview about raising money and his willingness to "prostitute" himself to do it. "You run the risk of deciding whether or not you're going to prostitute yourself to give the answer you know they want to hear in order to get funded to run for that office," he explained. "I went to the big guys for the money. I was ready to prostitute myself in the manner in which I talk about it, but what happened was they said, 'Come back when you're 40, son.' " [16]

Despite those early struggles, Biden was able to raise $276,000 for the Senate campaign, a significant sum in 1972 for an election in a small state like Delaware.[17] Much of the coordination work was done by his brother James, who as finance chairman worked to enlist "the support of national unions, political leaders, and financiers around the country." [18]

Joe's opponent was Congressman J. Caleb Boggs, a two-term Republican incumbent for the state of Delaware. He was a World War II veteran who had earned endorsements from labor. In 1972, Joe beat him, winning a close election by 3,000 votes out of 230,000 cast statewide.[19]

Thus began his thirty-six years as a U.S. senator until he became vice president.

Weeks after his 1972 electoral victory and entrance onto the stage of national politics, tragedy struck when, as mentioned earlier, his wife and daughter were killed in a car crash; his two sons were injured. His sister Valerie moved in to help with his boys, Hunter and Beau. Joe would commute home to Delaware from Washington almost every day on Amtrak to be home with them.[20] Riding the rails would become a powerful symbol of "Six-Pack Joe." According to Biden, he has made more than eight thousand trips on Amtrak—although not always in the commuter car. "I can say this now, since they can't do anything about it, I used to ride in the cab a lot with the engineers."[21] If he was running late, Biden pulled rank. "On many days" he would call the train conductor and the train would be held "until Joe came aboard." Other rail commuters would just have to wait.[22]

The clouds parted in Joe's personal life a few years later when his younger brother Frank gave him a phone number and suggested he call a girl named Jill. The two had met at school. "You'll like her, Joe," Frank said. "She doesn't like politics."[23]

Joe and Jill quickly became serious, and it was clear that this was going somewhere. The family noticed and brothers James and Frank took her to dinner for some straight talk. "They told me," Jill later recalled, "it was a dream of this family that Joe would be president, and did I have any problem with that?"[24] The dinner was a testament to how the family viewed its fortunes as being tied to Joe's political rise. Clearly, Biden's political career was very much a family operation.

In 1988, when Joe was running for president, he looked to be a favorite. But his campaign was derailed by allegations that he had plagiarized a speech from British politician Neil Kinnock. With the campaign in crisis, his wife Jill, brothers Frank and James, sister Valerie, his parents, and his children all gathered around Joe. The choice to withdraw from the race was a family decision.[25]

A Catholic priest married Joe and Jill in 1977 in a ceremony held at the United Nations chapel in New York City.[26] They had a daughter, Ashley, in 1981. As the kids grew, they moved into a mansion once owned by the DuPont Company in Greenville, Delaware.[27]

For the next three decades, Senator Joe Biden became a Washington fixture, accumulating a progressive voting record on a wide variety of issues.[28] Other aspects of his voting record suggest the pull of his family's commercial interests. Senator Biden pushed for the passage of a new bankruptcy law that put him out of step with most of his Democratic Party colleagues.[29] He voted against a bill that would require credit card companies to provide better warnings about the perils of making only minimum monthly payments. He was only one of five Democrats to do so.[30] During the same period (between 2001 and 2005), son Hunter was receiving consulting fees from the MBNA Corporation, a major Delaware bank and credit card company.[31] While sitting on the Senate Judiciary Committee, Senator Biden also worked hard on legislation to deal with asbestos-damage lawsuits.[32] It just so happened that son Beau was working for a Wilmington, Delaware, law firm that was handling asbestos litigation cases.[33]

In 2001, son Hunter jumped in with both feet when he became a lobbyist with the firm Oldaker, Biden & Belair LLP, with offices on Connecticut Avenue just blocks from the White House.[34] Their founder, William Oldaker, also served as a legal advisor to Joe Biden. The boutique firm specialized in "appropriations" lobbying, which meant shaking money loose from the federal government for their clients. They represented lawyers, American Indians, as well as the health care industry. It was located in the same office was the National Group lobbying firm, also run by Oldaker, whose clients included the University of Delaware. Part of their job was submitting "targeted spending items called 'earmarks' to Biden's office." The arrangement seemed to work quite well until 2006, when the Senate passed an ethics bill requiring senators to verify in writing that they or their families would not benefit from spending items or earmarks that they were pushing. Hunter had to shift gears and leave the appropriations lobbying game.[35]

However, Hunter was not done with other types of lobbying.

An online gambling company run out of Gibraltar named PartyGaming was under federal scrutiny. The Department of Justice had issued subpoenas to more than a dozen banks working with the company. The company needed help in Washington and hired Hunter Biden to lobby on their behalf. It probably did not hurt that his father was the chairman of the Senate Foreign Relations Committee and a senior member of the Senate Judiciary Committee, with oversight of the Department of Justice. In 2008, Hunter eventually dropped his lobbying clients when his dad was announced as Obama's running mate. Months later, a cofounder of PartyGaming pleaded guilty to violating the Wire Act and agreed to pay a $300 million fine to the U.S. government.[36]

During his years in the Senate, Biden's family benefited financially in other ways as he leveraged political power. Joe's sister Valerie ran all of his senate campaigns, as well as his presidential runs in 1988 and 2008. But she was also a senior partner in a political messaging firm named Joe Slade White & Company; the only two executives listed at the firm were Joe Slade White and Valerie.[37] The firm received large fees from the Biden campaigns that Valerie was running. Two and a half million dollars in consulting fees flowed to her firm from Citizens for Biden and Biden

For President Inc. during the 2008 presidential bid alone.[38] Keep in mind that Joe Slade White & Company worked for Biden campaigns over eighteen years.[39]

When Barack Obama selected Joe Biden as his running mate in 2008, it boosted the Biden family fortunes to another level. Now suddenly there were opportunities on a global scale. The executive branch offered an abundance of power to leverage, and the value of the Biden family's commercial deals, especially those of Hunter, James, and Frank, would skyrocket.

With the election of his father as vice president, Hunter Biden launched businesses fused to his father's power that led him to lucrative deals with a rogue's gallery of governments and oligarchs around the world. Sometimes he would hitch a prominent ride with his father aboard Air Force Two to visit a country where he was courting business. Other times, the deals would be done more discreetly. Always they involved foreign entities that appeared to be seeking something from his father. Often, the countries in question, including Ukraine, Russia, and Kazakhstan, had highly corrupt political cultures. In short, Hunter Biden was not cutting business deals in Japan or Great Britain, where disclosure rules and corporate governance might require greater scrutiny.[40] These were deals in the truly dark corners of the world.

In 2009, Hunter established a series of small investment vehicles with his friend and business partner Devon Archer. Biden and Archer had been at Yale University together. They launched Rosemont Seneca Partners in partnership with Rosemont Capital, an investment vehicle backed by the Heinz family. Chris Heinz, stepson of then-senator John Kerry, had been roommates with Archer at Yale.[41] Clearly, this would be an extremely well-connected firm in Washington, D.C.

As I recounted in my previous book, *Secret Empires,* on December 4, 2013, Hunter was riding on Air Force Two with his father to Beijing, China. For Vice President Joe Biden, effective diplomacy was about forming personal relationships with foreign leaders. "It all gets down to the conduct of foreign policy being personal."[42] The vice president had a series of important and tense meetings with Chinese officials on a variety of critical matters in the bilateral relationship. The trip coincided with an enormous financial deal that Hunter Biden's firm, Rosemont Seneca, was arranging with the state-owned Bank of China. What Hunter did during the official visit to Beijing we cannot know for sure. Other than a few photo ops with his father, he was nowhere to be seen.[43] After the publication of *Secret Empires,* Hunter Biden, through an attorney, claimed to ABC News that he did no business during his visit to Beijing aboard Air Force Two.[44] However, a Beijing-based company representative later claimed that Hunter had introduced his Chinese business partner, Jonathan Li, to his father during the visit.[45]

Approximately ten days after the Beijing trip, Hunter Biden's Rosemont Seneca Partners finalized a deal with the Chinese government worth a whopping $1 billion. The deal was later expanded to $1.5 billion.[46] As of this writing, the fund's website says its investments amount to more than $2 billion.[47]

It is important to note that this deal was with the Chinese government—not with a Chinese company, which means that the Chinese government and the son of the vice president were now business partners.

What they created was a joint venture called Bohai Harvest

RST (BHR). The name reflected who was involved: the "RS" was a reference to Rosemont Seneca; the "T" was the Thornton Group, a small U.S. investment firm that did business in China. It was a very unusual arrangement: the most powerful financial institution in China, the Bank of China, was setting up a joint venture with Rosemont Seneca Partners. BHR touted its "unique Sino-U.S. shareholding structure" as well as the fact that it was backed by the Chinese government.[48]

Hunter Biden actively cultivated these deals. He had visited China twice before, in 2010 and 2011, to meet with senior Chinese government officials in finance.[49] But he had no background in China, and other than a very brief and unsuccessful attempt to run a hedge fund with his uncle, no background in private equity.[50]

When the Chinese government's BHR was established, Hunter Biden was given a slot on the board of directors—supposedly unpaid while his father was vice president.[51] His actual compensation cannot be known; it is confidential.

Since *Secret Empires* was released in 2018, Hunter has claimed that he only received compensation from the Chinese after his father left the vice presidency in January 2017. He further claimed it came in the form of a 10 percent equity stake in the Bohai Harvest Financial Management Company.[52] Whether his claim is accurate or not is impossible to know—it cannot be independently verified. Furthermore, he has misled reporters about the Chinese deal in the past. Even if his account is accurate—that his compensation was deferred—it does not really make a difference. Deferred compensation from a Chinese government entity is still direct compensation from a Chinese government entity. He has never explained why he got this great opportunity from them in the first place.

BHR, with Hunter Biden on the board of directors and Devon Archer as the vice chairman and Investment Committee member, engaged in a series of financial deals that served the strategic interests of Beijing. In one of their first deals, the firm took an ownership stake in China General Nuclear Power Corporation (CGN), a nuclear energy company. The company was charged in 2016 with espionage against the United States. Also charged was an engineer who stole nuclear secrets from the United States. BHR also helped buy out the American precision machining company Henniges. They bought the company in a joint deal with Aviation Industry Corporation of China (AVIC), a military contractor owned by the Chinese government. Because Henniges's technology has military application, and therefore national security implications, the deal had to be approved by an interagency committee made up of Obama-Biden administration officials.[53] BHR also invested in military-related technology companies closer to home: they bought a stake in Face++, a major developer of facial recognition software commonly used in a phone application made by the Chinese government for surveillance of its own population.[54]

BHR was the first of a series of business relationships that Hunter Biden established with the Chinese government or Chinese government–connected entities. Another Hunter Biden–linked firm called Rosemont Realty struck a deal with a Chinese government–connected company in 2014. Hunter was an advisor and the "cofounder" of the company, which owned commercial real estate properties around the United States.[55]

Just as he had little or no background in private equity, Hunter also had no background in real estate.[56] Rosemont Realty openly touted its ties to Vice President Joe Biden. In a Rosemont Realty company prospectus for investors watermarked

"CONFIDENTIAL," there was the "key consideration" that "Hunter Biden (son of Vice President Biden) is on the advisory board."[57]

Better yet, Rosemont Realty had other political connections beyond Hunter Biden.

Rosemont Realty was headed by Daniel Burrell, a Yale grad who had worked on the John Kerry 2004 presidential campaign. A major investor in Rosemont Realty was an entity called Rosemont Real Estate GP, LLC.[58] Who exactly owns Rosemont Real Estate GP is unclear; however, in Securities and Exchange Commission (SEC) filings, the firm lists its address as that of the Heinz family office in Pittsburgh and shares a phone number with Rosemont Capital in New York City.[59] At the time of Rosemont Realty's arrangement with the Chinese firm, John Kerry, married to Heinz heir Teresa Heinz Kerry, was the U.S. secretary of state.

Just about a year after the massive deal with the Chinese government's Bohai Harvest, another Hunter Biden firm struck a pact with another Chinese government–linked firm called Gemini Investments. This deal involved a multibillion-dollar investment with Rosemont Realty.[60]

Who exactly is Gemini Investments? While Gemini is a publicly traded stock in Hong Kong, it is ultimately an "indirect subsidiary" under the control of a Chinese conglomerate called Sino-Ocean Group (formerly Sino-Ocean Land). Gemini Investments' director and honorary chairman is Li Ming. His corporate and political ties in Beijing go to the highest levels of the Communist Party. Indeed, he served several terms running as a member of the Chinese Communist Party's elite People's Political Consultative Conference. Before the name change, Sino-Ocean Land was "one of the largest real estate companies in Beijing," and it is directly connected to a company called China Ocean Shipping

Company (COSCO). Formed in 1961, COSCO is a state-owned company with strong organizational links to the Chinese navy.[61]

By December 2014, Gemini Investments inked the new partnership with Rosemont Realty, under which they would acquire an interest in the company and its underlying properties.[62] Eight months later, the newly christened Gemini-Rosemont announced its plans for $3 billion worth of new acquisitions.[63]

In short, Hunter Biden was involved in two billion-dollar deals with Chinese government–connected firms in a twenty-month period while his dad was vice president of the United States. Hunter was apparently eager to strike other deals with the Chinese—business implicitly leveraged on who his father was.

Consider the case of Patrick Ho, who was arrested in late 2017 by federal agents in New York for money laundering and violating the Foreign Corrupt Practices Act. Ho was an assistant to Chinese oil tycoon Ye Jianming, who ran the energy company CEFC. The company has strong ties to the Chinese military.[64] Hunter Biden would later admit Ye sent him a "large diamond" after one of their meetings. Biden says that he did not keep it.[65] Ho was also the secretary-general of the nonprofit China Energy Fund Committee, which many observers view as a government-directed entity.[66] In March 2019, Ho was jailed in the U.S. on bribery charges stemming from oil deals in Africa.[67] According to the *New York Times*, it appears that Ho's first phone call while in the custody of U.S. officials was an attempt to reach Hunter Biden.[68]

CEFC officials had met multiple times with Hunter Biden beginning back in 2015. In May 2017, Hunter met with Ho in Miami, where they reportedly discussed joint energy and infrastructure deals in the United States. The night of his arrest, Ho called James Biden, Joe's brother. Why Ho had James Biden's number is not clear. According to James Biden, the call was a surprise; he believed Ho was trying to contact Hunter so he gave him his nephew's number.[69]

During Ho's trial, prosecutors presented evidence that he was an arms dealer on the side, running guns to conflict zones around the world.[70] He was sentenced to three years in jail. If in fact Ho did intend for his first call while in custody to reach the son of the former vice president, it speaks volumes about how juiced in Hunter Biden was with some Chinese officials.

With Hunter's deals in China, Joe Biden's attitude toward China seemed to soften. In 2011, the Obama administration announced a strategic shift called the Asia Pivot.[71] Based on the idea that the main military and strategic challenges facing the United States are emanating from China, the Obama administration shifted military resources toward Asia.[72] Yet Biden continued to strike a relatively soft posture toward Beijing, much to the chagrin of U.S. allies in the region.[73] He continued to minimize the challenges posed by China in the spring of 2019 while on the campaign trail. "Come on, man," Biden said. "They're not bad folks, folks, but guess what. They're not competition for us."[74]

Hunter Biden's foreign deals were not limited to China, as strategically generous as that country was to the vice president's son. Ukraine, Kazakhstan, and even Russia offered him other wealth opportunities.

Ukraine boasts an abundance of energy resources, especially oil and natural gas. Burisma, a top Ukrainian natural gas producer, has deep political ties in the country. It was created in 2006 by Mykola Zlochevsky and has a Cypriot registration. He became the ecology and natural resources minister under the pro-Russian government of Viktor Yanukovych. As natural resources minister, Zlochevsky conveniently gave himself licenses to develop abundant natural gas fields. His oversight allowed Burisma to become the second-largest private natural gas company in the country. They currently rank first.[75]

As previously noted in *Secret Empires*, on April 16, 2014, Devon Archer made a private visit to the White House for a meeting with Joe Biden. The day prior, Burisma had deposited more than $112,000 into a Rosemont bank account marked "C/O Devon Archer." Six days later, on April 22, it was announced that Archer was joining the board of directors of Burisma. In short succession, on May 13, it was announced that Hunter Biden would join the Burisma board, too. Neither one had any background or experience in the energy sector, or in Ukraine for that matter.[76]

We now know based on financial records that each man appears to have been paid $83,333.33 *per month* by Burisma, or a total of $1 million a year.[77]

The timing of their appointment to the Burisma board and the payments is more than interesting. The day before Archer's official appointment, on April 21, Vice President Biden landed in Kyiv for meetings with Ukrainian officials, bringing with him terms for a United States Agency for International Development (USAID) program to assist the Ukrainian natural gas industry.[78]

Even in a country abounding with corruption, Burisma stands out. Burisma founder Zlochevsky was in legal crosshairs when Biden and Archer joined the company board. By February 2016, Ukrainian authorities seized Zlochevsky's property on suspicion that he was engaged in "illicit enrichment."[79] Zlochevsky found himself on Ukraine's wanted list and fled the country.[80] The Ukrainian prosecutor general's office seized Burisma's gas wells. Tax authorities began investigating him for suspicion of tax evasion.[81]

Hunter Biden used his contacts in Washington to help Zlochevsky in his corruption case. Burisma hired a former Obama Department of Justice lawyer named John Buretta and Blue Star Strategies, a consulting firm run by former Clinton administration officials, to help.[82]

Buretta would later recount how he interacted directly with Ukrainian prosecutors with the expressed purpose of getting the charges dropped. According to Buretta, the charges were dismissed in September 2016.[83]

Under pressure from Joe Biden, Ukrainian officials fired the Ukrainian prosecutor who was investigating Burisma. Joe Biden later bragged that he had the prosecutor fired by threatening to withhold one billion dollars in U.S. aid assistance to Ukraine.[84]

On January 16, 2017, Air Force Two descended toward Boryspil International Airport, just southeast of Kyiv. It was Joe Biden's last foreign trip as vice president. Under Biden's direction, the Obama administration had poured some $3 billion into the country.[85] Four days before Biden arrived, Burisma announced that the Ukrainian government prosecutors had ended the criminal investigations into the company and its founder Zlochevsky.[86]

There is no complete public record of Hunter Biden's foreign financial deals while his father was vice president, because neither he nor any other members of the Biden family, beyond Joe and Jill, had any federal disclosure requirements of their finances. However, court documents, including financial records from a trial involving Hunter's business partner Devon Archer, offer some tantalizing clues involving other deals Hunter Biden made around the world during the time his father was vice president.

A Morgan Stanley investment account from which Hunter

regularly received funds shows money arriving from mysterious sources around the world. There is a $142,300 deposit in April 2014 from Kazakh oligarch–controlled Novatus Holdings. Kenges Rakishev, whose father-in-law is the former vice prime minister of Kazakhstan and a close ally of Kazakh dictator Nursultan Nazarbayev, runs the offshore firm.[87] In August 2014, $1.2 million arrived into the account from an anonymous LLC via a small Swiss bank called BSI S.A. In 2016, BSI was one of several companies that were part of an embezzlement and money-laundering investigation spanning ten countries and at least $4.2 billion in irregular transactions.[88]

The financial documents also demonstrate that someone in the Biden family has other LLCs set up to receive payments. In August 2015, for example, $150,000 was transferred into an account controlled by something called MFTCG Holdings LLC Biden. It is unclear what that account is or who controls it.[89]

In another corporate record released as part of the court trial, Devon Archer describes a financial relationship with Russian oligarch Yelena Baturina. A billionaire with extensive political connections in Moscow and notorious links to Russian organized crime, Archer said Baturina invested $200 million into "various investment funds" with which he was involved.[90]

Not all of Hunter Biden's wealth accumulation during his father's vice presidency was international. Some deals occurred within the United States and benefited from taxpayer dollars steered by his father's closest aides.

Consider the case of something called mbloom, a joint venture that Hunter Biden and Devon Archer set up in Hawaii. Mbloom was a "public-private partnership" in which Hunter's firm invested $5 million and the other half came from the Hawaii Strategic Development Corporation (HSDC).[91] But where did HSDC get its money for mbloom? It came from a program back in Washington, D.C., called the Treasury Department State Small Business Credit Initiative. Three million dollars of the HSDC money came from the program, which was run by a longtime Biden aide named Don Graves.[92]

It is hard to find someone tighter in the Biden orbit than Graves. Over the course of his career, he has served as counselor to Vice President Biden, his domestic and economic policy director, and as his traveling chief of staff. After Joe Biden left the White House, he appointed Graves to the policy advisory board of the Biden Institute.[93]

The bottom line is that Hunter Biden's joint venture with mbloom was partly funded by taxpayer dollars through a program run by his father's longtime aide.

Things ultimately did not go well for mbloom. Almost immediately, the company became embroiled in an ethics scandal when it was revealed that the two men running the fund were steering dollars to their own companies.[94]

Beyond his numerous Rosemont-branded entities and ventures like mbloom, Hunter was also deeply involved with a troubling entity called Burnham Financial Group, where his business partner Devon Archer also sat on the board of directors.[95]

As they had with Rosemont, Hunter Biden and Devon Archer used Burnham to make foreign deals with governments and oligarchs, including Nurlan Abduov, an associate of Kazakh oligarch Kenges Rakishev.[96] As mentioned, Rakishev is the son-in-law of the former vice prime minister of Kazakhstan. His father-in-law,

Imangali Tasmagambetov, was also formerly the defense minister of the country and is now the Kazakh ambassador to Russia.[97] Kazakhstan is an important country not only for its vast energy resources but also because of its geostrategic position.

The financial ties between this foreign government and Biden appear to go deeper than just the investment in Burnham. As one business associate put it in an email released at the court trial, "Rosemont is deeply involved in Kazakhstan. The SWF [Sovereign Wealth Fund] of Kazakhstan is involved with Rosemont Seneca Technology Partners, Rosemont's technology investment vehicle."[98]

Between the Rosemont entities and Burnham, Biden and Archer's business dealings in Kazakhstan were extensive, although specific financial data remains undisclosed. What can be discerned from emails obtained through the Freedom of Information Act (FOIA) is that there was back-channel communication between Kazakh officials and then–secretary of state John Kerry via Devon Archer. Recall that Kerry's stepson Chris Heinz was a business partner with Biden and Archer in some of their ventures. In an email from July 11, 2013, Kerry chief of staff David Wade writes to Devon Archer, "Devon: understand you spoke to the Secretary re having him call [Kazakh] Foreign Minister Idrisov today, can you let me know topics Idrisov wants to talk about/any requests he'll have of the boss, so we can get paper prepared for a call. Hopefully, the situation on the home front will leave him time to do it."[99] This email alone makes clear that Archer had direct access to the secretary of state, without the knowledge of his chief of staff, and that Archer acted as a liaison for the Kazakh foreign minister with the secretary of state, all the while receiving funds for his and Hunter's private deals.

In addition, two Chinese companies also became involved

with Burnham. Kirin Global Enterprise Limited, a mysterious investment vehicle run by Xiangyao (or Yaojun) "Larry" Liu and Guo Jianfeng, was one that invested in Biden's company. Very little is known about Kirin or its two principals, other than the fact that they invest heavily in mainland Chinese real estate.[100] Another firm, Harvest Global Investors, a Chinese investment firm linked to the government in Beijing, also worked with Burnham, although it is unclear whether they invested money.[101]

Kazakhstan and China aside, Burnham Asset Management became the center of a federal investigation involving a $60 million fraud scheme against one of the poorest Indian tribes in America, the Oglala Sioux. Devon Archer was arrested in New York in May 2016 and charged with "orchestrating a scheme to defraud investors and a Native American tribal entity of tens of millions of dollars." Other victims of the fraud included several public and union pension plans.[102] Although Hunter Biden was not charged in the case, his fingerprints were all over Burnham. The "legitimacy" that his name and political status as the vice president's son lent to the plan was brought up repeatedly in the trial.[103]

The scheme was explicitly designed to target pension funds that had "socially responsible investing" clauses, including pension funds of labor union organizations that had publicly supported Joe Biden's political campaigns in the past. Indeed, eight of the eleven pension funds that lost their money were either government employee or labor union pension funds.[104] Joe Biden has "a long-standing alliance with labor." He closely identifies with organized labor. "I make no apologies," he has said. "I am a union man, period."[105] And many public unions have endorsed him over the years.

The defrauded pension funds included:

- Birmingham (Alabama) Water Works Pension Plan
- Chicago Transit Authority
- Management International Longshoreman's Association
- Milk Drivers Local 246 (an affiliate of the Teamsters)
- Omaha, Nebraska, School Employees' Retirement Fund
- Philadelphia Housing Authority
- City of Richmond (Virginia) Retirement System
- Washington Suburban Sanitary Commission[106]

Transcripts from Devon Archer's trial offer a clearer picture of Hunter Biden's role at Burnham Asset Management, in particular the fact that he used his father's name and political status as a means of both recruiting pension money into the scheme and alleviating investors' concerns.[107]

Hunter Biden had an office at Burnham's New York City offices on Fifty-Seventh Street.[108] During the trial, numerous witnesses came forward describing Hunter's involvement with the firm. Tim Anderson, a lawyer who did legal work on the issuance of the tribal bonds, recounts seeing Hunter while visiting the Burnham office in New York City to meet with Bevan Cooney, who was later convicted in the case.[109]

The political ties that Biden and Archer had were considered key to the Burnham brand. As stated in an August 2014 email, Jason Galanis, who was convicted in the bond scheme, agreed with an unidentified associate who also thought the company had "value beyond capital" because of their political connections.[110]

In the closing arguments at the trial, one of Devon Archer's defense attorneys, Matthew Schwartz, explained to the jury that it was impossible to talk about the bond scheme without mentioning Hunter Biden's name. "Mr. Archer responded to further questions. They wanted to know about this too, and one of the reasons—by the way, it was perfectly sensible—was because Hunter Biden was part of the Burnham team. You remember that. You saw on that Teneo slide deck he was going to be the vice chairman. You heard testimony that he was in the office. Mary Moynihan from the BIT board told you they had questions about his commissions and how much he was going to bring in in terms of clients. He was part of this deal. It was sensible to talk about him." Beyond son Hunter, other family members saw their commercial fortunes rise as they leveraged Joe Biden's position for their personal benefit.[111]

It would be a dream for any new company to announce their launch in the Oval Office at 1600 Pennsylvania Avenue.

StartUp Health is an investment consultancy based out of New York City, and in June 2011 the company barely had a website. The firm was the brainchild of three siblings from Philadelphia. Steven Krein is CEO and co-founder, while his brother, Dr. Howard Krein, serves as chief medical officer. Sister Bari serves as the firm's chief strategy officer. A friend named Unity Stoakes is a co-founder and serves as president.[112]

StartUp Health was barely up and running when, in June 2011, two of the company's executives were ushered into the Oval Office of the White House. They met with President Barack Obama and Vice President Joe Biden.[113]

It was an "amazing moment," recalled Unity Stoakes. "We were pinching ourselves." The following day the new company would be featured at a large health care tech conference being run by the U.S. Department of Health and Human Services (HHS). The meetings at the White House were crucial. Afterward, according to Stoakes, they felt "the wind to our backs."[114]

StartUp Health would continue to enjoy access to the highest levels of the White House as they worked to build up the business. Indeed, StartUp Health executives became regular visitors to the White House. According to 2011 White House visitors' logs, Howard Krein attended the China State Dinner, a White House Staff barbecue, and President Obama's Motown event. His brother, Steven, had half a dozen other meetings with White House officials.[115] Executives were back in June 2014 for a meeting with sixty "health transformers."[116] Howard even had another visit with President Obama on September 25, 2015.[117]

That first White House meeting in the Oval Office would remain an important touchstone for the company and was a key component in the way they presented themselves to potential investors and partners. In 2019, they were still touting it publicly as part of the company's mythology.[118]

How did StartUp Health gain access to the highest levels of power in Washington? Their status as a health care incubator was hardly unique. In fact, there were thirty-one similar companies operating in the state of California alone, and another eleven in the state of New York.[119]

So how did the hookup actually happen? At this point, it is important to point out that the chief medical officer of StartUp Health, Howard Krein, is married to Joe Biden's youngest daughter, Ashley.

"I happened to be talking to my father-in-law that day and I mentioned Steve and Unity were down there [in Washington, D.C.]," recalled Howard Krein. "He knew about StartUp Health and was a big fan of it. He asked for Steve's number and said, 'I have to get them up here to talk with Barack.' The Secret Service came and got Steve and Unity and brought them to the Oval Office."[120]

Advancing the commercial interests of StartUp Health using the Oval Office and Air Force Two would continue over the next half-decade while Biden was in office. Dr. Krein, who started dating Ashley in 2010 and married her in 2012, joined the Biden inner circle, even serving as a pallbearer at Beau Biden's funeral in 2015.[121]

StartUp Health describes itself as an investor in health care companies and an incubator. This is no charity. The firm offers to provide new companies technical and relationship advice in exchange for a stake in the business. Newly launched health-technology companies that want help from StartUp Health are expected to offer the firm 2 to 10 percent equity in their company.[122] Demonstrating and highlighting the fact that you can score a meeting with the president of the United States certainly helps prove a strategic company asset: high-level contacts.

Vice President Joe Biden continued to help Krein promote his company through his last months in the White House. In 2016, the vice president took his son-in-law to the Vatican for a conference on regenerative medicine attended by Pope Francis. Hunter Biden was also on the trip. After arriving on Air Force Two, Vice President Biden gave a keynote speech. Pope Francis also offered his thoughts on the challenges of health care and decried profit-driven research. Conference attendees included a who's who of scientific researchers in medicine from around the world.[123]

The vice president was still not finished helping to boost his son-in-law's business.

The following month, Krein was given the honor of introducing Vice President Biden at a major data conference first organized by the Obama administration in 2016 called Health

Datapalooza.[124] Then, in October 2016, Biden made a joint appearance with StartUp Health's Steve Krein at the Cleveland Clinic's Medical Innovation Summit.[125] In January 2017, in his final days in the Obama administration, Biden made a surprise appearance at the StartUp Health Festival in San Francisco. The corporate event, which is open only to StartUp Health members, included the vice president chatting in a closed session with the 250 people in attendance.[126]

Once Biden left the vice presidency, he continued to speak for his son-in-law's company. In January 2018, the now-former vice president delivered the keynote at the StartUp Health Festival. The following year it was Jill Biden's turn to deliver a speech there.[127]

Joe Biden's younger brother, James, has been an integral part of the family political machine from the earliest days when he served as finance chair of his 1972 Senate campaign. Joe and James have remained close. After Joe joined the U.S. Senate, he would bring his brother James along on congressional delegation trips to places like Ireland, Rome, and Africa.[128]

James Biden's beach house on Keewaydin Island, Florida, was a Biden gathering place during the vice presidential years. An exclusive island off the coast of Naples, Florida, the five-acre property became known locally as the Biden Bungalow. During the Christmas 2013 holiday, for example, the vice president and the Biden family gathered there.[129] As might generally be expected, James was welcome as well to the White House, including attending the visit of Pope Francis in September 2015. How many times James Biden visited the White House is not clear even by examining the White House visitors' logs. In 2011, for example, he was photographed attending a state dinner at the White House, but his name did not appear in visitors' logs for the event.[130]

Where James Biden's visits to the White House become pertinent to this analysis is where Joe secured James's inclusion at important White House functions that dovetailed with James's overseas business dealings. As we will see, James Biden's commercial opportunities flourished when his brother became vice president, continuing to show a pattern of Joe's public power being leveraged for his family's material gain. As with Hunter and Ashley, James profited handsomely during Joe's tenure as vice president.

Consider the case of HillStone International, a construction firm created in 2010 as a subsidiary of Hill International. Hill International began losing money in 2011. It had been launched back in 1976, and founder Irv Richter quickly became a major campaign contributor to the New Jersey Democratic Party. He was not shy about the fact that political connections had built his construction business. As he once told the *Philadelphia Inquirer*: "If your competition has access because they've been political contributors, and you don't, you're going to be at a serious disadvantage."[131]

The president of HillStone International was Kevin Justice, who grew up in Delaware and was a longtime Biden family friend. He was friends with lots of Bidens, especially Joe's sons Hunter and Beau. On November 4, 2010, according to White House visitors' logs, Justice visited the White House and met with Michele Smith in the Office of the Vice President. Smith was an advisor to the vice president.[132] Less than three weeks later, Hill-Stone announced that the vice president's brother James would be joining the firm as an executive vice president. James appeared to have little or no background in housing construction, but that did not seem to matter to HillStone. His bio on the company's website noted his "40 years of experience dealing with principals in business, political, legal and financial circles across the nation and internationally" that "enable him to understand the needs and perspectives of government, financial and development leaders to effectively negotiate and implement low-cost housing objectives both domestically and abroad." His company bio added that at "the age of 22, [James] Biden was the finance chairman of his then 29-year-old brother's bid for a U.S. Senate seat in Delaware and successfully enlisted the support of national unions, political leaders and financiers across the country." [133]

James Biden was joining HillStone just as the firm was starting negotiations to win a massive contract in war-torn Iraq. Six months later, they announced a contract to build 100,000 homes. It was part of a $35 billion, 500,000-unit project deal won by TRAC Development, a South Korean company. HillStone also received a $22 million U.S. federal government contract to manage a construction project for the State Department. [134]

David Richter, founder Irv's son, was not shy in explaining HillStone's success in securing government contracts. It really helps, he told investors at a private meeting, to have "the brother of the vice president as a partner," according to someone who was there. [135]

David Richter talked about having James Biden on the payroll and what it meant. "He knows how to deal with government officials; that's his skill," he said. "He makes people from foreign countries comfortable we're not going to steal their money. After all, he's also been with his brother a long time." [136]

The Iraq project was massive, perhaps the single most lucrative project for the firm ever. In 2012, Charlie Gasparino of Fox Business reported that HillStone officials said that the Iraq project was expected to "generate $1.5 billion in revenues over the next three years." That amounted to more than three times the revenue the company produced in 2011.[137]

A group of minority partners, including James Biden, would split about $735 million. "There's plenty of money for everyone if this project goes through," said Irv Richter.[138]

A South Korean construction company won the contract on which Hill and HillStone would work. Only months after the deal's announcement, James Biden and his wife, Sara, showed up at the White House as guests for an official state dinner. It just happened to be a state dinner honoring the then-president of South Korea, Lee Myung-bak.[139]

The deal was all set, but HillStone made a crucial error. In 2013, the firm was forced to back out of the contract because of a series of problems, including a lack of experience by Hill and TRAC Development, according to Irv Richter. But it continued doing significant contract work in the embattled country, including a six-year contract with the U.S. Army Corps of Engineers.[140]

James Biden remained with Hill International, which accumulated contracts from the federal government for dozens of projects, including projects in the United States, Puerto Rico, Mozambique, and elsewhere.[141]

The Bidens leverage political power not only for generating deals, but also for the opportunities to quietly develop the financial resources of wealthy friends for the benefit of the family. Friends that help the Bidens can count on Joe to grant them governmental favors. Consider the case of a businessman named John Hynansky.

A car dealer from Delaware, Hynansky and his family have

officially poured tens of thousands of dollars into Joe Biden's campaign coffers over the years. More than just a donor, he is a Biden friend and has helped the Biden family out financially as well.

On July 22, 2009, Vice President Biden was in Kyiv, Ukraine, as part of his first visit to the country during the Obama administration. A large crowd of citizens and businessmen gathered on a beautiful warm summer morning to hear him speak. During his speech, Biden singled out John Hynansky as "my very good friend," describing him before the large crowd as "a very prominent businessman from Delaware . . . I had breakfast with him the other day." [142]

Hynansky is well known in Ukraine. Shortly after the fall of communism, he moved into the country as an automobile importer and car dealer.[143]

Hynansky had ambitions to expand his business in Ukraine and the Obama-Biden administration was willing to help. Three years after that speech, in July 2012, the federal government's Overseas Private Investment Corporation (OPIC) announced that it was providing Hynansky's company with a $20 million loan so that he could grow his import dealership in Ukraine. According to OPIC, the loan was to "expand Winner Import Ukraine's automobile business, [and] construct and operate 'Winner Autocity,' which will have two new, state-of-the-art dealership facilities for Porsche and Land Rover/Jaguar Automobiles." What is unusual, and as OPIC made clear, is that the loan would not actually create any American jobs; the cars to be sold in Ukraine were European luxury vehicles built in other countries. The best it could claim was that the taxpayer-backed loan would not cost any American jobs.[144]

The Biden family friend benefited from taxpayer-backed loans provided by the Obama-Biden administration. Why Hynansky needed the loans is unclear, given his vast business empire. Indeed, in 2015, Hynansky told reporters, "I have a ton of companies in the Ukraine."[145] Why OPIC granted a taxpayer-backed loan for a business that would not create jobs in the United States and would simply sell expensive European-made vehicles to the Ukrainian elite is also unclear.

What is clear is that Joe Biden helped a friend who would later help another Biden.

In June 2015, James Biden had a federal tax lien placed on the Biden Bungalow on Keewaydin Island, Florida, by the Internal Revenue Service (IRS). According to tax filings, he owed nearly $590,000 to the federal government in back taxes. In late 2014, there was also a $74,700 lien placed on the home by a contractor called Gator Pressure Cleaning & Custom Painting.[146] In mid-2015, help arrived when James received two mortgages totaling $900,000. The mortgages came from an obscure Delaware entity called 1018 PL LLC. According to corporate records, John Hynansky controls that company.[147]

The mortgages Hynansky provided seemed to do the trick. The amount James owed to the IRS dropped to just $30,000 by the end of 2015.[148] Six days after he received the mortgages from Hynansky, Gator was paid, too.[149]

Even after Joe left office, James Biden continued to tout his ties to his brother. At a meeting in 2018, James told a group of potential business partners that the Biden Cancer Initiative, a nonprofit launched in 2017 by Joe and Jill Biden, would help promote their new business.[150]

———

In July 1999, Joe's other younger brother, Frank Biden, was living in San Diego and driving—with a suspended Florida license—a rented Jaguar XK8 sedan. On August 14, 1999, Frank drove the Jag to a friend's house and later, around 11:15 p.m., they decided to go to a concert at the Belly Up Tavern in Cardiff, California. According to court documents, he gave the keys to his young friend Jason Turton; three others piled into the backseat. Frank rode shotgun, handled the stick shift, and provided instructions as they cruised down the highway. At one point, Frank shifted into high gear and told Turton "punch the car and leave it in third gear" until told otherwise. Frank then gave the command for fourth gear and the Jaguar picked up speed. Soon they were humming along between 70 and 80 mph in a 35-mph zone. Michael Albano, a thirty-seven-year-old single father, was crossing the street, having just left a beachside bar, when the Jaguar slammed into him. Albano was first struck by the right headlamp, which sent him crashing into the windshield, over the top of the car, into a backseat passenger's face, and then onto the Jaguar's trunk before landing on the asphalt. In depositions two of the witnesses sitting in the backseat recall Frank Biden telling Turton to "keep driving" after Albano hit the ground.[151]

Albano died at the scene. He left behind two young daughters, who would later describe him as a "perfect" father.[152]

Turton pleaded guilty to felony hit and run.[153] The guardians for Albano's daughters sued Frank Biden in court in a "wrongful death" civil lawsuit on August 14, 2000, but Frank never showed up at the courthouse. Nor did he reply to any legal correspondence from the court, including a court final judgment in September 2002 that Frank owed each of the girls $275,000 for his role in the tragedy.[154]

In October 1999, the guardians for the two Albano girls had hired a private investigator to find Frank. They spoke to his ex-wife, the broader Biden family, and eventually the Biden family attorney, who refused to provide any information about Frank's whereabouts or to accept service of documents. Investigators also noted that they had "received information indicating that the Subject appears to stay with his brother, Joseph, occasionally," and that people nearby claimed to have seen him at Joe's house in Delaware.[155]

The quest for paying the judgments began. Investigators could not find any bank accounts connected to Frank "because of his apparent evasive actions"; they suspected that perhaps he had accounts "in another name or DBA."[156]

Eight years after the court's ruling, in September 2008, an attorney for the girls reached out to Senator Joe Biden in Washington, asking for assistance in locating his brother and getting him to pay the debt. Joe Biden, of course, had lost his own wife and daughter in an automobile accident so perhaps there was the hope that he would be sympathetic. Joe Biden did not respond. Instead, his chief of staff at the time wrote back in what can only be described as a businesslike—even cold—letter, revealed publicly here for the first time. "Senator Biden has received your letter of September 16 regarding a judgment by your clients against his brother Frank," he wrote on Biden's official Senate stationery. "The Senator wishes to express his deep sympathy with the Albano daughters over their loss. While it is correct, as you state, that Senator Biden was not involved in the accident and bears no legal liability for the judgment, the Senator would certainly encourage his brother to pay the judgment if his personal financial circumstances made that at all possible. As you are aware, however, Frank has no assets with which to satisfy the judgment. The Senator regrets that this is where matters stand and that he cannot be more helpful."[157]

But Frank Biden was earning money. Indeed, seven days before Joe Biden's office sent that letter, his brother was slapped with a tax lien from the IRS for $23,638.59 in unpaid taxes. In total he owed more than $32,000 at the time, a clear indication that Frank had income. In 2013, he paid off the tax lien in full.[158]

As of the time of this writing, in September 2019, the Albano daughters have still not collected their money from Frank Biden. With interest, that judgment debt is now more than $900,000.[159]

As we have already observed, loyalty to family is a virtue until it becomes an excuse for unethical use of public power. Here, we also note the irony that loyalty to his family would become an excuse to disregard someone else's family—despite having the power to take compassionate action for a just cause.

Although Joe appears unwilling to help the Albano sisters collect a legitimate debt from Frank, as we will see, he has been busy helping Frank accumulate wealth through far-flung business deals.

In late March 2009, Vice President Joe Biden was headed to Costa Rica aboard Air Force Two. He went for a series of meetings with officials as a preamble to the Fifth Summit of the Americas Conference. Biden went to the Costa Rican presidential palace for a one-on-one with President Oscar Arias. Daniel Ortega, the strongman leader of neighboring Nicaragua, criticized Biden for being "too chummy" with Arias. The Biden visit had symbolic significance. The last time a high-ranking American official had visited the country was back in 1997, when Bill Clinton had come.[160]

Biden and Arias met with a number of associates present. Biden invited "Arias to work with him personally to develop" education policy for Central America, but also underscored that "foreign direct investment would help Costa Rica's economy more in the short term." During the meeting, Arias gave Biden a letter to pass on to President Obama requesting additional U.S. aid dollars to assist with Costa Rica's education system.[161] Later, the Arias administration declared that it was "a clear recognition of the trajectory of Costa Rica as the United States' strategic partner in the region."[162]

Joe Biden's trip to Costa Rica came at a fortuitous time for his brother Frank, who was busy working deals in the country. Conveniently, any assets Frank might hold in Costa Rica would be out of reach of U.S. courts and the Albano family. Frank, who had studied law and practiced real estate in Florida, had ambitions in Costa Rica. In the months that followed, the opportunities for Frank Biden arose courtesy of the Costa Rican government. Just months after Vice President Biden's visit, in August, *Costa Rica News* announced a new multilateral partnership "to reform Real Estate in Latin America" between Frank Biden, a developer named Craig Williamson, and the Guanacaste Country Club, a newly planned resort. The partnership, which appears to be ongoing, was wrapped in a beautiful package as a "call on resources available to the companies and individuals to reform the social, economic and environmental practices of real estate developers across the world by example." Frank Biden declared, "Prioritizing the health and wellbeing of employees, members of the local community and protecting the breathtaking beauty that is Costa Rica is a money maker."[163]

In real terms, Frank's dream was to build in the jungles of Costa Rica thousands of homes, a world-class golf course, casinos, and an antiaging center. The Costa Rican government was eager to cooperate with the vice president's brother.[164]

As Joe Biden would later recount in his book *Promise Me, Dad*, he was a central player in Obama administration policy toward

Latin America and the Caribbean. "The President asked me to take over the job of repairing our wobbly relations across the entirety of the Americas—the Northern Triangle, Brazil, the Caribbean, everything." He was the go-to guy in the White House for Latin America policy.[165]

The Costa Rican National Power and Light Company (CNFL) unveiled the conceptual design for what would later become the Guanacaste Solar Park. The new facility would provide energy for Frank's plans for a massive resort being built just north of the town of Liberia. CNFL picked Frank's company, Sun Fund Americas, as their partner for the solar park. Frank did not have any background in solar energy, but it was quite clear who he was when he pitched the project to investors. His brother Joe's name figured prominently in his biography.[166]

Frank's partner in the deal, as in the Guanacaste Country Club, was a real estate investor in Costa Rica named Craig S. Williamson, an American army veteran who now lived in the country.[167] Williamson was arrested in 2014 for failing to appear in court related to a fraud charge.[168] Long active in selling real estate to Americans in Central America, Williamson describes himself as a "Central American Real Estate Investment Advisor for many North American based Institutional Real Estate Investors as well as hundreds of Private Investors, including the family of US Vice President Joseph Biden."[169]

Frank's vision for a country club in Costa Rica received support from the highest levels of the Costa Rican government—despite his lack of experience in building such developments. He met with the Costa Rican ministers of education and energy and environment, as well as the president of the country. Costa Rican president Luis Guillermo Solís Rivera even penned a letter to

Frank Biden praising the project. The letter found its way onto the internet seeking presales for the project to investors back in the United States.[170]

On October 4, 2016, the Costa Rican Ministry of Public Education signed a letter of intent with Frank's company, Sun Fund Americas. The project involved allowing a company called GoSolar to operate solar power facilities in Costa Rica. The previous year, the Obama-Biden administration's OPIC had authorized a $6.5 million taxpayer-backed loan for the project.[171]

Despite Frank's MIA status concerning the Albano debt, Joe and Frank Biden have remained close over the years. As Frank explains in his bio, "Throughout his career Mr. Biden worked as an unpaid senior advisor on all of his brother Joe Biden's senatorial campaigns, culminating in the Presidential election of 2012. He is currently senior advisor to the former VP's 2020 political action committee."[172] During Joe's tenure as vice president, Frank frequently visited the White House. On May 1, 2014, Frank sat in on a small meeting with Barack Obama in the Oval Office.[173] In 2016, Frank was a guest at the Singapore State Dinner in the White House.[174]

Frank's company, Sun Fund Americas, had ambitions beyond Costa Rica. The company states that it "teams with governments and local partners and provides debt and equity financing, as well as world-class brands, operators and equipment suppliers" for projects.[175] Here, too, Joe could help.

In June 2014, Vice President Joe Biden announced the launch of the Caribbean Energy Security Initiative (CESI). The program called for increasing access to financing for Caribbean energy projects that he strongly supported. American taxpayer dollars were dedicated to facilitating deals that matched U.S. government financing with local energy projects in Caribbean countries, including Jamaica.[176] In January 2015, Biden hosted CESI in Washington, D.C., bringing together leaders from across the region to discuss energy issues and in particular, renewable energy.[177] One primary focus of the conference was local and international dealmakers needing help to bring renewable energy projects to the Caribbean region. USAID announced that it would be spending $10 million to boost renewable energy projects in Jamaica over the next five years.[178]

After Joe Biden brought together leaders for CESI, brother Frank's firm Sun Fund Americas announced that it was "engaged in projects and is in negotiations with governments of other countries in the [Caribbean] region for both its Solar and Waste to Energy development services." [179] As if to push the idea along, the Obama administration's OPIC provided a $47.5 million loan to support the construction of a 20-megawatt solar facility in Clarendon, Jamaica. When the deal was announced, U.S. ambassador to Jamaica Luis G. Moreno noted that the project "wouldn't be possible without OPIC financing." [180]

Frank Biden's Sun Fund Americas later announced that it had signed a power purchase agreement (PPA) to build a 20-megawatt solar facility in Jamaica.[181]

Many of Frank's commercial ventures sidecar with government initiatives driven by his famous brother, and so far, those described have been international.

Closer to home, one of Frank's largest business ventures involves education. Just as the lack of a background in large-scale real estate developments did not deter him in Costa Rica, and lack of a background in renewable energy did not deter him in Jamaica, lack of a professional background in education was no roadblock in Florida. In 2008, with his brother on the verge of becoming vice president, Frank became involved in the lucrative commercial real estate side of the charter school movement.

His older brother had a history of supporting charter schools in the U.S. Senate. Back in 2001, for example, he cosponsored the "Charters and Choice" bill, one of only eight Democrats to do so.[182] In the 2008 campaign, the Obama-Biden ticket had vowed to double funding for charter schools.[183] Charter schools are public schools established with taxpayer funding but, unlike traditional public schools, have greater flexibility in experimenting with different teaching models. Charter school methods have shown significant success in turning around some troubled public schools.[184]

Beginning in 2009, there was a lot of taxpayer money available for starting charter schools. As part of the federal stimulus, the Obama-Biden administration made $5 billion available for "education innovations," which opened the door to more charter schools.[185]

Frank's interest was in the business side of the schools, in particular, the underlying real estate associated with them. He discovered early on that charter schools pay rent using taxpayer dollars. Managed correctly and with the right connections, this created profitable opportunities.

In Joe Biden's first year as vice president, Frank became involved with a for-profit management company for charter schools called Mavericks in Education Florida LLC. Frank says that his involvement grew out of a chance encounter in a coffee shop when he bumped into a South Florida businessman named Mark Rodberg. Mavericks built schools for at-risk students who had trouble in class. The schools themselves would be nonprofits, but Mavericks in Education Florida LLC would be a for-profit company that charged the schools management fees, while the related School Property Development LLC owned and charged high rents for their buildings. The funds would come from taxpayer money and federal grants. Whether the school failed or succeeded, the for-profit company owned the real estate assets.[186]

It was not long before Frank was flying around Florida in a private jet, lobbying local politicians and school officials to allow Mavericks to manage charter schools in their communities. Eventually, he became president and director of development for the company. Whenever the company shared his biography for a business proposal, the fact that he was the brother of the vice president of the United States was in the first or second sentence.[187]

"I'm a salesman," Frank said. "I'm nothing but a P. T. Barnum for these kids."[188]

From 2009 to 2011, Mavericks opened eight schools in Florida.[189] When Mavericks set up a school in Fort Lauderdale, they acquired the building from a controversial Broward County power broker named Jesse P. Gaddis.

Known as "Fort Lauderdale's Taxi King," Gaddis "had ties to mobsters and major drug smugglers." As a young man, Gaddis was charged and convicted of armed robbery, and went to jail. In a later case, he was charged with kidnapping and robbery, although the charges were eventually dropped. Authorities also investigated Gaddis in connection with a drug-smuggling operation in which his brother and business partner, Donald Gaddis, was killed. His brother was found in a shallow grave in southwest Florida.[190]

The deal between Mavericks and Gaddis had extraordinarily lucrative terms for Gaddis: Gaddis exchanged the building for a $2 million promissory note attached to the mortgage at an initial interest rate of 12 percent (lowered to 10 percent in 2014). The term was originally for five years and was twice extended, in 2014 and

2017. The first extension reveals that the interest-only monthly payments for the note's second term were nearly $16,700.[191]

Mavericks LLC was a business. "Are there people making money in charter schools? Absolutely," Frank Biden explained in one interview. "I don't apologize for them at all. Just run good schools for kids who need them."[192]

Mavericks ran with its own unusual teaching model: students would interact with teachers for only a few hours a day. The rest of the time, they would sit in front of computers as part of self-directed learning.[193]

According to the Florida Department of Education, the performance record of Mavericks Schools in Florida was abysmal. These were not what one would regard as "good schools for kids." The best-performing Mavericks school was in Kissimmee, near Disney World. The graduation rate at that school was just 43 percent in 2011. Things were worse at Mavericks' other Florida locations: in Largo, the graduation rate was an astonishing 7.2 percent; in Homestead, it was an incredible 4.5 percent.[194]

The schools continued to receive poor marks from state regulators. From 2009 to 2014, individual schools received " 'declining' ratings three times and one F."[195]

The graduation rates also did not really improve over time. In 2019, the *Miami Herald* reported continued basement-level performance. Mavericks High of North Miami Dade had a 9 percent graduation rate; Mavericks High of South Miami Dade was 13 percent.[196]

Mavericks was also accused by state auditors in Florida of inflating their enrollment numbers. As the *South Florida Sun Sentinel* noted, "In South Florida, three probes released by the state Auditor General's office in 2013 and 2014 found Mavericks schools in Fort Lauderdale, Pompano Beach, Palm Springs and Homestead were collecting dollars for students who did not attend the school and not teaching enough hours to meet state requirements."[197] Why inflate the enrollment numbers? The more students enrolled, the more taxpayer funding collected.

The key to understanding Frank Biden's business is that the real money was *not* in the operation of the schools themselves— but in the underlying real estate for charter schools. "It's all about the buildings we buy," he explained in another interview. "Certainly the operation of the schools isn't profitable."[198]

In addition to Mavericks in Education, Frank also became a partner in School Property Development, which provided "building services" to charter schools and owned buildings connected to Mavericks. They were soon building charter schools in West Palm Beach, Royal Palm Beach, Glen Ridge, Pembroke Pines, and elsewhere in Florida.[199] He also lists himself as a partner in DelMarva LLC, based in Washington, D.C. "These entities are responsible for over 12 billion dollars in school financing placed with over 200 schools built and operated in Florida," reads his account. "His companies provide a turnkey, single source of responsibility to acquire, finance, design, build and lease K-12 public schools."[200]

The strategy was charging the schools high enough rent to pay off the mortgage on the property. In Homestead, Florida, for example, Mavericks' school building had a market value of just $1.2 million. The school was scheduled to pay $1.75 million in rent over just five years.[201] In short, the schools were a vehicle for School Property Development LLC to profit from buying or leasing real estate for rental by Mavericks in Education LLC. Because the schools were using taxpayer money and receiving grants to pay for the buildings, they were probably less concerned with the cost of rent.

By 2014, the Mavericks schools had received more than $70 million in state money. Nine million of that went to the management company.[202] As we will see, the Obama administration also lavished the failing Mavericks schools with federal grants.

During this time, Frank enjoyed access to the highest levels of the White House. Indeed, on May 1, 2014, he attended an education event at the White House with top education officials from the National Education Association. That day he was also in a small meeting of just ten people with President Barack Obama in the White House to talk about charter schools. Other participants included Stephen Bittel, a Florida real estate developer who would later become the chairman of the Florida Democratic Party.[203]

Getting a charter school approved can be a tricky political feat. There is clearly going to be opposition from local teachers' unions, and some politicians are going to be suspicious of who is actually going to be running the school. Frank Biden had an advantage that other competitors did not have: a powerful and famous brother whose name he could leverage.

Frank dropped his brother's name and position to vouch for his honesty. When he appeared before the city commission of Sunrise, Florida, in 2015 to pitch a school, he casually explained who he was. According to the official minutes of the meeting, the recorder tells of Frank's testimony, saying, "Whatever he [Frank] does, because of the honor of being the Vice President's brother, he has to watch himself. Whomever he was involved with was fully vetted."[204] He never explained exactly how his business activities were vetted and by whom. Was he simply making it up? It is impossible to know. Regardless of what explanation he might provide, he was capitalizing on his relationship as the vice president's brother to confer integrity to his company. In an instance several years earlier, he told skeptical local politicians that his school would work by "invoking his family's political power." "I give you my word of honor, on my family name, that this system is sustainable," Frank said. "This school will be sustainable." Local officials approved the deal.[205]

During the Obama presidency, Frank Biden's charter schools received millions of dollars in federal grants. These were "discretionary grants" given through the U.S. Department of Education's (DOE) State Educational Agencies (SEA) grant program.[206] Applications were filed with Education Department headquarters in Washington.[207] As of 2012, the department was sending each Mavericks school approximately $250,000 a year in taxpayer money.[208] In 2015, Mavericks schools received just under $2.7 million in grants from the DOE—an average of almost $300,000 per school.[209]

Shortly after he announced his 2020 campaign for president, Joe Biden was on the campaign trail in Texas. He told a crowd, "I do not support any federal money . . . for for-profit charter schools—period," Biden said to the crowd's approval. "The bottom line is it siphons off money from public schools, which are already in enough trouble."[210] He never mentioned Frank's profitable charter school businesses and, ironically, the legitimacy that his own name gave them.

On June 4, 2019, presidential candidate Joe Biden released a campaign video announcing his views on how to deal with climate change. Joe explained that his plan provided for "an enormous opportunity to hold polluters accountable for the damage they've caused, particularly in low-income communities and communities of color."[211]

On the same day, about 1,600 miles from Joe, who was campaigning in New Hampshire, brother Frank stood before the assembled media in South Florida with a similar message. He, too, was making an announcement concerning pollution and "communities of color." But Frank was part of a legal team that was suing twelve sugar growers in a class-action lawsuit.[212] The tenor was remarkably similar to what his brother had spoken about in his campaign video.

The Berman Law Group in South Florida hired Frank in 2018 to serve as a "Senior Advisor." "He brings a prestigious combination of accomplishments and experience," the firm noted in a press release. They said of Frank, he is "highly regarded in the business and government sectors" and boasts "one of the most respected names in the U.S. and abroad."[213]

The Berman Law Group features as its director of government relations former Democratic Florida state senator Joseph Abruzzo, who had worked with then–vice president Joe Biden on legislation.[214]

Frank had never filed a legal case before. On that day, the Berman firm filed a class-action lawsuit against the United States Sugar Corporation and eleven other defendants on behalf of poor minority residents in Belle Glade, Pahokee, and South Bay, Florida, who claimed that they had suffered health problems related to the burning of sugarcane fields.[215] To help make their case, the law firm released a six-and-a-half-minute video/infomercial about the lawsuit. Frank figured prominently throughout and finished it off by walking with the group in slow motion, wearing black sunglasses, through a ring of fire while dramatic music played.[216]

Biden's campaign video appeared to be perfectly synchronized with his brother's lawsuit.

When asked by a reporter at his press conference whether he had coordinated his announcement with that of his brother, Frank explained, "There was absolutely no coordination. It was serendipitous that Joe's environmental policy came out today. . . . Our thoughts are the same, but there was no coordination."[217]

The environmental plan that Joe Biden unfurled in his campaign video had policy nuggets that would help Frank's businesses in very specific ways. Joe Biden's plan calls for strengthening international collaboration and investment in clean energy infrastructure in the Americas, and supplying clean energy across the entire Central American energy grid and in the Caribbean, which is of course what Frank was doing in the region.[218]

Coordinated in this case or not, the overall pattern here is that the Biden family members see that Joe's vested public power is convenient for the creation of business opportunities for personal wealth.

It would be easier to dismiss these entanglements if they only involved one of the Bidens. The fact that it involves five family members indicates that there is a culture within the Biden family that trades off Joe's power. And Joe appears willing to act on their behalf whenever he can.

The Bidens leverage Joe's power to their financial benefit. But as we will see in the next chapter, others are also prepared to go to extraordinary lengths to leverage their power in creative and destructive ways.

4

CORY BOOKER

Cory Booker is a rock star senator with a cultivated persona, heroic mystique, and a crowd of celebrity friends. He hangs out with Oprah Winfrey and Spike Lee, and does big financial deals with Facebook founder Mark Zuckerberg and Eric Schmidt, the former executive chairman of Google. On camera, he performs fits of derring-do, including saving people from burning buildings and rescuing puppies.[1] To his admirers, he is a sensei of sorts. "He's a vegan and a Rhodes Scholar, and he never touches alcohol or tobacco," notes one admiring journalist. "He meditates daily, and Tweets quotes from Jewish scholars and Buddhist priests."[2]

As a senator, Booker has demonstrated a penchant for rhetorical flourish. When U.S. Supreme Court nominee Brett Kavanaugh was up for Senate confirmation, Senator Booker famously threatened to break ethics rules by releasing confidential records about him. "This is about the closest I'll probably ever have in my life to an 'I am Spartacus' moment," he declared. The disclosure was far less dramatic than Booker would claim; he knew in advance that the documents had been cleared for release.[3]

While on the national stage, Booker has consistently identified himself as a progressive, a reformer, a hero for the people. As he told one reporter back in 2013, "There's nothing in that realm of progressive politics where you won't find me."[4]

Yet his meteoric rise, first to Newark city council member, then to Newark mayor, and now to U.S. senator, has left a trail of enriched friends. Booker's public persona may be virtuous, but a look at his political climb reveals a politician who has leveraged his power for the benefit of his friends and supporters.

Booker himself is knit together as a tapestry of American history. Harvard professor and historian Henry Louis Gates Jr. once tested Booker's DNA for an episode of his PBS show *Finding Your Roots*. Gates discovered that Booker was 47 percent African, 45 percent European, and 7 percent Native American. Booker himself researched his ancestors and found a remarkable lineage, which seems to inform his pronouncements about national "unity." As Booker writes in his book *United*, "I am descended from slaves and slave owners. I have Native American blood and am also the great-great-great-grandson of a white man who fought in the Creek War of 1836, in which Native Americans were forcibly removed from their land. I am the great-great-grandson of many slaves, and I am also the great-great-grandson of a corporal who fought in the Confederate Army. . . ."[5]

Booker grew up in the white, upper-class New Jersey suburb of Harrington Park, less than an hour outside of Newark. Booker's father poetically described his family in their neighborhood as "four raisins in a tub of sweet vanilla ice cream."[6] He excelled in high school as both a student and as an athlete and was named Gatorade New Jersey Football Player of the Year. His athletic prowess and academic skills meant a scholarship to attend Stanford University, where he graduated in 1991. Later he attended Oxford University as a Rhodes Scholar, where he studied United States history before going on to Yale Law School.[7]

At Oxford, his religious views expanded in an unusual manner. Amid the graceful spires, he struck up a close friendship with

Hasidic rabbi Shmuley Boteach, who founded the L'Chaim Society, an organization for Orthodox Jewish students. Boteach is a member of a unique branch of Judaic teaching that embraces the spiritual teachings of the Lubavitchers. Much of the spiritual guidance came from the work of Rabbi Menachem Schneerson, who died in 1994. Lubavitchers are part of Chabad, a Hasidic sect known for its "celebratory approach to the Jewish faith." Booker, although raised Baptist, embraced (at least for a while) the Lubavitchers. When he returned to the United States, he maintained a close relationship with Rabbi Boteach. At Yale Law School, he cofounded a Jewish society with a rabbi. Booker visited Schneerson's grave site, where he reportedly prayed three times. It is not clear if there were multiple visits or multiple prayers on one. When scholar Robert Curvin asked him about the gravesite visit(s) later, Booker oddly deflected his answer and avoided the subject.[8]

After he graduated from Yale Law School in 1997, the super law firm Skadden, Arps, Slate, Meagher & Flom offered Booker a two-year fellowship to practice public interest law in Newark. For a $37,000 annual salary, he would be filing complaints against slumlords. Booker won some legal victories.[9] It was during this time that the young lawyer would claim to experience a crucial turning point in his life. As he explained it later, he encountered a powerful woman named Virginia D. Jones, who was the head of the tenants' association at Brick Towers, one of the worst housing projects in Newark. Jones explained to him the realities of urban life in Newark, showing him "drug dealers, a crack house, and rundown projects." When Booker asked how he could help, she retorted, "Well, you can't help me." His takeaway was that he could help if he was prepared to stay there and make a real change. According to Booker, she and other tenant leaders eventually challenged him to seek political office, spurring his interest in running. Jones, however, offered a different version of events. She claims Booker asked her to support his candidacy for city council after he had been collecting signatures to get on the ballot.[10]

In 1998, Booker threw his hat in the ring and was on the ballot for Newark Municipal Council as the representative from the Central Ward. It would be a tough race. In the general election with three candidates, a rival named George Branch was ahead by more than 300 votes in the first round of voting, but since no one held a majority, there was a runoff. Booker struck a deal with local political boss "Big Steve" Adubato Sr., who "poured all of his troops behind Booker."[11] Adubato was the rough-talking, legendary boss of Newark's North Ward. A fixture in Newark since 1962, Adubato served as Democratic Party chairman of the North Ward and sat on the executive board of the Newark Teachers Union. Big Steve also ran a collection of nonprofits and schools, operating out of the Clark Mansion, an imposing twenty-eight-room Queen Anne–style house.[12]

In the second round of voting, Booker won by 659 votes. Adubato would help Booker win reelection four years later, as well as become elected mayor. Adubato and his machine were an important component of Booker's political rise culminating, so far, in his election to the U.S. Senate. Adubato would prove to be critical for Booker's hold on power. As Professor Robert Curvin of Rutgers University puts it, "the Booker/Adubato relationship has been the most critical factor in building a path for Booker's future victories in Newark. Adubato may, in fact, be Booker's most important horse."[13]

Over the years, Booker would return favors to Adubato. When the Oprah Winfrey Foundation sent $1.5 million to Cory Booker for distribution by his Newark Now nonprofit, $500,000 went to Adubato's charter school. As Professor Curvin observes, when connecting Adubato's support for Booker and the flow of money in return, "The timing was exquisite." [14]

Although never personally accused, Adubato would be caught up in a swirl of ethics scandals. In 2009 and 2010, eleven people who were part of his political machine "were convicted of voting fraud and related crimes." Booker aides were charged, too, "for improper handling and voting of several hundred messenger ballots." Then a test cheating scandal broke out at a charter school that Adubato founded, the one that had received half a million dollars from Booker's nonprofit. Sixth-grade students' standardized tests answers were changed to improve the school's test scores. [15]

On the one hand, Booker's early tenure as a member of the Newark Municipal Council was marred by his general absence at meetings. He often spent time attending meetings of the Stanford University Board of Trustees, where he was a member, and giving speeches on college campuses around the country. [16] Councilman Booker also excelled at publicity events that gave him national media attention. In 1999, he dramatically announced that he was going to set up a tent and live in a crime-ridden area in Newark until the city cleaned up the area. The media presented it as an act of sacrifice; Booker was prepared to put himself on the line to help his community. The New York Times and New York magazine described the scene with drug dealers throwing feces at the tent along with nighttime "catcalls and threats" that reportedly kept Booker awake. [17] In actuality, Booker was not exactly roughing it. The tent was "ballroom size." Two people who participated in the event later revealed, "Booker seldom stayed in the tent overnight but would often leave after dark and return early the next morning. The press was led to believe that he camped at the site overnight."[18]

By 2002, Booker was ready to aim higher, putting his sights on the mayor's office. His main impediment was a powerful and corrupt incumbent who had been in office for more than a decade and a half.

Newark mayor Sharpe James was straight out of central casting. As one journalist put it, he was "a gap-toothed, gold-chain-wearing caricature of a corrupt, urban New Jersey politician"—a smart talker who had ruled over Newark for sixteen years.[19] James actually held two political positions at the same time: He was both mayor and a New Jersey state senator, so he was drawing two salaries. Even the $250,000 he earned, though, could never fully explain how the public servant was able to buy properties in Newark and Florida, as well as a Rolls-Royce and a yacht.[20]

Drawing on his network of supporters around the country, Booker raised huge sums of money for the race. By Election Day, of the more than $3 million in total he had raised for the campaign, only $47,550 of it actually came from Newark.[21] There were more problems than just where the money came from. After the race, Booker's campaign was charged with more than 1,500 election-law violations. It received the largest campaign fund-raising fine in New Jersey political history to that point. Sharpe James held the record previously.[22]

Booker had impressive credentials—and Mayor James quickly used his pedigree against him. "You have to learn to be black," he lectured Booker, "and we don't have time to teach you."[23] There were also savage and slanderous personal attacks. According to Booker's people, James smeared his opponent as a "faggot white boy."[24] James appeared impervious to any sense of shame. During the campaign, the mayor was forced to admit that he had visited a strip club that the police alleged was a brothel where underage prostitutes were working. The mayor responded that he had been at the club only in his "official capacity" to make sure that the club would be shut down. It did not help Booker's cause that his own campaign chief of staff, Jermaine James, was also at the club when the police arrived, waiting in a line to get in.[25]

However crude and offensive Sharpe James's attacks against Booker might have been, they proved effective: Booker lost the election by about 3,500 votes. Booker, however, got the last laugh. James was indicted on thirty-three counts of fraud. His crimes included charging Newark city credit cards with $58,000 worth of personal expenses. Convicted and sent to jail, James added his name to a long parade of corrupt Newark mayors. Every other mayor in Newark over the past forty-five years had been indicted.[26]

Booker and his allies turned the 2002 election defeat into another national media opportunity. Defeat at the ballot box did not dent national enthusiasm for Booker. Indeed, he found his celebrity status only rising. Part of it was the result of an extraordinary documentary film called *Street Fight*, which covered the 2002 race. A gritty, street-level look at urban politics, *Street Fight* positioned Booker as the the Reformer fighting the Establishment. Many in Hollywood championed it as a sort of organic citizen film. It was even nominated for an Academy Award. But the film was less grassroots than it might appear. In fact, Marshall Curry, one of Booker's closest friends, produced the film. Curry's family owned the investment firm Eagle Capital Management, and the family was among the most generous of his campaign donors.[27]

The Curry connection would prove to be an interesting one.

Booker was a champion of charter schools, which he viewed as the best option for improving the performance of failing public schools. Booker pushed aggressively for charter schools, not only in Newark, but also on the national stage. For Curry and Eagle Capital, charters schools were a commercial opportunity, suggesting their support for Booker was in part a calculated investment. Ravenel Boykin Curry IV of Eagle Capital Management told the *New York Times* that charter schools are "exactly the kind of investment people in our industry spend our days trying to stumble on, with incredible cash flow, even if in this case we don't ourselves get any of it."[28]

Still, there were ways to profit. Like Frank Biden, they discovered there were a variety of means to take an educational reform and profit from it. Hedge funds like Eagle enjoyed a lucrative tax credit called the New Markets Tax Credit (NMTC), which Bill Clinton established in 2000. The tax credit allowed hedge funds to take a 39 percent tax credit on money they contribute to charter schools and to collect interest on those payments. According to Investopedia, "A hedge fund could double its money in seven years" with the NMTC. Not bad for what some would consider an altruistic investment.[29]

In the wake of the 2002 defeat, Booker joined the local law firm Rabinowitz, Trenk, Lubetkin, et al. (hereafter Trenk). The firm, later renamed Booker, Rabinowitz, Trenk, et al., specialized in government contracts and services, thriving on its ties to local politicians. What Booker did at Trenk is unclear. An examination of legal records suggests that Booker had a light footprint at the law firm. He appears to have spent much of his time giving speeches around the country and continuing to build his political machine. As part of that effort, he also set up a nonprofit organization called Newark Now, which shared an address with the law firm.[30] Newark Now stacked its board and staff with Booker's political aides and the family members of local machine politicians. He chose Modia "Mo" Butler, a close political aide, to run the organization. Butler would be a fixture at Booker's side going forward. Mo's ex-wife, Nicole, was later on the payroll of another Booker nonprofit, Newark Charter School Fund.[31] Once Cory was elected mayor, Newark Now would become an important conduit for money from city contractors and others wanting favors from the mayor's office. Leverage requires a pathway for payment.

With his partnership at Trenk and his new nonprofit, Booker began almost immediately campaigning for the 2006 election. This time Booker would leave no room for error; he was raising an astounding $6 million and solidifying his relationship with the "Big Steve" Adubato political machine. His opponent this time was a long-in-the-tooth politician named Ronald Rice Sr. He raised a small fraction of Booker's war chest—variably reported at $150,000 and $250,000—a pittance either way. Predictably, Booker won the 2006 mayoral race going away, capturing 72 percent of the vote. His major support came out of the North and East Wards of the city, which were controlled by his political ally Adubato's bloc of voters.[32]

Booker's victory meant he was now running the state's largest urban government, dubbed by some at one time as "the Worst American City."[33] Newark, rife with crime, poverty, decay, unemployment, and corruption, felt like it had never quite recovered from the violent 1967 riots.[34]

On election night, Booker shone as the Reformer declaring that things were about to change. "This is the beginning of a new chapter in the life of our city."[35]

But his tenure involved more continuity than change, especially as it concerned corruption and cronyism. Indeed, it appeared to many that a new machine was replacing the old—both corrupt, but the upgrade was finely tuned and running at peak efficiency.

Booker's years in the mayor's office were controversial, a mix of policy successes and failures. He tightened the city's belt, cutting the workforce by 25 percent. He also doubled the amount of affordable housing in the city. Yet even admirers admitted serious flaws. "The Newark police," wrote one journalist, "on Booker's watch, accumulated a horrifying record on race and brutality that prompted federal intervention in 2016."[36]

As mayor, Booker continued the pattern of absences from Newark that had marred his time as councilman. In one year, he was gone almost three months total, giving speeches and appearing on national television. During his eight-year tenure, he gave nearly 100 speeches around the country, for which he was paid. In all, he collected over $1.3 million, donating a significant but unknown percentage to charity, keeping the rest for himself. Like Bernie Sanders, Booker discovered that speaking fees would be a very helpful way to collect outside income while in political office. In addition to the podium, he was also a regular fixture on national television, hanging out with Oprah and Ellen DeGeneres, as well as on *Meet the Press*.[37] Indeed, Booker seemed to spend an extraordinary amount of time doing national publicity instead of governing Newark. Even his former campaign manager, Carl Sharif, admitted, "He can't sit still for a day without having a press conference or giving a speech."[38] But while his record on policy was mixed, the corruption and cronyism in Newark city politics would prove to be downright alarming. The mayor of Newark had substantial powers, especially when it came to lucrative contracts and making decisions involving real estate development. Booker masterfully managed this intersection of money and power, passing out favors while collecting checks for his political machine and friends.

When Booker took his seat at the mayor's office on 920 Broad Street in Newark, he quickly went about building up his political base and leveraging his newfound powers. Despite his platform as a reformer, he ran the city much as any city political boss would. As one reporter put it, "The legacy of political corruption Booker inherited in Newark is the stuff of gangster movies and mob lore."[39] Booker added a more sophisticated political gloss, but, according to many, the extortive system remained.

Booker was quick to reward friends and donors with Newark taxpayer money. In his first few months in office, Booker gave his campaign manager's son a sole-source contract to update a website for the city. However, the son's company was new and had no background doing such work. The contract was sizable—more than $2 million—and after two years the project was still incomplete, so the city had to hire another firm to clean up the work.[40]

Booker also hired friends to join him in the mayor's office amid complaints of cronyism. Alarm bells went off in some Newark circles almost immediately when Booker appointed a campaign aide named Pablo Fonseca as his first chief of staff. Before joining forces with Booker, Fonseca had been an "operative" for notoriously corrupt and future convict Sharpe James. Indeed, even after James went to prison, Fonseca remained "close" to him. With Booker traveling in and out of town, Fonseca "wielded an inordinate amount of power in the administration," says Professor Andra Gillespie in her study of Booker as mayor of Newark. "To many current and former city hall insiders . . . Fonseca was the real mayor during the first half of Booker's first term."[41]

In addition to his chief of staff, Booker signed on Oscar James

Sr. as another advisor who had been close to former mayor Sharpe James, but was no relation. Oscar James Jr. was a city councilman. Oscar James Sr. would later plead guilty to tax evasion charges over failing to pay taxes while he was advising Booker.[42]

Booker quit the law firm where he had been working, but they continued to pay him throughout his tenure. He had been at Trenk just four years, much of the time out of Newark, overseeing his nonprofit, and giving speeches. In short, he had a scant presence at the firm, but Trenk paid him nearly $700,000 over the next five years in what they claimed was a payout for his share of the law firm.[43]

The trouble is that while his old law firm was paying Booker, Booker's office was steering contracts back to the firm.

Trenk received more than $2 million in work from city departments, including Newark's Housing Authority, a public wastewater treatment agency, and the Newark Watershed Conservation and Development Corporation (NWCDC). As one New Jersey Democrat put it, "That's almost like Sharpe James–type shit."[44] The local newspaper, the *Star-Ledger,* also made comparisons to the previous administration, warning about Booker's boss-like tactics: "We hope Booker is not starting to look like James, The Sequel."[45]

For the money to flow for the benefit of friends and supporters, Booker relied on his political aide Mo Butler, who had been running his nonprofit Newark Now. After Booker became mayor, he appointed Butler as chairman of the Newark Housing Authority, a perch that would have allowed him to steer contracts to Booker's friends and donors.[46]

Butler also served on the board of the Brick City Development Corporation, a city-owned corporation Booker established when he became mayor. Brick City had the authority to help with development plans and provide taxpayer-financed loans. Auditors later discovered that 40 percent of the loans issued had not been repaid.[47] Further consolidating his power, Butler became Booker's chief of staff in 2008.[48]

Lucrative city contracts were doled out to political donors as well. Law firms, who had been among his largest financial supporters, won big with new contracts when Booker became mayor. Eight law firms were slated to receive more than $2.4 million in legal contract increases—six of those had contributed to his campaign. Booker pushed for and got $1.3 million in legal contracts for allied law firms known to be "Booker boosters."[49]

Beyond contracts, Booker was willing to do other favors for big donors. In principle, Booker was opposed to the city using eminent domain to force landowners to sell their properties for big developers and their new construction projects. However, when one condo developer who had donated $53,000 to allied campaigns wanted it invoked, Booker conveniently made an exception, offering no rationale. Perhaps none was needed.[50]

Booker had campaigned as a reformer in 2006. Among his promises were bold commitments to eliminate the several "deputy mayor" positions that had become magnets for cronyism at City Hall. He also pledged to halt donations from city contractors to political campaigns, to limit campaign contributions by city employees, and to install an anticorruption official in the mayor's office.[51] Booker would honor only some of these promises. Even when he did fulfill them, circumventions were available—often to his benefit. For example, while he did ban campaign contributions from city contractors, those same contractors could and did donate to the nonprofits he controlled. While the law caps campaign contributions, there was no cap on the amount they could give to his nonprofits.

According to Professor Curvin, Newark Now "apparently became the place for donations by contractors who sought business from the city." The *Star-Ledger* discovered that they populated Newark Now donor events. At one golfing event, for example, nine contractors gave $19,500 to Booker's charity. Over the next twelve months, the companies received $21.5 million in city contracts.[52]

Booker might have promised that he was going to eliminate the positions of deputy mayor, but he appointed Margarita Muñiz, the wife of an allied councilman, as one of his deputy mayors. He picked David Giordano as Newark's fire director, even though he had no senior management experience. Giordano, a longtime Booker supporter, had served as the head of the firefighters' union.[53] In the early months of his mayoral administration, many of his appointees negotiated six-figure salaries with Booker, which sometimes exceeded the amount allowed by law. Booker issued executive orders increasing their salaries retroactively.[54]

Another deputy mayor appointee was Ronald Salahuddin, who had been active in local politics. Booker tapped him to be in charge of public safety. Unfortunately, within a month of his appointment, Salahuddin was already steering contracts in exchange for bribes.[55] Within four years, Salahuddin was indicted on federal charges involving bribery and extortion. U.S. Attorney Paul Fishman laid out how Salahuddin had shaken down business owners for money, not just for himself, but also donations for Booker's nonprofit Newark Now.[56]

Local businessman Nicholas Mazzocchi owned a demolition firm and had been implicated in a case of bribing city officials in exchange for contracts.[57] He agreed to wear a wire for federal officials to avoid going to jail on bribery and tax evasion charges. He met with Salahuddin, who offered to steer city demolition contracts to his companies in exchange for contributions. Mazzocchi made clear that he thought the deputy mayor was "shaking him down" at the behest of Booker. A thirty-five-page federal indictment mentioned a Newark official seven times, which was later confirmed to be Booker chief of staff Pablo Fonseca.[58] Salahuddin explained how he would pressure the right city bureaucrats to funnel contracts to Mazzocchi's firm. (Neither Booker nor Fonseca was charged in the case.) Federal officials accused Salahuddin of steering demolition contracts to a local businessman named Sonnie Cooper, who donated $6,300 to Booker's campaign. They also charged him with steering business to Mazzocchi and Joseph Paralavecchio, who was an East Ward political boss.[59]

Booker declared his innocence saying that Salahuddin was a good friend and advisor, but that he did not know anything about the arrangements.[60] Salahuddin was found guilty of conspiring to commit extortion and went to jail.[61] He would not be the only one.

As mayor, Booker pushed for strengthening the Newark Watershed Conservation and Development Corporation, a city-owned entity that managed Newark's water resources and sewers. Booker appointed Linda Watkins-Brashear, a donor and close ally, to the post in 2007. Spending at the city-owned corporation exploded, especially funds paid to outside consultants. In 2005, the corporation spent $6.7 million; five years later, it was $10 million. Some of those funds were going to consultants tied to Booker, including $812,000 sent to his old law firm, Trenk, which was of course still paying him. There were also consulting fees going to a board member's father. But the money flowed both ways: of the thirty-six contracts that were awarded by the Watershed, sixteen of those vendors gave to a political action committee aligned with Booker called Empower Newark.[62]

At the same time, Watkins-Brashear used the entity's considerable financial resources to dole out contracts to her friends and ex-husband. Cory Booker's old law partner, Elnardo Webster, was also put under contract to act as the corporation's lawyer. His firm received more than $200,000 as a result. Elnardo had also been Booker's campaign treasurer.[63]

A state audit by the comptroller would later reveal that there were widespread financial problems, including "siphoning millions of public dollars and making illegal payments and sweetheart deals." Watkins-Brashear "was using the Watershed like her own personal bank account" and confessed to using taxpayer money to fund her gambling addiction. Mayor Cory Booker was an ex officio board member of the Watershed, but he did not attend a single board meeting. Soon the Watershed was under investigation by both the U.S. attorney and the FBI. Watkins-Brashear would later plead guilty to a kickback and corruption scheme.[64]

A state audit found problems not just at the Watershed, but also throughout the Booker administration. Indeed, auditors found that, like the Sharpe James administration, there was "a long list of problems and violations of regulations and city ordinances, many indicating that there is little or no competent supervision in many areas of the city."[65]

Ironically, Booker also apparently had no problem leveraging city resources for his political campaigns after he had decried the practice in James's campaign. During his 2010 reelection bid, Booker used city money to have banners placed on public buildings, which proclaimed, "Cory Booker, Newark: building a stronger, safer, prouder City." Clearly, these were political campaign materials, but the city of Newark had paid for them. Even worse, the city's youth basketball league and other recreational sports teams received T-shirts to wear paid for by the city that read "Mayor Cory A. Booker—here to win in 2010." Again, it was a clear campaign slogan—on banners produced using taxpayer dollars. Eventually the city halted production because of the outcry from recreation department employees.[66]

Booker also apparently used city human resources as "some city employees alleged that they were pressured to sell fundraising tickets for Booker campaign events."[67]

The Booker administration set up family counseling services around the city and called them Family Success Centers. Jointly run by the city and his nonprofit Newark Now, the centers offered poor residents advice about personal health and other matters, but the centers were not simply altruistic. "Mayor Booker also intended the centers to have a political role, in terms of helping him reach out to the communities and win electoral support," according to Professor Curvin. Indeed, he says, "Center staff attempted to mobilize residents to support administration political battles."[68]

In short, Booker erected a political machine in Newark, which was fueled by the flow of taxpayer money to friends and contributors. Then he also directly used taxpayer dollars to bolster his own campaign for reelection.

While mayor, Booker often advertised his acts of heroism and empathy to develop his media brand and deflect attention from the deeper issues of corruption miring his tenure. While some of these acts appear to be genuine, upon closer examination many of the stories resemble stunts or attempts to cover up larger political failures.

Booker would often regale out-of-town audiences with tales of his dangerous work as mayor. During a speech in suburban

Summit, New Jersey, for example, he explained to the audience how he was "dodging bullets in Newark," comparing himself to the character in the movie *The Matrix*, all the while twisting his body and reenacting the maneuvers of Keanu Reeves.[69]

In December 2010, after a major snowstorm hit Newark, Mayor Booker got a call on his cell phone reporting the fact that there were no snowplows on the street. "We are going to get the plows there," he told the caller. "Give us an hour or so." The snowplows did not show up. When the caller turned on the local news that evening, he heard "a report that the mayor of Newark was out shoveling driveways for elderly people." Curvin later wrote, "The management of the cleanup effort was a near disaster. However, on the airwaves and in the newspapers, Booker was being praised as a leader who knew how to handle a snowstorm."[70]

During the same snowstorm, a Newark resident went on Twitter and reported that his sister's family was trapped in their house and were running out of diapers. Booker tweeted, "I'm on it." Booker showed up at the Byers house with Pampers and the media. Again, Booker received a lot of praise for his personal heroism. Tellingly, Barbara Byers later noted, "The only reason he brought me Pampers was that it had been three days and our street hadn't been plowed. . . . All we wanted was for him to plow our streets. It's about knowing how to manage a city."[71]

As a progressive with an elite background, Booker was eager to demonstrate his connection and empathy with poor residents in Newark. At one point, he challenged himself to live on $33 worth of food a week, based on the amount of money that an individual would receive under the federal government's Supplemental Nutrition Assistance Program (SNAP). Never mind that SNAP was a "supplemental" program, not designed to provide all of one's nutritional needs. Booker was trying to make the valid point of how difficult it would be to live in poverty, but his execution of the experiment left people perplexed. The menu of items he chose to buy (which he announced to the world via Twitter) included organic olive oil and an expensive bag of mixed greens, among other items; not exactly tight-budget dining. Critics noted that while the stunt got media attention, Booker never really did anything to attempt to improve the program. "Booker has the annoying habit of transforming others' personal distress into fuel for his personal marketing machine," wrote one author.[72]

When Booker spoke to audiences around the country or met with reporters, he would often speak about his encounters with a Newark drug dealer named "T-Bone," who he said was a neighbor. Booker claimed that they had long conversations about the struggles of life on the streets. At one point Booker claimed T-Bone threatened to "bust a cap [bullet] in" his ass. Booker used this story for years until he announced for the U.S. Senate and reporters began swarming the mean streets of Newark in search of T-Bone. Journalists even talked to undercover narcotics cops, but no one could find T-Bone. Later it became clear that T-Bone was not really a person—even though Booker had for a long time insisted that he was. Booker would later admit, "although T-Bone's corporeal being is '1,000 percent real,' he's an 'archetype' of an aspect of Newark's woe whose actual nom de crack may not actually be T-Bone."[73]

One of Booker's most famous moments as mayor occurred when he ran into a burning building and rescued a woman from the blaze. The genuinely heroic act received enormous national attention and even garnered an appearance on Ellen DeGeneres's television show, where the host presented him with a Superman costume. Critics noted, however, that Booker had shut down three of Newark's fire companies, so when it came time to rescue the woman, "perhaps no one else was around to do it."[74]

It is one thing to lay down one's own life or interests to act heroically; it is completely another thing to self-promote. In 2008, *Esquire* magazine ran a profile of Booker after reporter Scott Raab spent several months following him around the city. Raab likened Booker to Will Smith's character in the newly released movie *I Am Legend*. In the film, Will Smith is combating zombies who are trying to annihilate the world. Where did he get the idea to compare Booker to Will Smith fighting Zombies? According to Raab, he got the idea after Booker took him to see the movie the first night that he began following him. Raab admitted that Booker intentionally framed himself as the savior of the city, and candidly called him a "bullshit artist."[75]

Other favorable press continued. In 2011, *Time* selected Booker as one of their 100 World's Most Influential People, a remarkable selection for the mayor of Newark. Oprah Winfrey penned a tribute titled "Saving Newark with a Smile," where she described how Booker "defines [the term] *servant leader*." In *Men's Health*, Booker wrote a "Celebrity Fitness" column, where he described his fitness routines and advised, "don't run from hard; run toward it" and "be the change you want to see in the world." Around the same time, *Vogue* magazine christened him an "urban superhero."[76]

In September 2010, Facebook founder Mark Zuckerberg was on national television sitting next to Cory Booker and New Jersey governor Chris Christie. On a chair nearby sat Oprah Winfrey. As the nation watched Oprah's show, Zuckerberg calmly announced that he was making a $100 million commitment to Newark to help improve the city's schools. Newark residents learned about the bold gesture the same way everyone else did—by watching *Oprah*.[77]

Zuckerberg had no direct ties to Newark—other than his relationship with Cory Booker. Critics noted that the Facebook founder made his commitment to Newark shortly after the release of the movie *The Social Network,* which portrayed him as an obnoxious and insecure techie who craved social acceptance.[78] Regardless of the motive, $100 million could dramatically help just about any school system, if used appropriately.

Unfortunately, examining Booker's use of those funds raises serious questions. Instead of being used to upgrade the schools of Newark for the benefit of children, much of the money, as we will see, was diverted to other interests.

Booker's machine was already leveraging donors to give to his nonprofits, which would steer funds to friends and allies. Organizations such as Newark Now served that purpose well. Now Booker created new nonprofits to dispense the money coming from Zuckerberg.

One of those nonprofits was PENewark. The other was Foundation for Newark's Future (FNF). To run FNF, he hired Greg Taylor, an executive with the Kellogg Foundation. Taylor did not live in Newark, but was paid $382,000 a year for three or four days of work per week. Booker then started hiring consultants to conduct surveys and organize coffee klatches to find out what people wanted out of Newark schools. Many of the consultants hired had ties to Booker. One that came on board was Bradley Tusk, of Tusk Strategies. Tusk was New York mayor Michael Bloomberg's reelection campaign manager, and Bloomberg was a major Booker financial supporter. A Booker aide would later admit that Tusk's work was "a boondoggle." An FNF board member observed, "It wasn't real community engagement. It was public relations."[79]

Booker also hired SKDKnickerbocker, a national public affairs firm whose Washington, D.C., office is headed by Anita Dunn, formerly a White House communications director for Obama, along with several other connected consulting firms.[80] Over the next couple of months, they would burn through $2 million on consultants who conducted the survey. Critics called the project "wasteful and a boondoggle for Booker's friends."[81]

Newark's public schools were in terrible shape. The funds were supposed to go to improving and revamping them. The state of New Jersey had taken over control of the schools before Booker became mayor because of mismanagement.[82] New Jersey governor Chris Christie had agreed to turn over some control of the schools to Booker as part of the Zuckerberg gift.[83]

A good deal of the money ended up in the pocket of consultants.[84] The biggest chunk of the gift—$33 million—did not go to the schools but instead to provide back pay to teachers.[85]

As mayor, Booker's sprawling network of activities included speaking fees (for as high as $30,000 a pop), nonprofits, the Zuckerberg gift, and a commercial venture called Waywire.[86] In June 2012, Booker launched the new video-sharing social media company that he promised would give "marginalized voices," including "high school kids," a hearing. Booker put a public service gloss over the venture: "What was exciting to me was that it was expanding entrepreneurial, economic, and educational opportunities for so many." Booker got the project easily funded by tapping his wealthy friends Oprah Winfrey, Google's then–executive chairman Eric Schmidt, and Jeff Weiner, the CEO of LinkedIn, among others to invest. Waywire amassed an advisory board that included CNN president Jeff Zucker's then-fourteen-year-old son.[87]

The Waywire deal was highly unusual and controversial for several reasons. Booker was still mayor of a major American city, and yet he was launching a business with people who in numerous cases had been campaign donors. The terms of the deal were also unusual. Booker received the largest ownership stake in the company, even though he had likely invested comparatively little capital, and was not working on the project full-time. Booker used Waywire as a place to provide jobs for some friends and associates. The son of a top supporter and his social media consultant were put on the payroll.[88]

The mystery of the arrangement with Waywire deepened, as he was late to disclose on both state and federal financial disclosure forms that he was involved with the company. It would soon become such an issue in his budding Senate campaign that he was, reluctantly, forced to step away.[89]

Booker was by now a national figure, not only in the media, but also within the Democratic Party. In 2012, he served as the co-chairman of the Democratic Party platform committee at the national convention.[90] Months later, he made his national ambitions clear when he announced his bid for the U.S. Senate, filing papers to run for the Senate in January 2013.[91]

At the time, the aged Senator Frank Lautenberg occupied the seat. A month after the mayor announced his bid, Lautenberg declared that he would not seek reelection.[92] Booker hit the campaign trail, but he also hit the lecture circuit, pulling in close to half a million dollars in speaking fees across the country between January and September of 2013.

By June, Lautenberg was dead of viral pneumonia.[93] Initial polls had Booker in the lead by as much as 25 percent, but the race narrowed.[94] Booker was suddenly in a tighter race for the seat, barely leading a no-name Republican in the polls.[95] It was an unusually tight race by New Jersey standards, where the Democratic Party had long been dominating U.S. Senate races.[96] With controversy swirling about Waywire, he resigned from the board and donated his shares in the company to charity.[97] A portion of them ended up in a troubled charity run by his brother.[98] Booker won by the lowest margin that any of the polls had indicated: 10 percent.[99]

What Booker counted on to carry him to victory was a corrupt political machine. For his Senate run, "Booker sought and received the backing of political bosses like George Norcross in South Jersey and Essex County Executive Joseph DiVincenzo."[100] In return, Booker was prepared to support these and others, even though they were mired in corruption.[101]

In May 2013, there were contentious elections in Hackensack, New Jersey. Fed up with local corruption, a coalition of residents launched a ticket against the political establishment. Booker recorded a robocall for the political establishment urging people to vote for them. His support failed to get the desired result; the reformers defeated them.[102] Likewise, in Jersey City, Booker backed the reelection of Mayor Jerramiah Healy. According to the *Star-Ledger*, Healy's "administration has been proved to be thoroughly corrupt. Healy is one of the few survivors in his inner circle who was not convicted in the famous 2009 FBI bust known as 'Operation Bid Rig.'"[103] Booker also backed Passaic mayor Alex Blanco, who later pleaded guilty to taking bribes. He was sentenced to twenty-seven months in jail.[104] Booker built his Senate campaign on favors and ties to corrupt political establishments rather than reformers.

Booker, the newly minted senator from New Jersey, had

changed his zip code, but not his relationships and manner of operation, which remained largely the same as in New Jersey. Special favors for friends and allies; the flow of money to friends and allies.

Facebook executives had been some of his largest donors during the Senate campaign. Zuckerberg and his wife, Priscilla Chan, gave the maximum combined contribution of $20,800. Chief operating officer Sheryl Sandberg, general counsel Colin Stretch, former chief privacy officer Chris Kelly, and VP of advertising Andrew Bosworth were also large donors.[105] That flow of money would continue—more than $44,000 into his campaign coffers from Facebook between 2014 and 2018.[106] Of course, the depth of those ties extended back to the Zuckerberg gift to Newark schools, which ended in failure.[107]

One of Booker's hires was for the critical position of his chief of staff. For that position, he slotted in Louisa Terrell, who had been the director of public policy at Facebook.[108] This would lead to a consistent pattern of Booker proposing legislation that would benefit both Facebook and Zuckerberg's other investments. Booker's committee assignments included a slot on the subcommittee on Communications, Technology, and the Internet.[109] Booker has supported a whole host of proposals that would benefit big tech, including net neutrality, also favored by Facebook.[110]

While in the U.S. Senate, Booker's political machine has continued to run smoothly as his top aides slid from their campaign duties for him, to his Senate staff and to lobbying firms. Booker appointed his old political hand, Mo Butler, to the all-important position of New Jersey state director of his Senate office, which put the dealmaker at ground zero for doling out favors and money to allies in the Garden State.[111] The Newark Charter School Fund, a nonprofit Booker helped to launch and fund, sent $87,000 to a lobbying firm called Mercury Public Affairs in 2016.[112] That same year, Mo Butler joined the Mercury Public Affairs lobbying team. Butler became a partner at Mercury and then the city of Newark used taxpayer dollars to hire Mercury for a $225,000 contract to help the city with "messaging."[113]

The machine that Booker ran in Newark was now established in the nation's capital. With Cory Booker as the state's most visible public figure, close aides and donors benefited from his newfound powers as a United States senator—including Mercury, the controversial lobbying firm that was at the center of the Robert Mueller investigation into Russian influence in the United States.[114] As a highly lucrative and successful lobbying operation, Mercury, because of its ties to powerful officials, enjoys access to the highest levels in Washington.

No current politician in America has deeper ties to Mercury than Cory Booker. Two of the lobbying firm's partners are Booker confidants. Michael Soliman was a campaign strategist to the Booker senate campaign. He joined Mercury shortly before Booker was elected, serving as managing director beginning in 2013. By 2016 he was a partner at the firm.[115] Mo Butler, Booker's longtime consigliere, joined Mercury in February 2016 and became a partner in 2018.[116] It is hard to find someone closer to Cory Booker than Mo Butler.

Booker has emphasized how important Mo Butler is to him. As he told one reporter, "I get so much attention and very few people know who Mo is, but the reality is I wouldn't be doing the things I'm doing if it wasn't for Mo Butler." He likened his confidant to a boxing champion. "When the time comes to punch someone in the nose when it's necessary, even though he looks like a lightweight, he's Muhammad Ali." In short, "Mo's the man," he said.[117]

Mercury prospered with the addition of the two Booker advisors. According to Open Secrets, the firm's billing for lobbying activity jumped 35 percent the year after Mo Butler was hired.[118]

Mercury, and specifically Soliman and Butler, have lined up clients that correspond to Cory Booker's Senate committee assignments, and likewise, Booker has introduced legislation that would benefit Mercury clients. New client Horizon Blue Cross and Blue Shield of New Jersey paid Mercury $160,000 in 2018 for work on various unspecified health care issues. Booker was also active on health care, cosponsoring S.974, "Creating and Restoring Equal Access to Equivalent Samples Act." This bill also went through his committee.[119]

In late 2016, Booker cosponsored the "First Responder Anthrax Preparedness Act" to authorize anthrax vaccine purchases, which were produced by a firm called Emergent Biosolutions. The legislation passed and was a financial boon to the company. In total, the firm received orders of at least $900 million. The following year, the firm hired Mercury to represent their interests in Washington and paid them $190,000 over 2017–18.[120]

In 2017, the Morganza Action Coalition hired Mercury to lobby and paid them $170,000. They lobbied specifically on "water resource issues." Booker sits on the Senate Committee on Environment and Public Works, which deals with water matters.[121]

In 2017, insurance giant Primerica hired Mercury and paid them $200,000 over the next two years to lobby the U.S. Senate. Booker sits on the subcommittee with oversight on consumer protection and insurance.[122]

In 2017, the pharmaceutical company Amerisource Bergen hired Mercury to represent their interests on Capitol Hill. They paid the firm $120,000 in 2017 and $170,000 in 2018.[123] Booker had voted against an amendment that would allow for the importation of pharmaceuticals from outside the United States, which brought him a lot of heat from progressives.[124] Pharmaceutical companies like Amerisource were obviously opposed to the idea. Booker also cosponsored two bills on which Amerisource lobbied. One was S.469, "The Affordable and Safe Prescription Drug Importation Act."[125] While the bill would allow for the possible importation of pharmaceuticals, it set up a labyrinth of regulatory requirements that would make it financially draining for many companies. Amerisource Bergen executives and its corporate PAC are major Booker donors.[126]

Another new client was the Spanish company Cosentino Group. They hired Mercury in 2017 and over the next two years paid them $320,000.[127] Cosentino was dealing with issues involving tariffs and the Commerce Department. Booker at the time served on the Commerce Committee with oversight of that department.[128] The Spanish firm had never hired a lobbyist before.[129]

Perhaps most startling is the rise in foreign clients that hired Mercury beginning in 2017. It was in December 2016 that Cory Booker joined the Senate Foreign Relations Committee.[130] Those clients included the government of Qatar, a small monarchy in the Persian Gulf. The government of Qatar paid the firm $1.2 million in 2017 alone.[131] Another client was the government of Turkey, which hired Mercury in 2017 for $100,000 and by the next year was paying the firm almost $1.2 million. Additionally, the Turkey-US Business Council paid Mercury close to $2 million in 2018.[132] It is interesting to note that Booker's foreign trips as a member of the Senate Foreign Relations Committee included visits to both Turkey and Qatar.[133] During committee hearings in March 2018, Booker urged the United States to help mediate the dispute between Saudi Arabia and the United Arab Emirates with Qatar.[134] On another occasion, he favored Qatar by suggesting that the United States needed to "reexamine" its "entire relation-ship" with Saudi Arabia.[135]

In short, all of these were new clients for Mercury and all had direct ties to Booker's responsibilities in the Senate. The Booker machine has leveraged his position in the Senate for more lobbying clients.

When the PennEast Pipeline, a consortium of five energy utilities, proposed to build a 120-mile pipeline through New Jersey, they realized quickly that they needed help in Washington, so they turned to Mercury. The pipeline was controversial, particularly to Booker's base of progressive voters. PennEast was proposing to construct a pipeline to deliver fracked natural gas from Pennsylvania to Mercer County, New Jersey. The utility companies argued that the pipeline was necessary so they could meet the energy needs of their consumers. Critics argued that the pipeline would be harmful to the environment and was unnecessary.[136]

Michael Soliman was the registered lobbyist for the contract with PennEast. The pipeline company spent $740,000 on lobbying fees to Mercury over four years to secure approval for the pipeline.[137] One might assume that given his credentials as a progressive supporter of environmental causes, Booker would oppose the deal, but he was initially quiet.[138] It was only after public opposition mounted and the project's approval came into question that Booker came out against the project.[139] One might argue it was for show, not substance, too little, too late.

Mercury also did substantial lobbying work for the marijuana industry. By 2015, the firm represented multiple medical marijuana interests, including biopharmaceutical company KannaLife Sciences Inc.[140] Later Mercury signed on PharmaCann, which paid the firm $10,000 per month.[141] In 2018, Mercury had signed on two new clients as part of "the New Jersey weed lobby."[142]

With his friends' lobbying firm taking on a plethora of marijuana clients, Booker jumped in and introduced legislation pushing for the legalization of marijuana. His first attempt came in 2017. By 2019, he was at it again with the so-called Marijuana Justice Act, which would legalize marijuana nationwide.[143] The Marijuana Justice Act would not allow for the free and unregulated production of marijuana. Instead, it would legalize the consumption of weed, but production would be by only certain government-approved manufacturers who obtained a federal license, which would presumably include those who were lobbying for the legislation in the first place.

Cory Booker represents the link between leveraging power for the financial benefit of friends and ambition for one's own political career. As both an executive, while mayor, and as a legislator in the U.S. Senate, he has wielded power to secure donations for his political machine, including his nonprofits. In the U.S. Senate, he has offered his close aides a path to great wealth as lobbyists by using his position on Senate committees for their commercial benefit.

Cory Booker is not the only professed reformer in the Senate to function in this way. As we will see next, Elizabeth Warren used her position in the Washington, D.C., revolving door to make her family wealthy, and continues to do so today.

ELIZABETH WARREN

In the wreckage that was the 2008 financial crisis, there were plenty of people who got burned. One who rose from the financial ashes was Elizabeth Warren. The Harvard professor, despite her slender frame and academic demeanor, emerged as a booming and powerful proponent of reform. Fans such as Suzanna Andrews of *Vanity Fair* have likened her to Jimmy Stewart's character in the movie *Mr. Smith Goes to Washington*, declaring, "She had become like a modern-day Mr. Smith, giving voice to regular citizens astonished at the failure of Washington to protect Main Street."[1] Others describe her as "perhaps the most recognizable leader of what has been called a resurgent progressive movement."[2] Her supporters see her greatest strength as her "outsider's perspective."[3]

Warren recounts an interesting story of when she had dinner with Obama economic advisor Larry Summers:

> Late in the evening, Larry leaned back in his chair and offered some advice. . . . He teed it up this way: I had a choice. I could be an insider or I could be an outsider. Outsiders can say whatever they want. But people on the inside don't listen to them. Insiders, however, get lots of access and a chance to push their ideas. People—powerful people—listen to what they have to

say. But insiders also understand one unbreakable rule: *They don't criticize other insiders.*[4]

Warren supporters place her in a category far removed from the typical politician. "What elevates her brand is that she is not a politician but a complete honest broker," proclaimed Ari Rabin-Havt, who worked for Media Matters for America.[5] In contrast to progressives like Joe Biden, Bernie Sanders, and many other national political figures, she has spent far less time in elective office.

Warren's legend grew when she appeared in Michael Moore's film *Capitalism: A Love Story.* Moore proclaimed, "Capitalism is an evil and you cannot regulate evil," and portrayed Warren as a heroine in the film, standing on the ramparts and shrewdly fighting powerful corporations.[6]

Warren directs her political message squarely at the middle class. She recalls a time when America was "big, solid, boring, hardworking" and the middle class could "play by the rules" and get ahead. Now, she argues, the middle class is "chipped at, hacked at, squeezed and hammered." America's economic reality is that "booms and busts will come and millions of people will lose their homes, millions more will lose their jobs, and trillions of dollars in savings retirement accounts will be wiped out. The question is, do we have a different vision of what we can do?"[7]

Critics argue that she does poorly on style points. "I want her to sound like a human being," one Democratic analyst told WBUR radio in Boston, "not read the script that makes her sound like some angry, hectoring schoolmarm."[8] But Warren has become a public figure to be reckoned with, slashing large corporations with razorlike criticism and taking Wall Street to task for their excesses.[9]

In 2011, the Occupy Wall Street movement was born and activists protested loudly in front of the homes and offices of Wall Street executives. The movement began in New York's Zuccotti Park, just a couple of blocks from Wall Street, but quickly spread to cities across the country. Warren was an inspiration for the movement that sometimes became violent.[10] "I created much of the intellectual foundation for what they do," she said.[11] It was fitting with her theme that the economic system in the United States was "rigged." As she would write in her book *A Fighting Chance*, "Today the game is rigged—rigged to work for those who have money and power." "Rigged" would become a catchword for much of her rhetoric about business.[12] At the center of it is what some would call the "Wall Street–Washington nexus."[13]

The American middle class was "the turkey at Thanksgiving dinner," which large banks and corporations would feast on so they "could make a profit," she would say.[14]

Fueled by such rhetoric and timing during the economic crisis, Elizabeth Warren's trajectory to political prominence has been remarkable. While Bernie Sanders had spent decades slogging his way through the political jungle to claim his mantle as the leading social democrat in America, Elizabeth Warren, in the span of approximately two years rose from Harvard professor, to a major voice of the national progressive movement, to United States senator.[15]

Much of the booster fuel that has propelled Warren has been the sense that, like Jefferson Smith in that famous movie, she has been untainted by corrupt interests; that her motivation is idealistic. Warren claims that her message is part of a lifelong quest to fight corporate power. "This is not a change for me," she told supporters in her first campaign. "This is what I've worked on all my life."[16]

But Warren's image as an outsider and progressive reformer

is not matched by the realities surrounding her actions, interests, and commercial ties that have enriched her family. Her family's accumulation of wealth, even while she has risen to power championing attacks on corporate America, has been deeply dependent on those same corporations. Indeed, in the 1990s she effectively leveraged her position working as a government consultant on bankruptcy issues to reap a rich financial harvest as a legal consultant for the biggest corporations in America. And her family has benefited from other corporate ties. The fundamental contradictions between what she presents herself to be and what she has done provide for remarkable contrasts.

Elizabeth Warren was born in Oklahoma, the daughter of Donald Herring and Pauline (Reed) Herring.[17] Financial instability clouded her childhood, she recalls, and there was little encouragement to pursue academic achievement. She recounted vividly later in life the repossession of her family's station wagon.[18] She was not the best student, but excelled at speech and forensics. That led to a debate scholarship to attend George Washington University and a way out. Marriage to a high school sweetheart cut short her undergraduate studies at George Washington, and she moved with Jim Warren to Houston, where she finished her studies at the University of Houston. It was a traditional life. She did her studies and had two children, daughter Amelia and son Alex. She was interested in law, and when her husband took the family to New Jersey, she enrolled at Rutgers University Law School and graduated with a J.D.[19]

Growing up in the Warren household, her daughter Amelia recalls a tightly run ship, including a dinner table with "napkin rings with our names on them that made it clear who was supposed to sit where."[20]

In 1978, Warren and her husband split up. She began seeing

Professor Bruce Mann, who was teaching at the University of Connecticut. Warren and Mann taught law at the University of Houston and then moved to the University of Texas in 1983. She continued to move up the ladder of the university system. By 1987, both she and Bruce had moved to the University of Pennsylvania Law School. She was now in the Ivy League.[21]

The story of Elizabeth Warren's academic success cannot be divorced from her claimed status as a Native American; they are deeply intertwined.

Barely one year before her appointment to the University of Pennsylvania faculty, Warren began to list herself as a "minority" Native American law professor in the directory of the Association of American Law Schools.[22] Her claim as a Native American, she would later say, was based on family lore about their ancestry.[23] When it became an issue during her 2012 Senate campaign, she turned up a great-great-great-grandmother who was designated as Cherokee in an online ancestry posting of a marriage license back in 1894. In 2018, she took a DNA test that demonstrated that she had some Native American DNA. If her account is true, she is, at a maximum, 1/32nd Native American. If, however, the heritage she claims was a few generations further back, she is as little as 1/1024th Native American.[24]

Warren says that she claimed Native American status in the directories not to benefit her career, but instead "I listed myself in the directory in the hopes that it might mean that I would be invited to a luncheon, a group, something that might happen with people who are like I am."[25] But there is no record at Texas, Penn, or Harvard that she joined any groups or organizations that would bring her in contact with people "who are like I am." Furthermore, the directory is used explicitly to make "diversity-friendly hires," something that Warren undoubtedly would have known.[26]

Warren, by declaring herself a Native American law professor, was a rare find for the University of Pennsylvania. They made a point of publicizing her alleged ethnic roots. The law school's federal affirmative action reports listed a sole "Native American female professor" (presumably Warren) while she taught there.[27] Penn's "Minority Equity Report," for example, identified her as an ethnic minority.[28]

At Penn, she caught the attention of Harvard. They recruited her, offering Warren an endowed chair position on the faculty (the Leo Gottlieb Professor of Law) that would make her the third-highest-person on the payroll at Harvard.[29] Her recruitment to Cambridge came at a time when Harvard Law School "was under intense pressure to diversify its faculty with more minorities." Harvard contends that she was not hired because of her claimed ethnic background.[30] As the University of Pennsylvania had done, Harvard was eager to tout her as a minority recruit. A Harvard University spokesman described her as Harvard Law School's "first woman of color."[31] She was repeatedly identified as an example of minority hiring at Harvard Law. "Harvard Law School currently has only one tenured minority woman, Gottlieb Professor of Law Elizabeth Warren, who is Native American," noted the *Harvard Crimson*.[32]

But something curious happened after Warren secured her new position at Harvard Law School. She stopped listing herself in the directory as a minority the same year Harvard hired her to a tenured position.[33]

A corporate law firm named Cleary Gottlieb funded her endowed chair. They set up the chair to honor one of the firm's founding partners—a Harvard graduate. Cleary Gottlieb is a global firm that counts foreign governments and multinational corporations as its most lucrative clients. The firm specialized in commercial and financial law, representing a variety of corporate firms and Wall Street investment houses.[34] In addition to funding her chair, Warren also credited them with providing funds for research on various writing projects.[35] As we will see, her ties to Cleary Gottlieb spilled over into her roles as a government official.

While at Harvard, Warren taught classes in stately red sandstone law buildings like Austin Hall, with its Romanesque architecture and graceful arches.[36] But her teaching load was light, affording her other opportunities to generate income, many of which seem to contradict her 2008 public persona.

Oklahoma's economy is heavily tied to energy prices and has experienced booms and busts over the decades. A depressed energy market meant that jobs were scarce and real estate values were down. People lost their homes, unable to pay their mortgages.[37] It was the sort of economic calamity and hardship for the middle class about which Warren has eloquently spoken. In her books, she wrote about victims of the housing bust.[38] But Warren and her husband took advantage of the economic tumult, buying foreclosed properties at rock-bottom prices and then flipping them for profit. Warren knew what she was talking about when she later wrote a book titled *The Fragile Middle Class*, noting that foreclosures are "notorious for fetching low prices."[39] In all, the two law professors worked to supplement their income and net worth through a number of real estate deals that netted the family serious profits once they "flipped" the homes. Warren and her husband bought properties in their own names, but they also financed the purchase of properties by her relatives. (In those instances, she charged her family high interest rates for her investment.) For example, in June 1993 they purchased a foreclosed home from the U.S. Department of Housing and Urban Development (HUD) for $61,000 and then sold it eighteen months later for a 56 percent profit. In another instance, they bought a house on N.W. 16th Street in August 1993 for just $30,000. Five months later they sold it for $145,000—a 383 percent gain.[40]

In all, over the course of fifteen years, Warren either purchased or financed $1.2 million in real estate deals, according to Oklahoma real estate records.[41]

Warren and her husband were engaging in the sort of profit-making activity that is certainly legitimate, but also ironic, given that their profit margin was at times predicated on the financial misfortune of others. In short, for herself, she was comfortable with the sort of economic behavior for which she would later famously condemn others.

Warren, like many law professors, had the opportunity to seek additional sources of income beyond her already high salary.

In the mid-1990s, Warren began advising the U.S. Congress on bankruptcy laws. It was her academic specialty and by 1995 she was tapped to advise the National Bankruptcy Review Commission, which had been set up by Congress to rewrite U.S. laws.[42] In a 2002 court document, she would explain the role she played: "I provided assistance to various Congressional staff people . . . tried to help them understand the issues involved and to evaluate the various statutory proposals as they arose." She was also a key advisor on an obscure but profoundly important section of the bankruptcy law called U.S.C. 524(g), which dealt with mass tort bankruptcies of corporations and had to do specifically with asbestos companies, but had broad ramifications for other corporations as well. Could large companies who were facing class-action lawsuits because of defective products shield themselves from these legal claims by declaring bankruptcy? How would corporate bankruptcies and the money owed to legal claimants be handled? Large corporations stand to gain or lose a lot based on how these bankruptcy laws are written. As Warren recounted in a legal brief involving a later corporate bankruptcy:

> When the Commission formed working groups, I assisted the mass tort group, supervised the research on the subject, developed an agenda to consider mass tort issues, prepared a number of position papers, invited witnesses and participants to Commission meetings, and helped craft a proposal that was ultimately adopted unanimously by the Commissioners.[43]

In short, Warren was at ground zero in rewriting corporate bankruptcy laws.

The revisions to the laws that she helped to pen had enormous positive ramifications for America's largest corporations. The new laws allowed financially healthy corporations to start using bankruptcies as a way to avoid liability from legal suits. As the *New York Times* explained, the legislation pushed by Warren led "Fortune 500 companies with otherwise solid balance sheets" to use "the bankruptcy courts as part of a broad strategy to resolve potentially ruinous legal woes."[44]

The new bankruptcy laws were a big win for large corporations, from asbestos producers to manufacturers of breast implants.[45] Warren's role in writing these new rules created enormous financial opportunities for her. With large corporations still being sued, she was positioned to provide legal advice and services to those same companies for a high fee. Who better for them to hire than the person who helped to write the new laws?

It was the ultimate Washington leverage move.

Warren was walking a well-worn self-enrichment path in the nation's capital, whereby the people who write the rules interpret those same rules in order to use them for their benefit. What makes Warren's case unusual is that she has continued to insist that she is an outsider, not part of the madding crowd in Washington who were cashing in on public service and leveraging it for profit.[46]

Warren claims that she has been consistent for years in her advocacy for families and workers. "I've been out there working for families," she said when asked about her legal work in 2012. "I've been out there working for people who've been injured by big corporations. I've been out there working for people who've been injured by asbestos. I've been doin' that for years and years and years."[47]

But a detailed examination of her legal consulting record shows otherwise. Indeed, of the known cases where she did legal consulting, her work on a number of those cases was on behalf of major corporations. Each of these companies was facing major liability involving pensions or class-action lawsuits, which she helped them avoid.[48] She was extremely well compensated. In a legal brief, she described her "customary billing rate" as $700 per hour back in 2002. Today in 2019, that equates to about $996 per hour.[49]

Let us consider what she was paid to do and who was paying her.

In one of her earliest cases, Warren represented corporations seeking release from a law that required them to pay health benefits to coal miners. One of those clients was LTV Steel, which was trying to overturn a court ruling that required the company to pay its former employees and dependents $140 million in retirement benefits. LTV was trying to avoid its responsibilities under the 1992 Coal Act, which established a fund to pay retired coal workers. The appellate court sided against Warren's clients, and Warren filed a brief with the Supreme Court seeking to overturn the decision. The Supreme Court never took up the case.[50]

Warren argued that since LTV Steel was coming out of bankruptcy, it should not have to pay into the coal fund. Mineworkers, of course, were opposed to her position, fearing that if LTV did not pay its fair share, it would allow other coal companies to get out of their obligations. "That's what the people who didn't want to pay always wanted to say," said Peter Buscemi, a lawyer who represented the retirees in the case. "They wanted to say someone else will pay and the benefits won't be in jeopardy. But if one employer doesn't pay then another and then another, then who knows what will happen?"[51]

When asked publicly about her work on the LTV matter, Warren tried to obscure her role in the case, arguing through a spokesperson that she was simply standing up for "bankruptcy principles."[52] In 2006, she actually gave an interview with the Public Broadcasting System (PBS) where she attacked the company for treating employees "like paper towels. You use them and you throw them away." She never disclosed in that interview that the company paid her to help them avoid some of their liabilities.[53]

Warren was paid $10,000 for her work, but she was just getting started.[54]

In the same PBS interview, Warren tried to distance herself from the rules she had helped write. Now, after she had made large sums of money helping corporations, she denounced the rules. "Congress [wrote] the rules, and the rules say the employees don't come first." She wanted new rules quite different from those she had helped to write a decade earlier and that had benefited her financially. "What we need is a new set of rules that does not permit corporations to put their short-term immediate profits ahead of the employees that have invested in these businesses for 20 and 30 years." However, she continued to represent corporations in bankruptcy proceedings even after this interview.[55]

Warren also did legal work for Fairchild Aircraft Corporation (FAC), which produced small aircraft. The company went into bankruptcy in 1990, and a group of investors bought it and formed Fairchild Acquisition Incorporated (FAI). The asset purchase was supposed to be free and clear of any liabilities. In 1995, the families, estates, and/or businesses of four people who had died tragically in a plane crash sued FAC and FAI. The victims' families believed that the aircraft was "defectively manufactured by FAC." FAC hired Warren to argue to a Texas court that the families could not legitimately sue the companies. The bankruptcy court rejected her legal theory.[56]

Warren claims that her motive in defending the company was to save jobs. In fact, though, the company hired her to protect their assets, not jobs. Their worry was that the case would affect future claims that others might have against them. In addition, there is no evidence to indicate that the suit would result in lost jobs. Instead, she essentially argued that these families did not have legal recourse against these companies.[57]

Warren's legal consulting work radically contradicts the claims she makes that she is a fighter for the middle class and against corporate America. Indeed, she was well compensated for more than a decade providing legal testimony for corporations attempting to avoid pension obligations and paying victims.

Consider the work Warren did as a legal consultant for Southwest Electric Power Company, a utility in Louisiana. A large power company wanted to shut down a rural energy cooperative, Cajun Electric Power, and acquire its major asset, a large coal-fired electric plant. When asked about her work for the utility during her 2012 Senate campaign, Warren claimed that she "represented a company that offered a plan to help save a bankrupt rural power cooperative." The opposite was true, according to a New Orleans lawyer involved in the case. The power company was looking to use bankruptcy to liquidate the rural cooperative. As a bankruptcy expert, she provided legal assistance.[58]

In 1995, Warren also provided expert legal advice to Dow Chemical. The chemical giant owned 50 percent of Dow Corning, which was in a bankruptcy case. The bankruptcy followed lawsuits involving reportedly faulty silicone breast implants causing health problems. Dow was seeking to shield itself from taking any responsibility. As law professor William Jacobson of Cornell University puts it, "in the early days of the Dow Corning breast implant litigation Elizabeth Warren was providing legal advice to Dow Chemical, which was denying liability and [would be] fighting breast implant claims for many years to come."[59] As one lawyer involved in the case put it, "Warren's expertise was used by a company fighting in court to limit its liability and payments to women."[60]

Her involvement in the Dow case is clearly something she has tried to avoid having in the public light. During her 2012 campaign for the U.S. Senate, Warren avoided including the Dow case in a list of her legal consulting work that she provided to the media.[61]

In 2009, she defended insurance giant Travelers against the claims of asbestos victims. Travelers was fighting to gain immunity from some asbestos-related lawsuits by establishing a $500 million trust for victims, but on the precondition "that other insurers [would] give up their claims against Travelers." Warren worked to protect the settlement for victims that other insurance companies would invalidate if they were able to retain their claims. Travelers avoided paying the $500 million settlement by losing the fight with the other insurers. Warren claimed that she was working on behalf of asbestos workers, but her client was the insurance giant; they were paying her fee for advice on protecting their interests. For her services, Travelers paid Warren a whopping $212,000. As Professor Jacobson puts it, "Warren got paid, Travelers got to keep its settlement money, and the asbestos workers were left out in the cold."[62]

Her husband, Bruce Mann, a law professor who focuses on bankruptcy in American history, also did legal work on the case. According to the couple's 2009 financial disclosure, Travelers paid him an undisclosed sum.[63]

Warren worked similarly with Armstrong World Industries, a massive producer of wall and ceiling products for construction, which was also dealing with asbestos liabilities. The company used a reorganization plan to establish a trust and avoid direct payments to asbestos claimants.[64] Warren was their paid consultant, and she helped them navigate rule 524(g), which she had helped to write.[65]

Warren's legal consulting work was on behalf of large corporations who were using bankruptcy laws or bankruptcy trusts to avoid liabilities.

Much of Warren's legal work for these clients came through the white-shoe corporate law firm Caplin & Drysdale, which represented a myriad of large companies that were going through bankruptcies.[66] Warren often provided legal advice to the corporations, which meant that her ethical and legal obligations were to look out for the interests of the corporation, not their employees or claimants.

Warren did do some legal work for nonprofit organizations such as AARP (formerly the American Association of Retired Persons). She also served as a consultant for lawyers who were suing major corporations.[67] In all, most of her work outside Harvard was for the benefit of large corporate clients. And her corporate work provided the bulk of her legal income.[68]

Warren's regular and lucrative work for major corporations continued even as she sought to position herself as a consumer advocate. Along with her daughter Amelia, she co-wrote two books that presented a more populist view of the economy. The first book, *The Two-Income Trap*, argued that middle-class couples, even with two incomes, had a hard time getting ahead. A key part of the problem was real estate prices—driven up by families looking to live in neighborhoods with good schools. The declining quality of public education had pushed up the price of housing in the best school districts, they argued. Parents had to overextend themselves to get a good education for their kids.[69] The most radical solution they offered in the book was providing each family with a voucher that would allow parents to send their children to any public school regardless of where they lived. It would be, they said, "a shock to the educational system." But the competition would be good, and it would allow parents to "take control over schools' tax dollars."[70]

Despite her claims to be a consumer advocate, Warren's legal work for large corporations was helping to make both her and her husband rich. Financial disclosures by the time she ran for the Senate in 2012 showed that her net worth was as much as $14.5 million. Her house alone was worth $5 million. The couples' investment stock portfolio was worth as much as $8 million, according to her own disclosures. Yet she steadfastly insisted that she was not "wealthy." "I realize there are some wealthy individuals—I'm not one of them, but some wealthy individuals who have a lot of stock portfolios," she told MSNBC's Lawrence O'Donnell.[71]

A peek inside the couple's investment portfolio also contradicts her public persona as a liberal reformer and populist. While Warren has been downright brutal in her criticisms of major corporations from Wall Street to the health care industry, the couple has the bulk of her wealth invested in the very same companies—Fortune 500 and other traditional corporations.

In 2008, for example, Warren and her husband held between $1 million and $5 million in global equities through their TIAA CREF retirement fund, and another $500,000 to $1,000,000 in a Vanguard 500 Index Fund. They had no investments in "socially responsible investment funds." At the same time, Warren's husband also held an interest in a gas well in Latimer County, Oklahoma.[72]

Warren was teaching at Harvard Law School when the financial quake of 2008 struck. The financial crisis jolted even Harvard Law, with its massive endowment and storied halls. With the stock market plunging, the Harvard endowment was down 30 percent, although it was still tens of billions of dollars. In 2009, Harvard Law School officials had some financial decisions to make. The choice came down to salary reductions for the high-paid faculty or letting low-level employees at the Law School go. Warren made $349,375 in 2009.[73]

Reportedly, a petition was circulated among Harvard Law

faculty that called for salary reductions to save jobs. When job cuts came, Harvard trimmed the staff by 10 percent. *Harvard Magazine* noted that "faculty and senior administration members" had agreed to waive some compensation to help with the job cuts, but according to Warren's tax returns, she did not waive any compensation. Warren's salary actually went up in 2009.[74]

In her memoirs, Warren recounts how tight she is with her daughter Amelia Warren Tyagi, and how they have worked so closely. Having written two books together, they are certainly still in regular communication. Supporters acknowledge that mother and daughter are not just close personally, but they are also "longtime accomplice[s]" professionally.[75] While Elizabeth Warren moved from Harvard academic to government official and U.S. senator, Amelia has been involved in a business venture that has run parallel to her mother's career like railroad tracks. As Warren came to play a central role in the regulation of the financial industry in the Obama administration, her daughter was seeking and securing partnerships and deals with some of those same investment firms. As Warren served in the U.S. Senate, she would take curious positions on a number of issues that would seem to benefit her daughter's corporate clients.

The integrated relationship between Warren and her daughter is made apparent during a critical turning point in Warren's career. In November 2008, then-professor Warren was at home in the evening when Senate Majority Leader Harry Reid called on the phone. Financial markets were in turmoil and Congress was in the process of creating mechanisms to inject huge sums of money into financial institutions. Reid had never met Warren before, but he knew her by reputation. He had read her book *The Two-Income Trap*. Congress was setting up a five-member congressional oversight panel to keep track of the government bailout that would make available $700 billion to investment banks and other financial institutions. Reid asked her to come to the capital to discuss the possibility of her serving as the chair. Warren agreed to meet, and then she asked Amelia to join her in Washington. Amelia was the cofounder of a business in 2007 called the Business Talent Group (BTG) and she was in search of capital investors, board members, clients, and partners. As Reid later recalled, Warren "came down to DC and met me with her daughter, and did the deal."[76]

Warren became chair of the Troubled Asset Relief Program (TARP) oversight committee, which played a central role in the federal government's bailout of financial firms. *Time* magazine described Warren as a new sheriff in town, who "wielded her clout like a cudgel."[77] Warren would hold highly publicized hearings, offer advice to Congress on the oversight program, and call out large financial institutions and Treasury Department officials. Warren turned her committee "into a tough, prosecutorial committee" and "issued blunt monthly reports demanding more accountability from banks."[78]

At the same time that Elizabeth Warren was meeting and talking with major Wall Street investment firms, her daughter's firm BTG was adding high-profile advisors with connections to the same companies who would benefit and face possible scrutiny from TARP. According to BTG's website in late 2008 these included:

- Robert A. Kindler—Global head of Mergers and Acquisitions at Morgan Stanley, former global head of M&A at JPMorgan Chase.[79] Ironically, Kindler boasted a vanity license plate for his Porsche that read "2BIG2FAIL."[80] Morgan Stanley would receive $10 billion from TARP.[81]

- Edward J. Mathias—Managing director at the Carlyle Group, former member of management committee and board of directors at T. Rowe Price.[82] The Carlyle Group grabbed $154 million in TARP funds for an affiliate.[83]
- William I. Jacobs—Former senior executive vice president and chief operating officer at MasterCard International.[84]

Amelia founded BTG along with business partner Jody Greenstone Miller. The company is essentially a temp firm for specialized and highly skilled employees. BTG proudly positions itself as a mechanism for the "gig economy," where people are hired for part-time jobs rather than full-time employment. As Miller put it in the *Wall Street Journal*, "The surge in temp hiring is not a sign of a malfunctioning economy. It is the face of the future."[85] Curiously, this business model runs totally contrary to Senator Warren's positions. Warren has been highly critical of the "gig economy," arguing that part-time workers rarely get the benefits or the workplace authority that they would as full-time employees.[86]

In its early years, the firm struggled. Executives admitted that they had to be "extremely resourceful" in order to find new business.[87] Executive recruitment and the temp business are largely about corporate connections. As Clare Malone of the Daily Beast pointed out, BTG is "a hybrid headhunting and consulting firm—industries whose bread and butter is leveraging connections."[88] Now they appeared to have some in abundance.

In 2009, BTG had two hundred people in its talent pool available for hire, just $4 million in revenue, and only one salesperson. By 2012, BTG had 1,800 independent professionals in the network and almost triple the revenue, at over $11 million.[89] As we will see, they were doing business with some of the largest corporations in the country, as well as government agencies.

From chair of the TARP oversight committee, Warren moved to the White House in September 2010 when President Obama appointed her as assistant to the president and special advisor to the Secretary of the Treasury. Her new job focused on setting up a consumer protection bureau.[90]

In the wake of the 2008 financial crisis, the mortgage meltdown, and all the instability that went with it, there was a natural appeal for such a bureau. President Obama and congressional Democrats were soon on board. Because it had been Warren's idea, she was the natural person to play a central role in establishing the organization and running it.[91]

The new $550 million agency would have enormous power.[92] It was created to enforce rules on banks, collection agencies, Wall Street brokerage firms, credit unions, payday lenders, student loan servicers, and others. As the Treasury secretary at the time, Timothy Geithner, put it, "It got the authority to write and enforce consumer rules for much of the financial system."[93]

Warren was eager to establish direct lines of communication with the executives of the most powerful financial firms in the country. Her first assignment to one staffer, Will Sealy, was "collecting the cell phone number for every Wall Street CEO."[94]

In her new role, Warren was publicly blunt and aggressive when describing corporate America and the failures of corporate executives. "Wall Street CEOs, the same ones who wrecked our economy and destroyed millions of jobs, still strut around Congress, no shame, demanding favors, and acting like we should thank them," she said during her speech at the Democratic National Convention in August 2012. "Does anyone here have a problem with that?"[95]

However, privately she offered a softer, more friendly tone in her communications with the large Wall Street firms. Indeed, she seemed eager to work with the same titans that she was lambasting in public. "You all gave us a great deal to think about, and we are all appreciative," she wrote to Richard Davis, the president and CEO of U.S. Bancorp, in a March 2011 email obtained through the Freedom of Information Act. "I value your help—and your friendship—more than you know." Communication with the CEOs of major Wall Street firms was in "stark contrast to the battle that [was] waged in public." [96] Warren has met in private with Wall Street moguls that she publicly criticizes. This duality in her public utterances and private tone continued well into her tenure in the U.S. Senate. In July 2017, she joined a private donor retreat held at the Martha's Vineyard home of Robert Wolf, the former UBS Investment Bank CEO. [97] Wolf told the *New York Times*: "I think she is very different in a conversation than when she's on the stump." She also held private meetings with JPMorgan Chase CEO Jamie Dimon. [98] In public, she has excoriated Dimon and pointedly asked for his resignation from the New York Federal Reserve Bank's board of directors. [99]

Elizabeth Warren's softer tone in private occurred while her daughter Amelia was building BTG.

Warren's daughter Amelia is married to Sushil Tyagi, who moved to the United States from India after studying civil engineering in Delhi. Amelia and Sushil met at Wharton Business School while pursuing their MBAs. Sushil had been in the United States for a while, and had studied at the Rosenstiel School of Marine and Atmospheric Science and the University of California at Berkeley. [100] Sushil Tyagi is a somewhat mysterious figure. He is generally media-shy and appears in few publicly available Warren family photographs. And he enjoys business ties in India and elsewhere that are hard to trace.

Elizabeth Warren is close to Sushil. She mentions him on her website and credits him in the acknowledgments of the book she wrote with Amelia called *All Your Worth*, stating, "Sushil Tyagi offered tremendous support and intelligent insight."[101] Warren recounts in her memoir attending Sushil's brother's wedding in India, but offers scant information about the Tyagi family. Indeed, finding details about Tyagi's background is quite difficult. Warren and her husband, Bruce Mann, also have some familiarity with Sushil's business activities. In December 2009, they served as witnesses for a power of attorney corporate document he filed in India.[102]

Since his marriage into the Warren family, Sushil has been involved in a series of curious—even troubling—business ventures around the world. Tyagi runs Tricolor Films, which formerly boasted a small website with few details of his activities.[103] In 2004, he was an executive producer on an Indian film called *Hari Om*, produced with a company called Tips Industries, which is run by Kumar and Ramesh Taurani. The two brothers are well known in Indian film circles; in 1997, Ramesh was accused of hiring a hit man to take out a film rival named Gulshan.[104]

But Sushil Tyagi has demonstrated a willingness to work with global bad actors in business ventures.

Tyagi was the producer on a 2008 film funded by the Iranian government. The film was called *The Song of Sparrows* and was directed by Iranian filmmaker Majid Majidi. The film's synopsis: "After being let go from his job on an ostrich farm a man leaves his small village to find work in the big city. As a motorcycle taxi driver, he soon becomes consumed with his passengers' lives and is swept up in a world of greed. Now it is up to his family back home to *help restore his caring and generous nature*" (emphasis added).[105] A *New York Times* review of the film called it Majidi's "most religious" film released in the United States.[106]

On April 8, 2009, Sushil Tyagi was listed as the sole producer in the credits for *The Song of Sparrows* on the *New York Times* film page. Now his entry on the *New York Times* film page has been removed.[107]

The full credits of the film, for some reason, seem to also have been scrubbed from the internet. We obtained a copy by using the Wayback machine and made a startling discovery: the movie's chief investors included none other than the social deputy of the State Welfare Organization (SWO) of Iran (SWO-"معاونت اجتماعی سازمان بهزیستی کشور") as well as the Cultural and Artistic Organization of Tehran ("سازمان فرهنگی و هنری شهرداری تهران").[108]

These two investors in the film might appear at first glance to be innocuous cultural organizations—but they are not. Both are funded and controlled by the Islamist Iranian government.

The Cultural and Artistic Organization of Tehran states: "This organization was founded in 1996 and [does] its activities under the supervision of a board of trustees composed of various cultural institutions such as IRIB and Islamic propaganda organization."[109] Their home page promotes several events, like one for schoolchildren entitled "The Seal of Hostages," attended by several top Iranian officials.[110]

Another event that this "cultural organization" promotes is the inherently anti-Semitic Quds Day on the last day of Ramadan. The Cultural and Artistic Organization of Tehran openly acknowledges that they organize marches and create the posters, cartoons, and caricatures for Quds Day. They write: "A new plan for the destruction of Israel will be launched, and the Quds Cultural Radio station will be located at the Radio Station. Also, the 'I love the fight against Israel' is distributed among the people."[111]

Quds Day typically features massive crowds organized by the Iranian government chanting "death to America" and burning effigies, with full media coverage.[112]

The film credits for Sushil's *The Song of Sparrows* read like a who's who of prominent Iranian government institutions. They include a thank-you to the Iranian Revolutionary Guards Air Force.[113]

Tyagi's connection to the Iranian government came at a troublesome time for U.S.-Iranian relations. Washington had accused Iran of assisting in the killing of five American soldiers based in Iraq.[114] The country's president, Mahmoud Ahmadinejad, had repeatedly threatened the United States, which he declared a "satanic power," and warned that Israel would disappear from the face of the earth.[115]

Sushil Tyagi also produced another film by Majid Majidi called *Najva Ashorai*. Even less information is available about this film than for *The Song of Sparrows*.[116]

A now shut-down Web page describes Sushil's production company this way: "Leveraging their relationships with studio executives, access to top creative talent, and *the high-level support that they enjoy from numerous foreign governments*, this Los Angeles–based production company is developing a number of major international-themed projects for feature films, television, and interactive media" (emphasis added). It is not known what foreign governments those might involve beyond Iran.[117] Why the website was shut down is also unknown.

Would Sushil Tyagi's international business ties ever influence Warren's decision making? That is hard to know. What can be known is that his businesses could stand to benefit from her advocacy and proposed policies.

One of Elizabeth Warren's themes about anticompetitive practices in corporate America involves her critique of the beer industry. "If you've bought a six-pack recently," she wrote in 2017, "chances are you're paying more for fewer options. That's because just two companies control the lion's share of America's beer, buying up the craft brewers and independent breweries that have created a vibrant beer market and jacking up beer prices in order to stuff more money into their own pockets." She has pushed federal regulators to go after large brewing companies. "The thing is, we already have laws that prevent companies from doing just that. It's time to start enforcing them. Antitrust agencies can start by telling aspiring monopolies: keep your hands off of our beer!" [118]

Warren describes herself as a "beer lover." [119] But nowhere does she mention that Sushil Tyagi, her son-in-law, runs two beer-related businessses. The first is an enterprise in India: Kali Gori Breweries in Uttarakhand province. [120] The brewery name matches several business registrations in March 2011 under the name Kali Gori Breweries, both with Sushil's name on them. [121] Tyagi had been seeking to open the business since at least 2009. In fact, he authorized a power of attorney, describing the prospective business, to an Indian attorney (possibly his brother). What makes that interesting is that the power of attorney was notarized in Los Angeles, and witnessed by Elizabeth Warren and husband Bruce Mann. [122] In December 2010, Tyagi registered another beer-related business, this time stateside in Delaware, but operated out of his California home. [123] Called Craftbev International Amalgamated, it appears to have no other employees or executives. Its only public footprint was its purchase of the legacy Celis beer brands in June 2012.[124] In November 2013, Craftbev sold for an undisclosed amount the domestic production rights for Celis to Total Beverage Solutions, a firm run by a former Guinness executive. Craftbev retained the international distribution rights until February 2017, when the Celis family repurchased all trademark rights. By Tyagi's own statements at the time, he remains involved in the brands' international marketing.[125]

Warren has written over the years about her concerns that regulatory agencies would be "captured" by outside interests, with regulators no longer focused on the proper regulation but instead doing the bidding of those outside interests.[126]

Cleary Gottlieb was at the center of the effort to fight against the creation of Warren's new bureau. Cleary Gottlieb served as the lobbyist for a host of financial firms looking to weaken Dodd-Frank. This includes Barclays, Bank of America, Citigroup, Credit Suisse Group, Nomura Holdings, BNP Paribus, Credit Agricole Corporate and Investment, Deutsche Bank AG, and the Securities Industry and Financial Markets Association.[127] Cleary Gottlieb was working behind the scenes to see that the new financial reform bill worked for the interests of their clients. It is important to note that Elizabeth Warren called out several institutions and individuals for trying to undermine the financial reforms: she took Securities and Exchange Commission (SEC) chair Mary Jo White to task, for example, calling her work "extremely disappointing."[128] Warren apparently held her fire and never publicly attacked or condemned Cleary Gottlieb, who funded her work at Harvard, or their clients.[129]

Ever since Warren had stepped onto the national stage in the Obama administration, powerful Democrats had been encouraging her to run for office. Senator Chuck Schumer and Senate Majority Leader Harry Reid were early enthusiasts.[130] An organization called the Progressive Change Campaign Committee set up a fund-raising effort to draft her, so when she announced her Senate campaign in 2011, she had plenty of friends and allies.[131] One of the most important was daughter Amelia, who had built up relationships within the progressive movement. In the early stages of the Democratic primary in Massachusetts, it was a crowded field. Several other candidates announced early for the run against Republican senator Scott Brown. Meanwhile, the organization connected to Amelia quietly went about boosting her status inside the progressive movement. Amelia sat on the board of directors of a left-wing organization called Demos, becoming chairman in 2010. New York–based Demos had championed Elizabeth Warren to head up the Consumer Financial Protection Bureau (CFPB), never disclosing that Amelia was chairing the organization.[132] Demos now applauded her run for the Senate, calling her "a figure of rare integrity" and declaring, "She and this republic are better served by Warren making the Senate run." Miles Rapoport, then president of Demos, said in July 2011, "Demos has long been a vocal supporter of Elizabeth Warren and commends her for working tirelessly to set up the CFPB all while defending it from unrelenting and unfounded attacks." In 2010, the group even presented her with a "Transforming America" award. In their statements of praise, though, Demos never mentioned that her daughter, Amelia, was a board member and then chairman of the organization.[133]

Eventually the other candidates for the Democratic primary bid melted away and Warren beat Republican incumbent Scott Brown. As Warren's political star rose, so would Amelia's business. Beginning in 2012 and 2013, shortly after Warren took her seat in the Senate, BTG began growing rapidly, according to a Stanford University Business School history of the company. Eventually, there was an interesting overlap between the clients that hired BTG and Senator Elizabeth Warren's legislative work.[134]

In 2014, Senator Elizabeth Warren pushed for more funding for the National Institutes of Health (NIH). In 2015, her daughter's BTG landed a contract with the Foundation for the National Institutes of Health for $808,000. The following year, they received another for $467,000.[135]

Senator Elizabeth Warren sits on the Senate Health Education Labor and Pensions Committee, which has passed legislation providing funds for the Corporation for Public Broadcasting, which funds PBS. In 2015, the committee passed the Ready to Learn program to help fund PBS. Also in 2015, her daughter's firm began listing PBS as a client.[136]

BTG's list of clients generally overlaps with those who have matters sitting before Elizabeth Warren in the U.S. Senate, and she at times has appeared to take positions or actions that would benefit her daughter's clients. Consider Warren's attitude toward the medical device industry. Warren sits on the powerful Health Education Labor and Pensions Committee, with oversight of the medical industry. Warren has consistently bashed other large industries for excessive profits and failure to pay their "fair share" in taxes. "The most profitable corporations should have to pay their fair share," she says. While the medical device industry would certainly fit that definition, Warren has been very supportive of it. As a senator, she pushed for the repeal of the medical device taxes that were part of Obama's Affordable Care Act. She also introduced something called the Medical Innovation Act, which would take fines paid by the pharmaceutical industry and steer them for the benefit of "med-tech" companies. Warren has also favored rewriting Food and Drug Administration (FDA) rules for the benefit of med-tech companies and wants certain tax credits made permanent for the industry.[137]

Observers have taken note of her wild inconsistencies when it comes to this one industry. One Democratic Senate staffer told *Time* magazine, "The idea that Elizabeth Warren thinks that one industry should get a sweetheart deal from paying their fair share for providing healthcare to poor Americans is repulsive." Observers note that several medical device manufacturers are based in Massachusetts.[138] What no one mentions is the other significant tie between the medical device industry and Warren's family. Her daughter's firm has more than half a dozen medical device manufacturers as clients. The BTG client list includes two of the largest medical device companies—Johnson & Johnson and General Electric. It also lists as clients Emerson, Pfizer, McKesson, Hologic, and Hitachi—all of which are in the field affected by the medical device tax. The Carlyle Group, another BTG client, spent $4.15 billion to buy a medical device company (Ortho Clinical Diagnostics) in 2015.[139]

In short, the Warren family's legacy of deep financial ties to major corporations continues. It began with Warren's corporate legal work and now extends to providing staffing solutions to major corporations. Despite Warren's continued vocal criticism of corporate America, the family has prospered in its close association with the same.

Likewise, Warren's political campaigns have been fueled by campaign donations from major corporate law firms who represent the Wall Street firms and the major corporations that she often criticizes. Warren has three entities collecting campaign contributions while she serves in the Senate. She had a campaign committee, a leadership PAC named PAC for a Level Playing Field, and a joint fund-raising committee called the Elizabeth Warren Action Fund. Each received large contributions from white-collar criminal defense and financial industry law firms, as well as individuals working in the private equity and securities and investment industries. Lawyers and law firms are together the largest group of contributors to the Action Fund. Included contributions are sizable checks from Brown Rudnick, Cotchett Pitre & McCarthy, and others. Her campaign committee funds for the Senate reflect a similar story. Indeed, for her first election in 2012, among her top contributions were high-powered white-collar criminal defense and financial attorneys at Ropes & Gray and at Goodwin & Procter.[140]

There were other conflicting relationships, too. Elizabeth Warren describes her close relationship with Richard Trumka, who would become president of the AFL-CIO. During her days at the TARP Commission, she describes an encounter with him. Trumka recalls, "She doesn't see me, and I lean up and I say to her, 'Don't worry, Elizabeth, I have your back,' and she turned around and smiled and said, 'Yes, you do, and I'll always have the back of the workers.' "[141] At the same time, Trumka's union was a donor to Amelia's organization Demos.[142]

As a United States senator, Elizabeth Warren advocated for projects that were of interest to those corporate law firms to which she was closest. These projects would seem to contradict her stated positions on important issues. In 2018, Warren cosponsored the Mashpee Wampanoag Tribe Reservation Reaffirmation Act, which would overturn a federal court decision and allow the Mashpee Wampanoag Tribe in Massachusetts to open a casino.[143] The idea of allowing the tribe to open the casino was rather odd, in part because it was new—first recognized by the federal government in 2007 after a vigorous lobbying effort that included Washington super-lobbyist Jack Abramoff, who later went to prison on fraud and bribery charges. The tribe was also small: it had roughly 2,600 members. The tribe wanted to open a casino called First Light Casino and Resort, in the blue-collar town of Taunton, Massachusetts.[144] What was most unusual about the project was Warren's support for it. Going back to 2012, she had consistently taken the position of opposing legalized gambling in Massachusetts. In 2014, she supported efforts to repeal legalized gambling in Massachusetts. "It's a tough call here. People need jobs, but gambling can be a real problem economically for a lot of people," she said. "I didn't support gambling the first time around and I don't expect to support it [now]."[145]

The Mashpee Wampanoag casino ran into legal problems in 2016 when U.S. district judge William G. Young halted the tribe's plans for the casino. Judge Young blocked the Department of Interior's decision to take land into trust on behalf of the tribe, which was a prerequisite for Indian gaming.[146]

But in 2018, Elizabeth Warren completely reversed her long-held position by supporting legislation to overturn the federal court's decision. Her support for the casino was also unusual in that the town where it was to be built was largely opposed to the Mashpee Wampanoag project. Mayor William Carpenter of nearby Brockton actually went to Washington to meet with lawmakers to oppose the bill. The proposed casino would "destroy his community's [own] plans for a casino." In short, Warren had long opposed Massachusetts's desire for casinos providing blue-collar jobs, but now appeared in favor of one for the Mashpee Wampanoag Tribe.[147]

Warren's move puzzled most observers, who assumed that she reversed course on the issue of gambling in an effort to heal her relationship with Native Americans after the fallout over her bogus claims of Native American ancestry. Other reasons might also explain why she would support the deal.

The First Light Casino and Resort was to be on Mashpee Wampanoag tribal land, but running the casino (and vacuuming up 40 percent of the gross profits) was a massive Malaysian gambling conglomerate called Genting. The Malaysian company had already reportedly sunk $400 million into the deal. In short, they stood to lose a lot.[148]

Representing Genting in the Mashpee Wampanoag casino deal was Cleary Gottlieb. In fact, the law firm was extremely close to Genting, representing the Malaysian company in several deals, including the financing of a $3 billion casino in Las Vegas, as well as projects in New York City and Miami.[149]

Elizabeth Warren's efforts to leverage her positions for her own financial and political benefit are not unusual. As we will see in the next chapter, one of her closest Senate colleagues has been doing so for decades.

SHERROD BROWN

Sherrod Brown has always relied on a certain roguish charm when in the public spotlight. Described by the media as a "handsome, gravelly-voiced defender of the working class; perpetually mentioned in presidential conversations," he has spent almost his entire adult life either serving in political office or running for it.[1] The unique appeal to his supporters, in addition to that charm, is the fact that he viewed "himself as a progressive before it was cool."[2] While most progressives on the national stage hail from the coasts—think California, Oregon, Massachusetts, or New York—Ohio-born Sherrod Brown has his feet firmly planted in the American heartland.

Brown carries with him all the accessories of a midwestern populist. He speaks of hard-hewn midwestern values and his Lutheran faith. Chapter 25 in the Bible's book of Matthew features prominently in his speeches and interviews, normally translated to indicate Jesus' kudos for those who have served "the least of these." (He takes umbrage at the "least" language, so he reads a version called the "Justice and Poverty Bible," which apparently translates more to his egalitarian liking.) Brown is, in many respects, a throwback. As one writer puts it, he "often seemed a politician from the radio era."[3] Brown loves telling reporters that he wears suits made just ten miles from his house in Cleveland, and, of course, he drives an American-made Jeep. Brown does not dress like the typical U.S. senator; his "perpetually wrinkled suits and shaggy hair" are standard on the campaign trail or behind the podium.[4]

Brown displays his working-class sentiments in his Senate office reception area, where he has a miner's safety lamp sitting on the table, as well as a beer stein from the United Mine Workers. On the wall, there is a plaque of a caged canary. In earlier times, miners used the birds to detect toxic air in the mine.[5]

Brown's progressive message has been consistent over the nearly fifty years he has been in political office: he is a fighter for the working class. "It has been a 100-year battle between the privileged and the rest of us," he thunders like an Old Testament prophet.[6]

Brown's supporters and family express his political work in heroic terms. His wife, Connie Schultz, once sent an email to a colleague at the Cleveland *Plain Dealer* who had drawn a political cartoon critical of him. She wrote: "For 30 years, Sherrod has fought for those who would have no voice and *no future without him* . . . (and he) remains a hero to so many. Especially to me" (emphasis added).[7]

But Brown himself, as we will see, grew up privileged. While he has campaigned with a hole in one shoe (and drawn the media's attention to it with an early, infamous reelection advertisement), his roots are far from working class. His identification with workers has more to do with his reading material than actual working-class experience. As George Packer has pointed out, Brown likes to cite Leo Tolstoy's *Resurrection* as an inspiration for his understanding of the degradation of society's poor. He read Tolstoy at Yale; he never lived a working-class life. "In other words," writes Packer, "Brown discovered Tolstoy before he discovered the working class."[8]

Brown's approach to politics has been remarkably consistent—and successful—over the course of his more than four and a half decades in public office. Sherrod Brown's friend John Eichinger jokingly explained at a Democratic Party roast back in 1982 that Brown's approach is to "get money from the rich and votes from the poor by promising to protect them from each other."[9]

It is a formula that has worked in American politics for more than one hundred years.

However, a closer examination reveals a far more complex picture than that of a conventional progressive politician. More than simply using that political strategy to win office, Brown seems to have used his government office to benefit his family, in particular, his brother's legal practice, which has engaged in what some might consider strange and suspect lawsuits. Additionally, Brown's advocacy for "workers" appears to be far more about protecting union leaders who donate to his campaigns than rank-and-file union workers. Indeed, when the interests of union leaders and the union members clash, Brown consistently sides with the bosses who have underwritten his many political campaigns.

Brown was born in Mansfield, Ohio, a town midway between Columbus and Cleveland. The son of a doctor, his mother was a staunch Lutheran and progressive social activist; Sherrod inherited both from her.[10] While in high school, young Sherrod organized a march in his hometown to celebrate the first Earth Day in 1970. "We did this really cool march and we had a really big crowd," he recounted later. "But we get down to the square and none of us had thought about what you do when you get down there. We didn't have any speakers, and it was like, 'Oh, shit.' So we just disbanded."[11]

He is the youngest of three brothers and is especially close to his brother Charlie. Indeed, as we will see, Brown has seemed to use his political office on regular occasions to help one of his brother's class-action lawsuits against everything from dentists to vaccine companies.

Sherrod left Ohio to attend Yale University, where he majored in Russian studies.[12] Before graduating in 1974, he was recruited during his senior year at Yale by a local Democratic Party leader back in Ohio named Donald Kindt to run for the state legislature. Brown agreed to toss his hat in the ring despite the concerns raised by his father. During that first campaign, Sherrod described himself to voters as a "farmer," even though he had launched his primary campaign while a senior at Yale. While Brown's family had owned Ohio farmland since the early 1800s, it is doubtful he did much work with livestock or crops in the hallowed fields of the Yale campus in New Haven, Connecticut.[13]

Brown worked hard that first election, walking the precincts, knocking on doors, and shaking hands. According to Brown, he knocked on 20,000 doors—about half of the entire district—a claim that is easy to believe. The hard work paid off: he beat a Republican incumbent in a conservative district. At just twenty-one, he was seated in the state legislature.[14] It was the beginning of a long political career: eight years in the state legislature; eight more as Ohio's secretary of state; fourteen years in Congress; and three terms in the U.S. Senate and counting.[15]

In short, Brown has never held a full-time job outside of government service. Local sportscaster Mike Greene once joked that Brown had a "lifelong quest to avoid gainful employment." [16]

Ohio had a part-time legislature, but Brown was one of the few legislators who did not hold an outside job.[17] Instead, in those early years, he toiled away in Columbus pushing legislation. Dogs, for some reason, did not fare well in his early bills, perhaps because he claims to have been bitten eight times by dogs while campaigning during his first four years in the state legislature.[18] Whatever the reason, Brown supported legislation to allow animal shelters to put down dogs with sodium pentobarbital. He also voted for a bill imposing fines and jail time for dog barking.[19]

More important, Brown fused himself with the leaders of local unions in his district, to the point that he became embroiled in their internecine leadership battles. In 1981, he was accused by officials of the United Steelworkers of improperly interfering in a local election. By 1982, the battles became so heated that local union leader Dan Martin, of the United Steelworkers Subdistrict 27, complained of "verbal harassment from Sherrod Brown's mother." She reportedly verbally attacked him after a party meeting because he did not want to endorse Brown for reelection. There was also a late-night phone call from Brown himself, who according to Martin "used language which was not very becoming to a person who is a state representative."[20]

Nevertheless, unions continued to be an important power base when in 1982 he ran for his first statewide office: secretary of state. When he won he was just twenty-nine years old.[21]

As secretary of state Sherrod devoted much of his time to voter registration efforts. He persuaded McDonald's to put voter registration forms on their tray liners.[22] His other major responsibility included writing language for state ballot initiatives. He was criticized for tilting language in favor of ballot initiatives he liked, and against those he did not.[23]

His tenure was also marked by tragedy and scandal. When troubles or scandal struck, Brown seemed to use his power to squelch investigations to avoid bad publicity.

On August 30, 1983, someone walked up to the fifth floor of the Frank J. Lausche State Office Building in downtown Cleveland. Sherrod's deputy director Colleen Shaughnessy had an office there. By noon, the twenty-seven-year-old aide would be dead. She was murdered in a particularly brazen manner: in a state office building in the middle of a typical workday. It was also a notably brutal crime: Shaughnessy was found beaten, strangled, tied up, and murdered with a metal spike stabbed into her heart. "This was a sickening display of violence in broad daylight," said the deputy coroner.

Just hours after Shaughnessy was murdered, a former Sherrod Brown campaign employee received a threatening phone call, according to the police file.[24]

As details emerged from the crime scene, there appeared to be more questions than answers. Shaughnessy reportedly kept her steel office door locked and there was no sign of forced entry. This led some investigators to speculate that she may have known her killer.[25] As the *Akron Beacon Journal* put it, "The circumstances surrounding Colleen's death suggest the plot of an Agatha Christie mystery."[26] Shaughnessy was close to Sherrod Brown. She had helped to manage Brown's 1982 statewide campaign for secretary of state and was one of his closest aides.[27] During the course of the murder investigation, troubling accusations began to emerge. It was reported by a witness that the 1982 Brown campaign had kept two sets of books pertaining to campaign finances. The police files also reveal that Shaughnessy was allegedly one of two female staffers who knew about it.[28]

Police also heard from several witnesses that Shaughnessy also received a letter from a former Sherrod Brown campaign worker; one reported that the ex-worker was threatening to expose "illegal payoffs" involving the campaign unless the person was given a job.[29]

At the same time, witnesses close to Shaughnessy explained

to the police that the victim was "very upset with Sherrod" and "wanted to change jobs."[30] Another reported that she was "very disenchanted with her job and as the primary election went on she became troubled with Sherrod Brown's family."[31]

Beyond working for Sherrod Brown, there were other ties. Shaughnessy had also dated Sherrod's brother, Robert Brown, for a year.[32]

Prosecutors eventually charged a teenager in the case.[33] During the trial, though, they presented little evidence actually linking him to the crime. A jury acquitted him.[34] Brown had his office, including the room where Colleen Shaughnessy was murdered, closed because of the tragedy.[35]

Police never solved the case.[36]

While he was secretary of state, Brown's office also apparently became a center of drug activity. A retired undercover narcotics officer came forward to report that she had once bought drugs from someone on Brown's staff at the secretary of state's office.[37] Brown himself asked the state police to investigate after he found a bag of drugs under the front seat of his state-assigned car. In 1990, Michael Miller, a prosecutor who investigated the case, explained that there was "undeniable drug activity" occurring in Brown's office, but too much time had passed to prosecute.[38]

The narcotics investigation ran into roadblocks and Brown and his aides worked to kill the investigation, according to a former Ohio state police officer. At the center of it was Don Kindt, the Democratic Party county chairman who had first recruited Brown to run for the state legislature. Brown had brought Kindt on as the assistant secretary of state. According to Joseph Hopkins, a now-retired state patrolman assigned to investigate the case, Brown tried to halt the investigation because the 1986 election was on the horizon. "In my view, there was probable cause to believe there was inappropriate interference by someone in this case," he said. In a written report to his superiors, Hopkins explained, "I called [then–assistant secretary of state] Don Kindt . . . and learned that Brown wants to drop the investigation . . . Brown feels it should be dropped as it is going into the next year [1986]." Hopkins also said that one of his investigative reports was changed to make the offenses look less serious. Hopkins had written that the alleged offenses were felonies, but the reports were altered to claim they were misdemeanors. The Hopkins report has since been destroyed.[39]

The police eventually dropped the investigation.

In 1990, Brown suffered his only electoral defeat when he lost the secretary of state's position to Republican Bob Taft. After the loss, without skipping a beat, Brown pulled up stakes and moved back to northeastern Ohio to jump into a primary for a congressional seat that had just opened up near Cleveland.[40]

Brown campaigned as a progressive populist and outsider. He was promising change and the opportunity to upend the establishment, and claimed to back term limits, restricting how long politicians could serve in office. Indeed, he even supported the idea that a twelve-year term limit should be "retroactive," meaning if a term limit law was passed, one's time served in office would already count against the limit. He denounced "old-timers" who stayed in Washington too long. "Voters support term limits because they want to get rid of the people who have been here for 20 or 30 years," he proclaimed.[41]

Brown went on the win the seat, but he would never honor his commitment to term limits. After serving for twelve years in Washington, Brown reversed course, explaining now that suddenly longevity in office was a good thing. Being in the nation's capital longer was actually beneficial. Elected to the U.S. Senate in 2006, Brown has now been in Washington more than twenty-five years and counting.[42]

Brown's congressional career—in both the House and Senate—is marked by a devotion to progressive causes before they become widely supported within the Democratic Party. Brown's efforts in the minutiae of health and medical issues—those that seem designed to help put a lot of money in the pocket of his brother—are less well known.

Sherrod is extraordinarily close to both of his older brothers, Charlie and Robert. After Brown was first elected to the U.S. Congress, he recounted how he celebrated the following morning with "the people I care about the most." It is a short list, including his parents (who have since passed away), his brothers, his daughters, and a niece. These were not simply polite words about family. When he set up his congressional office, he relied on a team of three individuals to screen senior staff. One of those was his brother Charlie.[43]

They remain close to this day. So much so that Charlie is actively involved in Sherrod's political career. During Brown's 2018 Senate reelection, for example, Charlie served as a surrogate on the campaign trail, making appearances at Democratic Party events in Greene County and Montgomery County, where he shared his "insights into Sherrod's 2018 re-election campaign."[44]

Charlie Brown was, like Sherrod, elected to public office at a young age. In his case, it was attorney general of West Virginia back in 1984, making him the youngest state attorney general in the country at that time. Sherrod traveled to West Virginia from Ohio to campaign for his brother.[45] Unfortunately, Charlie's tenure ended with multiple scandals, resulting in his resignation. First, he was indicted on charges of soliciting campaign contributions from his own staff in the attorney general's office. Brown argued that while it was illegal to solicit such donations, he was asking for donations to retire old campaign debts so the law did not apply. He was charged anyway.[46] Then there was the problem of perjury allegations stemming from his messy divorce case. While attorney general, Charlie Brown had allegedly impregnated his secretary and then paid her hush money after a supposed abortion—one she reportedly never had. The matter surfaced in his custody hearing involving his ex-wife and their five-year-old daughter. He was accused of lying under oath about the scandal involving his secretary.[47]

Charlie Brown left political office and became a class-action lawyer focused on a number of health care issues, many highly controversial at best, some would say dubious. He and his legal partners have sued over vaccines, dental fillings, artificial sweeteners, and other products. His brother Sherrod, while serving in both Congress and the U.S. Senate, has appeared to work hard to clear the litigation path for his brother by pushing legislation or federal actions that would benefit his cases.

Sherrod Brown has been a consistent supporter of trial lawyers during his Senate tenure. When legislation was introduced to limit attorney's fees in class-action lawsuits, the Class Action Fairness Act of 2005, Brown voted against it. When another piece of legislation was introduced to impose sanctions on attorneys and law firms who filed frivolous lawsuits, Brown voted against that, too.[48] This is not unusual in Washington; trial attorneys are major contributors to politicians, especially to progressive politicians.[49]

What makes Brown's ties different is the fact that his brother is in the class-action lawsuit business.

Since 1996, Charlie Brown has been affiliated with the law office of Swankin & Turner, a Washington, D.C., and Ohio–based firm that specializes in representing "businesses as well as individuals and consumer groups in a wide variety of regulatory matters concerning food, drug, health, environmental and product-safety matters."[50] The firm is headed by litigators and lobbyists who have been Sherrod Brown boosters. Among them is James S. Turner, who has himself charted a controversial legal path over the course of his career. He is also the founder and registered business agent for Anakosha, a "swingers club" in Florida, and a partner with the National Coalition for Sexual Freedom. Together they launched a "Swing Leadership Conference."[51]

Turner and his wife and son are decades-long donors to Sherrod Brown and Turner "aligns with the positions" of Sherrod, a political ally and friend.[52]

Charlie's work as an attorney has been challenged in the legal community. In 2007, the Washington, D.C., Bar Counsel found that he had shown "a disregard of certain ethical standards," including filing frivolous lawsuits against defendants and filing a lawsuit without stating any legal or factual basis for the claims. They issued an informal admonition. Several years earlier, an Arizona Court of Appeals had ruled that his claims against certain defendants were "groundless" in a separate case. Eventually, the State Bar of Arizona issued Charlie "an order of informal reprimand and costs."[53]

Seemingly in support of their class-action lawsuits, Charlie Brown and James Turner run several health advocacy nonprofits out of the law firm and work closely with dozens of others. The organizations have official-sounding names like Citizens for Health; National Institute for Science, Law, and Public Policy; and Consumers for Dental Choice. Citizens for Health has gone after childhood vaccines (on the theory that they cause autism), fluoride in drinking water, artificial sweeteners, antibiotics in livestock, cell phone tower radiation, the cancerous risks of using mobile phones, and more.[54]

There is a reason that these nonprofits are run out of the law firm: the groups may have altruistic motives, but the net effect is that they help advance the law firm's litigation by raising medical issues and concerns. And Charlie Brown and his legal partners have latched on to every conceivable health issue or product and used it as an opportunity to litigate: vaccines, aspartame, and amalgamated dental fillings, to name a few.[55] As we will see, Sherrod Brown has moved the levers of government in a manner beneficial to these lawsuits.

It is important to note that the areas of Charlie's litigation almost entirely overlap with his brother Sherrod's committee assignments in Congress. Shortly after Sherrod was elected to Congress in 1992, he sought out a slot on the House Energy and Commerce Committee. The powerful committee "has jurisdiction over the world," bragged a former congressman, because it had a voice in anything dealing with commerce and energy broadly defined.[56] Congressional Democrats granted him the post and gave Sherrod a perch on the Investigations and Oversight Subcommittee.[57]

His committee and subcommittee assignments also placed him in the perfect position to help his brother's litigation, which would proceed against a variety of companies and interests. After the Republican sweep of Congress in the 1994 elections, he became the top Democrat on a powerful Commerce subcommittee that oversees health and environmental laws.[58] These were precisely the areas that Charlie would be litigating.

Almost as soon as he was in Congress, Sherrod was in a position to take actions that could benefit his brother's litigation. In 1996, Charlie started Consumers for Dental Choice (CDC), which would lobby for "mercury free" dentistry.[59] As with Citizens for Health, CDC would be run out of Swankin & Turner.[60] In the spring of that same year, a subcommittee of Sherrod's Committee on Commerce sent a series of letters to the Food and Drug Administration (FDA) concerning delayed rulemakings in several areas including "dental amalgam ingredient labeling." They wanted the FDA to expedite the rewriting of rules concerning possible warning labels for dental fillings.[61]

Charlie began working with class-action attorneys around the country who sought large damages from the dental industry on the grounds that they had failed to disclose the ingredients in dental fillings. One lawsuit in Georgia alone sought damages that could potentially exceed $100 million.[62]

Charlie's legal cases rested on the widely disputed claim that dentists are poisoning millions of Americans by using amalgam fillings for cavities. Because the amalgam includes mercury, Brown claims that they are dangerous.[63] Never mind that the practice has been widely used for decades and there is little or no scientific evidence to back up his claims.[64] But if the FDA was to issue warning labels about the contents of amalgam, that might introduce consumer doubt—and potentially sway jurors.

The lawsuits against dentists soon followed. In 2004, Charlie moderated a panel at the Association of Trial Lawyers concerning Mercury Silver Dental Fillings as the Next Mass Tort. Speakers included a Los Angeles–based class-action attorney who would partner with Charlie: Shawn Khorrami.[65] The Khorrami firm was described as "one of the country's most successful mass tort firms," with verdicts and settlements worth some $2.5 billion.[66] But it was also highly controversial: Khorrami has faced nineteen counts of misappropriating the funds of clients and in 2016 was disbarred by the California State Bar Association.[67] Charlie was "of counsel" at Khorrami's California-based firm. According to

Khorrami's website at the time, Charlie Brown "actively works on the Khorrami Firm's cases relating to mercury fillings."[68] Khorrami later served as the lead national counsel at Consumers for Dental Choice.[69]

At the association meeting in 2004, Charlie Brown explained: "This development puts every dentist in America on notice that if they continue to place mercury fillings in children or young women, they may well end up in a court of law."[70]

On September 8, 2005, Sherrod took another step that would directly benefit his brother and his law partners. He introduced a bill called the Medical Advertising Reform Act.[71] The legislation would create new rules on prescription drug and medical device advertising directly to consumers. It was particularly focused on drugs like Celebrex and Bextra. Indeed, Sherrod mentioned them both by name. He went on: "This is a matter of life and death for millions of consumers. When lives are at risk, the stakes are too high to cross our fingers and hope drugmakers do the right thing."[72]

What Sherrod did not mention is that the same day he introduced the bill, a group of class-action attorneys merged thirty-one legal cases against Bextra and Celebrex from large federal cases into another group. The lawyer at the center of it? Shawn Khorrami, from the firm where Charlie was "of counsel." The lawsuits were about Celebrex and Bextra and allegations that they had made false claims in their advertising, the same subject as Sherrod's bill in Washington.[73]

The lawsuits over pharmaceutical advertising ran into another problem in early 2006 when the FDA claimed that because of federal preemption, the lawsuits citing state laws would be moot. This, of course, undermined the entire case against the makers of Bextra and Celebrex. Sherrod and other members sent a letter to the secretary of the Department of Health and Human Services opposing the FDA's position and demanding that it be overturned.[74]

Sherrod's actions—both in introducing legislation and his letter to the HHS secretary—appear to be timed to directly benefit his brother Charlie and Charlie's legal partner Shawn Khorrami.

The pattern continued with a drug called Vioxx.

In December 2004, Brown was one of the twenty-two members of Congress who signed a letter to the FDA requesting more information on a Dr. David Graham, a "Vioxx Whistleblower" who was being punished by the agency for his testimony before a Senate committee. Graham testified that the FDA "fumbled in its handling of the arthritis drug Vioxx," among other things. In the letter, Congress said that if these actions against Graham were true, they were "out of line and may very well be illegal."[75]

By May 2004, Shawn Khorrami had already begun investigating *individual and class lawsuits* against Vioxx, and by December they were already prosecuting individual and class-action cases.[76] Both Charlie Brown and James S. Turner were listed as attorneys at Khorrami's firm at the time.[77]

With Khorrami's class-action lawsuits in play, Sherrod was continuing his fight for Vioxx lawsuits. He asked to send a portion of SB 5, or the Class Action Fairness Act of 2005, to the committee for consideration.[78] If passed, the law would address abuses of class actions by expanding federal jurisdiction over these suits and would limit attorney fees in class-action lawsuits.[79] Sherrod opposed the bill on the grounds that it would make Vioxx lawsuits more difficult and would betray "the public's trust."[80] In short, he wanted the Vioxx cases to continue. His efforts failed.

Sherrod voted nay on the bill, but it became law with a final vote of 279 to 149.[81]

In 2007, the FDA began receiving complaints about jerky treats from (or with ingredients from) China making their dogs sick. Complaints jumped from 2011 to 2013.[82] In February 2012, Senator Brown wrote a letter to the FDA commissioner, which claimed that pet owners in his home state of Ohio had reported numerous cases of their dogs getting sick or dying after eating jerky treats imported from China. Brown railed against the problem in numerous media outlets and demanded that the FDA investigate the matter, test the dog treats imported from China, and ban anything found to be toxic.[83] One of these large class-action lawsuits was introduced by attorney Shawn Khorrami, who sued treat makers in January 2013.[84]

Beyond the activities of his brother as a class-action lawyer, Sherrod Brown enjoys large contributions from lawyers, no doubt including those operating in this area of the law.[85] He continues to push for legislation that would benefit the entire class-action industry. In 2019, he introduced legislation that would add restrictions on arbitration and allow more class-action lawsuits in consumer contracts.[86]

The other major entanglement for Brown is his close relationship with labor leaders. Richard Trumka, president of AFL-CIO, says that Brown is "not just an ally, but a champion."[87] Few American politicians have received more financial support from labor union political funds than Sherrod Brown. He can count on the support of the leadership of every major union: the AFL-CIO; the Teamsters; United Food and Commercial Workers; Service Employees International Union; American Federation of State, County, and

Municipal Employees (AFSCME); the United Steelworkers; and others.[88] He attends rallies that consistently feature appearances on the podium with the "labor movement glitterati."[89] National labor leaders like Teamsters head Jimmy Hoffa Jr. are regular fixtures by his side at campaign events. And they stuff his campaign coffers with funds. His embrace of unions is also part of political reality in Ohio and "reflects the power of the Ohio organized labor movement, particularly in the Cleveland area."[90]

As a member of Congress and as a U.S. senator, he has received financial support not only from local unions in Ohio and national headquarters in Washington, D.C., but also West Coast unions who see him as their champion.[91] The funds have been a major foundation of his electoral success. During his 1998 congressional campaign, two of his top five contributors were unions.[92] Unions not only donate to his campaign, but they also provide campaign services. For example, they pay for polls during election years.[93]

On a personal level, his older daughter has worked for the Service Employees International Union (SEIU).[94]

Beyond the money, his political operation is fused with labor leaders. The head of his Ohio operations, John Ryan, was the former head of Cleveland's AFL-CIO office. He was Brown's Senate campaign manager in 2006 and has headed up his Ohio office ever since.[95]

Far less discussed is the role he plays to help union *leaders*. The distinction between union *leaders* and union *members* is an important one because the interests of the two can and do clash. And when they clash, Brown appears to consistently side with union leaders. He has worked during his time in public office to protect the interests of union leaders from transparency rules that would allow union members to track how their dues are being spent. He has also pushed a union pension plan that helps union leaders at the expense of union workers, and proposed legislation that makes it easier for union leaders to intimidate workers.

Consider the simple question of transparency about how much union leaders are paid and how they spend their members' money. The Department of Labor has required since 1959 that union officials make certain financial disclosures about how much they are paid, and how they spend union funds.[96] The Department of Labor eventually updated those rules to require "increased reporting on compensation amounts of union leaders, identifying the buyers and sellers of union assets, and expanding on the reporting of cash receipts."[97] Given the long history of union corruption and financial malfeasance over the decades, the rules would seem to make sense.

Sherrod Brown, though, considers these rules unreasonable. During a Senate hearing in November 2007, Brown made clear that it would be burdensome for the Department of Labor to require greater financial disclosures by union officials. He characterized the disclosure requirements as unreasonable since even "volunteer union activists [would] have to disclose about their financial lives."[98] The reality is, of course, otherwise. Indeed, the law covers many union leaders who have fueled his political rise—and they are hardly "volunteers." Many are extraordinarily well paid. Lennie Wyatt, the president of the United Food and Commercial Workers Local 75 in Ohio, had over $480,000 in compensation in 2015. The secretary-treasurer of that same union, Steve Culter, received more than $500,000 for the same year.[99] The union leaders are major Brown allies: the UFCW has bragged about "its statewide outreach efforts" securing victory for Sherrod Brown in his Senate run.[100] It is hard to see why asking union leaders to explain how much they are paid and how they spent union dollars is burdensome.

A major problem for organized labor and millions of Americans is the failure of union pension funds over the years. The pension funds have been poorly funded, leaving workers holding the bag. Brown places the pensions' failing on Wall Street. "Wall Street turned around and stole the pensions Ohioans worked for," he said.[101]

But the causes are not so simple. Some of the blame lies with union leaders themselves.

One of Brown's closest alliances is with the Teamsters, which is headed by Jimmy Hoffa Jr., son of the mob-tied former Teamsters' leader. His father mysteriously disappeared under suspicious circumstances in 1975.[102] The Teamsters' pension fund, the Central States Pension Plan, is in deep financial trouble today thanks in part to poor management and corruption involving union leaders. The Central States fund was only 38 percent funded as of December 2018. The fund started in 1955 and has been linked to the mob over several decades. In 1963, the elder Hoffa and six other union officials were indicted in federal court for diverting $25 million in pension fund loans and then siphoning off $1.7 million of that for their personal use. They were convicted and went to jail. But the travails continued. In 1967, Hoffa and others were implicated in a real estate scandal whereby they received 10 percent kickbacks on "highly questionable" loans. In 1972, the stepson of Teamster local boss Paul "Red" Dorfman was convicted "for illegally obtaining a $55,000 kickback from a recipient of a Central States loan." In 1974, "He was indicted for fleecing the fund out of $1.4 million." An audit of the pension fund by Price Waterhouse in the 1970s found that 90 percent of the pension funds were invested in real estate. Many of these were related to organized crime investments. As a Justice Department official put it: "The thing that's absolutely frightening is that through the Central States Pension Fund, the mob, quite literally, has complete access to nearly a billion dollars in union funds."[103]

The Teamsters are not alone in having these problems with their pensions. Other pension funds in Ohio that are in trouble include the United Mine Workers of America Pension Plan, the Ironworkers Local 17 Pension Plan, the Ohio Southwest Carpenters Pension Plan, and the Bakers and Confectioners Pension Plan. All, Brown said in early 2018, "are currently on the brink of failure."[104]

In general, while nonunion private pension plans must use a government-prescribed and realistic interest rate, unions have enjoyed regulatory favoritism that allows them to use—in effect—whatever interest rate assumptions they want when running their pension plans.[105] The problem, in short, has less to do with Wall Street than it does the union leaders who manage and run the plans.

The question is, what to do about these pension problems? How best to ensure that union members who paid into these pensions have retirement funds?

Some have called for the federal government-supported Pension Benefit Guaranty Corporation (PBGC) to take over some of these pension funds. This would ensure payment to workers, essentially backed by the federal government.[106]

Senator Sherrod Brown, however, is opposed to that. He is the co-chairman of the federal bipartisan committee to "solve the pension crisis." Brown does not want union workers to have their pensions handled by the federal government; instead, he wants the federal government to loan the money to union leaders and let them manage it.[107]

He introduced a bill called the Butch Lewis Act, which would have taxpayers lend money to the union-run pension funds to cover the shortfall.[108] But those same union pension funds were poorly run in the first place, creating the crisis that exists today. Brown does not propose any additional accountability for union leaders to run the pension with a taxpayer bailout. Instead, he proposes that taxpayers provide thirty-year loans to the unions with interest-only payments for twenty-nine years. In year thirty the union would be expected to pay off the principal. Observers expect that would never happen.[109]

The distinction between Brown's alliances with union bosses as opposed to rank-and-file members is further demonstrated by his apparent lack of interest in highlighting and dealing with financial malfeasance by union officials. Although he has spoken about the importance of labor unions in American society, he has demonstrated a remarkable lack of interest when congressional hearings focus on the actions of corrupt officials who created financial hardships for his own constituents. In October 2005, Sherrod Brown was in Congress and a member of the Committee on Energy and Commerce in the House of Representatives. Labor organization members, including at least one Ohio resident, testified on how they had paid dues only to see organization officials use those dollars for exorbitant "office expenses." (They discovered the financial misconduct by using those disclosures required by the federal government that Sherrod Brown opposes.) When one disabled member needed his permanent disability payments, they found that the account had been raided to make temporary disability payments. Brown, a member of the Subcommittee on Oversight and Investigations, never asked a single question or made a single statement at the hearing. Indeed, there is no evidence that he even attended the hearing.[110]

Senator Brown has pushed other legislation favored by union bosses but opposed by rank-and-file members. Brown has vigorously advocated for "card check" unionizing. The current system allows that if 30 percent of workers sign cards saying they want a union, a secret ballot is held. If 50 percent of employees vote yes on a secret ballot, a union is formed. But card check dramatically changes those rules. Under card check, if 50 percent of employees turn in cards saying they want a union, it will automatically be organized. But here's the rub: surveys consistently show that more than 70 percent of union members want a secret ballot. Only 13 percent want a change to the law. The main reason: union intimidation. There are numerous examples of those who do not support the formation of a union being threatened with physical violence. In one instance from 2008, for example, the National Labor Relations Board (NLRB) heard testimony from an employee who received an anonymous phone call in which the caller threatened to "get even" with him if he "backstab[bed] us." Another group of employees experienced threats that corroborated that story.[111]

Sherrod Brown has, over the course of his political career, denounced the terrible influence of lobbyists on policy making in Washington, D.C. He even proposed renaming the Washington Nationals baseball team the "Washington Lobbyists."[112] But when Brown ran for reelection to the U.S. Senate in 2018, he received more campaign contributions from lobbyists than any other senator: more than $430,000.[113]

BERNIE SANDERS

The Last Chance Saloon was a gathering place in mid-1980s Burlington, Vermont, and then-mayor Bernie Sanders would visit while making his rounds. One night he showed up while an Irish band belted out "green alligators and long-necked geese"—lyrics from "The Unicorn Song."[1] Sanders ordered the bar's special, "Fat Man Bud." Bob Conlon recalls that night he was tending bar. Bernie dropped a dollar on the bar to pay for his ninety-five-cent drink. Conlon remembered that the mayor stood there "waiting four [people] deep to get his nickel change back."

The incident made an impression on Conlon, who made part of his money on tips. "I'd vote for O. J. Simpson before I'd vote for Bernie," he later said.[2]

Bernie Sanders is one of the most polarizing figures in modern American politics. Sanders fans are likely to view this event as evidence of his frugality. Critics will no doubt label his demands for a nickel (with no apparent effort to tip) as "cheap." And so it goes with so much about Bernie Sanders. People are divided about his message: fans consider him a truth-teller about capitalism and income inequality; critics see him as a grandstander and a hypocrite. His brusque and blunt style means he is being candid and honest in the eyes of his supporters; detractors see his holier-than-thou attitude as a turnoff. Even some friends and acquaintances joke that his hectoring and sermonizing can be a bit much. Professor Garrison Nelson, who taught for decades at the University of Vermont and has known of Sanders almost as long, warns that "Bernie's the last person you'd want to be stuck on a desert island with. Two weeks of lectures about health care, and you'd look for a shark and dive in."[3]

Beyond his difficult and gruff style, there is little doubt that Sanders has become a major force in American politics. He has well-honed progressive credentials. As Professor Michael Kazin describes him, "Sanders resembles his hero, Eugene V. Debs—the Socialist who ran five quixotic races for president, the last time, in 1920, from a prison cell—far more than he does a standard-issue career politician. Other pols identify with 'revolution' and claim their campaign is a 'movement.' But Bernie really means it." Sanders deeply identifies with Debs and even has a plaque of him on his Senate office wall.[4]

Many of the policy prescriptions that Sanders has called for over the past several decades have become main planks of the Democratic Party. Although he steadfastly insists that he is an independent, there is little doubt that they have moved closer to him than he has to the main tenets of the party. The dominance of progressives within the ranks of the Democratic Party is a testament to the power of Bernie Sanders and his brand. His approach to politics has been remarkably consistent in one respect: the need for an enemy. According to Dennis Morrisseau, a "lifelong Vermonter" who has followed Sanders's career for decades, he "always had a common enemy in each of his more than twenty political campaigns—namely, the wealthy." In the 1970s, he railed against the Rockefeller family; today it is the billionaire class. Morrisseau adds, "If Bernie didn't have an enemy or scapegoat, he created one."[5] In 2017, researchers at the University of

Vermont named a new spider species after Sanders: "Spintharus berniesandersi."[6] The naming is apt because Sanders has become adept at spinning a web of financial ties and relationships that remain largely hidden from the public.

There are serious financial mysteries swirling around Sanders, concerning both his own wealth and the funds that have been pouring into his political movement. They raise fundamental questions that have yet to be aired, questions that Sanders and his wife, Jane, have worked to avoid addressing. Beyond the mysterious flow of funds, there is also the reality of his close, mutually beneficial financial ties to powerful financial figures—those that belie his image as David taking on Goliath. As we will see, Sanders has worked hard to obscure his financial arrangements.

Sanders is a son of Brooklyn, New York, born to Jewish parents. His father, Eli, was from Poland and immigrated to the United States in 1921. Mother Dorothy Glassberg was a native New Yorker, whose parents arrived off the boat earlier from Poland and Russia.[7] Among the extended Sanders family, he had relatives killed in the Holocaust. Sanders spent his early childhood in a three-and-a-half-room apartment. He was a "pretty good student" and attended the University of Chicago, where he became politically active. He was involved in the civil rights movement of the 1960s and more left-wing politics like the Young People's Socialist League.[8]

After college, Sanders drifted around before heading to Israel to work on a kibbutz in 1963. The kibbutz movement was wide and varied, and for years, Sanders refused to reveal the exact kibbutz to which he was connected. During the 2016 presidential campaign, intrepid journalists discovered that he spent his time at a settlement connected to an Israeli political party called Mapam. This was a particularly political settlement, Kibbutz

Sha'ar Ha'amakim, connected to a "Soviet-affiliated political faction." Kibbutz members admired Joseph Stalin until his death, calling him "Sun of the Nations." They would celebrate May Day with red flags.[9]

Sanders spent several months there in 1963, where he wore a uniform of khaki slacks with a matching button-down shirt. He would wake up every morning at 4:10 a.m. to pick fruit. The kibbutz had strict rules: members were not allowed to wear skirts or neckties, and social activities like playing cards and ballroom dancing were forbidden.[10]

The kid from Brooklyn, via Chicago and the Israeli desert, eventually found his way to rural Vermont. By his own account, how he ended up in the Green Mountain State was surprisingly happenstance.

As a teenager, he was walking through midtown Manhattan when he had an encounter that would change his life. "We stopped near the Radio City Music Hall and at that point the state of Vermont had a storefront there, advertising Vermont land," he recalled. "We picked up the brochures. We read them and we saw farms were for sale." More than ten years later, he pooled together some inheritance money with his brother and his first wife to buy eighty-five acres in the north woods of Vermont for $2,500.[11]

"I had always been captivated by rural life," he would later say.[12]

Sanders settled in the small town of Stannard, a hippie enclave with a population hovering around 150 people just forty-five minutes from the Canadian border.[13]

Sanders and his wife moved to Vermont, but he spent very little of his time in the decade and a half following college with gainful employment. He worked briefly as a researcher with the Vermont Tax Department, before trying his hand as a carpenter. (One acquaintance admitted, "He was a shitty carpenter.")

Mostly he was a political activist and agitator, who occasionally wrote essays, one displaying his "affinity for Sigmund Freud." [14]

Throughout the 1970s, Sanders continued to avoid consistent employment and was endlessly running for political office. (He derided basic working-class jobs as "moron work, monotonous work.") He ran two campaigns for the U.S. Senate as part of a minor political party called Liberty Union. The campaigns were bare-bones and during his 1974 campaign for the U.S. Senate, he actually collected unemployment while a candidate. His campaign rhetoric could be downright apocalyptic and conspiratorial. "I have the very frightened feeling that if fundamental and radical change does not come about in the very near future that our nation, and, in fact, our entire civilization could soon be entering an economic dark age," he thundered as he announced his 1974 Senate run. Later that same year, he sent a public letter to President Gerald Ford, declaring that America would face a " 'virtual Rockefeller family dictatorship over the nation' if Nelson Rockefeller was named vice president." [15]

Rockefeller did become vice president. The dictatorship, of course, never emerged.

During this period, while he was laying out his policies for reorganizing the entire American economy, Sanders quite literally had trouble keeping the lights on in his sparse apartment. "He was living in the back of an old brick building," recalled Nancy Barnett, an artist who lived next door. "And when he couldn't pay the [electric bill], he would take extension cords and run down to the basement and plug them into the landlord's outlet." Eventually, the landlord kicked him out of the apartment. He moved in with a friend.[16]

In 1980, at age thirty-nine, Sanders made a decision to run yet again for political office. This time he set his sights lower than the U.S. Senate. He wanted to be mayor of Burlington, Vermont, a picturesque and bucolic town on the shores of beautiful Lake Champlain, and the largest town in the state. It was his newly adopted home and he entered the crowded field as a socialist, leveling many of his attacks at a local developer named Tony Pomerleau. On Election Day, Sanders upset the political establishment by winning the race by ten votes out of 8,650 votes cast.[17]

"The whole Bernie Sanders phenomenon all comes down to ten votes," says Sam Hemingway, a columnist for the *Burlington Free Press* who covered Sanders for decades. "If he had failed to win that race, he would have been history."[18]

The win rocked local politics. A self-professed socialist had beaten back both Republicans and Democrats. As one local politician described Sanders, "He's the puppy that caught the car."[19]

But Sanders would prove to be no puppy.

Ten days after election night, Sanders held an official victory party at which he would forge perhaps his most important personal and political alliance. He was divorced from his first wife, and among the young activists who showed up at the party that night was a campaign worker and young mother named Jane Driscoll. They would soon start dating.

Jane would go on to be Sanders's consigliere. They would eventually marry in 1988.[20]

"She's one of his most trusted advisers, if not the most trusted adviser," says Sanders political consultant Tad Devine.[21] "They are a team; they always were a team," said Carina Driscoll, her daughter. "They have been a really amazing example of a partnership based on building something extraordinary together."[22]

From the outset, having finally achieved political office, Sanders established a pattern of benefiting himself and his allies. Shortly after taking office, he appointed his new girlfriend, Jane, to head up the Mayor's Youth Office. (The office organized "youth dance troupes," among other things.) It was initially a volunteer position that later became salaried. The job was never advertised so that others could apply. A local paper noted that Sanders never bothered to provide evidence as to her "qualifications" for the position. Conveniently, the Mayor's Youth Office was under his chain of command. It was not under the jurisdiction of the Parks and Rec Department.[23]

The appointment would remain a source of controversy for Sanders. After Bernie and Jane got married, his new wife received a big pay increase. As one local newspaper reported, "Political sparks flew at Burlington's annual city meeting Monday night as Democratic aldermen raised a series of questions concerning a hefty pay raise for Mayor Bernie Sanders' new wife and whether she should continue to hold her job as director of the Mayor's Youth Office."[24]

Sanders also created a powerful Community and Economic Development Office (CEDO) within the city government. In keeping with his practice, he put his friend Peter Clavelle in charge.[25] Sanders was not opposed to development; he just wanted to control it. CEDO would essentially pick business winners and losers in Burlington. As Greg Guma, a progressive journalist in the city, noted, "The administration's approach was essentially to stimulate certain types of business development while letting others fend for themselves."[26]

Despite his socialist rhetoric, to those with Bernie connections, he proved to be a man with whom you could do business. As the former director of the Burlington Square Mall, Nick Wylie, said at the time: "He has figured out that it's a cow to be milked. He wants to build his tax base. What he does as opposed to what he says are two entirely different things."[27]

Fellow progressives who had helped elect Sanders mayor were surprised at how he was consolidating power. He even put local charities on notice that he was in charge. Jon Svitavsky, who ran a local homeless shelter, said the new mayor rejected the charity's well-established shelter rules. The homeless shelter, for example, had a policy of refusing entry to anyone who was drunk or high on drugs. Sanders did not like that rule, so he had the city set up its own competing shelter.[28]

Sanders went further still. In search of tax dollars, he sent Burlington's nonprofit hospital, the Medical Center Hospital of Vermont (MCHV), a $2.8 million property tax bill. Never mind that as a nonprofit charity, it was exempt from paying property taxes. Sanders was challenging the hospital's tax-exempt status. Mayor Sanders wanted some of the charity's money for tax revenue. The charity had to take the mayor to court. The court sided with the charity.[29]

Sanders made clear that in general, he was not a big fan of charities. As mayor, he went to the local United Way and delivered the infamous "I Don't Believe in Charity" speech, which left the audience "in stunned silence." Perhaps that explains why Sanders has given sparingly to charities over the years, even when he has enjoyed a high income.[30]

But perhaps the most surprising move Sanders made as mayor was on real estate development. Bernie had run an explicit campaign as a socialist fighting against the rich. He had campaigned on real reform in Burlington. "Burlington is not for sale," he said.[31] He had directed much of his ire at Pomerleau, who owned shopping centers across Vermont. The white-haired French Canadian had planned to develop Burlington's industrial waterfront into a condominium and shopping area. During his 1981 campaign, Sanders attacked Pomerleau for wanting to create a waterfront for the wealthy with his development plans, and denounced the waterfront project as an "enclave for the rich."[32]

While he had demonized the Pomerleau family during his 1981 election as heartless greedy developers, Sanders soon struck an alliance with the wealthy family formerly in his gun sights—an alliance that would last decades. Sanders tamped down his rhetoric and started collaborating on various projects; at the same time, the wealthy family funded Sanders family projects, including those involving his wife. The Pomerleaus supported Jane's projects at the Youth Office by helping "generate business support and money."[33] Later, Pomerleau would make Jane's $10 million Burlington College venture possible.

As local progressive journalist Greg Guma recalls, fighting real estate development was largely why Sanders had been elected. A coalition of progressives in the city believed that Burlington was changing through "gentrification." As he writes, "Low-income people were being driven out of town, they protested, by condominium and office conversions and by high rents. They were being replaced by upwardly mobile, young professionals with disposable income."[34]

As mayor, Sanders suddenly embraced a new development plan for the waterfront that was just as exclusive as the one he had earlier opposed. Indeed, the new project, called Alden, "would dwarf the $30 million Pomerleau project." Outside investors who were pushing for Alden included an heir to the Dow Jones fortune. When supporters discovered that Mayor Sanders was holding "secret meetings" with these developers, they erupted. He had railed against the political establishment for doing just this sort of thing.[35]

To make the project appear different to the public, some of the language was changed. "The condominiums were called 'neighborhood housing' in their campaign literature, the hotel became a 'Lakeside Inn.' " Former Sanders allies were outraged over the new plan. When Citizens Waterfront Group pushed for transparency and an end to the secret meetings between Sanders and the developers, Sanders "blasted the group." Other progressives from the green movement accused him of "collusion with business interests." [36]

The Sanders-backed Alden plan was not so different from the one he had campaigned against in the 1981 mayoral election. As author Steven Soifer puts it, "Sanders's original campaign theme, that the waterfront should not become 'a rich man's paradise and an enclave for the wealthy,' was violated as much by the Alden project as it was by the Pomerleau one." [37]

In the end, Sanders pushed for a city referendum to approve municipal bonds to make the project happen, but voters rejected it. [38]

Despite the defeat over the municipal bond referendum, Sanders remained generally popular as mayor. A major component of his political success was the booming Burlington economy—fueled by the "profligate military spending that occurred during the Reagan Administration." [39] (Never mind that Sanders supporters applauded that he would "challenge Reaganism and imperialism in its every manifestation.") [40] General Electric, one of the nation's largest defense contractors at the time, had a plant in Burlington employing three thousand workers. [41] By 1986, the armaments plant had nearly doubled its defense contracts. The *Burlington Free Press* blared a headline: "Pentagon Spent Big in Green Mountains." [42]

The Burlington plant produced Vulcan Gatling guns, a rotating rapid-fire gun that was mounted on attack helicopters and fighter jets. The guns were also exported overseas.[43]

Many of Bernie's progressive allies were, of course, opposed to what the plant produced and represented, and showed up at the plant gates with banners and signs. Sanders has been outspoken throughout his political career about the military-industrial complex. So much so that protesters were shocked when Sanders appeared to side with General Electric executives and denounced the protest.[44] More shocking still, he had protesters arrested.[45] His actions would represent the beginning of an emerging pattern for Sanders. A harsh critic of the wealthy and powerful corporations, he would happily join forces with them if it served his own political interests. It was that way with the developers and it would be that way with military contractors, especially when he joined the U.S. Senate.

Being mayor of Vermont's largest city was perhaps the first steady job Sanders had ever held. "It's so strange, just having money, things like that," he said. Being mayor and creating a city post for his girlfriend, and then later his wife, meant a good income. They would supplement these salaries through tens of thousands of dollars in teaching and speaking fees. In 1989, the Sanderses actually sold two houses and claimed capital gains. Their primary Vermont residence included upscale amenities, which as one observer noted, "incongruously [made] Bernie perhaps one of the few socialists in the country with a built-in swimming pool."[46]

But for Sanders, being mayor of Burlington was a stepping-stone. He spent his tenure at city hall perpetually running for office. He ran for governor in 1986, Congress in 1988, and Congress again in 1990. He had come a long way from his insurgent campaigns in the 1970s, when he had run for the U.S. Senate as a member of the Liberty Union Party. For his successful 1990 bid, he raised more than half a million dollars, including large checks from developers, investment managers in Manhattan, and trust fund families.[47]

Reporters who covered Sanders on the campaign trail saw how he threw out varied ideas depending on his audience. Daniel Bellow, who worked as a reporter for several Vermont papers and covered Sanders, noticed that "Bernie would say one thing in Brattleboro and another in White River Junction."[48]

His broader campaign themes remained remarkably consistent: attacks on the rich and a call for greater socialism to deal with income inequality. When it came to that campaign, he found ways to save money even at the expense of his own staff—despite his extensive campaign resources. Sanders's campaign staffers were classified as consultants rather than employees to avoid paying Social Security taxes and workers' compensation taxes. A Vermont state audit in August 1990 found that seven of his campaign workers were inaccurately classified as "consultants" so the Sanders campaign could avoid having to pay the employee portion of their taxes. Sanders's campaign opponent charged hypocrisy, declaring, "That kind of selfish behavior has no place in Vermont, especially when Sanders touts himself as the champion of the working class." Sanders paid the back taxes and won in November.[49] The controversy did not seem to matter to many voters.

Once elected, Sanders moved to Washington and his wife, Jane, became a top aide, serving at various times as his chief of staff, press secretary, and political analyst.[50] After a decade in Congress, Jane and family went about setting up a company that operated under three different names to provide income tied to Bernie's political career. On September 27, 2000, the family formed Sanders & Driscoll LLC, a for-profit consulting company run by Jane, her daughter Carina, and son David. The business also operated under two trade names: Leadership Strategies and Progressive Media Strategies.[51]

The fact that this entity and its aliases were formed just weeks before the 2000 election is significant. The Sanderses ran these out of their home on Killarney Drive in Burlington. These entities served as financial conduits to run cash to the Sanders family. It is impossible to know precisely how much because on Sanders's financial disclosure forms, which he is required to release as a member of Congress, they only listed "more than $1,000" as the amount of income they earned from these consulting firms. We do know that some of Bernie's campaign dollars flowed through the LLCs. While running for House reelection in the early 2000s, critics claimed that "Sanders doled out more than $150,000 to his wife and stepdaughter for campaign-related work between 2000 and 2004."[52]

The LLCs are just part of a web of murky financial threads in the Sanders family that are difficult to track. For example, on one of Bernie's financial disclosures Jane lists herself as a "self-employed Antique dealer" making simply more than $1,000, but a search of Vermont business licenses turns up no antiques business registered to Sanders in the state.[53]

Some of the campaign money flowing to the family from Bernie's campaign came as Jane served as a "media buyer" for his reelection. Media buying is a murky but potentially highly lucrative stream of income for those involved in political campaigns. Modern American political campaigns spend large sums of money on television and other forms of media. A media buyer handles the purchase of airtime and secures the contracts with media outlets. Typically, a media buyer receives a commission of about 15 percent of the cost for a media campaign.[54] So if a campaign were to spend, say, $1,000,000 on television ads, the media buyer would pocket a $150,000 commission. But here's the kicker: the media buyer commission is not actually disclosed anywhere. Filings with the Federal Election Commission (FEC) only require disclosure of the bulk amount of the media buy.[55] In this example, the FEC report will only disclose the $1,000,000 media buy. And as for the fact that Jane Sanders is the spouse of a politician, she is only required to disclose that she earns "more than $1,000" from her businesses.

What is interesting about the Sanders family foray into media buying, in particular, is that Jane Sanders has no apparent background in media buying. But she worked with two media buyers named Barbara Abar Bougie and Shelli Hutton-Hartig.[56] Those names are significant. Remember them.

We do not know exactly how much Bernie's wife and daughter made working on his campaigns. We ultimately have to rely on what his campaign says. Jeff Weaver, his chief of staff at the time and a longtime friend, says that Jane was paid "about $30,000" from 2002 to 2004 and Carina Driscoll got "about $65,000" between 2000 and 2004.[57] There is no way to verify this on Federal Election Commission (FEC) records. FEC rules when it comes to the moneymaking of campaigns are minimal. Throughout his more than twenty-five years in Congress and later the U.S. Senate, Sanders has been secretive about his personal finances and tax returns. It was not until he announced his candidacy for the White House a second time in 2019 that he released his tax returns.[58]

The Sanders family consulting business was at the headwaters of what would become a common Sanders move: use Bernie Sanders's political position and power to provide income stream opportunities for the Sanders family. Later, as he set up his nonprofit organizations funded by his political supporters, he would again pay members of his family.

———

In 2004, tiny Burlington College announced that it had a new college president. Jane Sanders would be taking the helm of the private college with less than two hundred students. Professor Steward LaCasce founded the school in 1972. It was an unconventional place, to say the least: no classrooms or grades, the faculty was heavily adjunct, and students designed their own curriculum.

"You've got to remember: It was the 1970s," LaCasce later said.[59]

Burlington College positioned itself as a unique school where students who might not succeed elsewhere could prosper academically. The school, however, had problems. Shortly before Jane took over as president, the college was implicated in a scandal involving phony diplomas. For suspicion of fraud, forgery, and other crimes, police arrested five executives of a consulting company that ran schools in Israel that included an extension of Burlington College in the diploma fraud. The head of a teachers' union actually resigned over accusations that he was "soliciting teachers to purchase degrees from local branches of Burlington College" and another school.[60]

The fact that Jane was the wife of a U.S. congressman was an important factor in the school's decision to hire her. Robin Lloyd, a member of the college's board, says she and others supported Jane's appointment partly because "[w]e felt that her connection with Bernie would be helpful, certainly in terms of fundraising."[61]

Jane went about trying to develop international ties. In 2007, Jane traveled to Cuba and the college started a program to bring students to the communist country to attend classes at the University of Havana.[62] Burlington College officials visiting Cuba enjoyed access to the highest levels of the Cuban government. During one visit to the island, college officials met with Cuban Senate president Ricardo Alarcón, the third most powerful official in the country. "That's kind of exciting," recalled Jane, "because we've been able to make the kind of connections that are unusual."[63] Of course any faculty members of the University of Havana would be required to be in good standing with the Cuban government in order to teach there.

Because Cuba was under U.S. sanctions, the college had trouble getting the Treasury Department in Washington to sign off on the exchange program. Then someone made a phone call. They achieved a breakthrough when "Sanders—wife of U.S. Senator Bernard Sanders—simply called the Treasury Department herself."[64]

The Sanderses had long-standing ties in Cuba. In 1989, Bernie and Jane visited Havana and met with a leader of the city's "social brigades" and the mayor. (They attempted a meeting with Cuban dictator Fidel Castro, but the bearded one did not make himself available.[65]) Burlington College's relationship with Cuba included workshops for teachers, including one attended by Armando Vilaseca, the Cuban-born Vermont secretary of education.[66]

With no sense of irony, Burlington College touted the study abroad program as a "singular opportunity to question, debate, and discuss" numerous issues. This, including "politics," even though the university was located smack in the middle of a country that allows no free press.[67] There was no mention of the suppression of free speech, the arresting of political dissidents, or the imprisonment of human rights activists. Instead, Jane touted the program as something that would be beneficial to humanity.

"We encourage students to become actively engaged in fostering a just, humane society and sustainable communities."[68] This was not, of course, an exchange program. Burlington College students went to Havana. No Cuban students spent time in Burlington.

Unfortunately, Jane steered Burlington College resources in the same direction as Bernie did his campaign money: it went to the family. Burlington College was not cheap; tuition was over $23,000 a year in 2014–15.[69] In addition, the college received millions in federal money over the years and students could apply for federal government–supported student loans.[70] That flow of money provided funds that could be directed into family enterprises. Beginning in 2009, the nonprofit Burlington College agreed to a deal with the for-profit Vermont Woodworking School to set up a carpentry program. The school was not accredited and happened to be owned by Jane's daughter, Carina.[71] Burlington College had never had a woodworking program before, and apparently never sent out a public notice asking for proposals from people who might want to set one up through the college.[72]

Like Bernie hiring Jane to a city job while he was mayor, those outside the family were never invited to apply.

Carina had launched her Vermont Woodworking School less than two years earlier. That first year, the college gave her daughter's school $56,474 for "materials charges and lease of bench space." By 2010, the cash flowing from the college to the family business was more than $133,000. Payments ballooned to $182,741 in rental costs alone by 2012. In total, Burlington College would funnel more than $500,000 to Carina's woodworking school.[73]

The transactions stick out because Burlington College at the time was struggling to pay its own faculty and bills.[74]

Carina's school also received at least one federal grant from the U.S. Department of Agriculture (USDA) to install biomass heating.[75] At the time, Senator Bernie Sanders sat on the powerful Senate Budget Committee, with financial oversight of the USDA budget.[76] Other insiders who benefited from Burlington College money included the Leopold family. Bernie Sanders described longtime friend Jonathan Leopold as part of his "family."[77] Leopold's son had purchased a small resort in the Bahamas called Andros Beach Club. The college contracted with the club to host students during spring break at the suggestion of Jane Sanders. Burlington College paid the club close to $70,000 between 2009 and 2011.[78]

Despite Burlington College's high tuition and small student population, the college's graduation rate was abysmal. Students who enrolled in the college in 2007, for example, had a graduation rate of 22 percent—six years later. A higher percentage, 30 percent, actually transferred out of the college.[79]

There were other problems as well. Complaints mounted from faculty and students that Jane's leadership style was creating a campus with a "toxic and disruptive environment." Professor Genese Grill, a popular faculty member and one of Jane's first hires, made the mistake of sending a letter to the Academic Affairs chair Bill Kelly complaining of an "atmosphere of fear and censorship."

Jane Sanders denied the charge and then chose not to "reappoint" Grill.[80]

Despite the academic failings of the college, its continuing financial difficulties, and the growing river of funds that were flowing to her daughter's business, Jane's salary as president continued to rise. By 2009, she was making $160,000, including benefits.[81] Her income combined with Bernie's meant that they were starting to accumulate wealth. Despite Bernie's outspoken attacks on corporate America, the Sanderses became quite comfortable investing in those same companies with their growing investment portfolio.

They held many of their investments in mutual funds under Jane's name. Although her retirement plan provided the option of investing in so-called Socially Responsible Funds, the Sanderses had little interest. In 2012, for example, they held assets in only one "socially responsible fund." Much of the rest was in mutual funds invested in large corporations.[82] In 2014, they held investments in thirty-four separate mutual funds. Only four were "social conscience" funds.[83] Burlington College, despite its avant-garde vibe, was also decidedly bourgeois when it came to its investments. According to tax filings, the college's meager investment portfolio included shares in cigarette makers Philip Morris and Altria; chemical giant DuPont; financial goliaths HSBC Holdings and Merrill Lynch; and the petrochemical equipment firm Ameron International. None of the investments listed in their tax filings hint at anything remotely anticorporate.[84]

In 2010, Jane announced ambitious plans for Burlington College. Like many small colleges, Burlington was facing serious challenges attracting students. Jane wanted to expand the campus to make it more attractive to prospective students. She wanted to buy some property along the Lake Champlain shoreline from the Roman Catholic diocese. It was a prime piece of Burlington real estate and was therefore expensive: it would cost more than $10 million. How was a small institution with less than 200 students and an annual budget of less than $4 million going to manage that? It remains a source of great controversy.[85]

The deal was complicated and tough to pull off. Jane Sanders turned to the powerful and wealthy Pomerleau family. Not only did Tony Pomerleau help negotiate the deal on her behalf, he also provided a bridge loan of $500,000 to make the deal happen. The half-million dollars from Pomerleau was key. A wire transfer was arranged outside of normal banking hours on New Year's Eve in 2010 to get the deal done. As one local reporter put it, "Pomerleau rescued the entire Burlington College land deal." [86]

With the Pomerleau family backing certain Sanders family projects, both Bernie and Jane decreed that as far as this rich family was concerned, they were different. At the annual Pomerleau Holiday Party held in Burlington, local observers found it surprising that Bernie Sanders, a "notorious critic of the One Percenters," was the "most effusive" of all the politicians present when talking about Pomerleau. Jane also explained to reporters that this rich family was in her eyes a good rich family. "It's not that people are bad because they're millionaires or billionaires," she offered. "It's the ones who are pressing to get more and more at the expense of the people. Tony is the antithesis of that. He doesn't care about getting more. He cares about giving more." [87]

"He [Pomerleau] understands relationships," Jane would say on another occasion. [88]

With Pomerleau's help, Jane patched together a financial deal that included a $6.5 million loan from a bank and a $3.6 million mortgage from the Roman Catholic diocese. Financing was secured through the Vermont Educational and Health Buildings Financing Agency (VEHBFA), a state-backed organization. Sitting on the board of VEHBFA at the time was Vermont secretary of education Armando Vilaseca, who would later sit on the board of Burlington College. [89] Recall, Vilaseca made at least one trip to Cuba as part of the college's foray into that country.

The backing of VEHBFA was important: it made the interest paid on the bonds that financed the purchase of the property exempt from federal taxes. Curiously, VEHBFA, when approving the bonds, applied a credit rating of "none" to Burlington College.[90]

To secure the loan from the bank, Jane had claimed that she had nearly $2 million in confirmed donations. These donations, though, were not what she made them out to be. One million of it was a bequest from a woman not yet dead—hardly "confirmed." Another $1 million was from a donor who would match that bequest. These gifts could not be expected anytime soon, "unless [the first donor] were assassinated," joked Yves Bradley, a later board member at the college.[91]

It quickly became apparent that the college did not have enough money coming in to pay for its loans, and it started falling behind in its loan payments. The board of directors asked Jane to leave in 2011. She received a $200,000 severance on the way out.[92] When it was all over, the college would collapse.

It was later revealed that those were not the only financial misrepresentations that Jane had put on the bank loan application. Several other donors she mentioned told a Vermont news outlet that "their pledge amount was overstated or misrepresented."[93]

Burlington College board trustee David Dunn was astonished to find himself listed as a donor who had made a commitment, even though he had never done so.[94]

When these misrepresentations came to light, the Federal Bureau of Investigation (FBI) and the Justice Department launched a fraud investigation.[95]

How Burlington College ultimately managed to get the bank loan remains a mystery.

A member of the college's board of trustees was mystified that the loan was granted. "How does a bank loan this kind of money to a school that has no money, how does that happen?" said Joel Miller.[96]

One of Jane's successors had her ideas. Carol Moore had decades of experience in higher education before she became the college's president.[97] She called the purchase an "appallingly inappropriate business deal," and believes that the loans were approved in part because Jane happened to be married to the U.S. senator. "What bank lends a small, private, unendowed college of that size and financial status an amount that so obviously outweighs its ability to repay?" she asked. She suggested that part of the answer is "a bank in the state of an influential senator—a senator, as it turned out, with bigger ambitions?"[98]

Burlington College closed its doors in 2016. Five years earlier, Jane had landed easily on her feet. She left Burlington College in deep financial trouble—with a considerable severance in hand in spite of that. While still in the two-year payout window of the $200,000, Jane listed her income from Burlington College on her husband's annual financial disclosure form as greater than $1,000, and the type as "sabbatical."[99] The FBI began looking into the loan applications that Jane Sanders had filed. Fraud is a very complex legal concept, but if you purposely misrepresent financial information to a lending institution, it could constitute financial fraud. In 2017, federal investigators began questioning college officials and others in an attempt to get to the bottom of it.[100]

———

Then, with the FBI investigation swirling, the saga of Burlington College took an unusual turn. In the summer of 2016, a mysterious burglary took place when an intruder broke into the college's North Avenue building on the night of July 24. The only reason the crime has received any attention is the terrific reporting done by Morgan True of the nonprofit VTDigger.com.

Just hours after the burglary, a suspect was arrested in Troy,

New York. A young man named Brett Seglem had backed into a fence with a stolen Burlington College van. The police found the back of the van stuffed with electronics stolen from the college's main building.[101]

Once the Burlington police began investigating the crime, they found several strange elements to the incident. Seglem, who had no known connection to the college, seemed to know what he was doing when he broke in. He entered through a back door to the building (which was apparently unlocked) and then disconnected the security cameras. One school official told the police that someone had "removed the exact cables needed to disable the video surveillance of the areas which would have been accessed in gaining entry to the building." The intruder then went to another room "to disable the remainder of the system." Three former Burlington College employees believed that Seglem had prior knowledge of the building layout.[102]

Having disabled the security cameras, he gained access to the room that stored the college's computer servers. He then poured a "large amount of water" over some of the servers, effectively destroying them. The main server and an external hard drive were among the items taken. The intruder somehow found the van keys (the employee whose office they were in wonders how) and made off with close to $50,000 worth of property.[103]

When police found Seglem in the stolen van, they seized the computers in the back. Mysteriously, crucial components were missing. The main server and an external hard drive were not in the van. Documents taken from a Burlington College safe concerning those bogus diplomas awarded by the Israeli extension of Burlington shortly before Jane took the helm of the college were also missing.[104]

"There are still lots of unanswered questions as to motive and other things," said Burlington police detective Jeffrey Beerworth almost a year after Seglem's arrest. These questions would go unanswered because, oddly, Seglem was never charged.[105]

Other materials related to Burlington College disappeared, albeit in a more conventional, if still troubling, manner. After Burlington College closed, their records were placed for safekeeping with the Vermont Agency for Education (VAE). In November 2015, Vermont attorney Brady Toensing requested college records held by the VAE. On December 16, three days before rejecting his request, state officials wrote to Burlington College asking if they should destroy the records. Eventually the records were destroyed and they were never released to the public.[106]

One of the most curious and mysterious elements of Bernie Sanders is the movement of funds and his efforts to obscure the flow of money, whether into his political operation or his own pocket.

For a U.S. senator, there is really only one legal way to supplement your income. Formerly, politicians could take speaking fees—as Sanders did when he was mayor of Burlington. In 1991, Congress halted this practice of self-enrichment, at least for members of Congress.[107] As Bernie Sanders realized, a U.S. senator can boost their income by writing books.

Sanders dismisses criticisms of his newfound wealth as an author. "I wrote a best-selling book," he told the *New York Times*. "If you write a best-selling book, you can be a millionaire, too."[108]

Sanders, however, has not just written *a* book. Indeed, while sitting in the U.S. Senate, he has been one of that body's most prolific authors, penning more books than anyone except for the late John McCain. (In contrast to Sanders, McCain donated a portion of the proceeds of his book sales to charity.)[109] Indeed, during his tenure in the U.S. Senate, Sanders has actually written more books than he has written successful and substantive pieces of legislation. According to the U.S. government's GovTrack, Sanders had passed seven pieces of legislation over the course of his entire career in Washington, spanning close to thirty years. Two of those pieces of legislation were the naming of post offices and one was to declare a "Vermont Bicentennial Day."[110]

In contrast, between 2015 and 2019 alone, Sanders released three new books: *Where We Go from Here* (2018), *Our Revolution* (2016), and *Bernie Sanders Guide to Political Revolution* (2017). In 2015, he also rereleased a previous book with a new title: *Outsider in the White House*.[111] In one instance, Bernie did not even write the book; Nation Books transcribed and published one of his long speeches on the Senate floor and appropriately titled it *The Speech*. Then his campaign committee, Sanders for Senate, paid Nation's parent publisher, Perseus Books, more than $60,000 to purchase copies.[112] The campaign then gave the books to supporters for donations. The Bernie 2016 campaign also paid Verso Books more than $440,000 for copies of his book *Outsider in the White House*.[113]

As Sanders's book sales have boomed, his book advances have ballooned. He received a $795,000 advance for his book *Our Revolution*. He earned another $63,750 for his teen book titled *Bernie Sanders Guide to Political Revolution*.[114] (*Teen Vogue* shared an "exclusive" sneak peek with its readers, calling his tome "Your Next Beach Read.")[115]

Sanders pockets profits from his book sales as the law and Senate rules allow. As a result, Bernie and Jane's annual income in 2016 and 2017 topped $1 million.[116]

Critics note that while Sanders once railed against "millionaires and billionaires" in his speeches, he has now seemed to drop references to millionaires as he has joined their ranks. He now goes after just the billionaire class.[117] Still, Sanders tries to obscure the fact that he has become wealthy because of his position as a U.S. senator writing books.

In April 2016, Senator Sanders loudly proclaimed, "I remain one of the poorer members of the United States Senate."[118] However, several months later he and his wife dropped more than half a million dollars in cash to purchase a vacation home.[119]

In addition to their investment portfolio, with stakes in America's largest corporations, the Sanderses have managed to amass a substantial real estate portfolio. In addition to the vacation home, they own a four-bedroom house in Burlington and a town house on Capitol Hill in Washington.[120] They purchased the vacation home through a private trust, called Islands Family Trust, which provides certain tax benefits. The irony of Sanders owning three homes was not lost on critics who noted that Bernie had once chided the rich, asking, "How many cars do they need?"[121]

The Sanderses' vacation home sits on picturesque North Hero Island, on Vermont's Lake Champlain, and boasts five hundred feet of lake frontage. They purchased it just months after Burlington College closed its doors forever. When the deal was disclosed, questions were immediately raised about where the money for the purchase came from. Jane Sanders tried to explain it away, saying that she sold her share in a Maine family property she held with her brothers. But real estate records from Maine reveal that property accounted for only $150,000 of the purchase price.[122]

What makes the Sanders case unusual is the effort to which the family has gone to obscure their income. When Bernie Sanders announced his run for president in 2015, the Federal Election Commission (FEC) required him to file a personal financial disclosure that is more detailed than the one he is required to file as a U.S. senator. Rather than actually file the disclosure, Sanders repeatedly filed for extensions to avoid having to release his financial information. (On the campaign trail, Sanders promised to release his tax returns, but only disclosed a summary of his 2014 filing.) When he failed to get the nomination in mid-2016, he said the filings were no longer necessary. He effectively "beat the clock," according to the Center for Public Integrity.[123]

One of Bernie Sanders's most popular themes with his supporters has been the rule that financial ties between politicians and the rich lead to favors for the wealthy at the expense of the average American.[124]

Bernie Sanders has enjoyed those ties as well, despite his best efforts to obscure them.

Bernie Sanders has been a regular fixture at a high-bar fund-raising meeting with big-dollar donors held by the Majority Trust, a project of the Democratic Senatorial Campaign Committee (DSCC). Sanders is an Independent, not a Democrat, and has no obligation to attend these events, but chooses to do so. He is a regular attendee along with his wife, Jane. For an invitation to these events, supporters have to donate the maximum allowed by law to the DSCC itself: $33,400. These Majority Trust events occur at exclusive locales such as Martha's Vineyard in the summer and Palm Beach, Florida, in the winter. Wealthy donors run the gamut and include lobbyists, lawyers, industrialists, and Wall Street executives. While Wall Street has been a particular target of Sanders's attacks over the years, one executive attending these events told CNN that when Sanders speaks at these events, "I don't recall him ever giving a speech attacking us."[125]

Bernie Sanders was an early and enthusiastic supporter of the Occupy Wall Street movement. He praised the movement for "shining a national spotlight on the most powerful, dangerous and secretive economic and political force in America."[126]

The ecosystem of political finances means that money is fungible. So Sanders can raise money from Wall Street for a Democratic Party committee (a party to which he professes to not actually belong) and then the Democratic National Committee (DNC) can funnel that money back into his campaign. The origin of the funds—Wall Street, large financiers—does not have to be disclosed. In short, Sanders can declare that he does not receive donations from wealthy investors while he actually benefits from them. In 2006, when he first ran for the Senate, the party spent $60,000 on ads for his campaign, another $100,000 to the Vermont Democratic Party, and the DSCC gave $37,300 directly into his campaign. For his part, Sanders has his PAC send his donor dues to the DSCC so he can attend these events.[127]

Unlike the money that flows courtesy of the Majority Trust, some of those financial ties with rich donors are traceable. And those ties present a familiar if troubling picture: wealthy donors back a candidate who in return pushes for subsidies and taxpayer grants that enrich the already wealthy donor.

David Blittersdorf is the founder of NRG Systems, a large power company in the United States. Blittersdorf lives in Vermont and is now the head of a green energy business called AllEarth Renewables.[128] His company operates with the help of generous federal and state tax credits and subsidies.[129]

Sanders has been outspoken for years about rich investors who are beneficiaries of corporate welfare. Blittersdorf certainly appears to fit that profile, receiving generous tax credits and benefits for his company. Blittersdorf financially and politically backs Sanders; Sanders supports legislation and champions grants that make Blittersdorf even wealthier.[130]

Blittersdorf is a controversial figure in Vermont, even among renewable energy advocates, because of his aggressive tactics against residential landowners and his desire to build large, industrial-scale wind and solar projects even in the face of local opposition. Sanders has sided with Blittersdorf in these disputes.[131]

Blittersdorf was accused of bullying residents who live near his projects and misrepresenting the size of his wind farms. When he announced plans to build massive wind turbines in Irasburg, a small northern Vermont town with about 1,000 people, he reportedly put false information on the application seeking approval, claiming that there was only one home within a mile of his proposed project. In fact, there were dozens of residents in the area. In another instance, he actually sued residents for being on their own property while he was constructing massive wind turbines nearby.[132]

In addition to his wind projects, Blittersdorf has also constructed two community-scale solar farms in the Green Mountain State.[133]

These projects have all enjoyed rich subsidies from both the federal and state governments. Many renewable energy advocates in Vermont are fed up, though, complaining about how ordinary taxpayers are subsidizing wealthy investors. "The people who are putting up the projects are millionaires or corporations held by very wealthy people, and the tax dollars are paid by all of us," says Vermont state senator John Rodgers, a Democrat.[134]

Doug Tolles, a then–select board member in New Haven, Vermont, said, "Corporate welfare is all it is."[135]

Sanders has remained steadfast in support of Blittersdorf and his projects, steering money to renewable energy and supporting legislation that benefits Blittersdorf's companies. That support has made Blittersdorf even richer. In 2013, when Vermonters mounted a campaign to limit the size of massive wind projects in the state, Sanders opposed them and supported wind developers like Blittersdorf.[136] Many landowners and longtime residents be-lieved that the massive wind turbines would blight their beloved Green Mountains. In 2017, Vermont's governor sought a morato-rium on wind projects over 500 kilowatts, the very industrial-size wind projects that Blittersdorf wanted.[137] Sanders sided with the wind developers like Blittersdorf.

Over the years, Sanders has procured taxpayer money that has ended up benefiting Blittersdorf's company. In 2013, Sanders took credit for securing $3 million in taxpayer money to fund the Vermont Regional Test Center (RTC), a solar energy testing facility. The center involved three Vermont businesses, one of which was owned by Blittersdorf. In 2018, Sanders took credit for securing another $4 million for the RTC.[138] Some years earlier, when Sanders chaired Senate hearings on "green jobs," he had Blittersdorf testify.[139]

As we have learned, Sanders has consistently cosponsored or voted for tax subsidies and grants that happened to benefit Blit-tersdorf's companies. For his part, Blittersdorf was an early en-dorser of Sanders's 2016 presidential campaign.[140]

As a U.S. senator, Sanders has consistently railed against large defense corporations at rallies. But when it has come to bringing defense dollars into his state, he is all in favor of them, particu-larly for the benefit of those who are aligned with him. Much like when he was mayor, his rhetoric has been harsh toward the defense industry. On October 2, 2009, Senator Sanders stepped onto the floor of the U.S. Senate and gave one of his customary barnburner speeches. He took defense contractors to task for their "systemic, illegal, and fraudulent behavior, while receiving hun-dreds and hundreds of billions of dollars of taxpayer money." [141] During the 2016 presidential campaign, he explained, "We need a strong military, it is a dangerous world. But I think we can make judicious cuts." He also added, "There is massive fraud going on in the defense industry. Virtually every major defense contractor has either been convicted of fraud or reached a settlement with the government." [142] During a Q&A in New Hampshire in 2014, he said, "In very clever ways, the military-industrial complex puts plants all over the country, so that if people try to cut back on our weapons system what they're saying is you're going to be losing jobs in that area. We've got to have the courage to understand that we cannot afford a lot of wasteful, unnecessary weapons systems, and I hope we can do that." [143]

Just as when he was mayor, Sanders sees the political benefits he accrues when supporting military projects in his own state.

By far the biggest project for Lockheed is the F–35 Joint Strike Fighter, which is the largest budget project in the history of military aviation. The total budget is reportedly $1.5 trillion. [144]

The project has been plagued with cost overruns and some important technological issues. These are the sorts of problems you would expect Bernie to rail against. And while he has declared that it is an example of the Pentagon's "long record of purchasing weapons systems from defense contractors with massive cost overruns that have wasted hundreds of billions of taxpayer dollars," he has lined up for Vermont's piece of the pie. [145] Sanders pushed for and endorsed the idea of deploying eighteen of the fighters to Burlington, Vermont. The fighters are to be deployed at the Burlington International Airport and flown by the Vermont Air National Guard. Despite fierce local opposition to the deployment by locals over environmental and noise concerns, Sanders has been steadfast in supporting the deployment because of the money it brings to Vermont. "My view is that given the reality of the damn plane, I'd rather it come to Vermont than to South Carolina," he said at a town hall meeting in 2014. "And that's what the Vermont National Guard wants, and that means hundreds of jobs in my city. That's it."[146]

Sanders's ties to Lockheed go deeper than the F-35. About a month after he lambasted defense contractors on the Senate floor, Sanders was hosting a delegation of a subsidiary of Lockheed Martin, a major defense contractor. (He had mentioned Lockheed in that Senate floor speech decrying military contractor corruption.) The delegation from Sandia National Laboratories was in Vermont at Sanders's invitation to talk about coming to the state to set up a satellite lab. The Department of Energy funds Sandia, which is managed by Sandia Inc., a Lockheed subsidiary. Sanders was supportive of creating a research facility in Vermont, but made efforts to distance Sandia from Lockheed Martin. One can only guess why. Interestingly, one of the delegation members who participated in those talks was Dave Blittersdorf, Sanders's ally.[147]

Sanders has made the flow of campaign dollars to political candidates a major part of his critique of modern American politics. Such issues have often been obscured and blurred, however, when it comes to his own campaigns.

During the 2016 Sanders campaign, we saw more evidence of blurred financial lines. Presidential candidates are required to file campaign donation disclosures and there are restrictions on how much an individual can contribute to a campaign. Sanders's campaign seemed to ignore those rules. The Sanders campaign received excess donations from more than 1,500 donors— "unprecedented" in American politics.[148]

Under federal law, individuals can make $2,700 in total donations per election. (That means in the 2016 presidential election, the most you could give was $2,700 for the primary and $2,700 for the general election to the same candidate.) The Federal Election Commission (FEC) threatened to audit the Sanders campaign. (Recall that Sanders's previous run for Congress had been the subject of audits by election officials as well.) The FEC argued, "The illegal contributions should have been easy to identify."[149] And of course, the Sanders campaign was staffed by experienced professionals who certainly knew how to run campaigns. In the best light, the Sanders campaign was sloppy. "At the point they realized this person maxed out, they should have stopped accepting any contributions from them," explains Larry Noble, the former general counsel for the FEC. "So at the very least, it's sloppiness. But you question whether they had any safeguards to make sure people weren't making excessive contributions."[150]

The Sanders campaign touted that its coffers were filled with small-dollar donations and the data seemed to confirm that 62 percent of Sanders's donations were small—less than $200.[151] But there is more to those numbers than meets the eye. Many wealthy donors chose to give numerous small donations rather than a single large one, creating the impression of an army of smaller donors. Houston lawyer and apparent Sanders fan James Bartlett gave fifty donations to the Sanders campaign on November 28, 2015, in increments from $5 to $414, creating the same impression. Katherine Klass of Wisconsin made thirty-eight separate donations. Even larger donors, like Ahmed Abdelmeguid, made multiple contributions—in his case totaling more than $12,000 over the course of a few months.[152]

The FEC also found other problems. They investigated and discovered that the Australian Labor Party sent a delegation of volunteers to help the Sanders campaign. This was also a clear violation of election rules because the Labor Party had paid for their flights. Beyond the reach of the FEC, Australians in Sydney held "phone banking parties" and called tens of thousands of Americans encouraging them to vote for Sanders. As one Australian paper reported it, "the group would use Google Hangouts to call Americans with an automated dialing service to gain support for the Vermont senator." [153]

Bernie Sanders's insurgent 2016 campaign brought in a huge sum of money. A large chunk of it—at least $83 million—flowed to a mysterious limited liability company with no website, no phone number, and no office space. Indeed, the LLC was registered to a private home on a cul-de-sac in suburban Virginia. [154]

The mysterious company is called Old Towne Media LLC. Two known political operatives who are connected to the shell company are Barbara Abar Bougie and Shelli Hutton-Hartig. These two political consultants have a history with Sanders; they did media buys for Bernie's 2006 Senate election. Back during the 2006 election, Sanders's political opponent had accused Jane of profiting from the arrangement. [155]

The Sanders campaign purchased a whopping $83 million in political ads through Old Towne Media, which could have earned the company a media fee of more than $12 million, based on the industry standard for ad buy commissions. Was Jane Sanders somehow involved in this financial arrangement? FEC disclosures make it easy to hide where media buying fees actually go. And Jane listed her income from her professional work at the time as simply "more than $1,000." [156]

When a highly respected Vermont reporter named Jasper Craven, working for the nonprofit VTDigger.com, asked Jane about Old Towne Media during a phone interview, she "hung up the phone." [157] The Sanderses have steadfastly refused to answer questions about the mysterious company and the tens of millions of dollars that flowed to it.[158]

From the ashes of his 2016 presidential campaign emerged the Sanders Institute, a nonprofit 501(c)(3) charity designed to advance Bernie's ideas.[159]

Bernie Sanders has a curious history with nonprofit charities and failing to file the necessary documents with the Internal Revenue Service (IRS). The first of these was the American People's Historical Society in 1977, which he launched before his first election as mayor. This nonprofit did not last long; the nonprofit status was eventually revoked.[160] It was the beginning of a trend that held for most of the Bernie nonprofits.

Sanders also was listed as one of the directors of the Vermont Patent and Trademark Depository Library in 1996. Unusually, this nonprofit managed to file a second time with Vermont in 2000, but still never filed the necessary documents.[161]

In keeping with the family's history when it comes to such things, Bernie's stepson David Driscoll emerged as executive director of the Sanders Institute, with an estimated salary of $100,000.[162] Jane Sanders insists that this is not nepotism. "Dave founded the institute. He's raised the money to keep it going. When you found something, how can it be nepotism?"[163]

It is unclear who actually runs the Sanders Institute, as corporate filings are wildly inconsistent. In corporate filings in Vermont, the directors of the Sanders Institute include his wife, Jane, David Driscoll, and close friend Huck Gutman. However, filings with the IRS during the same year tell a very different story. Here the board of directors includes chairman James Zogby and board members Meredith Burak and Sara Burchard.[164]

Zogby was an interesting choice to serve as the chairman of the organization. Zogby, a longtime Sanders ally who advised

Bernie in the 2016 campaign, has deep ties in the Middle East. He founded the Palestine Human Rights Campaign in Washington in the 1970s, but the organization apparently caught the interest of the U.S. Justice Department for its ties to Libya's foreign agent in Washington.[165] He has worked for the United Arab Emirates state-owned television network, and his research firm is Zogby Research Services. He counts among his largest clients the UAE's ministries of Labor, Federal National Council Affairs, and Foreign Affairs.[166]

Zogby is linked with foreign governments throughout the Middle East. As Obama transportation secretary Raymond LaHood explains, "[Zogby] knows all the Arab leaders, whether it's [Yasser] Arafat or the king of Jordan or the president of Egypt or the prime minister of Lebanon." But those close ties to Arab governments make him a controversial figure in Arab American circles. "Zogby is a TV host and columnist with several state-owned Arab media outlets [as of 2011]," said journalist Hussain Abdul-Hussain. "This puts Zogby on the payroll of Arab governments. When James Zogby addresses America, he does it on behalf of Arab autocrats, which makes him a foreign lobbyist." [167]

The Sanders Institute is a sister organization to another Sanders-run organization called Our Revolution. The Sanders Institute is a 501(c)(3). Our Revolution is a 501(c)(4) organization. Our Revolution got off to a rocky start when the staff revolted over the direction of the organization. On August 24, 2016, Bernie stood up and spoke at a community arts space in Burlington to announce the founding of a new political organization called Our Revolution. The speech was livestreamed to some 300,000 supporters. "Tonight I want to introduce you to a new, independent nonprofit organization that is called Our Revolution, which is inspired by the historic Bernie 2016 presidential campaign," he told the local crowd.[168]

But behind the scenes, not all was well. In what the *New York Times* described as a "staff revolt," eight members of the new group quit over their concerns about the focus of the organization. They wanted the focus to be on grassroots organizing. Jeff Weaver, Bernie's campaign manager, who was now leading the organization, had different plans. He wanted to raise money and buy a lot of advertising. With that, of course, would come all of the media buying fees going down some black hole.[169]

"We're organizers who believed in Bernie's call for a political revolution," said Claire Sandberg, a digital organizing director for Bernie who quit, "so we weren't interested in working for an organization that's going to raise money from billionaires to spend it all on TV."[170]

No word yet on who has those lucrative contracts for media buy commissions or whether the Sanders family will somehow get a slice of it.

AMY KLOBUCHAR

They call it "Minnesota Nice." Residents of the Land of Ten Thousand Lakes have a propensity for hospitality. On the other hand, Amy Klobuchar, Minnesota's senior senator, has a reputation for being anything but nice to her subordinates. Former Senate staffers recount humiliating and intense tongue-lashings from her. Emails reveal Klobuchar blasting a staffer in ALL CAPS, and she is prone to call staffers in the middle of the night. Others recount being sent over to her house to do the dishes, or to pick up her dry cleaning. Klobuchar reportedly threw a binder at another staffer.[1] One aide for then-senator Al Franken, also from Minnesota, recalls a Klobuchar staffer showing up to explain why her boss was late for a meeting. "I'm supposed to tell you," she reportedly explained with "terror on her face," that "Senator Klobuchar is late today because I am bad at my job."[2] Perhaps Klobuchar's most unique rumored humiliation? Forcing one female subordinate to dry shave her legs under the desk while she was on the phone. (Klobuchar denies that one.)[3] Perhaps it is no surprise then that Klobuchar has the highest level of staff turnover in the U.S. Senate, according to a review of Senate employment records between 2001 and 2016. (Her annual turnover was an astonishing 36 percent.) That makes her, according to Politico, one of the "worst bosses" on Capitol Hill.[4]

This is not something new. There have been complaints about

her conduct in the past. In 2006, when Klobuchar was running for the U.S. Senate, she faced opposition from lawyers working for her in the Hennepin County Attorney's Office, even though they might share her politics. Jim Appleby, an assistant Hennepin County attorney, who was also the head of the local chapter of American Federation of State, County and Municipal Employees (AFSCME), wrote a letter to the national union about her abusive behavior. Appleby accused her of denigrating office lawyers publicly and privately, taking credit for their work, damaging morale, and creating a hostile work environment. According to Appleby, her hiring practices meant "qualified personnel from her own and other public offices have been rejected because her priority has been to choose candidates who support her ambitions." He asked AFSCME headquarters not to endorse her candidacy because of the abuse. (They did so anyway.)[5] Klobuchar said that Appleby's complaints were just sour grapes over labor negotiations.[6] But they appear remarkably consistent with what her Senate staffers would later report.

Other Klobuchar staffers have defended her on these matters, explaining that she holds "the highest standards for her staff."[7] But perhaps the most remarkable feature of Klobuchar's career is not just her penchant for "punching down" at subordinates, but her willingness as a prosecutor, county attorney, or U.S. senator to go soft on powerful figures and interests that would benefit her political career. Those self-professed "highest standards" do not seem to apply to those who might be breaking the law or seeking special treatment. Indeed, Klobuchar has quietly built a legislative record that leads to the distribution of economic benefits to favored, politically connected businesses.

Klobuchar descends from Minnesota royalty. Her father, Jim, was a legendary sports reporter for the *Minneapolis Star Tribune*, the largest paper in the state.[8] He covered the beloved Minnesota Vikings of the National Football League but also wrote on other issues, including personal matters involving his family. At times, he would reference Amy in his columns; he would write candidly about his drinking problems and his divorce. He enjoyed a large following in the Land of Ten Thousand Lakes.[9]

From early adulthood, Amy fused herself with another branch of Minnesota power players, namely Walter Mondale. The U.S. senator and then vice president of the United States under Jimmy Carter is, other than perhaps Hubert Humphrey, Minnesota's most famous political son. Klobuchar first worked as an intern for his office in 1980 while he was vice president and volunteered for the campaign, canvassing locally for the Carter-Mondale ticket. (He ran against Reagan for the presidency in 1984 and lost.) Klobuchar graduated from Yale in 1982 and from law school at the University of Chicago in 1985.[10]

After law school, Amy joined the law firm of Dorsey & Whitney in Minneapolis, where she worked on utility law and represented large telecom companies like MCI, which were challenging incumbent monopolies.[11] She began immersing herself in local Minnesota Democrat-Farmer-Labor (DFL) Party politics and joined a club of young political types called Wednesday Night Democrats. Even at this age, she was calculating a political run for office. "She was always thinking of where to live, based on what office she could run for," recalled friend Amy Scherber.[12]

In 1987, she was reunited with Mondale when he joined Dorsey & Whitney. Klobuchar spent the next few years working part time with the former vice president on "business development, speeches, and other civic activities." The bond was tight, and she entered the orbit of the extended Mondale network, which we will see included the vice president's sons and their business ventures. How much of a role did Mondale play in Klobuchar's career? One hint might be that she mentions the former vice president no fewer than forty-eight times in her 2015 autobiography.[13]

The reunion with Mondale brought Klobuchar deep within the financial elite of Minnesota politics. By 1992 she became a Mondale Fellow at the University of Minnesota's Humphrey Institute. As she recalls, the fellowship allowed her "the chance to meet all kinds of national political types."[14]

The following year she married John Bessler, a man seven years her junior.[15] The wedding ceremony and the reception that followed oozed politics. They held the reception at the University of Minnesota's Humphrey Institute. "Guests wandered through the permanent exhibit chronicling the life of one of Minnesota's most beloved Democratic leaders," recalled the *Star Tribune*.[16]

Klobuchar clearly had the political bug. In the fall of 1993, she made plans to run for chief prosecutor of Hennepin County, the largest and most significant prosecutorial job in Minnesota. (Hennepin County incorporates much of Minneapolis.) However, she ended up deferring to a more established candidate, the incumbent Mike Freeman, just five months before the 1994 election. By 1998 she was ready to throw her hat in the ring again. Even though her legal experience at this point revolved largely around telecom companies, she went on to win a tight victory by less than 1 percent of the vote.[17]

As chief prosecutor, she was in charge of more than 150 lawyers. Klobuchar paints a portrait of her tenure as one involving hand-to-hand combat with white-collar criminals. It is a central component of her message as a progressive. "We really pushed the envelope in one other area: white-collar crime," she wrote in her autobiography. She describes how her office was taking many white-collar criminal referrals, "from investment swindles and contractor fraud to tax evasion and identity theft rings." According to her version of events, she triumphed and operated "without fear or favor."[18]

As we will see, that depends on what sort of white-collar criminal you were, and what sort of political connections you might enjoy. Indeed, she seemed in her prosecutorial record to punch down by throwing the book at smaller fish, while avoiding prosecutions of larger and more serious criminal operators.

Klobuchar aggressively went after small actors accused of financial crimes and fraud. There was the home remodeler in Burnsville, Minnesota, who pleaded guilty to eight felony counts for swindling homeowners out of $1 million—netting 75 percent of that. Klobuchar threw the book at him; he got two years in prison.[19]

She also took on airline pilots who worked for Minneapolis-based Northwest Airlines. According to Klobuchar and her office, forty-two Northwest Airlines pilots were investigated for not paying Minnesota income taxes by claiming residence in other states even though they spent much of their time in the state. They collectively owed some $321,000 in state taxes. Klobuchar charged seven pilots with tax evasion. The pilots argued that they lived in other states and would arrive in Minneapolis for their flight assignments. Klobuchar declared the airline pilots were "white-collar crooks" in her book—further proof that she was tough on white-collar crime.[20]

But the largest financial fraud by far in her jurisdiction involved a massive conspiracy that she never even appeared to investigate. It involved the second-largest Ponzi scheme in American history to date (surpassed only by Bernie Madoff).[21] It involved billions of dollars, dummy corporations, and an elaborate scheme that ripped off investors for hundreds of millions of dollars. The man at the center of it, however, happened to be in business with the Mondales, was a Klobuchar friend, and one of her largest financial backers. Indeed, Petters Group International (PGI) would prove to be her single largest campaign donor when she ran for the Senate in 2006. Despite plenty of warning signs, she appears to have looked the other way.

Tom Petters purported to be a billionaire and a philanthropist. His firm, Petters Group Worldwide, or its subsidiaries, employed family members of Minnesota's political elite. Bill Mondale, son of the former vice president, worked for Petters as the director of international business development of Petters Consumer Brands LLC.[22] Ted Mondale, the former vice president's eldest son and a former state senator, was vice president of a Petters company from 1999 to 2003. When Ted left to launch a software company, he received a $750,000 investment from Petters. Petters also gave him a $150,000 personal loan.[23]

Later, when federal officials charged Petters for his crimes, he admitted that he used the Mondale name to solidify his company's reputation. When he was trying to drum up business in Asia, for example, he would drop Walter Mondale's name because Mondale had served as ambassador to Japan. His ties to the Mondales "opened up incredible doors."[24]

It was his relationship with Klobuchar and her office that might have been even more important because they probably delayed his legal day of reckoning. When Klobuchar ran for county attorney in 1998, Petters and his employees gave her campaign $8,500. That was just the start. When she announced for the U.S. Senate in 2006, Petters Group Worldwide and its employees were some of her earliest and most enthusiastic donors. Just weeks after she announced her candidacy in February 2005, Petters and thirteen employees in his companies all gave her contributions in a single day (March 31, 2005). By the quarterly report released right before the 2006 election, they were her largest contributor by far—donating $71,600 or 32 percent more than her second-largest donor, her old law firm.[25] By the end of 2006, Petters Group Worldwide had contributed more than $120,000 toward her successful bid.[26]

One of the reasons Petters may have been able to operate is that the Hennepin County Attorney's Office reportedly had worked to expunge his records of a previous arrest on fraud charges. While living in Colorado, Petters was accused of forgery and fraud, the alleged crime involving some $75,000 worth of VCRs that apparently did not even really exist. Petters moved to Minnesota and made a financial restitution payment to avoid a fugitive warrant, but the arrest was still on his record. Obviously, it would be more difficult to launch a financial firm with this lurking on his record. He went to the Hennepin County Attorney's Office and with the reported help of an assistant county attorney named Nancy McLean got his record wiped clean. This happened under Michael Freeman, Klobuchar's predecessor. When Klobuchar replaced him in 1998, McLean stayed on as an assistant county attorney.[27] During Klobuchar's tenure as county attorney, there appear to have been early warning signs of what Petters was doing. In January 1999, just weeks into her tenure, potential evidence of the Ponzi scheme began to cross her desk. Officers from her office raided the home of Richard Hettler and Ruth Kahn. They were Petters investors. The documents seized reportedly offered clear evidence that "Hettler, Kahn, and Petters (were) engaged in a mutually beneficial and highly illegal financial scheme." Klobuchar threw the book at Hettler and Kahn, charging them with fraud. But she did not prosecute or apparently even investigate Petters.[28]

The Hennepin County Attorney's Office would issue a statement in 2012 defending Klobuchar's inaction regarding Petters. "At no time was the Hennepin County Attorney's Office presented by any law enforcement agency a case against Tom Petters."[29]

There were plenty of other warning signs as to what Petters was doing. There were numerous lawsuits against Petters for failing to repay money he owed. There were "criminal cases for allegedly writing bad checks."[30] Some clients who had invested money with Petters wanted to borrow from a bank to invest more and one of these clients openly claimed getting "in excess of 25 percent a month" return on their investment.[31]

Petters's associates also had histories that raised questions. One of Petters's business partners was Frank Vennes, who had pleaded guilty earlier in his life to money laundering and no contest to cocaine dealing and illegally selling firearms. He was also a Klobuchar campaign donor.[32]

In January 2005, when Petters's company bought Polaroid Holding Company, an amalgam of the assets of the bankrupt camera and film company, accusations swirled that he was making the purchase with stolen cash. Richard Hettler, Petters's convicted former investor who had his records seized by Klobuchar's office back in 1999, made the charge. The records seized documented Hettler's dealings with Petters. Hettler emailed information to Polaroid's CEO, federal and state regulators, and law enforcement officials about his allegations.[33]

It was not until late September 2008 that FBI agents raided both Petters's house in Wayzata, just outside Minneapolis, and his office. Days later, the FBI recorded a conversation between Petters and Robert White, a senior executive with his company. Petters explained to White his fears about going to jail, but then noted,

"We've helped a lot of people" (with political contributions). Klobuchar, he said, now a U.S. senator, had actually called him days after the raid. (He reports that Norm Coleman, Minnesota's other U.S. senator, did not call him.)[34] Reportedly Klobuchar's aides suggested a close family friend, Doug Kelley, a Minneapolis attorney provide legal help. Kelley had been a longtime friend of Klobuchar's father, both as a lawyer to help him with legal issues and as a mountain-climbing partner.[35]

Lawyers who were handling the prosecution of Petters expressed shock at how he had been able to operate so long. Joe Dixon, one of the prosecuting attorneys, explained, "It was like everyone knew PCI [Petters's umbrella company] was a fraud machine, and everyone knew here was a closet up on the third floor that only a few people could look into and nobody wanted to open the door."[36]

Richard Hettler, one of those investors arrested back in 1999 and charged by Klobuchar, claimed that she knew Petters was involved but elected to look the other way. "She took Ponzi money to get elected," he said.[37]

Others drew attention to the fact that Petters was a huge donor to Klobuchar and seemed to get favorable treatment while she was county attorney. "I mean, I know a prosecutor has discretion— and I don't have anything against her, I didn't know her, and I don't have any dog in the fight as far as that goes," attorney Garrett Vail told the Daily Caller. "But, it looks to me like he [Petters] had friends in high places. What I'm getting at is somebody was covering for him. The only way he ran a $3 billion Ponzi scheme was [that] he had politicians in his pocket."[38]

Investigator Randy Shain, executive vice president of First Advantage Litigation Consulting, was hired by four independent hedge funds to investigate Petters in the early to mid-2000s. "I've been doing this work since 1987, and I've never seen anyone who gave off more warning signals," he said.[39] It is important to note that Klobuchar's law firm, Dorsey & Whitney, did considerable legal work for Petters at this time, including the Polaroid acquisition, and was obviously familiar with the issue.[40]

Petters was found guilty on twenty counts of money laundering and wire and mail fraud in December 2009 in U.S. district court in St. Paul, Minnesota. In the end, the scam involved some $3.7 billion. He was sentenced to fifty years in prison.[41]

Politicians from both political parties who had gladly accepted Petters's checks when they were in office now felt obligated to donate those contributions to charity or send them to the Petters estate so that victims of his fraud could get some compensation. Since Amy Klobuchar had taken more money from Petters than anyone, she was obliged to return the most.[42]

Klobuchar's considerable political skills include her remarkable ability to raise money from large corporations and corporate lawyers. Early in 2006, Klobuchar recounts how the chairman of the Democratic Senatorial Campaign Committee, Senator Chuck Schumer, got in her face with his index finger and told her: "You're going to raise one million in the first quarter."[43] Klobuchar did not need advice on raising money. Indeed, she has become one of the Senate's most prolific fund-raisers and has done so in an unusual manner. While serving in the U.S. Senate, Klobuchar has a remarkably liberal voting record. To date in the 116th Congress, she has voted with Bernie Sanders 88 percent of the time.[44] However, unlike Bernie Sanders, she has also mined corporate donations in a manner that her Vermont colleague has avoided.

During her first term, Klobuchar was generally low profile and played it safe. Supporters touted her as a pragmatist, working the middle of the road. Minnesota critics saw her as "calculating, ambitious and gauzy on issues." Walter Mondale, her mentor, regards her as a "moderate, progressive," who fits perfectly the tone of Minnesota.[45] Klobuchar defines herself as a "progressive."[46] Part of her strategy was using her legislative agenda as a means of extracting donations from powerful corporations who wanted work done on Capitol Hill.

One of those techniques included the effective use of earmarks for her campaign funders.

During the 2006 Senate run, Klobuchar pounded her opponent because of his voting for earmarks and described the taxpayer-funded dollars as wasted on "the bridges to nowhere, the rain forest in Iowa, the waterless urinals in Michigan."[47] Klobuchar pledged during the campaign to cut earmarks because she claimed they were wasteful and reeked of cronyism. But once she was in office, Klobuchar quickly went about using them to great effect for the benefit of her largest supporters. According to Open Secrets, she sponsored or cosponsored 103 earmarks totaling more than $200 million in fiscal year 2008, her first full year in the Senate. (That put her near the top third in the U.S. Senate for earmarks.) She had another eighty-eight earmarks totaling more than $133 million in fiscal year 2009. In the last year that members of Congress could officially use earmarks, she had eighty-eight earmarks in excess of $117 million (fiscal year 2010).[48]

The earmarks were generous to her largest and most important political supporters. A key earmark was $89.1 million for two light-rail projects in Minneapolis over the three-year period.[49] The rail project would provide service for commuters running in and out of the downtown as well as to the new Minnesota Twins ballpark.[50]

The major financial beneficiaries of these earmarks were mega-donors to Klobuchar. Klobuchar's old law firm and her second-largest campaign contributor of all time, Dorsey & Whitney, was neck-deep in the project. The firm drafted the requests for proposal (RFPs) for more than $1 billion of public procurement contracts for these light-rail projects.[51]

Another major beneficiary of the project was the family that owned Major League Baseball's Minnesota Twins. The Northstar commuter rail runs right to Target Field, where the Twins play.[52] The Pohlad family owns the team.[53] Carl Pohlad, the patriarch, passed away in 2009, but he was a big supporter of the Northstar project because it would help bring more fans to the ballpark. He was a controversial figure in Minneapolis because he got Hennepin County taxpayers to pay for his new baseball stadium.[54] He died a year before Target Field opened.[55] The Pohlad family was a large financial supporter of Klobuchar and the DFL party.[56] Between 2006 and 2010, the Pohlad family donated tens of thousands to Klobuchar's campaign coffers.[57]

The light rail also benefited the Pohlad family in other ways, specifically their real estate company, United Properties. The Northstar commuter rail line, which stops near gate six at the stadium, helped boost real estate development in the area. United Properties owns the Ford Center, which is located across the railroad tracks from the stadium.[58]

The ties were so deep that Chris Pohlad, the grandson of Carl, served as a special assistant to Senator Klobuchar in Washington between 2009 and 2010 while she was issuing the earmarks.[59]

Klobuchar's legislative work for the benefit of large donors extends far beyond simple earmarks. From her perch on the powerful Senate Committee on Commerce, Science, and Transportation, she sits at the crossroads of corporate interests in Washington that wanted something from the federal government. We will see how she became adept at crafting specific legislation that would benefit powerful companies who write her checks either just before she introduces the legislation, or shortly after.

In May 2011, Klobuchar stepped forward and introduced a bold bill called the Commercial Felony Streaming Act (S. 978).[60] The bill was designed to stop piracy on the internet, specifically the streaming of songs and music online. According to critics, Klobuchar's was a draconian solution. Namely, individuals who illegally streamed TV shows or movies would be committing a felony. Entertainment industry executives loved the bill for obvious reasons. But it brought her criticism from online freedom advocates. Even those in the music business like Justin Bieber thought it went too far. He suggested that she should be "locked up" for proposing the bill.[61]

In the ninety days before she introduced the bill, something unusual started happening. Over a one-week period in February, seven executives from 20th Century Fox sent her donations. Three more wrote her checks in March. Other big entertainment companies opened up their wallets, too. Warner Bros., via its PAC, gave her a $20,000 contribution, and no fewer than fifteen other executives with the company sent her thousands in donations. The Motion Picture Association of America, the film industry association, gave $2,500 in late February.[62] Comcast, the cable giant based out of Philadelphia, which also strongly backed the bill, began giving and would become one of her largest campaign contributors for reelection in 2012, donating more than $26,000.[63] In all, the entertainment industry sent her more than $80,000, a flow of cash she had not experienced before; all of it was collected in the brief period before she introduced the bill.

In short, the entertainment industry "lined up to salute" her bill—and that salute meant cash.[64]

She was only getting started.

The entertainment industry was not the only one who would give her large concentrated donations in a short period, only to have her later introduce a bill that they liked.

At the end of September 2011, over a six-day period, no fewer than twenty-one executives from Xcel Energy wrote campaign checks to Klobuchar.[65] Weeks earlier, Klobuchar introduced legislation to amend the IRS code of 1986 to give a "renewable electricity integration" [tax] credit to utility companies.[66] The legislation would give utilities like Xcel Energy federal tax credits for producing renewable energy. Klobuchar was a sponsor of the bill. Xcel Energy lobbied for the bill.[67] She continued to go back to Xcel for more, and to introduce legislation that they favored.[68]

Beginning at the end of May 2017 over a ten-day period, twenty-eight executives from Xcel Energy sent her contributions totaling $12,500.[69] Just two and half weeks earlier, she had co-sponsored legislation called the Clean Energy for America Act, which would dramatically expand the tax credits available for companies like Xcel Energy.[70]

Despite a voting record remarkably similar to Bernie Sanders, she enjoyed the sort of corporate cash flow about which the senator from Vermont could only dream.[71]

Klobuchar likewise aggressively fought for the interests of medical device manufacturers. She pushed a bill that would loosen the conflict of interest rules for advisers to the Food and Drug Administration for approving new medical devices.[72] Klobuchar draws an artificial distinction between medical device manufacturers and pharmaceutical companies when it comes to regulations. She bristles at the power of big pharma. "The big pharma companies think they own Washington," she has said. "Well they don't own me."[73] But medical device manufacturers enjoy her unending support.

On March 17, 2016, Klobuchar introduced the Improving Medical Device Innovation Act, which would relax regulations for the medical device industry. Less than two weeks later, thirteen executives with medical device manufacturer Medtronic wrote her checks over a three-day period.[74] Back in 2011, Senator Klobuchar invited the CEO of Medtronic as her honored guest to President Obama's State of the Union address. She paid his company and industry homage in announcing the invitation.[75] Klobuchar supports the industry in part because it creates jobs in Minnesota. More to the point, they are large donors to her political campaigns and often cut checks close to when she writes legislation.[76]

Klobuchar is unique among progressives in her ability to raise enormous sums from giant corporations. For her reelection in 2018, she raised thirty-eight times the amount of her GOP challenger. She took in donations from the CEOs of eleven of Minnesota's twenty-five largest corporations. She has done particularly well with law firms and lobbyists—they have donated more than $3 million to her three Senate races.

Indeed, no industry has given her more.[77]

Lobbyists have been some of her most prolific fund-raisers. Lobbying shops such as McGuire Woods, Locke Lord Strategies, Holland & Knight, Flack Associates, Covington & Burling, have held fund-raisers in Washington for her.[78]

Klobuchar has tried to downplay the flow of corporate cash into her campaign coffers. Her announcement in February 2019 that her presidential campaign would not accept donations from corporate PACs was ironic, given that only months earlier she collected $1.9 million from corporate PACs for her 2018 Senate reelection campaign.[79]

This has led Klobuchar to apply her views on regulation and antitrust matters selectively. Klobuchar is the ranking member on the U.S. Senate Subcommittee on Antitrust, Competition Policy, and Consumer Rights.[80] The subcommittee is ground zero for large corporations seeking merger approval from the federal government. That power, of course, creates enormous opportunities to raise money from corporations who are donating out of either fear or favor. Klobuchar has always taken the position that she has no clear-cut position on mergers. As she announced in early 2008 during an interview about a potential airline merger, she proclaimed that she had no "blanket stance against mergers."[81] This case-by-case approach, which makes sense, also maximizes the opportunity to collect large sums of cash from companies seeking federal approval. Companies that are seeking approval for large mergers and acquisitions are some of her "most generous donors. Many of them have found themselves in the target of both the Justice Department's antitrust division or [sic] the Federal Trade Commission."[82]

Medtronic, for example, sought a "vertical" integration merger to buy a competing firm called MiniMed in 2011. The merger was highly criticized—but not by Klobuchar. Medtronic was her third-largest contributor from 2011 to 2016, which coincides with her first reelection bid in 2012.[83]

Cargill Inc. is a giant Minnesota-based food producer and distributor. Valued at approximately $60 billion, it has been one of Klobuchar's top donors. In 2013, it was the subject of a bipartisan probe by President Obama's Justice Department and some Republican attorneys general over its plans to merge with ConAgra Foods Inc. In the name of protecting consumers, the Obama Justice Department required Cargill to divest from four flour mills in order to approve the deal. Going back four decades, Cargill has faced major anticompetition investigations seven times.[84]

All said, "Klobuchar does not appear to have questioned many of [her corporate donors'] acquisitions."[85]

Klobuchar was also supportive of carve-outs for Cargill when it came to derivatives regulation. These complex investment vehicles on Wall Street have been highly controversial. Klobuchar supported legislation to rein in the trading of derivatives, but allowed for exemptions that would permit Cargill to continue to leverage them.[86]

When she organized an Innovation Summit with her National Innovation Agenda, two of the corporate speakers were the corporate VP of Cargill and the chairman/CEO of Medtronic, whose companies were major donors.[87]

ERIC GARCETTI

Mayor Eric Garcetti, longtime political fixture in Los Angeles, can run a star-studded campaign like few others. When he was running for mayor in 2013, he tapped his friend and supporter actress Salma Hayek to do a video about his merits as a leader. She talked about his skills as a dancer, the fact that he was a military officer, his culinary skills, his gardening acumen, and, finally, the job he was doing as president of the city council.[1] Then there was a fund-raiser at the Henry Fonda Theater featuring actor Will Ferrell, talk-show host Jimmy Kimmel, and the musician Moby. The campaign produced a list of two hundred "entertainment leaders for Garcetti," which included Michael Eisner, Jake Gyllenhaal, Kevin Spacey, and Michael Ovitz. His campaign finance chair was Sony executive Eric Paquette.[2]

Being mayor of the Entertainment Capital of the World means a melding of politics and celebrity like no place else. Mayor Garcetti, in addition to his apparent dancing skills, has also appeared on several television shows. He has appeared on *The Closer* and *Angie Tribeca*. And he is friends with rapper Jay-Z. When the city was planning to shut down the 6th Street Bridge for repairs, the mayor cut an R&B single called "101 Slow Jam" as a public service announcement.[3]

Eric Garcetti is one of the rising stars in national progressive circles. Journalists regularly point to his "solid progressive achievements" as mayor, and as one of the "potential pioneers of progressive policy" among America's big-city mayors.[4] In 2016, he was reportedly on the list of Hillary Clinton's vice presidential choices.[5] He remains a major player in the Democratic Party.

For Garcetti, it is all about a modern progressivism—with a pragmatic twist. In contrast with Elizabeth Warren and Bernie Sanders, his public persona and rhetoric appear to be far less hostile to corporations. He wants to make the machinery of government more efficient, bringing it into the "smartphone era."[6] Garcetti clearly sees his policies as setting a national agenda, which can be replicated around the country. "We've done it in L.A.," he told the Democratic National Convention in July 2016. "Now let's do it for our entire country."[7]

But behind the tinsel and celebrity Los Angeles has a corrupt political culture, as evidenced by two FBI raids on City Hall— one in November 2018, the other in July 2019.[8]

At the heart of LA politics is a hardened political operation fueled by an elaborate pay-to-play system where businesses and developers pay money to get their projects approved by the city. It appears to operate like a classic political machine, albeit less explicit than the old Tammany Hall system made famous in the nineteenth century. The way Garcetti's machine operates often looks like Tammany Hall in Ray-Bans: sleek, stylish, and sophisticated, but at its root a machine that leverages power for money.

Garcetti is an amalgam of Los Angeles. He describes himself as a "kosher burrito," because of his mixed Jewish and Mexican roots.[9] He grew up in a prominent Los Angeles family. His father, Gil Garcetti, who "grew up poor in South L.A.," was the famed district attorney whose office took on O. J. Simpson and lost. Eric's mother, Sukey, is the daughter of a financially successful clothier.[10] Garcetti's parents were an atheist and an agnostic. But he has embraced his mother's Jewish heritage, studying the Talmud and attending LA's "social-justice-minded" IKAR synagogue.[11]

Eric received an elite education, attending first the Harvard School, the elite prep school in Studio City, California. He then went off to Columbia University.[12]

As an undergraduate at Columbia University, Garcetti organized a protest against a nearby market that had forbidden the homeless from redeeming cans and bottles for the five- and ten-cent deposits. "We hope to resolve this without it getting messy," he declared, "but the managers seem to be assholes who have to be hit hard."[13]

From Columbia, he went to Oxford on a Rhodes scholarship. It was on his way to the city of spires that he met his future wife, Amy Wakeland. Raised in Indiana, Wakeland was a Rhodes Scholar, too. They formed a solid team and core from the beginning and today she is widely considered one of his closest advisors.[14] After they returned from England and had settled in Los Angeles, Eric ran for city council. Wakeland served as the campaign field director and was described as a "general charging into battle." In contrast to her husband's more laid-back style, Wakefield is tough. "She is fierce," a deputy mayor under Antonio Villaraigosa (Garcetti's predecessor) who has worked with Wakefield told Los Angeles magazine. She has remained a central component of his power structure, recruiting many of the top aides who serve with him in the mayor's office. She also reportedly has oversight of his schedule.[15]

Garcetti has been a longtime political fixture in Los Angeles. He was first elected to the Los Angeles City Council back in

2001, and then for six years served as the city council president, which essentially gave him "complete control" of the legislative agenda for the city.[16]

During his earliest days as a member of the city council, Garcetti aligned himself with the interests of Los Angeles's developers. Los Angeles has very strict zoning and environmental laws when it comes to construction projects. But the laws allow the city council and the mayor to make exceptions—and under Garcetti they have done so an overwhelming majority of the time.[17] If a builder can get these politicians to give them an exception, it can result in an enormous windfall. As we will see, the way builders get those exceptions is by showering politicians and their families with cash.

Garcetti also became a supporter of using eminent domain to push people out of their property so that newer, larger projects could be built. He once offered, "The city would not use its powers of eminent domain to force property owners to sell, unless the developers were unable to reach a deal with the landowners." *Reason*'s Matt Welch argues, in short, that the city is going to take your property; you had better take the deal.[18]

Even as the president of the Los Angeles City Council, Garcetti was a rising star in national politics. President Barack Obama tried to lure him to the White House, according to Garcetti, to serve as his "urban czar." They met in the Oval Office to discuss having him join the Obama administration. "He said I could oversee HUD [Department of Housing and Urban Development] and HHS [Health and Human Services] and Education and transportation. It would have been an amazing opportunity." But Garcetti had larger ambitions, including running for mayor. And, perhaps, further down the road, he hoped to be sitting on the other side of the desk in the Oval Office.[19]

From president of the Los Angeles City Council, Garcetti ran for mayor. He won both elections handily, but he benefited from voter apathy and low turnout. The 2013 election was a "very low-turnout election."[20] Indeed, so few people in Los Angeles voted, Garcetti was elected with just 222,300 votes, equivalent to what was needed in the 1930s when LA was half the size.[21]

He was reelected in 2017 in an election where just one in five eligible voters turned out.[22]

The move to the mayor's office brought him more broad-ranging powers that could affect the fortunes of developers and other businesses. In Los Angeles, the mayor and other elected officials have enormous power to make developers rich with changes to the zoning code, waivers to planning requirements, and other benefits for real estate projects. Tweaking the law can dramatically increase the market value of commercial parcels of land and buildings by expanding their possible use, or allowing larger buildings to be constructed than regulations allow.[23] They can also exempt future real estate projects from the California Environmental Quality Act.[24] These favors can, over a number of projects, translate into billions of dollars for builders and developers.

In August 2013, Rick Jacobs joined Garcetti's office as deputy chief of staff for operations. During the 2013 mayoral run, Jacobs was a major fund-raiser for the campaign.[25] He was the founder of a consultancy firm called RDJ Strategic Advisors, which "provides expertise to ultra-high net worth families, investors, non-profits and corporations." Earlier in his career, Jacobs was assistant to the chairman of Occidental Petroleum, which was headed by the controversial Armand Hammer. Jacobs says that he took sixty trips to the Soviet Union in the 1980s.[26] Hammer, it was later revealed, worked as a "virtual spy" for the Soviet Union and was "a conduit for money that financed Communist espionage operations."[27]

With his elevation to the mayor's office, Garcetti set up the infrastructure for a self-funding political influence machine. Each of the roles that Rick Jacobs played appear to be a gateway between those looking for favors from the city government and the mayor's own political and personal ambitions. The merging of Garcetti's political machine with the official powers of the LA mayor became more apparent when Jacobs, who was officially the deputy chief of staff, began to introduce himself as "Executive Vice Mayor" of Los Angeles. It was a nonexistent position in Los Angeles city government; the title was apparently inspired by a role common in China.[28]

In June 2014, Garcetti launched a nonprofit he called the Mayor's Fund for Los Angeles. The nonprofit was explicitly linked to the city's government and worked on Garcetti's projects. Jacobs claims to have created the organization and would go on to serve as the treasurer and director. Jacobs would remain attached to the Mayor's Fund, but on July 20, 2016, Jacobs left the mayor's office on a "leave of absence" to focus on "outside political and civic activities," including Garcetti's reelection campaign and another Garcetti pet project: Measure M, an initiative for a sales tax increase to fund infrastructure projects.[29] The initiative was a merging of interests. Jacob's company was paid almost $90,000 to advise on the initiative; the largest single donation to the "Yes on M" campaign was a political action committee (PAC) for the infrastructure firm HNTB, which stood to gain a lot from its passage. In November 2016, Measure M passed.[30] It was expected to raise $120 billion over a forty-year period for infrastructure projects.[31] In late October 2017, Garcetti launched a nonprofit called Accelerator for America (alongside South Bend, Indiana, mayor Pete Buttigieg), with Jacobs as CEO.[32] In November 2017, Garcetti launched the Democratic Midterm Victory Fund, a PAC to support Democrats in the 2018 midterms. Jacobs's firm, RDJ Strategic Advisors, was paid $231,797 by the PAC during the 2018 cycle—nearly 10 percent of what it raised.[33] Jacobs was accused of using extortion tactics against opponents of some of the mayor's initiatives. Opponents of Measure EE, a tax plan backed by Garcetti, were reportedly warned of voicing opposition. The *LA Times* reported, "Tracy Hernandez, founding chief executive of the Los Angeles County Business Federation, known as BizFed, said Measure EE campaign manager Rick Jacobs told her during a phone call last month that BizFed members who campaign against the measure won't do any business in the city of L.A. for the next four years." Jacobs denied the allegations.[34]

One mechanism for receiving money is a California loophole known as "behested payments." This allows politicians to establish nonprofits, and then solicit money for those nonprofits from businesses who want something from their office. Few in California politics have been more effective at doing this than Eric Garcetti. The contributions are often large—much larger than campaign contributions—and they are mostly unregulated. Observers note the irony that Garcetti excels at collecting large sums given that he is "a longtime critic of big money in local politics."[35]

Between 2009 and 2017, Garcetti took in $31.9 million in such payments from "individuals, businesses, and foundations, some of which have won sizable contracts and crucial approvals from the city in recent years." The bulk of those behested payments were directed to the Mayor's Fund, which fused together city government and his own political machine.[36]

To get a sense of the scale of Garcetti's money stream, that was twice what California governor Jerry Brown raised in behested payments during the same period, and more than forty times what the then lieutenant governor, Gavin Newsom, did. Behested payments provide "an ideal opportunity for the very wealthy and the lobbyist to buy access to lawmakers," said Craig Holman, with the group Public Citizen.[37]

Garcetti's use of behested payments is ironic given that back in 2011 he pushed for an initiative that was supposed to reduce the flow of big money. Charter Amendment H barred campaign contributions from those bidding on city contracts larger than $100,000. "Special interests are always trying to buy influence at City Hall," he said at the time. "Charter Amendment H will help stop them." But what was not included in that ban was behested payments. And while campaign contributions were capped at $1,400 for the Los Angeles mayor's race, behested payments have no restrictions. Politicians are required to disclose behested payments only if they are more than $5,000 a year per donor.[38]

Consider the case of AT&T. The telecom giant was a $30 million contractor with the city of Los Angeles, so it could not make campaign contributions. But Garcetti's fund collected three payments totaling $105,000 from the company over a six-month period. Likewise, in 2015, Verizon received a contract worth up to $15 million from the city. Again, they were not allowed to make a campaign contribution. But a little more than a month after they received approval for that contract, they donated $100,000 to Garcetti's fund.[39]

"If there's anyone that's paying attention, you realize that the company doesn't have to give the money to the legislator directly," notes broadband industry analyst Craig Settles. "You just basically funnel it into different activities where the elected official can get a great photo op and then, boom, there you go."[40]

Less well-known companies got into the game, too. An

LA landscaping company called Turf Terminators got behind Garcetti. They cashed in more than $23 million in rebates. In April, thirteen contributions were made to Garcetti's campaign and his nonprofit totaling $25,650. Just a month later, Garcetti mentioned the company in his 2015 State of the City address. He even pointed out the company's twenty-nine-year-old former CEO in the audience.[41]

The company, which converts lawns to less water-intensive landscaping, is a niche but lucrative business. Homeowners and the company receive rebates from the local utility or the water district. After Garcetti mentioned them in the State of the City address, they saw a business boom. As the local CBS affiliate put it, Turf Terminators "would go on to take in millions of dollars in ratepayer rebates."[42]

"Limits on the amount that a donor can give directly to a candidate are in place for a reason, and that's to limit corruption," says Brendan Fischer, an attorney with the Campaign Legal Center in Washington, D.C. "By a donor being allowed to support a public official above and beyond the legal contribution limits undermines the law's anti-corruption purpose." The reason is that the behested gifts are actually solicited by the politician. As Columbia law professor Richard Briffault notes, "A true gift may come out of the blue, unasked-for, and may not even be something the covered person wants. But a behested gift is one that the public servant has actually asked for. So the likelihood of actual gratitude is much higher."[43]

The Mayor's Fund often appears to sit on cash rather than passing it out to charities. The nonprofit only spent about 40 percent of the money donated during the first two full years.[44]

"People who have business pending in the city of Los Angeles shouldn't be making payments at the behest of the mayor," says

Bob Stern, a former general counsel of the California Fair Political Practices Commission.[45]

At one point during his 2013 mayoral campaign, Garcetti made a public declaration that he would not accept campaign contributions from Walmart on the grounds that they paid their workers low wages. But the following year, he collected a $100,000 check from Walmart for the Mayor's Fund—at his behest.[46]

The flow of money from those who got approval for projects was staggering. Developer Samuel Leung was seeking to clear a real estate project near the Port of Los Angeles. He wanted to construct a residential development in an industrial area of the city known as Harbor City. Leung was accused of then using "straw donors" to funnel hundreds of thousands of dollars to local politicians, including Garcetti. On the same day in February 2015, there were multiple checks written in what appeared to be the same handwriting from Leung's handymen, a gardener, and a chef for a hotel run by his company. Later, when asked about the contributions, these individuals either denied ever making them or said that they did not remember giving. Leung wanted to build apartments in an area zoned industrial. Residential properties, of course, offer much larger profit margins than industrial real estate. The city's planning commission had rejected the proposal in March 2014.[47] Janice Hahn, who was a U.S. representative at the time, received more than $200,000 in straw or real donations from those connected to Leung. Indeed, in 2013 Leung coughed up $60,000 for a committee seeking to elect Garcetti as mayor. The organization, dubbed Committee for a Safer Los Angeles, was an independent expenditure committee run for his benefit. Garcetti employed a rarely used mayoral prerogative that reduced the number of city council members needed to approve the project. That did the trick; the project was approved.[48]

Hahn later became a Los Angeles County supervisor. In December 2016, not long after the news broke of the payments from Leung, Hahn hired the mayor's sister, Dana Garcetti-Boldt, as a policy advisor.[49] After Garcetti's sister joined her staff, legal problems continued to follow Hahn. An aide for Hahn was convicted on bribery charges in an unrelated case in March 2018.[50]

As we will see, Dana Garcetti-Boldt's husband would also become enmeshed in controversial projects at the center of an FBI probe.

Leung has been indicted on bribery and money-laundering charges related to this case. He has denied the charges.[51]

The FBI launched investigations related to other real estate development projects approved in Los Angeles. These involved several Chinese-controlled companies. In 2018, the FBI issued a search warrant as part of a federal corruption probe into potential crimes involving Los Angeles City Council member Jose Huizar. The probe focused on high-rise development projects in downtown Los Angeles funded by Chinese investment companies. The warrant specifically named the Shenzhen New World Group, a Chinese real estate firm. Shenzhen is looking to build the tallest building in Los Angeles on the site of the Grand Hotel. The warrant also named Greenland USA, another Chinese firm, and sought email communications from Raymond Chan, an LA city official who served as Garcetti's deputy mayor for economic development. The FBI executed a warrant asking Google for all communications and data connected to Chan's Gmail account. The mayor named him interim head of the LA Department of Building and Safety in 2013, and the permanent director the following year. He was then appointed Garcetti's deputy mayor, lasting a year at that post. The warrant noted that it was seeking information on "other foreign investors not yet identified." The

FBI also raided council member Jose Huizar's house and office to look for evidence of money laundering, bribery, conspiracy, extortion, and kickbacks, among other possible crimes. Huizar, his family, and his staffers were included in the search warrant.[52] Another council member, Curren Price, was also named in the FBI investigation. Joel Jacinto, a Garcetti appointee who sat on the Board of Public Works, also resigned because of the investigation.[53] (No charges had been filed against any of the politicians being investigated as of the date this book was sent to press.)

As the *New York Times* put it, the "warrant described a sprawling web of possible corruption." Local observers saw the scandal as reminiscent of the 1974 movie *Chinatown,* about shady real estate deals.[54]

A citizens group called Coalition to Preserve LA sent a fifty-four-page complaint to the LA County Civil grand jury requesting an investigation into corruption involving Garcetti and developers. The group complained that Garcetti had closed-door meetings with developers who were putting money into the Mayor's Fund.[55]

City Councilman David Ryu tried to ban some contributions from developers, but his reforms were thwarted by the city council's decision to delay the vote.[56]

The Shenzhen New World Group purchased the Los Angeles Marriott Downtown and the Sheraton Universal Hotel for an estimated $150 million in 2010 and 2011, respectively.[57] Oceanwide Holdings, another Chinese firm, was developing Oceanwide Plaza, a housing and retail project near the Staples Center, where the Los Angeles Lakers play. The billion-dollar, three-tower complex high-rise would feature 504 condominiums, retail space, and a five-star hotel.[58] Zinner Consultants, an environmental firm that just happens to employ Garcetti's brother-in-law, Glenn Boldt, as an executive, listed the Park Hyatt, which is part of Oceanwide Plaza, as a project on which they consult.[59]

The aforementioned Greenland USA was approved for the Metropolis development. The four-tower complex was another $1 billion project. Again, Garcetti's brother-in-law's firm was retained as a consultant on the project.[60]

Projects linked to Garcetti's brother-in-law seem to do well in city hall. When the developers sought to redevelop the Century Plaza Hotel, Garcetti not only approved of the project, he also helped arrange international funding for the redevelopment.[61] Zinner Consultants was again hired as mitigation consultants for the project.[62]

Garcetti's ties to developers go even deeper. The Zolla family is a major developer of real estate in Los Angeles. Garcetti co-owns with the Zolla family a small boutique hotel called the Inn at Playa del Rey.[63] The Zollas also owned several properties on Manchester Avenue, located near the site of a redevelopment project along Los Angeles International Airport's northern rim, something called the LAX Northside Plan Update. The Inn at Playa del Rey is also not far from the project site. Garcetti has championed the project.[64]

Developer Rick Caruso donated $125,000 to Garcetti's nonprofit. Caruso wanted to develop a project that was too tall given zoning restrictions. A year later, his development project—with only slight modifications—got the necessary approvals to proceed.[65]

Garcetti's apparent willingness to look the other way when it comes to city corruption involving his political allies includes the Los Angeles Fire Department (LAFD). In late 2015, LAFD officials found that Inspector Glenn Martinez had claimed hundreds of hours of overtime for his inspection work. Internal investigators at the LAFD looked into his claims and discovered that no one had actually seen him where he had professed to work. For example, he claimed to have put in six and a half hours of inspection time at Our Lady Help of Christians School. But he was "not seen by anyone" on site. In another case, he claimed to have spent four hours inspecting two buildings at Occidental College. The problem: at the time, the campus was shut down for winter break. And again "nobody" saw him on the premises.[66]

Now, this might seem like just another case of government employees milking the system. But there is more to the story. Deputy fire chief John Vidovich investigated this and other cases of overbilling and brought the matter to the attention of his boss, LAFD chief Ralph Terrazas. Terrazas, Mayor Garcetti, and the mayor's chief of staff, Ana Guerrero, sat on the reports for nearly a year.[67]

Then Garcetti reassigned Vidovich. That reassignment "coincided with the donation of $350,000 to his re-election campaign, and those of his City Council successors, by the firefighters' union."[68]

Vidovich sued the city in January 2017, alleging that Mayor Garcetti and his aides, with the help of the fire chief, pushed him out of his office at the bidding of the firefighters' union. In his case, he claimed that he was pushed out because he exposed "illegal and fraudulent acts" by inspectors, particularly some who were padding their pockets by making implausible overtime claims. According to court documents, fire chief Terrazas told Vidovich that "the mayor's office has me over a barrel" and had to push him out. When asked who in the mayor's office pushed him, Terrazas reportedly said, "the mayor." Garcetti and aides denied the allegation.[69] But the city ended up settling with Vidovich and reportedly paid him $800,000 to make the case go away.[70]

Eric Garcetti has been at the center of Los Angeles political power since 2001. When Garcetti goes to his office at City Hall, on the south side of the building there is a quote from Cicero: "He that violates his oath profanes the divinity of faith itself." On the north side there is an etched quote from the nineteenth-century poet James Russell Lowell: "The highest of all sciences and services—the government."[71]

While during his tenure he has constructed an efficient political machine for extracting money from companies who are doing business with the city, the City of Angels continues to struggle. It does poorly in quality-of-life rankings. Richard Florida, the urban theorist, places the Los Angeles area dead last among the twenty largest metro areas in the country when it comes to rankings of inequality and poverty. According to a study conducted by the University of California, Los Angeles (UCLA), 25 percent of people in Los Angeles spend half of their income on rent, the highest of any major metropolitan area.[72]

And Los Angeles continues to be plagued with a massive and inefficient government. Because of red tape, as of 2016 it took an average of 373 days to hire someone. Also, nearly one out of every six employees on the city payroll is off the job on workers' compensation—and it is twice as bad for the police and fire departments.[73]

Another senior city official puts it more bluntly.

"You have to understand, it's a fucking miracle your trash gets picked up."[74]

CONCLUSION

Corrupt acts can take various forms. As we have seen, these can include using your political power to enrich your family; tilting the scales of justice for the benefit of friends; steering government contracts to friends and family; or using the machinery of your office to serve your interests rather than those of the people you are supposed to represent.

The progressive solution for every national problem is to give them and our political leadership more power. So, how have they managed the power they have already been granted?

The progressives featured in this book all profess to have the purest of motives in their quest for greater power. They seek that power for our benefit or to fix our problems, or so they claim. Even if we take them at their word, the reality is that, as economist and Nobel laureate Milton Friedman reminds us, "Concentrated power is not rendered harmless by the good intentions of those who create it."[1]

History teaches that corruption follows power. The more power you accumulate, the more likely you are to exploit that power for your own benefit. History also teaches that power tempts those who wield it into corrupt acts. Founding Father George Washington once worried, "Few men have virtue to withstand the highest bidder."[2]

But the problem is not just with accumulated power, but also with those who seek it. As scientist and author David Brin pointedly noted, "It is said that power corrupts, but actually it's more true that power attracts the corruptible."

Whichever is more true, the link between power and corruption is an iron rule of human history.

What political figures do with the power they enjoy reveals a lot about who they are. The great historian Robert Caro has written a masterful four-volume set of books on the public life of President Lyndon Baines Johnson. After he finished the fourth volume, he commented on the truths he uncovered in his decades-long study of public power. "What I believe is always true about power is that power always reveals."[3]

This book has hopefully served as a revelation of how power is exercised and how it can be twisted to serve the ends of those who seek more of it. It is, of course, very easy to blame our public figures for the state of public corruption. But ultimately the problem lies with us. We get the government we choose, the leaders we elect, and the corruption we tolerate. Novelist and essayist George Orwell wrote the masterpiece *1984* about a dystopian future. But he was also a shrewd observer of political life in democracies. He warned about the political choices people make regularly in an elective system of government. "A people that elect corrupt politicians, imposters, thieves and traitors are not victims, but accomplices."[4]

The progressive message continues to be "hand us more power." What they are asking us to do is ignore history—including *their* history—in how such power is actually exercised. We must ask ourselves: Why trust someone with more power when you cannot even trust them with the little they already have?

ACKNOWLEDGMENTS

This book, like many of the others I have written over the course of the past couple of decades, proved to be research intensive. I am blessed to have a great team of researchers who scour the planet for documents, financial records, and corporate materials. And a team of fact-checkers to make sure that our sources are top-notch and being accurately reported. In particular, I want to thank Steve Stewart, Tarik Noriega, Christina Armes, Joe Duffus, Jedd McFatter, Seamus Bruner, Caleb Stephens, Hannah Cooperman, and Brian Baugus for all their hard work. I also wish to thank all those members of the research team who wish to remain anonymous.

Special thanks are also due to Vermont attorney Brady Toensing, who shared his research on Bernie Sanders, and to Dave Bossie, of Citizens United, who shared emails he obtained through the Freedom of Information Act (FOIA).

I am also grateful for the leadership team that works with me at the Government Accountability Institute. Our board of directors, including chairman Rebekah Mercer and member Ron Robinson, provides courageous and wise leadership as we navigate the treacherous waters of investigating and exposing corruption involving powerful people. We are also blessed to have senior leadership staff, including Stuart Christmas, Eric Eggers, Steve Post, and Sandy Schulz. Thanks also to Sally Jo Roorda, my longtime assistant, for keeping me organized.

My agents Glen Hartley and Lynn Chu of Writers Reps always

steer me right, and I am grateful for their diligence on my behalf. This is my second book with Eric Nelson as my editor. He has a wonderful combination of both patience and commitment to excellence that makes him a delight to work with. Thanks also go to Hannah Long for her assistance. And Tina Andreadis of the Harper publicity team is quite simply the best in the business.

Finally, thanks and gratitude go to my family. This book is dedicated to my mother, Kerstin Schweizer, who since my earliest days encouraged me in my endeavors. My wife, Rhonda, has been loving and encouraging throughout this busy and difficult time. Joe, Maria, Dan, Adam, Raquel, and Ava—thanks for joining me on this wild ride. It's my hope that by fighting corruption we can make the world a better place for everyone, especially for my children, Jack and Hannah.

The author alone is responsible for the contents of this book.

NOTES

CHAPTER 1: THE CRANNIED WALL

1. "Top Arkansas Lawyer Helped Hillary Clinton Turn Big Profit," *New York Times*, March 18, 1994, https://www.nytimes.com/1994/03/18/us/top -arkansas-lawyer-helped-hillary-clinton-turn-big-profit.html?pagewanted =all.
2. "Whitewater: Time Line," *Washington Post*, 1998, https://www.washington post.com/wp-srv/politics/special/whitewater/timeline.htm.
3. Eric Lichtblau and Davan Maharaj, "Clinton Pardon of Rich a Saga of Power, Money," *Chicago Tribune*, February 18, 2001, https://www.chicagotribune .com/sns-clinton-pardons-analysis-story.html.
4. "Governance Memorandum," email from jreynoso@stblaw.com to john .podesta@gmail.com and brucerlindsey@aol.com, *Wikileaks*, December 3, 2011, https://wikileaks.org/podesta-emails/emailid/7769 (see attachment 12727757_4.pdf).
5. Anna Massoglia, "Clinton Foundation's Revenue Hit 15-year Low After 2016 Presidential Election," Opensecrets.org, December 13, 2018, https:// www.opensecrets.org/news/2018/12/clinton-foundation-revenue-low/.
6. Michael S. Schmidt and Amy Chozick, "Using Private Email, Hillary Clinton Thwarted Record Requests," *New York Times*, March 3, 2015, https:// www.nytimes.com/2015/03/04/us/politics/using-private-email -hillary-clinton-thwarted-record-requests.html.
7. Robert Penn Warren, *All the King's Men* (New York: Harcourt, 1946), pp. 234–35.
8. Ibid.
9. Jim Bettinger, "The Anger Journalists Never Fully Understood," Nieman Reports, Winter 2003, https://niemanreports.org/articles/the-anger-journal ists-never-fully-understood/.
10. Andra Brichacek, "Six Ways the Media Influence Elections," University of Oregon School of Journalism and Communication, n.d., https://journalism .uoregon.edu/news/six-ways-media-influences-elections.
11. Thomas E. Patterson, "News Coverage of Donald Trump's First 100 Days," Shorenstein Center, May 18, 2017, https://shorensteincenter.org/news-cov erage-donald-trumps -first-100-days/.

12. "6 Political Scandals the Press Doesn't Want You to Know About," *Investor's Business Daily*, October 17, 2018, https://www.investors.com/politics/edito rials/scandals-democrats-media-bias/.

13. Ken Doctor, " 'Profitable' Washington Post adding more than five dozen journalists," Politico, December 27, 2016, https://www.politico.com/media /story/2016/12/the-profitable-washington-post-adding-more-than-five -dozen-journalists-004900; Paul Bedard, "Washington Post assigns army of 20 to dig into 'every phase' of Trump's life," *Washington Examiner*, May 11, 2016, https://www.washingtonexaminer.com/washington-post-assigns-army -of-20-to-dig-into-every-phase-of-trumps-life.

14. "How Times Journalists Uncovered the Original Source of the President's Wealth," *New York Times*, October 2, 2018, https://www.nytimes .com/2018/10/02/insider/donald-trump-fred-tax-schemes-wealth.html.

CHAPTER 2: KAMALA HARRIS

1. Bonnie Eslinger, Aaron Kinney, and Mike Rosenberg, "President Barack Obama, in Ritzy Atherton, Raises Money, Compliments Kamala Harris," *Mercury News*, April 4, 2013, https://www.mercurynews.com/2013/04/04 /president-barack-obama-in-ritzy-atherton-raises-money-compliments -kamala-harris/.

2. Sharon Driscoll, "Tony and Maya: Partners in Public Service," *Stanford Lawyer* 82 (May 17, 2010), https://law.stanford.edu/stanford-lawyer/articles /tony-and-maya-partners-in-public-service/; Carla Marinucci, "In Obama afterglow, D.A. Harris set to run for attorney general," *San Francisco Chronicle*, November 12, 2008; Philip Matier and Andrew Ross, "State stars may shine with Obama," *San Francisco Chronicle*, November 6, 2008; Carla Marinucci, "D.A. Harris Plans Run for Attorney General," *San Francisco Chronicle*, November 12, 2008, https://www.sfgate.com/politics/article/D-A-Harris -plans-run-for-attorney-general-3262181.php.

3. Michael Martinez, "A 'Female Obama' Seeks California Attorney General Post," CNN, October 22, 2010, http://www.cnn.com/2010/POLITICS /10/22/california.kamala.harris.profile/index.html.

4. Matthew Artz, "Kamala Harris Taking Quiet Path to California's US Senate Seat," *Los Angeles Daily News*, October 22, 2016.

5. Mark Pulliam, "The Next Obama," *City Journal*, Winter 2016, https://www .city-journal.org/html/next-obama-14181.html; Shaila Dewan, "For California, Attorney General Insisted on Better Terms in Foreclosure Deal," *New York Times*, February 13, 2012, https://www.nytimes.com/2012/02/14/busi ness/how-kamala-harris-finessed-a-foreclosure-deal-for-california.html.

6. Molly Hensley-Clancy, "The Complicated Politics of Kamala Harris's First Book," Buzzfeed News, August 20, 2018, https://www.buzzfeednews.com /article/mollyhensleyclancy/kamala-harris-smart-on-crime-book.

NOTES

7. Scott Duke Harris, "In Search of Elusive Justice," *Los Angeles Times,* October 24, 2004; Artz, "Kamala Harris Taking Quiet Path to California's US Senate Seat"; George Joseph, "Community pins hopes next on Kamala Harris," *India Abroad,* November 28, 2003.

8. Aziz Haniffa, "Kamala Devi Harris," *India Abroad,* August 14, 2009.

9. Abby Aguirre, "Kamala Harris Is Dreaming Big," *Vogue,* April 2018, https://www.vogue.com/article/kamala-harris-interview-vogue-april-2018.

10. Joseph, "Community pins hopes next on Kamala Harris."

11. Ibid.; "UC Hastings Congratulates Kamala Harris '89: California's Next U.S. Senator," UC Hastings College of the Law San Francisco, November 9, 2016, https://www.uchastings.edu/2016/11/09/uc-hastings-congratulates-kamala-harris-89-californias-next-u-s-senator.

12. Harris, "In Search of Elusive Justice."

13. George Joseph, "It's time for new leadership: Harris," *India Abroad,* December 19, 2003.

14. George Joseph, "Six to the fore," *India Abroad,* October 31, 2003; Dan Morain and Paul Jacobs, "Worlds of Politics, Law Often Mix for Speaker: Capitol: Willie Brown's Legal and Speaking Fees from Corporations Far Outstrip His Public Salary. He Denies Any Conflict of Interest. The FBI Probes Some Dealings," *Los Angeles Times,* April 1, 1991, https://www.latimes.com/archives/la-xpm-1991-04-01-mn-1225-story.html; In the Court of Appeal of the State of California, Fourth Appellate District, 4th Civil No. D011997, 10, https://books.google.com/books?id=Lt18d2g43BMC&pg=PP25&lpg=PP25&dq=%22willie+brown%22++%22state+bar+investigation%22&source=bl&ots=XT9V2E1QqB&sig=ACfU3U3XzQARRwx7ihehPQkJyFdX-WulGQ&hl=en&sa=X&ved=2ahUKEwj-lMSS4vDiAhVBMqwKHTHACT0Q6AEwB3oECAsQAQ#v=onepage&q=%22willie%20brown%22%20%20%22state%20bar%20investigation%22&f=false, p. 10; "Investigators Say Lawmakers Broke No Law on Trip," *Los Angeles Times,* November 7, 1991, https://www.latimes.com/archives/la-xpm-1991-11-07-mn-1448-story.html; James Richardson, *Willie Brown: A Biography* (Berkeley: University of California Press, 1996), p. 353.

15. Richard C. Paddock, "Special Interests a large source of Brown's income," *Los Angeles Times,* March 13, 1987, https://www.latimes.com/archives/la-xpm-1987-03-13-mn-5616-story.html.

16. Weston Kosova, "The Real Slick Willie," *Newsweek,* December 3, 1995, https://www.newsweek.com/real-slick-willie-180166.

17. Lois Romano, "Tonight the Town Is Willie Brown's," *Washington Post,* July 16, 1984, https://www.washingtonpost.com/archive/lifestyle/1984/07/16/tonight-the-town-is-willie-browns/0484f4c3-aea5-43dd-b788-f454141308bf/.

18. Elizabeth Lesly Stevens, "The Power Broker," *Washington Monthly,* July/August 2012, https://washingtonmonthly.com/magazine/julyaugust-2012/the-power-broker/.

19. Peter Castro, "No Mere Mayor," *People*, June 24, 1996, https://people.com /archive/no-mere-mayor-vol-45-no-25/; Joseph, "Six to the fore."

20. Peter Byrne, "Kamala's Karma," *San Francisco Weekly*, September 24, 2003, http://www.sfweekly.com/news/kamalas-karma/.

21. Ibid.; William Carlsen, "Lawmakers put cronies in plum jobs / Big pay, few hours on 3 state panels," *San Francisco Chronicle*, March 10, 2002, https:// www.sfgate.com/politics/article/Lawmakers-put-cronies-in-plum-jobs-Big -pay-few-2864693.php.

22. Ann E. Marimow, "Davis' friends land on their feet; board salaries getting scrutiny," *San Jose Mercury News*, November 2, 2003; Carlsen, "Lawmakers put cronies in plum jobs"; Patrick Hoge, "D.A. Race: Hallinan, Harris, make runoff—Fazio loses for third time to S.F. incumbent," *San Francisco Chronicle*, November 5, 2003; David Siders, " 'Ruthless': How Kamala Harris Won Her First Race," Politico, January 24, 2019, https://www.politico.com/magazine /story/2019/01/24/kamala-harris-2020-history-224126.

23. Byrne, "Kamala's Karma."

24. Alana Goodman, "Kamala Harris Launched Political Career with $120K 'Patronage' Job from Boyfriend Willie Brown," *Washington Examiner*, June 1, 2019, https://www.washingtonexaminer.com/politics/kamala-harris -launched-political-career-with-120k-patronage-job-from-boyfriend-willie -brown.

25. Richardson, *Willie Brown*, pp. 389–90, 405.

26. Ibid., p. 390.

27. Ibid., p. 404.

28. "Hollywood's Epidemic of Mid-Life," *Ebony*, September 2001.

29. Lance Williams and Chuck Finnie, "Willie Brown, Inc.: How SF's mayor built a city based on 'juice' in politics," *San Francisco Chronicle*, April 29, 2001.

30. "Kamala Harris Biography," Biography.com, n.d., https://www.biography .com/political-figure/kamala-harris.

31. Siders, " 'Ruthless': How Kamala Harris Won Her First Race."

32. Patrick Hoge, "Harris Playing Catch-up in 3-Way Race to Be D.A. / Spend- ing Violation, Low Name Recognition Dog Ex-Hallinan Ally," *San Francisco Chronicle*, October 9, 2003, https://www.sfgate.com/politics/article/Harris -playing-catch-up-in-3-way-race-to-be-D-A-2583420.php.

33. Phillip Matier and Andrew Ross, "Wine, Dungeness Crab, Rice-a-Roni on Line in Bicoastal Bets," *SF Gate*, October 4, 2000.

34. Phillip Matier and Andrew Ross, "Feinstein 1, Mayors Brown 0 on South- ern Crossing Proposal," *San Francisco Chronicle*, January 21, 2000; Lance Williams, "D.A. dismisses ethics charges; Judge had earlier ruled in favor of ex-planning commissioner," *San Francisco Chronicle*, September 3, 2004; Lance Williams and Chuck Finnie, "Lawyer says S.F. official tried to force hiring of consultant," *San Francisco Chronicle*, November 18, 2002 (all Nexis).

35. Rachel Gordon, "The Mayor's Legacy: Willie Brown / 'Da Mayor' Soared

During Tenure That Rivals City's Most Notable, but Some Critical Goals Not Met," *San Francisco Chronicle*, January 4, 2004, https://www.sfgate.com /politics/article/THE-MAYOR-S-LEGACY-WILLIE-BROWN-Da-Mayor -2832960.php; Siders, " 'Ruthless': How Kamala Harris Won Her First Race"; Brittany Martin, "Kamala Harris Dated Willie Brown Decades Ago and Her Critics Claim It Matters," *Los Angeles Magazine*, January 29, 2019, https://www.lamag.com/citythinkblog/willie-brown-kamala-harris/.

36. Harris, "In Search of Elusive Justice."

37. Ibid.; "Rebecca Prozan," LinkedIn profile, accessed July 2, 2019, https:// www.linkedin.com/in/rebeccaprozan/; Ken Ludden, *A San Francisco Journalist* (Morrisville, NC: Lulu Press, 2011), p. 100.

38. Byrne, "Kamala's Karma."

39. Ibid.

40. Ibid.

41. Ibid.

42. Kevin West, "In her court: Being San Francisco D.A. has put Kamala Harris in the public eye," *W Magazine*, November 1, 2004.

43. Demian Bulwa, "Harris denies being indebted to donors; Political machine made challenger, D.A. Hallinan says," *San Francisco Chronicle*, November 25, 2003.

44. Patrick Hoge, "D.A. Files campaign complaint; Hallinan says opponent broke spending law," *San Francisco Chronicle*, October 1, 2003; Hoge, "Harris Playing Catch-up in 3-Way Race to Be D.A. / Spending Violation, Low Name Recognition Dog Ex-Hallinan Ally"; Demian Bulwa and John Wildermuth, "No-holds-barred debate in D.A. race," *San Francisco Chronicle*, December 5, 2003.

45. Bulwa and Wildermuth, "No-holds-barred debate in D.A. race."

46. Rachel Gordon, "D.A. candidate to pay up to $34,000 for 'unintentional' mistake," *San Francisco Chronicle*, October 7, 2003; Patrick Hoge, "Upstart in D.A. race: Harris poses threat to Hallinan," *San Francisco Chronicle*, November 6, 2003.

47. Bulwa and Wildermuth, "No-holds-barred debate in D.A. race."

48. John Roemer, "Harris Takes Money from Hotel Owners," *Daily Journal*, November 11, 2003.

49. George Joseph, "Kamala Harris picks up more support," *India Abroad*, December 5, 2003.

50. Ilene Lelchuk, "Campaign probe names S.F. official; Workers testify he told them to help Newsom," *San Francisco Chronicle*, October 22, 2004.

51. Lance Williams and Chuck Finnie, "Mayor's patronage army; Brown fattens payroll with loyalists, colleagues, friends," *San Francisco Chronicle*, April 30, 2001.

52. Anastasia Hendrix, "City Workers: We Were Told to Vote, Work for Newsom / S.F. City Attorney Probes Campaign Charge by 9 Street Clean-

ers," *San Francisco Chronicle*, January 15, 2004, https://www.sfgate.com/poli
tics/article/City-workers-We-were-told-to-vote-work-for-2812182.php.

53. Lelchuk, "Campaign probe names S.F. official; Workers testify he told them
    to help Newsom."

54. Larry Bush, "Lee vs. Nuru: Not Happening!" CitiReport, March 25, 2012,
    http://www.citireport.com/2012/03/lee-vs-nuru-not-happening/.

55. Patrick Hoge, "D.A. Race: Hallinan, Harris Make Runoff—Fazio Loses for
    Third Time to S.F. Incumbent," *San Francisco Chronicle*, November 5, 2003,
    https://www.sfgate.com/news/article/D-A-race-Hallinan-Harris-make
    -runoff-Fazio-2579061.php.

56. Leah Garchik, "Daily Datebook," *San Francisco Chronicle,* January 8, 2004;
    George Joseph, "Kamala Harris sworn in, vows to get smart on crime," *India
    Abroad,* January 16 2004.

57. Anastasia Hendrix, "Mayor says he wants full probe of allegations by city
    workers," *San Francisco Chronicle,* January 16, 2004; Bush, "Lee vs. Nuru: Not
    Happening!"; Hendrix, "City Workers: We Were Told to Vote, Work for
    Newsom."

58. Alanna Vaglanos, "Kamala Harris on Alex Acosta: We Don't Need Leaders
    Who Protect Predators," Huffington Post, July 9, 2019, https://www.huff
    post.com/entry/kamala-harris-alex-acosta-jeffrey-epstein-plea-deal_n_5d
    24b415e4b0583e4827eede; Shira Tarlo, "Kamala Harris Criticized Law
    Firm Behind Epstein's Plea Deal—Then Accepted Money From It: Re-
    port," Salon, July 16, 2019, https://www.salon.com/2019/07/16/kamala
    -harris-criticized-law-firm-behind-epsteins-plea-deal-then-accepted
    -money-from-it-report/.

59. Jaxon Van Derbeken, "Accused Abusers Freed in Bay Area / 16, Including
    Ex-Priests, Released After Court Ruling," *SF Gate*, June 28, 2003, https://
    www.sfgate.com/bayarea/article/Accused-abusers-freed-in-Bay-Area-16
    -including-2577085.php; "Archdiocese Sues Former Monsignor," Associated
    Press, September 16, 1999, https://www.apnews.com/101dbb097fe09eca4f24
    9a300891edb8.

60. Mark Clayton, "What Vatican Sex Abuse Summit May Achieve," *Christian
    Science Monitor,* April 22, 2002.

61. Matt Smith, "A Secrecy Fetish," *San Francisco Chronicle* (archive), June 2,
    2010, https://archives.sfweekly.com/sanfrancisco/a-secrecy-fetish/Content
    ?oid=2177326; Elizabeth Fernandez, "Victims' Group Irate over Prosecu-
    tors' Deal with Catholic Church," *San Francisco Chronicle*, September 9, 2002,
    https://www.sfgate.com/news/article/Victims-groups-irate-over-prosecutors
    -deal-with-2799997.php; Ron Russell, "Zipped Up," *San Francisco Chronicle*
    (archive), January 19, 2005, https://archives.sfweekly.com/sanfrancisco
    /zipped-up/Content?oid=2154654; Ron Russell, "See No Evil," *San Fran-
    cisco Chronicle* (archive), May 21, 2003, https://archives.sfweekly.com/sanfran
    cisco/see-no-evil/Content?oid=2148092.

62. Ron Russell, "Blind Eye Unto the Holy See," *San Francisco Weekly*, July 13, 2005, http://www.sfweekly.com/news/blind-eye-unto-the-holy-see/.

63. Russell, "Zipped Up"; Fernandez, "Victims' Group Irate over Prosecutors' Deal with Catholic Church"; Lee Fang, "As San Francisco District Attorney, Kamala Harris's Office Stopped Cooperating with Victims of Catholic Church and Child Abuse," *Intercept*, June 9, 2019, https://theintercept.com/2019/06/09/kamala-harris-san-francisco-catholic-church-child-abuse/.

64. Russell, "Zipped Up."

65. Fang, "As San Francisco District Attorney, Kamala Harris's Office Stopped Cooperating."

66. Russell, "Zipped Up."

67. St. Ignatius College Preparatory, Facebook post, September 10, 2018, https://www.facebook.com/St.IgnatiusCollegePreparatory/posts/california-governor-jerry-brown-55-signs-a-landmark-energy-and-environmental-bil/10160801814360453/; "The Gettys Host St. Ignatius Chairmen," *San Francisco Magazine*, n.d., photograph, https://www.modernluxury.com/san-francisco/scene/the-gettys-host-st-ignatius-chairmen/img281623; "In Memoriam: Judge William A. Newsom III '51," St. Ignatius College Preparatory, December 12, 2018, https://www.siprep.org/about-us/si-in-the-news/in-memoriam/in-memoriam-story/~board/in-memoriam/post/judge-william-a-newsom-iii-51.

68. "List of Jesuits from Jesuits West Province with Credible Claims of Sexual Abuse of a Minor or Vulnerable Adult," Jesuits West, December 7, 2018, https://jesuitswest.org/assets/publications/file/JW_List_1207_English.pdf; "Database of Publicly Accused Priests in the United States," Bishop Accountability, n.d., http://jesuitswest.org/assets/publications/file/JW_List_1207_English.pdf; https://bishop-accountability.org/priestdb/PreistDBbylastName-A.html.

69. "Catholics & Molestation Victims Want Lawyer to Quit National Post," Survivors Network of those Abused by Priests, March 4, 2005, press release, http://www.snapnetwork.org/snap_press_releases/2005_press_releases/advisory_march4_lawyer.htm.

70. Michael R. Merz, "A History of the National Review Board," United States Conference of Catholic Bishops, April 2011, p. 30, http://www.usccb.org/issues-and-action/child-and-youth-protection/upload/NRB-History-5-17-2011.pdf.

71. Dennis Opatmy, "Harris Pledges to Repair Relationship with SFPD," *Daily Journal,* December 24, 2003; Campaign Finance Disclosure, https://sfethics.org .

72. Harriet Chiang, "Veteran Alameda Prosecutor to Be Harris' Deputy / He Has Prevailed in Major Drug Cases," *San Francisco Chronicle*, December 23, 2003, https://www.sfgate.com/politics/article/Veteran-Alameda-prosecutor-to-be-Harris-deputy-2508282.php; Pam Smith, "Harris Reaches Across Bay

to Fill Top Slot," *Recorder*, December 23, 2003, https://www.achlaw.com /articles/recorder_11–23–2003.pdf; Campaign Finance Disclosure, https:// sfethics.org; Partner Cristina Arguedas was the defense attorney for Father Milton T. Walsh, a priest who was arrested and charged by D. A. Hallinan in 2002 for sexual abuse, and then removed from active ministry. Charges were dropped in 2003 due to the change in the statute of limitations law. Walsh was formerly an advisor to Bishop John Quinn, who first introduced Walsh to the boy who later claimed he was victimized.

73. Campaign Finance Disclosure, https://sfethics.org.

74. Kamala Harris, *Smart on Crime: A Career Prosecutor's Plan to Make Us Safer* (San Francisco: Chronicle Books, 2010), p. 204; Jim Herron Zamora, "Renne to Lead Newsom Team," *San Francisco Chronicle*, December 16, 2003, https:// www.sfgate.com/politics/article/Renne-to-lead-Newsom-team-2509028 .php; Pat Lynch, "This DA Makes a Difference for Women," Womensradio .com, on Internet Archive, accessed June 26, 2019, https://web.archive.org /web/20101219095441/http://www.womensradio.com/articles/This-DA -Makes-a-Difference-for-Women/559.html (the screenshot of the site was captured on December 19, 2010).

75. "Commission Members," City & County of San Francisco Ethics Commission, n.d., https://sfethics.org/ethics/2009/05/commission-members.html; "Joseph Russoniello," LinkedIn profile, accessed September 10, 2019, https:// www.linkedin.com/in/joseph-russoniello-a8652b7/.

76. Russell, "Zipped Up."

77. Fang, "As San Francisco District Attorney, Kamala Harris's Office Stopped Cooperating."

78. Smith, "A Secrecy Fetish."

79. John Roemer, "Victim Lashes Out at Harris," *Daily Journal*, December 6, 2003.

80. Homepage, Survivors Network of Those Abused by Priests, accessed July 3, 2019, http://www.snapnetwork.org/; Smith, "A Secrecy Fetish."

81. Smith, "A Secrecy Fetish."

82. Ibid.

83. Ibid.

84. Russell, "Zipped Up."

85. Fernandez, "Victims' Group Irate over Prosecutors' Deal with Catholic Church"; Don Lattin, "Levada Takes Heat over Abuse Injury / Panel Member Resigns, Says Church Suppressed Results," *San Francisco Chronicle*, November 12, 2004, https://www.sfgate.com/news/article/Levada-takes -heat-over-abuse-inquiry-Panel-2673017.php.

86. Larry B. Stammer, Richard Winton, and Jean Guccione, "Mahony: Protecting Minors 'Job 1,'" *Los Angeles Times*, February 18, 2004, https://www .latimes.com/archives/la-xpm-2004-feb-18-me-priest18-story.html; "Bishop Accountability," February 17, 2004, accessed July 18, 2019, http://www

.bishop-accountability.org/usccb/natureandscope/dioceses/losangelesca.
htm; "Report to the People of God: Clergy Sexual Abuse Archdiocese of Los
Angeles 1930–2003," Archdiocese of Los Angeles, February 17, 2004, http://
www.bishop-accountability.org/usccb/natureandscope/dioceses/reports/los
angelesca-rpt.pdf.

87. Maria Dinzeo, "Priest Accused of Abusing Children for Decades," Court
housenews.com, October 1, 2012, https://www.courthousenews.com/Priest
-Accused-of-Abusing-Children-for-Decades/.

88. "Sunshine Ordinance Task Force: Complaint Committee," City & County
of San Francisco, March 8, 2011, https://sfgov.org/sunshine/ftp/meeting
archive/sunshine_complaint_committee/Modules/030811item2-document
id=D37842.pdf.

89. Eliza Relman, "Kamala Harris Is Running for President in 2020. Here's
Everything We Know About the Candidate and How She Stacks Up Against
the Competition," Business Insider, accessed July 4, 2019, https://www
.businessinsider.com/who-is-kamala-harris-bio-age-family-key-positions
-2019-3; Gustavo Arellano, "Column: California Needs to Take Another
Look at Its Catholic Church Sexual Abuse Cases," Los Angeles Times, September
12, 2018, https://www.latimes.com/opinion/op-ed/la-oe-arellano
-catholic-church-sex-abuse-california-20180912-story.html.

90. "Bishop Accountability," BishopAccountability.org, n.d., http://bishop
-accountability.org/member/ (search for "charged" or "convicted" for major
cities' dioceses).

91. Philip Matier and Andrew Ross, "Cops, D.A. tangle over strip club raids,"
San Francisco Chronicle, July 12, 2004, https://www.sfgate.com/bayarea/mati
er-ross/article/Cops-D-A-tangle-over-strip-club-raids-3324156.php.

92. Ibid.

93. Ibid.

94. Phillip Matier and Andrew Ross, "Strip club doors drawing lots of attention
in D.A. probe," San Francisco Chronicle, July 19, 2004, https://www.sfgate
.com/bayarea/matier-ross/article/Strip-club-doors-drawing-lots-of-atten
tion-in-3324137.php.

95. John King, "Nightclub Operator Sam Conti Dies," San Francisco Chronicle,
November 11, 2009, https://www.sfgate.com/bayarea/article/Nightclub
-operator-Sam-Conti-dies-3210907.php; Sarah Phelan, "The Mitchell Sister," Guardian (archive), May 19–25, 2010, http://sfbgarchive.48hills.org
/sfbgarchive/2010/05/18/mitchell-sister/; Lee Romney, "In S.F., Weighing
Strippers' Rights," Los Angeles Times, December 19, 2004, https://www
.latimes.com/archives/la-xpm-2004-dec-19-me-stripper19-story.html; Katie
Dowd, "Police Investigating Four SF Strip Clubs for Allegedly Stealing
Thousands from Patrons," San Francisco Chronicle, February 8, 2017, https://
www.sfgate.com/bayarea/article/Police-investigating-four-SF-strip-clubs
-credit-10917966.php#photo-12337271; Jaxon Van Derbeken, Michael Bott,

and Jeremy Carroll, "San Francisco Strip Club Patrons Allege Rip-Off," *NBC Bay Area*, February 7, 2017, https://www.nbcbayarea.com/news/local /SF-Strip-Club-Patrons—413081593.html; Bruce Bellingham, "Belling ham by the Bay," Northside San Francisco, December 2009, http://www .northsidesf.com/dec09/op_bellinghambythebay.html; David Steinberg, "Lap Victory," *SF Weekly*, September 8, 2004, http://www.sfweekly.com/news /lap-victory/; Phil Bronstein, "Is It Porn—Or Just an Odd Couple Spat?" *San Francisco Chronicle* (blog), August 17, 2009, https://blog.sfgate.com/bron stein/2009/08/17/is-it-porn-or-just-an-odd-couples-spat/.

96. Byrne, "Kamala's Karma"; Hoge, "Harris Playing Catch-up in 3-Way Race to Be D.A. / Spending Violation, Low Name Recognition Dog Ex-Hallinan Ally."

97. Williams, "D.A. dismisses ethics charges."

98. Chuck Finnie and Lance Williams, "Warrant for Ex-S.F. Planning Chief / He's Charged with Local and State Conflict-of-Interest Violations," *San Francisco Chronicle*, November 1, 2002, https://www.sfgate.com/news/article /Warrant-for-ex-S-F-planning-chief-He-s-charged-2776157.php.

99. Ibid.

100. Williams, "D.A. dismisses ethics charges."

101. Jaxon Van Derbeken, "Empire Built on Sand: Businessman allegedly poured inferior concrete into key projects," *San Francisco Chronicle,* July 6, 2006, https://www.sfgate.com/news/article/EMPIRE-BUILT-ON-SAND-Busi nessman-allegedly-2516190.php.

102. Ibid.

103. Ibid.; Jaxon Van Derbeken, "Big concrete case crumbles," *San Francisco Chronicle,* June 1, 2008.

104. Ibid.

105. Ibid.

106. Ibid.

107. Michael Finnegan, "State candidate's job program trained illegal immigrants; San Francisco's D.A., an attorney general hopeful, kept felons out of prison to learn work they were ineligible for," *Los Angeles Times,* June 22, 2009; Francie Diep, "A Pacific Standard Guide to Kamala Harris' Record on Criminal Justice Reform," Pacific Standard, January 22, 2019, https://psmag.com /news/kamala-harris-record-on-criminal-justice-reform.

108. Kamala Harris, Letter to the Editor: "Does this job program work?," *Los Angeles Times,* June 26, 2009; Finnegan, "State candidate's job program trained illegal immigrants; San Francisco's D.A., an attorney general hopeful, kept felons out of prison to learn work they were ineligible for."

109. Finnegan, "State candidate's job program trained illegal immigrants; San Francisco's D.A., an attorney general hopeful, kept felons out of prison to learn work they were ineligible for"; Jaxon Van Derbeken, "D.A.'s office let illegal immigrants go," *SF Gate,* June 23, 2009, https://www.sfgate.com /bayarea/article/D-A-s-office-let-illegal-immigrants-go-3226767.php.

110. Ibid.

111. Ibid.

112. Ibid.

113. Maeve Reston, "Kamala Harris Rips Up the Script," CNN, April 2017, https://edition.cnn.com/interactive/2017/politics/state/kamala-harris-rips-up-the-script/; "Kamala Harris for Attorney General," *Los Angeles Sentinel*, May 27, 2010, https://lasentinel.net/kamala-harris-for-attorney-general.html; Robert Gammon, "Where's Kamala Harris?" East Bay Express, July 18, 2012, https://www.eastbayexpress.com/oakland/wheres-kamala-harris/Content?oid=3289649.

114. McKenzie Jean-Philippe, "8 Things to Know About Senator Kamala Harris' Husband, Douglas Emhoff," *Oprah*, July 9, 2019, https://www.oprahmag.com/entertainment/a25905360/kamala-harris-husband-douglas-emhoff/; Dana Goodyear, "Kamala Harris Makes Her Case," *New Yorker,* July 22, 2019, https://www.newyorker.com/magazine/2019/07/22/kamala-harris-makes-her-case.

115. "Venable LLP," n.d., https://www.venable.com/files/Event/af34eab5-a39d-4fc3-b98d-318db6222890/Presentation/EventAttachment/74a6fe00-47f6-4472-a961-45a0d687837a/Post_Election_Review.pdf; "Douglas C. Emhoff," DLA Piper, accessed September 10, 2018, https://www.dlapiper.com/en/us/people/e/emhoff-douglas-c/?tab=experience.

116. Mitchell Evall, James E. Nelson, and James L. Shea, "Venable Names Douglas C. Emhoff Managing Director, West Coast and Mitchell Evall Partner-in-Charge of Its Los Angeles Office," Venable LLP, August 13, 2015, https://www.venable.com/about/news/2015/08/venable-names-douglas-c-emhoff-managing-director-w; "Venable Opens California Office with Lawyers from Two Los Angeles Firms," PR Newswire US, July 26, 2006.

117. Andrew Khouri, "14 States Ask Congress to Investigate the Herbal Supplement Industry," *Los Angeles Times*, April 2, 2015, https://www.latimes.com/business/la-fi-state-attorneys-herbal-investigation-20150402-story.html.

118. Julia La Roche, "Dietary-Supplement Stocks Are Getting Crushed," Business Insider, November 17, 2015, https://www.businessinsider.com/doj-to-take-action-against-dietary-supplement-company-2015-11.

119. Diane Bartz, "Herbalife Says FTC Opens Inquiry Long Sought by Ackman," Reuters, March 12, 2014, https://www.reuters.com/article/us-herbalife-ftc/herbalife-says-ftc-opens-inquiry-long-sought-by-ackman-idUSBREA2B1KS20140313.

120. "Consumer Watchdog Opposes California Sen. Hueso's Bill That Would Limit Criticism of Shady Business Practices; Shadow Sponsored by Herbalife," PR Newswire, June 23, 2016, https://www.prnewswire.com/news-releases/consumer-watchdog-opposes-california-sen-huesos-bill-that-would-limit-criticism-of-shady-business-practices-shadow-sponsored-by-herbalife-300289474.html.

121. "Herbalife Refunds," Federal Trade Commission, May 2019, https://www
.ftc.gov/enforcement/cases-proceedings/refunds/herbalife-refunds.

122. Khouri, "14 States Ask Congress to Investigate the Herbal Supplement Industry."

123. "Venable LLP," Law 360, accessed September 11, 2019, https://www.law360
.com/firms/venable-llp/clients.

124. Jessica Corso, "Walgreen Escapes False Ad Suit Over Homeopathic Ear
Meds," Law360.com, January 8, 2015, https://www.law360.com/articles
/609258/walgreen-escapes-false-ad-suit-over-homeopathic-ear-meds.

125. Re: Response to Request for Application to Serve as Independent Compliance Auditor for Herbalife, August 29, 2016, Venable correspondence to
Federal Trade Commission, Bureau of Consumer Protection, pp. 20, 21.

126. Matthew Handley, "Herbalife and the 1986 State of California Final Judgment," Seeking Alpha, December 3, 2014, https://seekingalpha.com/article
/2728325-herbalife-and-the-1986-state-of-california-final-judgment.

127. Alexander Nazaryan, "Why Did Kamala Harris Let Herbalife Off the
Hook?," Yahoo, March 18, 2019, https://news.yahoo.com/kamala-harris
-herbalife-accused-of-exploiting-latinos-090000896.html.

128. "Luncheon for Fundraiser for Kamala Harris for Senate," Political Party
Time, February 26, 2015, http://politicalpartytime.org/party/38907/;
"Rep. Bishop, Hill Veterans Launch Lobby Shop—Groups Lobby on Ex-Im,
RFS—Podesta Hosts Fundraiser," Politico, February 25, 2015, https://www
.politico.com/tipsheets/politico-influence/2015/02/rep-bishop-hill-vet
erans-launch-lobby-shop-groups-lobby-on-ex-im-rfs-podesta-hosts
-fundraiser-212543; Opensecrets.org, "Lobbyists Representing Herbalife
International, 2013," n.d., https://www.opensecrets.org/lobby/clientlbs
.php?id=D000022026&year=2013.

129. Nazaryan, "Why Did Kamala Harris Let Herbalife Off the Hook?"

130. Evall, Nelson, and Shea, "Venable Names Douglas C. Emhoff Managing Director, West Coast and Mitchell Evall Partner-in-Charge of Its Los Angeles
Office."

131. Christopher Cadelago, "Gov. Jerry Brown Endorses Kamala Harris' U.S.
Senate Bid," Sacramento Bee, May 23, 2016, https://www.sacbee.com/news
/politics-government/capitol-alert/article79332672.html.

132. Liza Tucker, "Brown's Dirty Hands," ConsumerWatchdog.org, August 2016,
https://www.consumerwatchdog.org/sites/default/files/2017–09/Browns
DirtyHands.pdf; Mihir Zaveri, "Corroded Well Lining Caused Aliso Canyon
Gas Leak That Displaced Thousands, Report Says," New York Times, May 17,
2019, https://www.nytimes.com/2019/05/17/business/porter-ranch-gas
-leak.html.

133. John Wildermuth, "In Senate Debate, Kamala Harris on the Hot Seat," San
Francisco Chronicle, May 11, 2016, https://www.sfgate.com/politics/article
/In-senate-debate-Kamala-Harris-on-the-hot-seat-7459059.php.

134. Susan Shelley, "Daughters of Charity Deal Carries Warning for the Future of Health Care," *Los Angeles Daily News,* December 8, 2015.

135. Ibid.

136. *Prime Healthcare Services Inc. and Prime Healthcare Foundation Inc. v. Kamala Harris,* Complaint, United States District Court Central District of California, Eastern Division, pp. 3–4, 29.

137. Ibid., pp. 3–4, 34, 36.

138. Ibid., pp. 9, 19.

139. Ibid., pp. 6–7.

140. Ibid., pp. 9, 36.

141. Ibid., p. 7.

142. Ibid., pp. 6–7.

143. Ibid,, pp. 7–8.

144. Shelley, "Daughters of Charity Deal Carries Warnings for the Future of Health Care."

145. *Prime Healthcare Services Inc. and Prime Healthcare Foundation Inc. v. Kamala Harris,* Complaint, United States District Court Central District of California, Eastern Division, pp. 8–9.

146. Ibid., p. 24.

147. Ibid., pp. 23–24, 27.

148. Ibid., p. 29.

149. Ibid., pp. 30–31.

150. Anthony Brino, "Daughters of Charity Gets $250 Million Lifeline from BlueMountain Capital Management," *Healthcare Finance,* July 17, 2015, https://www.healthcarefinancenews.com/news/daughters-charity-finds -savior-hedge-fund.

151. "Blue Mountain Freezes Its Largest Hedge Fund," *New York Times,* November 3, 2008, https://dealbook.nytimes.com/2008/11/03/blue-mountain -capital-freezes-its-largest-hedge-fund/.

152. *Prime Healthcare Services Inc. and Prime Healthcare Foundation Inc. v. Kamala Harris,* Complaint, United States District Court Central District of California, Eastern Division, pp. 46–49.

153. Banks Albachn, "Hospital Chain Deal Gets Approval, with Conditions," *Daily Journal,* December 8, 2015.

154. Federal Election Commission (FEC) data: see FEC.gov.

CHAPTER 3: JOE BIDEN

1. "Timeline of Biden's life and career," Associated Press, August 23, 2008, https://web.archive.org/web/20080925021142/http://www.sfgate .com/cgi-bin/article.cgi?f=%2Fn%2Fa%2F2008%2F08%2F22%2Fpolitics %2Fp222636D16.DTL (captured September 25, 2008).

NOTES

2. Phil Helsel, "Beau Biden, Son of Vice President Joe Biden, Dies After Battle with Brain Cancer," NBC News, May 30, 2015, https://www.nbcnews.com /news/us-news/vice-president-joe-bidens-son-beau-dies-n367171.

3. Joe Biden, *Promises to Keep: On Life and Politics* (New York: Random House, 2007), p. xix.

4. Alfred P. Doblin, "Joe Biden will be missed more than he knows," *North Jersey Record*, January 16, 2017, https://www.northjersey.com/story/opinion /columnists/alfred-doblin/2017/01/16/doblin-joe-biden-missed-more-than -he-knows/96544882/.

5. Salena Zito, "Joe Biden, Gritty Guy," *Pittsburgh Tribune-Review,* November 30, 2008, https://archive.triblive.com/news/joe-biden-gritty-guy/.

6. Marc Caputo and Ben Schreckinger, "Biden Pledges 'Absolute Wall' to Separate Relatives' Business Dealings," Politico, August 28, 2019, https://www .politico.com/story/2019/08/28/biden-brother-business-2020–1476815.

7. Doblin, "Joe Biden Will Be Missed More Than He Knows."

8. Sean Higgins, "Joe Biden: 'Visionary-in-Chief,' " *Washington Examiner,* June 5, 2014, https://www.washingtonexaminer.com/joe-biden-visionary -in-chief.

9. "Timeline of Biden's Life and Career."

10. Jules Witcover, *Joe Biden: A Life of Trial and Redemption* (New York: William Morrow, 2010), p. 58.

11. "James B. Biden Joins Hill International Subsidiary As Executive Vice President," Hill International, November 23, 2010, http://www.globenewswire .com/news-release/2010/11/23/434923/207583/en/James-B-Biden -Joins-Hill-International-Subsidiary-as-Executive-Vice-President.html.

12. Witcover, *Joe Biden,* p. 58; Ashley Parker, "Biden Relies on His Closest Adviser, His Sister," *New York Times,* October 1, 2008, https://www.nytimes .com/2008/10/02/us/politics/02valerie.html.

13. Curtis Wilkie, *The Fall of the House of Zeus: The Rise and Ruin of America's Most Powerful Trial Lawyer* (New York: Crown, 2010), p. 195.

14. Ryan D'Agostino, "Things My Father Taught Me: An Interview with Joe and Hunter Biden," *Popular Mechanics,* May 18, 2016, https://www.popular mechanics.com/home/a20655/things-my-father-taught-me/.

15. Katelyn Caralle, "Joe Biden Says He Was Like the 'Token Black' When He First Ran for Senate," *Washington Examiner,* March 27, 2019, https://www .washingtonexaminer.com/politics/joe-biden-says-he-was-like-the-token -black-in-his-youthful-run-for-senate-in-1972.

16. Ibid.

17. Ibid.

18. "James B. Biden Joins Hill International Subsidiary As Executive Vice President."

19. "Boggs, James Caleb," Biographical Directory of the United States Congress,

n.d., http://bioguide.congress.gov/scripts/biodisplay.pl?index=b000593; Biden, *Promises to Keep,* pp. 58, 74.

20. Witcover, *Joe Biden,* pp. 97–99.

21. Charlie Spiering, "Joe Biden Reveals He Rode in Amtrak Locomotive Cab as Senator," *Washington Examiner,* February 25, 2014, https://www.washingtonexaminer.com/joe-biden-reveals-he-rode-in-amtrak-locomotive-cab-as-senator.

22. News Journal, *Joe's Journey,* p. 8.

23. Witcover, *Joe Biden,* p. 123.

24. Ibid., p. 130.

25. Ibid., pp. 210–11.

26. Biden, *Promises to Keep,* p. 117.

27. News Journal, *Joe's Journey,* p. 54.

28. John A. Tures, "Is Joe Biden Actually Moderate or Is He More Progressive Than We Think?," *Observer,* May 2, 2019, https://observer.com/2019/05/joe-biden-moderate-progressive-voting-record/.

29. Emily Larsen, " 'Middle-class Joe' Cozied Up to Credit Card Companies and Made Filing for Bankruptcy Harder," *Washington Examiner,* April 18, 2019, https://www.washingtonexaminer.com/news/middle-class-joe-cozied-up-to-credit-card-companies-and-made-filing-for-bankruptcy-harder.

30. Walker Bragman, "The Case Against Joe Biden," Paste, January 10, 2018, https://www.pastemagazine.com/articles/2018/01/the-case-against-joe-biden.html.

31. Christopher Drew and Mike McIntire, "Obama Aides Defend Bank's Pay to Biden Son," *New York Times,* August 24, 2008, https://www.nytimes.com/2008/08/25/us/politics/25biden.html.

32. Chuck Neubauer and Tom Hamburger, "Biden Family Ties Pose Questions," *Los Angeles Times,* August 28, 2008, https://www.latimes.com/archives/la-xpm-2008-aug-28-na-biden28-story.html.

33. Witcover, *Joe Biden,* p. 418.

34. Lindsay Renick Mayer, "Biden's Son a Registered Lobbyist," Opensecrets .org, August 25, 2008, https://www.opensecrets.org/news/2008/08/bidens-son-a-registered-lobbyi/.

35. "Biden Hires Lobbyist to Advise Senate Run," ABC News, on Internet Archive, n.d., http://web.archive.org/web/20150927092311/http://abcnews.go.com/Politics/story?id=5819589&page=1 (captured September 27, 2015).

36. Joseph Menn, *Fatal System Error: The Hunt for the New Crime Lords Who Are Bringing Down the Internet* (New York: PublicAffairs, 2010), pp. 58, 93–94; Christopher Drew, "Campaign Says Biden Son Dropped Lobbying Clients," *New York Times,* September 13, 2008, https://www.nytimes.com/2008/09/13/us/politics/13resign.html.

37. "About Joe Slade White," Joe Slade White & Company, accessed August 19, 2019, http://joesladewhite.com/teamjsw/.

38. FEC data.

39. "Vice President Joe Biden," Joe Slade White & Company, accessed May 17, 2019, http://joesladewhite.com/project/joe-biden/.

40. "Business Extent of Disclosure Index," World Bank, n.d., https://data.world bank.org/indicator/IC.BUS.DISC.XQ.

41. Peter Schweizer, *Secret Empires: How the American Political Class Hides Corruption and Enriches Family and Friends* (New York: HarperCollins, 2018), pp. 22–26; "Rosemont Seneca Partners, LLC," OpenCorporates, accessed July 1, 2019, OpenCorporates, https://opencorporates.com/companies/us_de/4703140.

42. Steve Clemons, "The Geopolitical Therapist," *Atlantic,* August 26, 2016, https://www.theatlantic.com/international/archive/2016/08/joe-biden -interview/497633/.

43. Schweizer, *Secret Empires*, pp. 30–33.

44. Tom Llamas, Lucien Bruggeman, and Matthew Mosk, "Biden Sidesteps Questions About His Son's Foreign Business Dealings but Promises Ethics Pledge," ABC, June 20, 2019, https://abcnews.go.com/Politics/biden-side steps-questions-sons-foreign-business-dealings-promises/story?id=63820806.

45. Adam Entous, "Will Hunter Biden Jeopardize His Father's Campaign?," *New Yorker,* July 1, 2019, https://www.newyorker.com/magazine/2019/07/08 /will-hunter-biden-jeopardize-his-fathers-campaign.

46. Schweizer, *Secret Empires*, pp. 33, 45.

47. "Team," BHR Equity Investment Fund Management Co., Ltd., archived, http://webcache.googleusercontent.com/search?q=cache:jlyBL3xgrhcJ:www .bhrpe.com/list.php?catid%3D8%26page%3D1&hl=en&gl=us&strip=1&vw src=0 (captured October 5, 2019).

48. Ibid., pp. 28, 34.

49. Ibid., p. 29.

50. Kimberly Kindy and Joe Stephens, "Biden's Son, Brother Named in Two Suits," *Washington Post*, August 24, 2008, http://www.washingtonpost.com /wp-dyn/content/article/2008/08/23/AR2008082302200.html.

51. Lucien Bruggeman and Matthew Mosk, "Hunter Biden Tackles Cocaine Use, Diamonds and Alleged Business Conflicts in Candid Magazine Inter-view," ABC News, July 1, 2019, https://abcnews.go.com/Politics/hunter -biden-tackles-cocaine-diamonds-alleged-business-conflicts/story?id=640 64060.

52. Maggie Haberman, Annie Karni, Kenneth P. Vogel, and Katie Benner, "Trump's Demands for Investigations of Opponents Draw Intensifying Criti-cism," *New York Times*, May 20, 2019, https://www.nytimes .com/2019/05/20/us/politics/trump-hunter-biden-china.html.

53. Schweizer, *Secret Empires,* pp. 46–50, 70.

54. Lee Fang, "Chinese Fund Backed by Hunter Biden Invested in Technology

Used to Surveil Muslims," Intercept, May 3, 2019, https://theintercept.com /2019/05/03/biden-son-china-business/.

55. Schweizer, p. 38; "Board of Directors," Burisma, on archive.is, n.d., http:// archive.is/Ia4q4 (captured May 13, 2014); Rosemont Realty, LLC, "Gemini Investments and Rosemont Realty Form Joint Venture," PR Newswire, August 24, 2015, https://www.prnewswire.com/news-releases/gemini -investments-and-rosemont-realty-form-joint-venture-300132117.html.

56. Bloomberg page, accessed July 22, 2019, https://www.bloomberg.com/re search/stocks/private/person.asp?personId=31216428&privcapId=145391568.

57. Schweizer, Secret Empires, p. 38.

58. Ibid.; "Gemini Investments (Holdings) Limited," gemini.bmgdemo.com, accessed August 21, 2019, p. 16, http://gemini.bmgdemo.com/function/do clist/LTN201412311037_C.pdf p 25.

59. United States Securities and Exchange Commission, Form D, Rosemont Real Estate GP, LLC, May 7, 2010, https://www.sec.gov/Archives/edgar /data/1489627/000148962710000001/xslFormDX01/primary_doc.xml; Heinz Family Foundation Form 990-PF, 2015.

60. Schweizer, Secret Empires, pp. 39, 44.

61. "Gemini Investments (Holdings) Ltd. (0174)," MarketScreener, n.d., https:// www.marketscreener.com/GEMINI-INVESTMENTS-HOLDI-6165703/; "Sino-Ocean Group Holding Ltd. (3377)," Market Screener, n.d., https:// www.marketscreener.com/SINO-OCEAN-GROUP-HOLDING-1412649/; "Top Real Estate Brands in China," Global Brands, August 8, 2018, https:// globalbrandsmagazine.com/top-real-estate-brands-in-china/; Schweizer, Secret Empires, pp. 39–40.

62. "Gemini Investments (Holdings) Limited," p. 6, http://gemini.bmgdemo .com/function/doclist/LTN201412311037_C.pdf.

63. "Gemini Investments and Rosemont Realty Form Joint Venture."

64. Matthew Goldstein, "Ex-Hong Kong Official Convicted in Bribe Case Involving Chinese Oil Company," New York Times, December 5, 2018, https://www.nytimes.com/2018/12/05/business/cefc-china-patrick-ho .html; "Opaque Chinese oil group makes clear gains in former Soviet bloc," Financial Times, September 13, 2017, https://www.ft.com/content/e3f8cbd 2–983f-11e7-a652-cde3f882dd7b; Alexandra Stevenson, David Barboza, Matthew Goldstein, and Paul Mozur, "A Chinese Tycoon Sought Power and Influence. Washington Responded," New York Times, December 12, 2018, https://www.nytimes.com/2018/12/12/business/cefc-biden-china-washing ton-ye-jianming.html.

65. Entous, "Will Hunter Biden Jeopardize His Father's Campaign?"

66. Jenni Marsh, "The rise and fall of a Belt and Road billionaire," CNN, December 2018, https://www.cnn.com/interactive/2018/12/asia/patrick -ho-ye-jianming-cefc-trial-intl/; Brendan Pierson, "Ex-Hong Kong Official Found Guilty of U.S. Corruption Charges," Reuters, December 5, 2018,

https://www.reuters.com/article/us-usa-china-corruption/ex-hong-kong
-official-found-guilty-of-u-s-corruption-charges-idUSKBN1O42KE.

67. Jenni Marsh, "Disgraced former Hong Kong politician jailed for 3 years for bribing African leaders at the UN," CNN, March 25, 2019, https://www .cnn.com/2019/03/25/asia/patrick-ho-sentencing-intl/index.html.

68. Stevenson, Barboza, Goldstein and Mozur, "A Chinese Tycoon Sought Power and Influence. Washington Responded."

69. Ibid.

70. Alvin Lum, "Former Hong Kong Minister Patrick Ho Accused of Being Illegal Arms Dealer by US Prosecutors as They Turn Up Heat Ahead of New York Bribery Trial," *South China Morning Post*, October 3, 2018, https:// www.scmp.com/news/hong-kong/law-and-crime/article/2166847/former -hong-kong-minister-patrick-ho-accused-being.

71. Keith B. Richburg, "U.S. pivot to Asia makes China nervous," *Washington Post,* November 16, 2011, https://www.washingtonpost.com/world/asia_pa cific/us-pivot-to-asia-makes-china-nervous/2011/11/15/gIQAsQpVRN _story.html; Kenneth Lieberthal, "The American Pivot to Asia," *Foreign Policy,* December 21, 2011, https://foreignpolicy.com/2011/12/21/the-amer ican-pivot-to-asia/.

72. Jonathan Pearlman, "US Will Shift Focus from Middle East to Asia Pacific, Barack Obama Declares," *Telegraph* (UK), November 17, 2011, https:// www.telegraph.co.uk/news/worldnews/barackobama/8895726/US-will -shift-focus-from-Middle-East-to-Asia-Pacific-Barack-Obama-declares .html.

73. Mark Landler and Martin Fackler, "Biden Walks Fine Line in Japan: He Voices Concern About China's Air Zone, but No Call for a Reversal," *International New York Times,* December 4, 2013.

74. Michael Barone, "Joe Biden's China policy is stuck in the last century," *New York Post,* May 10, 2019, https://nypost.com/2019/05/10/joe-bidens-china -policy-is-stuck-in-the-last-century/.

75. Schweizer, *Secret Empires*, pp. 55–56; Homepage, Burisma group, accessed August 28, 2019, https://burisma-group.com/eng/.

76. *U.S.A. v. Galanis et al.*, Case No. 1:16-cr-00371, United States District Court for the Southern District of New York, Rosemont Seneca Bohai account statements from Morgan Stanley Private Wealth Management, Gx301; Schweizer, *Secret Empires*, pp. 60–61.

77. *U.S.A. v. Galanis et al.*, Case No. 1:16-cr-00371, United States District Court for the Southern District of New York, Rosemont Seneca Bohai account statements from Morgan Stanley Private Wealth Management, Gx301.

78. "Fact Sheet: U.S. Crisis Support Package for Ukraine," White House Office of the Press Secretary, April 21, 2014, https://obamawhitehouse.archives.gov /the-press-office/2014/04/21/fact-sheet-us-crisis-support-package-ukr aine; J. C. Finley, "Vice President Biden arrives in Kiev," United Press Inter-

national, April 21, 2014, http://www.upi.com/Top_News/World
-News/2014/04/21/Vice-President-Biden-arrives-in-Kiev/4651398098183/.

79. ACEU Staff, "GPO Seizes Property of Ex-Minister Zlochevsky," American
Center for a European Ukraine, February 5, 2016, http://www.europe
anukraine.org/home/2016/02/gpo-seizes-property-of-ex-minister-zlo
chevsky.

80. James Stafford, "Bribery, back room dealing, and bullying in Ukraine: The
origins of Burisma," ProKaivos, October 14, 2015, http://www.prokaivos
.fi/2015/10/14/bribery-back-room-dealing-and-bullying-in-ukraine-the
-origins-of-burisma/.

81. "The Court Repeatedly Seized Wells the Company Zlochevsky," NEWS.ru,
accessed March 1, 2017, http://en.few-news.ru/the-court-repeatedly-seized
-wells-the-company-zlochevsky.html.

82. Kenneth P. Vogel and Iuliia Mendel, "Biden Faces Conflict of Interest
Questions That Are Being Promoted by Trump and Allies," *New York Times*,
May 1, 2019, https://www.nytimes.com/2019/05/01/us/politics/biden-son
-ukraine.html.

83. Burisma Group, "John Buretta: For Us It Was Important to Close All Cases
Against Burisma and Nikolay Zlochevskyi in a Legally Sound Manner," *Kyiv
Post*, February 1, 2017, https://www.kyivpost.com/business-wire/john-bu
retta-us-important-close-casesagainst-burisma-nikolayzlochevskyiin-legally
-sound-manner.html.

84. Michael Kranish and David L. Stern, "As Vice President, Biden Said Ukraine
Should Increase Gas Production. Then His Son Got a Job with a Ukrainian
Gas Company," *Washington Post*, July 22, 2019, https://www.washington
post.com/politics/as-vice-president-biden-said-ukraine-should-increase
-gas-production-then-his-son-got-a-job-with-a-ukrainian-gas-company
/2019/07/21/f599f42c-86dd-11e9-98c1-e945ae5db8fb_story.html.

85. Pavel Polityuk and Alessandra Prentice, "U.S. Vice President Biden to Make
Swansong Visit to Ukraine," Reuters, January 12, 2017, http://www.reuters
.com/article/us-ukraine-crisis-biden-idUSKBN14W0QT.

86. Burisma Group, "All Cases Closed Against Burisma Group and Its President Nikolay Zlochevskyi in Ukraine. The Company Cooperated with Law
Enforcement Agencies and Paid in Full All Outstanding Fees," *Kyiv Post*,
January 12, 2017, https://www.kyivpost.com/business-wire/cases-closed
-burisma-group-president-nikolay-zlochevskyi-ukraine-company-cooperat
ed-law-enforcement-agencies-paid-full-outstanding-fees.html.

87. *U.S.A. v. Galanis et al.,* Case No. 1:16-cr-00371, United States District Court
for the Southern District of New York, Rosemont Seneca Bohai account
statements from Morgan Stanley Private Wealth Management, Gx301;
Novatus Holding PTE. Ltd.—'3' for 6/7/13 re: Net Element, Inc., June 10,
2013, File # 1–34887, http://www.secinfo.com/d141Nx.x1165.htm; Nicholas
Trickett, "Watch the Throne: Trans-Caspian Pipeline Meets Succession

Politics in Kazakhstan," *Diplomat*, February 16, 2017, https://thediplomat
.com/2017/02/watch-the-throne-trans-caspian-pipeline-meets-succession
-politics-in-kazakhstan/.

88. *U.S.A. v. Galanis et al.*, Case No. 1:16-cr-00371, United States District Court
for the Southern District of New York, Rosemont Seneca Bohai account
statements from Morgan Stanley Private Wealth Management, Gx301;
Shamim Adam and Laurence Arnold, "A Guide to the Worldwide Probes of
Malaysia's 1MDB Fund," Bloomberg, March 7, 2018, https://www.bloom
berg.com/news/articles/2018–03–07/malaysia-s-1mdb-fund-spawns-world
wide-probes-quicktake.

89. *U.S.A. v. Galanis et al.*, Case No. 1:16-cr-00371, United States District Court
for the Southern District of New York, Rosemont Seneca Bohai account
statements from Morgan Stanley Private Wealth Management, Gx301.

90. *USA v. Galanis, et al.*, Case No. 1:16-cr-00371, Gx758; "The Luzkhov Di-
lemma," Wikileaks, February 12, 2010, https://wikileaks.org/plusd/cables
/10MOSCOW317_a.html.

91. Jason Rushin, "State Pulls Plug On Mbloom, But Still Wants to Help
Tech Startups," *Honolulu Civil Beat*, June 29, 2016, https://www.civilbeat
.org/2016/06/state-pulls-plug-on-mbloom-but-still-wants-to-help-tech
-startups/.

92. Hawaii Department of Business, Economic Development and Tourism,
"HSDC Receives Final Disbursement of $13 Million Federal Investment
Program," on Internet Archive, November 10, 2014, https://web.archive
.org/web/20141116100606/https://hsdc.hawaii.gov/news/hsdc-receives
-final-disbursement-of-13-million-federal-investment-program/ (the screenshot of the site was captured on November 16, 2014).

93. "Profile: Don Graves," CRF USA, accessed August 10, 2019, https://crfusa
.com/board/don-graves/; Karie Simmons, "UD's Biden Institute Will 'Write
and Produce New Policy,' " *Newark Post*, March 13, 2017, https://www
.newarkpostonline.com/news/ud-s-biden-institute-will-write-and-produce
-new-policy/article_86cf024e-8434–5264–91ee-c428e714f175.html;
"Members of the Biden Institute Policy Advisory Board," Bidenschool.udel
.edu, n.d., https://www.bidenschool.udel.edu/bideninstitute/Documents
/Biden%20Institute%20Policy%20Advisory%20Board.pdf; Don Graves,
LinkedIn profile, accessed August 28, 2019, https://www.linkedin.com/in
/don-graves-8668887/.

94. Rushin, "State Pulls Plug on Mbloom, But Still Wants to Help Tech Startups"; Jason Ubay, "Maui fund mbloom in conflict-of-interest controversy
with first investments," *Pacific Business News,* July 17, 2014, https://www
.bizjournals.com/pacific/news/2014/07/17/maui-fund-mbloom-in-conflict
-of-interest.html.

95. Bloomberg page, accessed July 9, 2019, https://www.bloomberg.com/profile
/person/15174380; "Board of Directors," Burisma.

96. *U.S.A. v. Galanis et al.*, Case No. 1:16-cr-00371: transcript 667, p. 106 of 309; transcript 671, p. 247 of 257; "Shareholders of KKB Elected New Members of the Board of Directors," KazKom, April 28, 2016, press release, http://kase.kz/files/emitters/KKGB/kkgb_reliz_280416_eng.pdf.

97. "Powerful Kazakh Politician Sent to Moscow to Be Ambassador to Russia," RadioFreeEurope/RadioLiberty, February 16, 2017, https://www.rferl .org/a/kazakhstan-tasmaghambetov-ambassador-moscow/28314038.html; Trickett, "Watch the Throne: Trans-Caspian Pipeline Meets Succession Politics in Kazakhstan."

98. *U.S.A. v. Galanis et al.*, Case No. 1:16-cr-00371: transcript 671, p. 247 (quoting Jason Galanis email).

99. Email, David E. Wade, July 11, 2013, 8:04 a.m., RE: re Call, Obtained through Freedom of Information Act by Citizens United.

100. Nathan Vardi, "The $2.4 Billion Nasdaq Stock Headquartered in Apartment 2A," *Forbes*, June 13, 2017, https://www.forbes.com/sites /nathanvardi/2017/06/13/the-2-4-billion-nasdaq-stock-headquartered -in-apartment-2a/#7a888b5a730c; "Kirin International Names Real Estate Executive Jianfeng Guo, Chief Executive Officer and President," Globe Newswire, June 4, 2015, https://www.globenewswire.com/news-release /2015/06/04/742147/10137208/en/Kirin-International-Names-Real -Estate-Executive-Jianfeng-Guo-Chief-Executive-Officer-and-President .html.

101. *U.S.A. v. Galanis et al.*, Case No. 1:16-cr-00371: document 402–17, Filed 04/11/18, Page 1 of 37; Court document: Minutes of an Executive Session of the Independent Trustees of the Board of Trustees of Burnham Investors Trust.

102. *Andrew M. Calamari, et al., v. Devon D. Archer, et al.*, Case 1:16-cv-035 05, document 1, filed May 11, 2016, https://www.sec.gov/litigation/com plaints/2016/comp-pr2016–85.pdf; United States Department of Justice, "Seven Defendants Charged in Manhattan Federal Court with Defrauding a Native American Tribe and Investors of over $60 Million," United States Attorney's Office, Southern District of New York, https://www.justice.gov /usao-sdny/pr/seven-defendants-charged-manhattan-federal-court-defraud ing-native-american-tribe-and.

103. *U.S.A. v. Galanis et al.*, Case No. 1:16-cr-00371: transcript 649, pp. 149–50; transcript 655, p. 87; transcript 667, pp. 40, 50.

104. *U.S.A. v. Galanis et al.*, Case No. 1:16-cr-00371: document 1, pp. 15, 20.

105. Russell Berman, "Biden is betting on unions. They might bet on someone else," *Atlantic*, April 30, 2019, https://www.theatlantic.com/politics/archive /2019/04/biden-unions-labor-movement/588367/.

106. *U.S.A. v. Galanis et al.*, Case No. 1:16-cr-00371: transcript 647, p. 169.

107. *U.S.A. v. Galanis et al.*, Case No. 1:16-cr-00371: transcript 649, p. 149; transcript 655, p. 87.

108. *U.S.A. v. Galanis et al.*, Case No. 1:16-cr-00371: transcript 655, pp. 87–88, 183.

109. *U.S.A. v. Galanis et al.*, Case No. 1:16-cr-00371: transcript 649, p. 149; "Bevan Cooney Sentenced to 30 Months in Prison for the Fraudulent Issuance and Sale of More Than $60 Million of Tribal Bonds," United States Attorney's Office, Southern District of New York, press release, July 31, 2019, https://www.justice.gov/usao-sdny/pr/bevan-cooney-sentenced-30-months -prison-fraudulent-issuance-and-sale-more-60-million.

110. *U.S.A. v. Galanis et al.*, Case No. 1:16-cr-00371: transcript 671, p. 243.

111. *U.S.A. v. Galanis et al.*, Case No. 1:16-cr-00371: transcript 677, p. 148.

112. John George, "StartUp Health: We Want the Best of the Best," *Philadelphia Business Journal*, August 21, 2015, https://philadelphiapact.com/startup -health-we-want-the-best-of-the-best/; "Meet the Team Transforming Health," StartUp Health, https://www.startuphealth.com/team.

113. George, "StartUp Health: We Want the Best of the Best"; "Our Journey to Transform Health," StartUp Health, on Internet Archive, accessed on September 19, 2019, https://web.archive.org/web/20190403173320/https:/www .startuphealth.com/journey (captured April 3, 2019).

114. Dan Kendall, "Episode #038: Unity Stoakes, Part 1, The Journey from Tech Startups to Startup Health," August 15, 2017, https://digitalhealthtoday.com /podcast/startup-health-part1/ (around thirty-seven minutes and after).

115. White House Visitors Logs.

116. "Our Journey to Transform Health."

117. White House Visitors' Logs.

118. "The Founders of Athenahealth Are Back, This Time to Reimagine the Medicare Experience," StartUp Health Team, last updated March 15, 2019, https://hq.startuphealth.com/posts/the-founders-of-athenahealth-are-back -this-time-to-reimagine-the-medicare-experience.

119. California Healthcare Foundation, *Survival of the Fittest: Health Care Accelerators Evolve Toward Specialization*, October 2014, p. 3, https://www.chcf.org /wp-content/uploads/2017/12/PDF-SurvivalFittestAccelerators.pdf.

120. George, "StartUp Health: We want to be the best."

121. Sara Nathan, "Joe Biden's Newlywed Daughter Hits the Campaign Trail—in a Smock Shirt (Something to Tell Us, Ashley?)," *Daily Mail*, October 19, 2012, https://www.dailymail.co.uk/news/article-2220356/Joe-Bidens-new lywed-daughter-hits-campaign-trail—smock-shirt-tell-Ashley.html; "Here Is Everything You Need to Know About Joe Biden's Daughter Ashley Biden's Husband Howard Krein," ecelebritymirror.com, March 15, 2019, https:// ecelebritymirror.com/entertainment/know-joe-biden-daughter-ashley -biden-husband-howard-krein/; Lucia Blackwell, "Beau Biden Funeral: How the Day Unfolded," *News Journal* (Delaware), June 6, 2015, https://www .delawareonline.com/story/news/2015/06/06/beau-biden-funeral-saturday -wilmington-delaware/28594017/.

122. California Healthcare Foundation, *Survival of the Fittest: Health Care Accelerators Evolve Toward Specialization*, pp. 8–9.

123. Josh Lederman, "At the Vatican, Biden seeks common cause with pope on cancer," Associated Press, April 29, 2016, https://apnews.com/0666e070cd 194159befbdd6d173d59f2.

124. Nicole Fisher, "Biden Takes Stage at DC DataPalooza Event to Talk About His Moonshot on Cancer," *Forbes*, May 16, 2016, https://www.forbes.com /sites/nicolefisher/2016/05/16/biden-takes-stage-at-dc-datapalooza-event -to-talk-about-his-moonshot-on-cancer/#6331c42b1e0d.

125. Brian Zeltner, "Joe Biden Talks Cancer Moonshot at Cleveland Clinic Innovation Summit," *Plain Dealer*, October 24, 2016, https://www.cleveland .com/healthfit/2016/10/joe_biden_talks_cancer_moonsho.html.

126. Maria Lenhart, "Nimble Planning," Meeting Professional, May 2017, http:// www.themeetingprofessionaldigital.org/themeetingprofessional/may_2017 /MobilePagedArticle.action?articleId=1106259#articleId1106259.

127. "Words of Hope: Vice President Joe Biden's Keynote at the StartUp Health Festival," StartUp Health, February 14, 2018, https://hq.startuphealth.com /posts/words-of-hope-vice-president-joe-bidens-keynote-at-the-startup -health-festival-startup-health-now-169; "Together We Can End Cancer: A Keynote Conversation with Dr. Jill Biden," StartUp Health, event on January 7, 2019, https://hq.startuphealth.com/posts/together-we-can-end -cancer-a-keynote-conversation-with-dr-jill-biden.

128. "Codel Biden," Wikileaks, November 6, 1974, https://wikileaks.org/plusd /cables/1974STATE243883_b.html; "Codel to AAI Conference in Maseru," *Wikileaks*, November 18, 1976, https://wikileaks.org/plusd/cables/1976 STATE283152_b.html.

129. Jennifer Beeson, "Biden Family's Keewaydin Vacation Home Sold for $1.35 Million to Local Architects," *Naples Daily News*, June 27, 2018, https:// www.naplesnews.com/story/money/real-estate/2018/06/27/biden-familys -keewaydin-vacation-home-sells-1-35-m-architecture-firm-naples-buyer -florida/698194002/.

130. White House Visitors' Logs; "Stately Fashion: Outfits from the State Dinner," CBS, https://www.cbsnews.com/pictures/stately-fashion-outfits-from -the-state-dinner/21/.

131. Charlie Gasparino, "The Ties that Biden," Fox Business, October 22, 2012, https://www.foxbusiness.com/politics/the-ties-that-biden.

132. White House visitors' logs; "Michele Gioffre Smith," LinkedIn Profile, n.d., https://www.linkedin.com/in/michele-gioffre-smith-b3880872/.

133. "James B. Biden Joins Hill International Subsidary as Executive Vice President."

134. Gasparino, "The Ties that Biden."

135. Ibid.

136. Ibid.

137. Ibid.

138. Ibid.

139. "Stately Fashion: Outfits from the State Dinner"; Monica Hesse and Rox-anne Roberts, "White House State Dinner with South Korea," *Washington Post*, October 14, 2011, https://www.washingtonpost.com/blogs/reliable-source/post/white-house-state-dinner-for-south-korea-oct-13–2011/2011/10/14/gIQAdNA3iL_blog.html.

140. Beatrice Thomas, "US Construction Firm Admits Mistake Over Iraq Investment," Arabian Business, February 24, 2014, https://www.arabianbusiness.com/us-construction-firm-admits-mistake-over-iraq-investment-540113.html.

141. Hill International contracts found on usaspending.gov and govtribe.com.

142. "Kyiv International Airport (Zhuliany), Ukraine," Weather Underground, n.d., https://www.wunderground.com/history/daily/ua/kiev/UKKK/date/2009–7–22; Christopher Bedford, "Biden's Good Friend Donor Receives $20 Million Federal Loan to Open Foreign Luxury Car Dealership in Ukraine," Daily Caller, August 17, 2012, https://dailycaller.com/2012/08/17/bidens-good-friend-donor-receives-20m-federal-loan/.

143. "John Hynansky," Ukraine Business Feature, interview, accessed September 2, 2019, https://www.ukraine.the-report.com/interview/john-hynansky/.

144. "Public Summary—LLC Winner Imports Ukraine, LTD," OPIC, n.d., https://www.opic.gov/sites/default/files/files/072612-llcwinterimports.pdf; Bedford, "Biden's Good Friend Donor Receives $20 Million Federal Loan to Open Foreign Luxury Car Dealership in Ukraine."

145. Maureen Milford, "Battle over $5 million Chateau Country Estate Ends for Tigani," Delawareonline.com, April 10, 2015, https://www.delawareonline.com/story/news/local/2015/04/10/battle-million-chateau-country-estate-ends-tigani/25601795/.

146. Tax Lien and Mortgage records found on: Department of the Treasury—Internal Revenue Service, Form 668 (Y)(c), Notice of Federal Tax Lien, James B. Biden, Serial No. 161967815, https://www.collierclerk.com/CorPublicAccess/Document/View/5153212; Claim of Lien, State of Florida, County of Polk, property owned by James Brian Biden, Sr., and Sara Jones Biden, December 24, 2014, https://www.collierclerk.com/CorPublicAccess/Document/View/5027058.

147. Mortgages records from Collier County, Florida: Mortgage, property owned by James B. Biden and Sara Jones Biden, May 26, 2015, https://www.collierclerk.com/CorPublicAccess/Document/View/5136203; Release of Mortgage, property owned by James B. Biden and Sara Jones Biden, February 21, 2015, https://www.collierclerk.com/CorPublicAccess/Document/View/5791008; Mortgage records from Montgomery County, Pennsylvania.

148. Department of the Treasury—Internal Revenue Service, Form 668 (Y)(c), Notice of Federal Tax Lien, James B. Biden, Serial No. 189920815, Decem-

ber 10, 2015, https://www.collierclerk.com/CorPublicAccess/Document
/View/5277682.

149. Satisfaction of Claim of Lien, State of Florida, Claim of Lien by Gator Pressure Cleaning & Custom Painting, Inc. against James Brian Biden Sr. and
Sara Jones Biden, December 24, 2014.

150 Ben Schreckinger, "Biden's Brother Touted Biden Cancer Initiative Ties
in Investment Pitch," Politico, September 26, 2019, https://www.politico
.com/news/2019/09/26/joe-biden-brother-cancer-initiative-investment
-pitch-001675.

151. *Albano v. Turton et al.*, Case No. GIN 007199: Declaration of Richard Cornell
in Support of Order for Publication of Summons, Motion to Default Defendant Francis W. Biden, June 27, 2002.

152. Ibid., p. 6.

153. Case No. SCN 109170, Superior Court of California, County of San Diego,
p. 22.

154. *Albano v. Turton et al.*, Case No. GIN 007199: Declaration of Richard Cornell
in Support of Order for Publication of Summons, Superior Court of California for the County of San Diego North County Branch, 2; Judgment by
Default, Superior Court of California County of San Diego, p. 62.

155. *Albano v. Turton et al.*, Case No. GIN 007199: Declaration of Richard Cornell
in Support of Order for Publication of Summons, 3; Confidential Investigation Reports, Francis W. Biden, p. 2.

156. Ibid., p. 3.

157. Letter from Senator Biden's chief of staff to attorney Richard Cornell, September 24, 2008.

158. Certificate of Release of Federal Tax Lien, Department of Treasury, Internal
Revenue Service, Francis W. Biden, December 25, 2013.

159. *Albano v. Turton et al.*, Case No. GIN 007199, p. 10.

160. "Biden gets warm welcome in Chile, Costa Rica; Vice President Joe Biden
scored points with his 'nice guy' image during his Latin America trip," *Miami
Herald*, April 2, 2009.

161. "Vice President Biden's March 30 Bilateral Meeting with Costa Rican President Oscar Arias," April 6, 2009, Wikileaks, April 8, 2009, https://wikileaks
.org/plusd/cables/09SANJOSE298_a.html; "Biden and Latin American
Leaders in Costa Rica," White House archives, photograph, n.d., https://
obamawhitehouse.archives.gov/photos-and-video/photos/biden-and-latin
-american-leaders-costa-rica.

162. "Costa Rica: Background and U.S. Relations," May 22, 2009—February 22,
2010, EveryCRSReport.com, https://www.everycrsreport.com/reports
/R40593.html.

163. Andrew Conte, "Biden Name Drives Costa Rican Golf Dream," Trib Live,
April 26, 2014, https://archive.triblive.com/local/pittsburgh-allegheny
/biden-name-drives-costa-rican-golf-dream/; "New Partnership Seeks to

Reform Real Estate in Latin America," *Costa Rica News*, September 2, 2009, https://thecostaricanews.com/new-partnership-seeks-to-reform
-real-estate-in-latin-america/; "Board of Directors," crgbc.org, on Internet Archive, n.d., https://web.archive.org/web/20101115150837/http://www
.crgbc.org/About/BoardofDirectors.aspx (captured November 15, 2010).

164. Conte, "Biden Name Drives Costa Rican Golf Dream."

165. Joe Biden, *Promise Me, Dad: A Year of Hope, Hardship, and Purpose* (New York: Flatiron Books, 2017), p. 74.

166. Conte, "Biden Name Drives Costa Rican Golf Dream"; "About," Sun Fund Americas, on Internet Archive, n.d., https://web.archive.org/web/2015022
4043102/http://www.sunfundamericas.com/en-us/about.aspx (captured February 24, 2015); "Projects," Sun Fund Americas, on Internet Archive, n.d., https://web.archive.org/web/20150224062647/http://www.sunfund
americas.com/en-us/projects.aspx (captured February 24, 2015).

167. "New Partnership Seeks to Reform Real Estate in Latin America"; "Guanacaste Country Club, Management and Ownership," JD Realty Enterprise, Inc., accessed May 22, 2019, https://www.jdrealtyenterprise.com/custom8/; "Sun Fund Americas Signs Solar PPA in Jamaica," PR.com, February 25, 2016, https://www.pr.com/press-release/660018.

168. Michael Krumholtz, "Guanacaste Developer Detained Briefly in Fraud Case," A.M. Costa Rica, July 31, 2014, http://www.amcostarica.com/073114.htm.

169. "Guanacaste Country Club, Management and Ownership."

170. "Guanacaste County Club Sponsors," JD Realty Enterprise Inc., https://
www.jdrealtyenterprise.com/custom5/.

171. Republica De Costa Rica Ministerio De Educacion Publica, Circular DVM
-PICR-0028–07–2017, https://www.mep.go.cr/sites/default/files/descargas
_etica/circular-dvm-picr-0028–07–2017.pdf; "Loan Summary: Overseas Private Investment Corporation to GoSolar Energy Efficiency S.R.L.," USASpending
.gov, September 17, 2015, https://www.usaspending.gov/#/award/47340034; GoSolar "Information Summary for the Public," accessed September 3, 2019, GoSolar Energy Efficiency S.R.L., https://www.opic.gov/sites/default/files
/files/GoSolar_INFORMATION-SUMMARY-FOR-THE-PUBLIC.pdf.

172. "National Recovery Council Team," National Recovery Council, accessed June 12, 2019, http://nationalrecoverycouncil.com/national-recovery-coun
cil-team.

173. White House Visitors' Logs.

174. Veronica Toney, "Complete guest list for the State Dinner in honor of Prime Minister Lee Hsien Loong of Singapore," *Washington Post*, August 2, 2016, https://www.washingtonpost.com/news/reliable-source/wp/2016/08/02
/complete-guest-list-for-the-state-dinner-in-honor-of-prime-minister-lee
-hsien-loong-of-singapore/?noredirect&utm_term=.47254d73fb02.

175. "Sun Fund Americas Signs Solar PPA in Jamaica."

176. "US Vice President announces launch of Caribbean Energy Security Initiative,"

Caricom, June 25, 2014, https://caricom.org/communications/view
/us-vice-president-announces-launch-of-caribbean-energy-security-initiative.

177. "US Energy Boost—Jamaica to Benefit from US$90 million Clean Power
Project," *Gleaner* (Jamaica), January 27, 2015, http://jamaica-gleaner.com
/gleaner/20150127/lead/lead1.html; Maria Perez Arguello,"Recap: Caribbean Energy Security Summit," American Society/Council of the Americas,
January 27, 2015, https://www.as-coa.org/articles/recap-caribbean-energy
-security-summit.

178. Arlene Martin-Wilkins, "US$9-m Boost," *Jamaica Observer*, January 26, 2015,
http://www.jamaicaobserver.com/news/us-90-m-boost_18292215.

179. "Sun Fund Americas Signs Solar PPA in Jamaica."

180. "Loan Summary: Overseas Private Investment Corporation to Content Solar
Limited," USASpending.gov, July 30, 2015, https://www.usaspending
.gov/#/award/47340364; "OPIC to Support 20 MW Jamaican Solar Energy
Facility," OPIC, June 25, 2015, press release, https://www.opic.gov/press
-releases/2015/opic-support-20-mw-jamaican-solar-energy-facility.

181. Jaime Lopez, "Renewable Energy Fund Based in Costa Rica Expands to
Jamaica," *Costa Rica Star*, February 27, 2016, https://news.co.cr/renewable
-energy-fund-based-in-costa-rica-expands-to-jamaica/45108/.

182. "Carper, Gregg Announce 'Charters and Choice' Education Bill," Tom
Carper's Senate page, accessed September 3, 2019, https://www.carper.senate.
gov/public/index.cfm/pressreleases?ID=54E9555B-BF41–4940-ADC9-AC
1C6B4542D1.

183. Associated Press, "Obama Vows to Double Funding for Charter Schools,"
September 9, 2008, https://www.cleveland19.com/story/8976743/obama
-vows-to-double-funding-for-charter-schools/.

184. Roland G. Fryer Jr., "Executive Summary: Injecting Successful Charter
School Strategies into Traditional Public Schools: A Field Experiment in
Houston," NBER Working Paper No. 17494, revised in December 2013,
http://www.nber.org/papers/w17494.

185. Robert Tomsho, "Charter Schools gain in stimulus scramble," *Wall Street Journal*, July 17, 2009, https://www.wsj.com/articles/SB124778613357254605;
Amanda Michel, David Epstein, and Michael Grabell, "No-Bid Stimulus
Contracts for Military," ProPublica, July 17, 2009, https://www.propublica
.org/article/no-bid-stimulus-contracts-for-military-717#.

186. Lisa Rab, "Mavericks Charter Schools Don't Live Up to Big Promises," *Miami New Times*, December 29, 2011, https://www.miaminewtimes.com
/news/mavericks-charter-schools-dont-live-up-to-big-promises-6385627;
Lisa Rab, "Mavericks Charges Charter Schools $350K in Rent, Plus Fees,"
Broward Palm Beach New Times, December 21, 2011, https://www.broward
palmbeach.com/news/mavericks-charges-charter-schools-350k-in-rent
-plus-fees-6473527.

187. Rab, "Mavericks Charter Schools Don't Live Up to Big Promises"; "Frank

Biden," School Property Development Brochure, accessed September 4, 2019, p. 3, https://deutsch29.files.wordpress.com/2019/04/spd-company-info.pdf.

188. Lisa Rab, "UPDATED: Joe Biden's Brother Is President and 'P.T. Barnum' for SoFla Charter School Chain," *Broward Palm Beach New Times*, November 22, 2011, https://www.browardpalmbeach.com/news/updated-joe -bidens-brother-is-president-and-pt-barnum-for-sofla-charter-school -chain-6466011.

189. Ibid.

190. Buddy Nevins and Alan Cherry, "Taxi King Gambles and Usually Wins," *South Florida Sun Sentinel*, August 20, 2008, https://www.sun-sentinel.com /news/fl-xpm-2000-08-20-0008200214-story.html; Bob Norman, "The Sheriff's Criminal Association," *Broward Palm Beach New Times*, October 15, 1998, https://www.browardpalmbeach.com/news/the-sheriffs-criminal -association-6331789; Stefan Kamph, "The Hidden Real Estate Empire of Jesse Gaddis, Yellow Cab Magnet: Here's Our Map," *Broward Palm Beach New Times*, July 17, 2012, https://www.browardpalmbeach.com/news/the -hidden-real-estate-empire-of-jesse-gaddis-yellow-cab-magnate-heres-our -map-6445580.

191. All records related to the transaction, during a period approximately between June 10 and June 21, 2010, may be found at Broward County official records: https://officialrecords.broward.org/AcclaimWeb/search/SearchTypeName. Where Grantor is "Gaddis Capital" and grantee is "School Property Development, LLC."

192. Karen Yi, "Charter school leaders concede laws need to be tightened," *Sun Sentinel*, February 19, 2015, https://www.sun-sentinel.com/news/education /fl-pb-charter-school-panel-20150219-story.html.

193. Rab, "Mavericks Charter Schools Don't Live Up to Big Promises."

194. Ibid.; Yi, "Charter School Leaders Concede Laws Need to Be Tightened."

195. Karen Yi and Amy Shipley, "Mavericks in Education: Failing to make the grade," *Sun Sentinel*, October 10, 2014, http://www.sun-sentinel.com/news /education/fl-mavericks-charter-investigation-20141010-story.html.

196. "Mavericks High of North Miami Dade County," *U.S. News*, accessed September 9, 2019, https://www.usnews.com/education/best-high-schools /florida/districts/miami-dade-county-public-schools/mavericks-high-of -north-miami-dade-county-4939; "Miami-Dade County Public Schools District," *U.S. News*, n.d., https://www.usnews.com/education/best-high -schools/florida/districts/miami-dade-county-public-schools-110364.

197. Yi and Shipley, "Mavericks in Education: Failing to Make the Grade."

198. Rab, "Mavericks Charges Charter Schools $350K in Rent, Plus Fees."

199. "School Property Development: Company Information," School Property Development Brochure, accessed September 4, 2019, https://deutsch29.files .wordpress.com/2019/04/spd-company-info.pdf.

200. "National Recovery Council Team."

201. Rab, "Mavericks Charter Schools Don't Live Up to Big Promises."

202. Yi and Shipley, "Mavericks in Education: Failing to Make the Grade."

203. White House Visitors' Logs; Peter Olsen-Phillips, "DNC paid $4.5 million for events at White House," Sunlight Foundation, March 4, 2015, https:// sunlightfoundation.com/2015/03/04/dnc-payments-white-house/; Gray Rohrer, "Florida Democratic Party Leader Resigns After Report of 'Creepy' Behavior," *Orlando Sentinel*, November 17, 2017, https://www.orlandosenti nel.com/politics/os-fdp-chair-bittel-resign-20171117-story.html.

204. "Minutes Meeting of the Sunrise City Commission," City of Sunrise Florida, April 28, 2015, p. 47, http://sunrisefl.granicus.com/MinutesViewer.php?view _id=4&clip_id=468&doc_id=29c25f75–5899–11e5-ab53–00219ba2f017.

205. Lisa Rab, " 'The Hope Factory,' Part 2," *New Times Broward-Palm Beach*, January 23, 2012, https://www.theadvocate.com/gambit/new_orleans/news /article_1ac741e1–8fc6–50ed-81ad-60e9560616fd.html.

206. "Charter Schools Program State Educational Agencies (SEA) Grant," U.S. Department of Education, accessed on September 5, 2019, https://www2 .ed.gov/programs/charter/index.html.

207. Ibid.; Applicant Information, U.S. Department of Education (archived infor- mation), accessed on September 5, 2019, https://www2.ed.gov/programs /charter/2015archive.html.

208. Rab, " 'The Hope Factory,' Part 2."

209. "SPA Awards Database," excel file, accessed September 5, 2019, https:// www2.ed.gov/programs/charter/cspawardsdatabase.xls.

210. Patrick Svitek, "Biden Makes First Texas Trip as a 2020 Presidential Candi- date, Pitching New Education Plan," *Texas Tribune*, May 28, 2019, https:// www.texastribune.org/2019/05/28/joe-biden-first-texas-trip-2020-candi date-pitches-education-plan/.

211. George Bennett, "Lawsuit Seeks End to Sugar Cane Burning in the Glades," *Palm Beach Post*, June 4, 2019, https://www.palmbeachpost.com/news /20190604/lawsuit-seeks-end-to-sugar-cane-burning-in-glades.

212. Ibid.; "Joe Biden to Travel to New Hampshire on Tuesday," June 4, 2019, 4president.org (blog), accessed September 5, 2019, https://blog.4president .org/2020/2019/05/joe-biden-to-travel-to-new-hampshire-on-tuesday -june-4–2019.html.

213. "Berman Law Group Welcomes Francis Biden as Senior Advisor," Berman Law Group, August 10, 2018, https://www.thebermanlawgroup.com /blog/2018/august/berman-law-group-welcomes-francis-biden-as-senio/.

214. "Omnibus Budget Will End Chances of Horse Slaughter Plants Opening in US," PR Newswire, January 14, 2014, https://www.prnewswire.com /news-releases/omnibus-budget-will-end-chances-of-horse-slaughter-plants -opening-in-us-240039791.html; "Executive Staff at The Berman Group," Berman Law Group, accessed September 5, 2019, https://www.theberman lawgroup.com/about-the-firm/executive-staff/.

215. Dan Sweeney, "Sugar companies hit with federal class-action lawsuit over health effects of cane field burns," *South Florida Sun Sentinel,* June 4, 2019, https://www.sun-sentinel.com/local/palm-beach/fl-ne-sugar-cane-burn-lawsuit-biden-abruzzo-20190604-6rjj2mkr2va5zmggky43duieky-story.html.

216. Berman Law Group, "The Glades Burning," YouTube, June 4, 2019, https://www.youtube.com/watch?v=6inCWEUuxXE.

217. Bennett, "Lawsuit seeks end to sugar cane burning in the Glades."

218. "US Energy Partnerships with Caribbean Countries Will Herald Long-Term Benefits," Atlantic Council, accessed on September 5, 2019, https://www.atlanticcouncil.org/?view=article&id=31900:us-energy-partnerships-with-caribbean-countries-will-herald-long-term-benefits.

CHAPTER 4: CORY BOOKER

1. Leanna Garfield, "Mark Zuckerberg Once Made a $100 Million Investment in a Major US City to Help Fix Its Schools—Now the Mayor Says the Effort 'Parachuted' in and Failed," Business Insider, May 12, 2018, https://www.businessinsider.com/mark-zuckerberg-schools-education-newark-mayor-ras-baraka-cory-booker-2018-5; Vincent Lara-Cinisomo, "Newark Mayor Cory Booker Connects with Google's Schmidt on Waywire (Correction)," *Silicon Valley Business Journal,* August 12, 2013, https://www.bizjournals.com/sanjose/news/2013/08/06/newark-mayor-has-big-stake-in-startup.html; Olivia Nuzzi, "The Ugly Truth About Cory Booker, New Jersey's Golden Boy," Daily Beast, October 20, 2014, https://www.thedailybeast.com/the-ugly-truth-about-cory-booker-new-jerseys-golden-boy.

2. Tom Moran, "Booker is running. I've watched him for 20 years. Here's what I've learned," *Star-Ledger,* February 1, 2019, https://www.nj.com/opinion/2019/02/booker-is-running-ive-watched-him-for-20-years-heres-what-ive-learned-moran.html.

3. Ibid.; Jordain Carney, "Booker Releases 'Confidential' Kavanaugh Documents," Hill, September 6, 2018, https://thehill.com/homenews/senate/405345-booker-releases-confidential-kavanaugh-documents.

4. Matt Taylor, "Cory Booker Doubles Down," Salon.com, July 9, 2013, https://www.salon.com/2013/07/09/do_liberals_know_cory_booker/.

5. "Finding Your Roots," PBS, n.d., https://www.pbs.org/show/finding-your-roots/; Cory Booker, *United: Thoughts on Finding Common Ground and Advancing the Common Good* (New York: Ballantine Books, 2016), p. 12.

6. Jill Lepore, "Confessions of a Presidential Candidate," *New Yorker,* May 13, 2019, https://www.newyorker.com/magazine/2019/05/20/confessions-of-a-presidential-candidate.

7. Ben Jacobs, "Cory Booker: Ivy League elite or hunger-striking hero?,"

Guardian, March 13, 2019, https://www.theguardian.com/us-news/2019
mar/13/who-is-cory-booker-democrat-2020; Alexandra Moller, "Lyons
Award Honors Service," Stanford Daily Archive, on Internet Archive, February 28, 2001, https://web.archive.org/web/20120624011945/http://archive
.stanforddaily.com/?p=1000223 (the screenshot of the site was captured on
June 24, 2012); Benjamin Ball, "NJ Senator Cory Booker Announces Presidential Bid," *Daily Princetonian,* February 1, 2019, http://www.dailyprince
tonian.com/article/2019/02/nj-senator-cory-booker-announces-presidential
-bid.

8. Robert Curvin, *Inside Newark: Decline, Rebellion, and the Search for Transformation* (New Brunswick, NJ: Rutgers University Press, 2014), pp. 218–20; Yair
Rosenberg, "New Jersey Senate Candidate Cory Booker Knows His Torah.
So What?" Tabletmag.com, August 12, 2013, https://www.tabletmag.com
/jewish-news-and-politics/140767/cory-bookers-jewish-story.

9. Shelbi Austin, "10 Things You Didn't Know About Cory Booker," *U.S.
News,* March 16, 2017, https://www.usnews.com/news/national-news
/articles/2017–03–16/10-things-you-didnt-know-about-cory-booker; Peter
J. Boyer, "The Color of Politics," *New Yorker,* February 4, 2008, https://
www.newyorker.com/magazine/2008/02/04/the-color-of-politics-2.

10. David Skinner, "Home Is Where the Heart Is," *Education Next* 6, no. 4 (Fall
2006), https://www.educationnext.org/home-is-where-the-heart-is/; Andra
Gillespie, *The New Black Politician: Cory Booker, Newark, and Post-Racial America* (New York: New York University Press, 2012), p. 157.

11. Curvin, *Inside Newark,* p. 221.

12. Ken Schlager, "He's No Angel," *New Jersey Monthly,* October 13, 2009,
https://njmonthly.com/articles/jersey-living/hes-no-angel/; Guy Sterling,
The Famous, the Familiar and the Forgotten: 350 Notable Newarkers (Bloomington, IN: Xlibris, 2014), p. 2.

13. Curvin, *Inside Newark,* pp. 221–22, 235.

14. Ibid., pp. 235–36.

15. William Schluter, *Soft Corruption: How Unethical Conduct Undermines Good
Government and What to Do About It* (New Brunswick, NJ: Rutgers University Press, 2017), p. 176; "Moran: Steve Adubato Sr. tarnishes legacy with
cheating, ethics scandals," NJ.com, November 18, 2012, http://blog.nj.com
/njv_tom_moran/2012/11/moran_steve_adubato_sr_tarnish.html; Max
Pizarro, "In Newark, Oprah's $500,000 Little Pieces," *Observer,* February 3,
2009, https://observer.com/2009/02/in-newark-oprahs-500000-little-pieces/

16. Curvin, *Inside Newark,* p. 222.

17. Andrew Jacobs "Evicted, Newark's Mayor Finds Another Blighted Street,"
New York Times, November 20, 2006, https://www.nytimes.com/2006
/11/20/nyregion/20newark.html; Seth Mnookin, "The New Natural," *New
York Magazine,* April 22, 2002, http://nymag.com/nymetro/news/politics
/newyork/features/5921/.

18. Marc Peyser, "Taking It to the Streets," *Stanford Magazine*, March/April 2000, https://stanfordmag.org/contents/taking-it-to-the-streets; Curvin, *Inside Newark*, p. 222.

19. Nuzzi, "The Ugly Truth About Cory Booker, New Jersey's Golden Boy"; Jonathan L. Wharton, *A Post-Racial Change Is Gonna Come: Newark, Cory Booker, and the Transformation of Urban America* (New York: Palgrave Macmillan, 2013), p. 38.

20. Ibid., p. 40.

21. Associated Press, "Newark Mayor's Race Unusually Spirited," Asbury Park Press, April 7, 2002, https://www.newspapers.com/image/144886581; Scott Fallon, "Cory Booker's 2013 Rise to the Senate Was Fueled by Outsider Status and Insider Maneuvering," North Jersey Record, February 1, 2019, https://www.northjersey.com/story/news/2019/02/01/cory-bookers-2013 -senate-win-fueled-outsider-status-insider-moves-jj-abrams-sharpe-james -norcross/2741821002/.

22. Associated Press, "Record Fines for Newark Candidate," *Philadelphia Inquirer*, December 9, 2005, https://www.newspapers.com/image/201137286 /?terms=%22cory%2Bbooker%22; C-G 0714 07 04 M2002, *New Jersey Election Law Enforcement Commission v. Cory Booker and Elnardo J. Webster II*, Consent Order and Final Decision, November 29, 2006.

23. Jacobs, "Cory Booker: Ivy League elite or hunger-striking hero?"

24. Boyer, "The Color of Politics."

25. Jeffrey Gold, "Newark Mayor James Denies Strip Club Stops," *Journal News* (White Plains, NY), April 18, 2002, https://www.newspapers.com/image /166220568/?terms=%22cory%2Bbooker%22; Jim Geraghty, "Twenty Things You Didn't Know about Cory Booker," *National Review,* February 7, 2019, https://www.nationalreview.com/2019/02/cory-booker-20-things -you-probably-didnt-know/.

26. Fallon, "Cory Booker's 2013 rise to the Senate was fueled by outsider status and insider maneuvering"; Nuzzi, "The Ugly Truth About Cory Booker, New Jersey's Golden Boy"; Jeff S. Whelan, "Former Newark Mayor Sharpe James Reports to Prison on Monday," NJ.com, September 12, 2008, https://www.nj.com/news/2008/09/sharpe_james_to_be_behind_bars .html.

27. Curvin, *Inside Newark,* p. 224; Fallon, "Cory Booker's 2013 Rise to the Senate Was Fueled by Outsider Status."

28. Christian Barnard, "Cory Booker's Career Shows School Choice Is the Civil Rights Issue Where Most Democrats Come Up Short," Hill, March 2, 2019, https://thehill.com/opinion/education/432307-cory-bookers-career-shows -school-choice-is-the-civil-rights-issue-where; Nancy Hass, "Scholarly Investments," *New York Times*, December 4, 2009, https://www.nytimes .com/2009/12/06/fashion/06charter.html.

29. Stephen Vita, "Inside the Hedge Fund Infatuation with Charter Schools,"

Investopedia, March 9, 2016, https://www.investopedia.com/articles/invest
ing/030916/inside-hedge-fund-infatuation-charter-schools.asp.

30. Michael Gartland, "Booker Made $689K from Ex-Law Firm While Mayor,"
    New York Post, September 7, 2013, https://nypost.com/2013/09/07/booker
    -made-600k-from-ex-law-firm-while-mayor/; "Booker, Rabinowitz,
    Trenk, Lubetkin, Tully, DiPasquale & Webster, P.C.," US Lawyers DB,
    n.d., https://uslawyersdb.com/attorney82024; Ben McGrath, "The Talk of
    the Town," *New Yorker,* August 9, 2004; Paul H. Johnson, "Blacks must use
    history as a guide to confront evils, civic leader says; Likely Newark may-
    oral candidate presses for action," *Record* (Bergen County, NJ), February 6,
    2004.

31. Michael Gartland, "Newark Mayor Cory Booker Pocketed 'Confidential'
    Annual Payouts from Law Firm While in Office," *New York Post*, August 11,
    2013, https://nypost.com/2013/08/11/newark-mayor-cory-booker-pock
    eted-confidential-annual-payouts-from-law-firm-while-in-office/;
    "Councilman Donald M. Payne, Jr./City of Newark," Project Re-Direct,
    n.d., http://www.projectredirectnj25.org/services-2011.html; Newark Char-
    ter School Fund Inc., Internal Revenue Service, Form 990, 2014, p. 7

32. Curvin, *Inside Newark,* pp. 223–27; Fallon, "Cory Booker's 2013 rise to the
    Senate was fueled by outsider status and insider maneuvering."

33. Skinner, "Home is where the heart is."

34. Nuzzi, "The Ugly Truth About Cory Booker, New Jersey's Golden Boy."

35. Ibid.

36. Moran, "Booker is running. I've watched him for 20 years. Here's what I've
    learned."

37. Taylor, "Cory Booker Doubles Down"; Nuzzi, "The Ugly Truth."

38. Curvin, *Inside Newark,* p. 230.

39. Nuzzi, "The Ugly Truth"; Leanne Shear, "Booker's Balancing Act," *Nation,*
    May 23, 2007, https://www.thenation.com/article/bookers-balancing-act/.

40. Curvin, *Inside Newark,* p. 259; Gillespie, *The New Black Politician,* p. 170.

41. Gillespie, *The New Black Politician,* pp. 169–70; "The Fonseca Factor," Insider
    NJ, April 25, 2017, https://www.insidernj.com/the-fonseca-factor/.

42. Karen Yi and Marisa Iati, "No Prison for Ex-Booker Advisor Who Stole
    $113K from Gov't," NJ.com, March 1, 2018, https://www.nj.com/essex
    /2018/03/oscar_james.html; "Post-election Questions in Newark; New Jobs
    for Anne Milgram, Deborah Howlett," NJ.com, May 16, 2010, http://blog
    .nj.com/njv_auditor/2010/05/post-election_questions_in_new.html.

43. Nuzzi, "The Ugly Truth"; Gartland, "Newark Mayor Cory Booker Pocketed
    'Confidential' Annual Payouts from Law Firm While in Office."

44. Ibid.

45. Wharton, *A Post-Racial Change Is Gonna Come,* pp. 47–48.

46. "Councilman Donald M. Payne, Jr./City of Newark"; Gartland, "Newark
    Mayor Cory Booker Pocketed 'Confidential' Annual Payouts from Law Firm

While in Office"; Gartland, "Booker Made $689K from Ex-Law Firm While Mayor."

47. Naomi Nix, "Newark Development Agency Review Questions over $3 Million in Loans," NJ.com, December 11, 2014, https://www.nj.com/essex/2014/12/newark_corporation_owed_millions_in_late_loans.html; Brick City Development Corporation, Internal Revenue Service, Form 990, 2007, pdfs.citizenaudit.org/2009_08_EO/26–0829057_990_200712.pdf.

48. Jeffery C. Mays, "Booker Changes Staff to Ready for 2010 Campaign," NJ.com, November 2, 2008, https://www.nj.com/newark/2008/11/booker_changes_staff_to_ready.html.

49. Gillespie, *The New Black Politician*, pp. 166–67; Wharton, *A Post-Racial Change Is Gonna Come*, p. 86.

50. Wharton, *A Post-Racial Change Is Gonna Come*, p. 99.

51. Paul H. Johnson, "Winning Easy for Booker; Leading Newark Harder," *Record* (Hackensack, New Jersey), May 10, 2006, A16, https://www.newspapers.com/image/504638728/?terms=%22cory%2Bbooker%22.

52. Curvin, *Inside Newark*, p. 259.

53. Gillespie, *The New Black Politician*, p. 170.

54. Ibid., p. 164.

55. "Ex-Newark Official Facing Corruption Charge Brags About Contacts on Mayor's Staff," NJ.com, March 4, 2010, https://www.nj.com/news/2010/03/ex-newark_official_facing_corr.html.

56. Curvin, *Inside Newark*, p. 226; *United States of America v. Ronald Salahuddin and Sonnie L. Cooper*, 18 U.S.C. §§ 666(a)(1)(B), 1951(a) and § 2, Indictment, http://media.nj.com/ledgerupdates_impact/other/salahuddin-indictment.pdf; "Ex-Newark Official Facing Corruption Charge Brags About Contacts on Mayor's Staff"; Wharton, *A Post-Racial Change Is Gonna Come*, p. 142; David Giambusso, "Verdict in Newark Corruption Trial: Former Deputy Mayor Salahuddin Found Guilty of Conspiracy," NJ.com, October 14, 2011, https://www.nj.com/news/2011/10/verdict_in_newark_corruption_t.html.

57. Megan DeMarco, "Newark Corruption Trial: Contractor Says Businessmen Didn't Bribe Ex-Deputy Mayor," NJ.com, September 19, 2011, https://www.nj.com/news/2011/09/newark_corruption_trial_contra.html.

58. "Ex-Newark Official Facing Corruption Charge Brags About Contacts on Mayor's Staff"; Wharton, *A Post-Racial Change Is Gonna Come*, p. 142.

59. *United States of America v. Ronald Salahuddin*, Nos. 13–1464, 13–1751, Decided September 3, 2014, https://caselaw.findlaw.com/us-3rd-circuit/1677050.html; "Ex-Newark Official Facing Corruption Charge Brags About Contacts on Mayor's Staff"; David Giambusso, "Following a Life of Public Service, Former Newark Deputy Mayor Headed to Prison," NJ.com, February 12, 2013, https://www.nj.com/essex/2013/02/following_a_life_of_public_ser.html; Wharton, *A Post-Racial Change Is Gonna Come*, pp. 141–42.

60. Wharton, *A Post-Racial Change Is Gonna Come*, pp. 141–42.

61. Curvin, *Inside Newark,* p. 226.

62. Nuzzi, "The Ugly Truth"; David Giambusso, "Appointee for Failed Newark Water Agency Spent $16K to Pay Ex-Husband to Design New Offices," NJ.com, February 9, 2012, https://www.nj.com/news/2012/02/would-be _official_for_failed_n.html; David Giambusso, "Funds Flowing Through Newark Watershed Power Escalating Battle over City's Most Precious Asset," NJ.com, January 29, 2012, https://www.nj.com/news/2012/01/newark _water.html.

63. Nuzzi, "The Ugly Truth"; Gillespie, *The New Black Politician,* p. 174.

64. Nuzzi, "The Ugly Truth"; Karen Yi, "Ex-Newark Watershed Director Sentenced to 8 Years for Kickback Scheme," NJ.com, September 22, 2017, https://www.nj.com/essex/2017/09/newark_watershed_director_linda _watkins-brashear_s.html; Moran, "Booker Is Running. I've Watched Him for 20 Years. Here's What I've Learned"; U.S. Department of Justice, "Former Executive Director of Newark Watershed Conservation and Development Corp. Sentenced to 102 Months in Prison for Role in Nearly $1 Million Kickback and Fraud Scheme," press release, September 22, 2017, https://www.justice.gov/usao-nj/pr/former-executive-director-newark -watershed-conservation-and-development-corp-sentenced.

65. Curvin, *Inside Newark,* p. 259.

66. Wharton, *A Post-Racial Change Is Gonna Come,* pp. 142–43.

67. Ibid., p. 86.

68. Curvin, *Inside Newark,* p. 241.

69. Wharton, *A Post-Racial Change Is Gonna Come,* p. 77.

70. Curvin, *Inside Newark,* p. 231.

71. Timothy Meads, "Is Senator Booker Auditioning for the Presidency or a Daytime Drama?" Townhall, August 3, 2018, https://townhall.com/tip sheet/timothymeads/2018/08/03/untitled-n2506676; Scott McKay, "The Histrionics of Fraud," *American Spectator,* January 12, 2017, https://specta tor.org/the-histrionics-of-a-fraud/.

72. Wharton, *A Post-Racial Change Is Gonna Come,* pp. 181–82.

73. Curvin, *Inside Newark,* p. 222; Wharton, *A Post-Racial Change Is Gonna Come,* p. 78; Scott Raab, "The Battle of Newark, Starring Cory Booker," *Esquire,* July 16, 2008, https://www.esquire.com/news-politics/a4732/cory -booker-0708/.

74. Nuzzi, "The Ugly Truth"; Curvin, *Inside Newark,* p. 223.

75. Gillespie, *The New Black Politician,* pp. 178–79.

76. Wharton, *A Post-Racial Change Is Gonna Come,* pp. 183–84.

77. Dale Russakoff, *The Prize: Who's In Charge of America's Schools?* (Boston: Houghton Mifflin, 2015), p. 55; "Mark Zuckerberg Announces $100 Million Grant," *Oprah Winfrey Show,* aired on September 24, 2010, http://www .oprah.com/own-oprahshow/mark-zuckerbergs-big-announcement-video.

78. Wharton, *A Post-Racial Change Is Gonna Come,* pp. 159–60.

79. Curvin, *Inside Newark,* pp. 293–94; Russakoff, *The Prize,* pp. 58, 61, 63; David Chen, "Newark Mayor Backed Bloomberg, Then Got Funds," *New York Times,* October 27, 2009, https://www.nytimes.com/2009/10/28/nyregion /28booker.html.

80. Russakoff, *The Prize,* pp. 58–59.

81. Curvin, *Inside Newark,* p. 294; "Academics Say $1M Newark School Reform Survey Was Inconclusive," NJ.com, December 30, 2010, https://www.nj .com/news/2010/12/academics_say_1m_newark_school.html.

82. Steve Strunsky, "22 Years of State Control over Newark Schools: A Timeline," NJ.com, n.d., https://www.nj.com/essex/2017/09/timeline_22_years _of_state_control_of_newark_schoo.html.

83. Wharton, *A Post-Racial Change Is Gonna Come,* p. 159.

84. Russakoff, *The Prize,* p. 224; Dan Ivers, "Classrooms, Contracts and Consultants: How Was $200M Spent on Newark Schools?" NJ.com, September 10, 2015, https://www.nj.com/essex/2015/09/classrooms_contracts_and_con sultants_see_how_200m.html.

85. Curvin, *Inside Newark,* pp. 295–96.

86. Russakoff, *The Prize,* p. 85.

87. Tom Cheredar, "Cory Booker Confirms That LinkedIn's Reid Hoffman Is Among WayWire's Angel Investors," VentureBeat, March 11, 2013, https:// venturebeat.com/2013/03/11/waywire-investors/; Marc Tracy, "Cory Booker's Shady Role in Web Startup Waywire," *New Republic,* August 7, 2013, https://newrepublic.com/article/114197/cory-bookers-role-startup -waywire-shady-unsurprisingly; Sarah Jones, "Cory Booker is not your friend," *New Republic,* January 12, 2017, https://newrepublic.com/minutes /139825/cory-booker-not-friend; David M. Halbfinger, Raymond Hernandez, and Claire Cain Miller, "Tech Magnates Bet on Booker and His Future," *New York Times,* August 6, 2013, https://www.nytimes.com /2013/08/07/nyregion/tech-magnates-bet-on-booker-in-web-venture .html.

88. Halbfinger, Hernandez, and Miller, "Tech Magnates Bet on Booker and His Future."

89. Tracy, "Cory Booker's Shady Role in Web Startup Waywire."; Jones, "Cory Booker is not your friend."

90. Wharton, *A Post-Racial Change Is Gonna Come,* p. 174.

91. Reuters, "Newark Mayor Booker Files Papers to Run for Senate," *Chicago Tribune,* January 11, 2013, https://www.chicagotribune.com/news/ct-xpm -2013–01–11-sns-rt-us-usa-politics-newjerseybre90a18m-20130111-story .html.

92. Maggie Haberman, "Lautenberg Will Not Seek Reelection," Politico, February 15, 2013, https://www.politico.com/story/2013/02/lautenberg-will-not -seek-re-election-87669.html.

93. Adam Clymer, "Frank Lautenberg, New Jersey Senator in His 5th Term,

Dies at 89," *New York Times*, June 3, 2013, https://www.nytimes.com
/2013/06/04/nyregion/frank-lautenberg-new-jersey-senator.html.

94. David Giambusso, "Cory Booker's Legacy in Newark Under Spotlight as He
Looks to Senate," NJ.com, October 6, 2013, https://www.nj.com/politics
/2013/10/cory_bookers_legacy_in_newark_under_spotlight_as_he_looks
_to_senate.html.

95. Ashley Koning and David Redlawsk, "Polls, Media, and Polarization Have
Made New Jersey's Special Senate Election Between Cory Booker and
Steve Lonegan a Must-Watch," LSE US Centre (blog), October 15, 2013,
https://blogs.lse.ac.uk/usappblog/2013/10/15/new-jersey-special-senate
-election/.

96. Jonathan D. Salant, "Here Are All the Stunning Ways N.J. Republicans Lost
Senate Races over 40 Years. Can They Win Tuesday?" NJ.com, n.d., https://
www.nj.com/politics/2018/08/nj_republicans_have_been_losing_senate
_races_for_40_years_can_bob_hugin_break_the_losing_streak.html.

97. Raymond Hernandez, "Booker to End Association with Start-Up He
Founded," *New York Times*, September 6, 2013, https://www.nytimes
.com/2013/09/07/nyregion/booker-to-end-association-with-start-up-he
-founded.html.

98. Adam Clark, "Cory Booker's Brother Opened a School So Bad It Got Shut
Down. N.J. Just Gave Him a $150K Education Job," NJ.com, July 11, 2019,
https://www.nj.com/education/2019/07/cory-bookers-brother-opened-a
-school-so-bad-it-got-shut-down-nj-just-gave-him-a-150k-education-job
.html.

99. Elizabeth Titus, "Booker Wins New Jersey Senate Seat," Politico, October 16,
2013, https://www.politico.com/story/2013/10/cory-booker-new-jersey
-senate-election-098436.

100. Fallon, "Cory Booker's 2013 rise to the Senate was fueled by outsider status
and insider maneuvering."

101. Tom Moran, "NJ Political Bosses Pose a Hurdle to Reform of Repugnant
Payoff System," NJ.com, September 18, 2011, http://blog.nj.com/njv_tom
_moran/2011/09/nj_political_bosses_pose_a_hur.html.

102. Fallon, "Cory Booker's 2013 rise to the Senate was fueled by outsider status
and insider maneuvering."

103. Tom Moran, "Moran: Jersey City Mayor Jerramiah Healy Likes a Good
Fight—and He's Found One," NJ.com, May 5, 2013, http://blog.nj.com/njv
_tom_moran/2013/05/moran_jersey_city_mayor_jerram.html.

104. Fallon, "Cory Booker's 2013 rise to the Senate was fueled by outsider status
and insider maneuvering"; Thomas Moriarty, "Ex-Passaic Mayor Alex
Blanco Gets 2 Years in Prison in Bribery Scheme," NJ.com, April 18, 2017,
https://www.nj.com/passaic-county/2017/04/former_passaic_mayor_alex
_blanco_sentenced_for_tak.html.

105. Lauren Hepler, "Cory Booker's Silicon Valley Money Machine: Zuckerberg,

Andreessen, Hoffman," *Silicon Valley Business Journal,* October 22, 2013, https://www.bizjournals.com/sanjose/news/2013/10/22/corey-bookers-300k-silicon-valley.html.

106. "Facebook campaign contributions Mark Zuckerberg Congress donations," Verge, April 11, 2018, https://www.theverge.com/2018/4/11/17219930 /facebook-campaign-contributions-mark-zuckerberg-congress-donations.

107. Garfield, "Mark Zuckerberg Once Made a $100 Million Investment in a Major US City to Help Fix Its Schools."

108. "Booker hires chief of staff from Facebook," *New York Post,* October 23, 2013, https://nypost.com/2013/10/23/booker-hires-chief-of-staff-from -facebook/.

109. "Cory Booker," Ballotpedia, accessed June 14, 2019, https://ballotpedia.org /Cory_Booker.

110. "Senate Democratic Leaders Unveil Save the Internet Act to Restore Net Neutrality Protections," Ed Markey's Senate page, March 6, 2019, press release, https://www.markey.senate.gov/news/press-releases/senate-democratic -leaders-unveil-save-the-internet-act-to-restore-net-neutrality-protections; "Oops: Net Neutrality Advocates Just Made the Case for Regulating Google and Facebook," *Investor's Business Daily,* August 30, 2018, https://www.inves tors.com/politics/editorials/net-neutrality-google-facebook/.

111. "NJ Sen.-elect Booker Names Chief of Staff," *Trentonian,* October 22, 2013, https://www.trentonian.com/news/nj-sen—elect-booker-names-chief-of -staff/article_ef79e737-08f7-5c35-aa6f-78764bad5ebc.html; Matt Katz, "Mo' Butler, Newark Mayor Cory Booker's Behind-the-Scenes Guy," *Philadelphia Inquirer,* December 10, 2012, https://www.inquirer.com/philly/news /politics/nj/20121210_Mo__Butler__Newark_Mayor_Cory_Booker_s_be hind-the-scenes_guy.html.

112. "Newark Charter School Fund Budget Raises Questions," https://philan thropynewsdigest.org/news/newark-charter-school-fund-budget-raises -questions; Newark Charter School Fund, Inc., Internal Revenue Service, Form 990, 2016, p. 7.

113. Max Pizarro, "EXCLUSIVE: Booker COS Mo Butler Going to Work for Mercury," *Observer,* January 19, 2016, https://observer.com/2016/01/exclu sive-booker-cos-mo-butler-going-to-work-for-mercury/; David Wildstein, "Mo Butler Named Partner at Mercury," *New Jersey Globe,* June 8, 2018, https://newjerseyglobe.com/section-2/mo-butler-named-partner-at-mer cury/; Rebecca Panico, "Newark Contracts with PR Firm for $225K to Help with Lead Messaging," Tapinto.net, December 20, 2018, https://www .tapinto.net/towns/newark/articles/newark-contracts-with-pr-firm-for -225k-to-help-with-lead-messaging.

114. Theodoric Meyer, "Why the Russia Probe Demolished One Lobbying Firm but Spared Another," Politico, February 1, 2018, https://www.politico.com /story/2018/02/01/russia-probe-lobbying-podesta-mercury-380579.

115. "Michael Soliman," Mercury LLC, accessed June 5, 2019, http://www
.mercuryllc.com/experts/michael-soliman/#; "Mercury Welcomes Michael
Soliman," Mercury LLC, September 6, 2013, http://www.mercuryllc.com
/mercury-welcomes-michael-soliman/; "Michael Soliman Named Partner at
Mercury: Soliman is 10th Partner at Global Bipartisan Public Strategy Firm,"
Mercury LLC, May 13, 2016, http://www.mercuryllc.com/michael-soliman
-named-partner-mercury-soliman-10th-partner-global-bipartisan-public
-strategy-firm/.

116. "Modia 'Mo' Butler Joins Mercury," Mercury LLC, February 23, 2016,
http://www.mercuryllc.com/2653-2/; Wildstein, "Mo Butler Named Partner at Mercury."

117. Katz, "Mo' Butler, Newark Mayor Cory Booker's Behind-the-Scenes Guy."

118. Opensecrets.org, "Mercury: Summary," 2019, https://www.opensecrets.org
/lobby/firmsum.php?id=D000022461.

119. Opensecrets.org, "Mercury: Summary," 2018, https://www.opensecrets.org
/lobby/firmsum.php?id=D000022461&year=2018; Creating and Restoring
Equal Access to Equivalent Samples Act of 2018, S. 974, 115th Cong. (2017),
cosponsors, https://www.congress.gov/bill/115th-congress/senate-bill/974
/cosponsors; Creating and Restoring Equal Access to Equivalent Samples Act
of 2018, S. 974, 115th Cong. (2017), summary, https://www.congress.gov
/bill/115th-congress/senate-bill/974; David Wildstein, "Booker Gets Judiciary Panel Seat," New Jersey Globe, January 9, 2018, https://newjerseyglobe
.com/section-2/booker-gets-judiciary-panel-seat/.

120. "Senate Passes Bill to Give Anthrax Vaccines to First Responders," Emergent
Biosolutions, November 18, 2016, https://www.emergentbiosolutions.com
/story/senate-passes-bill-give-anthrax-vaccines-first-responders; First
Responder Anthrax Preparedness Act, S. 1915, 114th Cong. (2015), https://
www.congress.gov/bill/114th-congress/senate-bill/1915/cosponsors; Search
page, Emergent Biosolutions, p. 4, https://www.emergentbiosolutions.com
/node?page=4; Berkeley Lovelace Jr., "Emergent BioSolutions Clears Hurdle
for Anthrax Vaccine Facility," CNBC, June 21, 2016, https://www.cnbc
.com/2016/06/21/emergent-biosolutions-clears-hurdle-for-anthrax-vaccine
-facility.html; "BioThrax," Emergent BioSolutions, last revised November
2015, https://www.fda.gov/media/71954/download; Michael Fitzhugh,
"U.S. Federal Agencies Pledge Up to $1.1B for Emergent Biosolutions' An-
thrax Vaccine," BioWorld Today, December 8, 2016, http://www.bioworld
.com/content/us-federal-agencies-pledge-11b-emergent-biosolutions-an
thrax-vaccine-0; Opensecrets.org, "Emergent BioSolutions: Summary,"
2017, accessed June 5, 2019, https://www.opensecrets.org/lobby/clientsum.
php?id=D000025674&year=2017; Addy Baird, "Cory Booker Launches
2020 Campaign with Attempt to Rewrite Big Pharma History," Think Progress, February 4, 2019, https://thinkprogress.org/cory-booker-big-pharma
-history-bda560985168/.

NOTES

121. Opensecrets.org, "Morganza Action Cmte: Issues," 2017, accessed September 23, 2019, https://www.opensecrets.org/lobby/clientissues_spec .php?id=D000053955&year=2017&spec=ENV; Opensecrets.org, "Mercury: Summary," 2017, accessed August 19, 2019, https://www.opensecrets .org/lobby/firmsum.php?id=D000022461&year=2017; "Booker Announces Committee Assignments for 115th Congress," Cory Booker's Senate page, December 15, 2016, press release, https://www.booker.senate.gov/?p=press _release&id=510.

122. Opensecrets.org, "Mercury: Summary," 2017, accessed August 19, 2019, https://www.opensecrets.org/lobby/firmsum.php?id=D000022461&year=2017; Ballotpedia, s.v. "United States Senate Committee on Commerce, Science, and Transportation," accessed September 23, 2019, https://ballotpedia.org/United _States_Senate_Committee_on_Commerce,_Science,_and_Transportation.

123. Opensecrets.org, "Mercury: Summary," 2017, accessed August 19, 2019, https://www.opensecrets.org/lobby/firmsum.php?id=D000022461&year =2017.

124. Andrew Breiner, "Progressives Outraged over Booker, Democrats' Vote on Prescription Drugs from Canada," *Roll Call*, January 12, 2017, https://www .rollcall.com/politics/pharma-booker-canada.

125. Affordable and Safe Prescription Drug Importation Act, S. 469, 115th Cong. (2017), cosponsors, https://www.congress.gov/bill/115th-congress/senate -bill/469/cosponsors; Opensecrets.org, "AmerisourceBergen Corp: Bills," 2018, https://www.opensecrets.org/lobby/clientbills.php?id=D000021841& year=2018; Opensecrets.org, "S. 771: Sponsors," accessed August 19, 2019, https://www.opensecrets.org/lobby/billspons.php?id=s771–115.

126. FEC data.

127. Opensecrets.org, "Cosentino Group: Summary," 2017, https://www.open secrets.org/lobby/clientsum.php?id=F211654&year=2017; Opensecrets.org, "Cosentino Group: Summary," 2018, accessed September 20, 2019, https:// www.opensecrets.org/lobby/clientsum.php?id=F211654&year=2018; Open secrets.org, "Cosentino Group: Summary," 2019, https://www.opensecrets .org/lobby/clientsum.php?id=F211654&year=2019.

128. "Booker Announces Committee Assignments for 115th Congress"; Open secrets.org, "Cosentino Group: Issues," 2018, accessed September 23, 2019, https://www.opensecrets.org/lobby/clientissues_spec.php?id=F211654& year=2018&spec=TRD; Opensecrets.org, "Cosentino Group: Agencies," 2018, accessed September 23, 2019, https://www.opensecrets.org/lobby /clientagns.php?id=F211654&year=2018.

129. Opensecrets.org, "Cosentino Group: Lobbyists," 2017, accessed September 23, 2019, https://www.opensecrets.org/lobby/firmsum.php?id=D00 0022461&year=2017.

130. Herb Jackson, "Booker Adds Foreign Relations to Senate Assignments," *North Jersey Record*, December 15, 2016, https://www.northjersey.com

/story/news/new-jersey/2016/12/15/booker-adding-foreign-relations
-assignments/95470566/.

131. Opensecrets.org, "Mercury Public Affairs: Registrants," 2017, accessed
June 16, 2019, https://www.opensecrets.org/fara/registrants/D000071638?
cycle=2017; "Engineered Stone Group Supports U.S. Tariffs," Stoneupdate
.com, December 26, 2018, https://www.stoneupdate.com/news-info/indus
try/1656-engineered-stone-group-supports-u-s-tariffs.

132. Opensecrets.org, "Mercury Public Affairs: Registrants," 2018, accessed
June 16, 2019, https://www.opensecrets.org/fara/registrants/D000071638?
cycle=2018.

133. "Booker Travels to Turkey, Afghanistan, Lebanon to Talk Regional Security,
Stability," Cory Booker's Senate page, June 4, 2018, https://www.booker
.senate.gov/?p=press_release&id=799; Jonathan D. Salant, "N.J.'s Booker,
Visiting Mideast, Says U.S. Must Do More to Help Syrian Refugees,"
NJ.com, August 21, 2016, https://www.nj.com/politics/2016/08/njs_booker
_visiting_mideast_says_us_must_do_more_t.html.

134. "Candidate Briefing: What a Cory Booker Presidency Could Mean for the
Gulf," Gulf International Forum, February 1, 2019, https://gulfif.org/candi
date-profile-what-a-cory-booker-2020-run-could-mean-for-the-gulf/.

135. Hunter Walker, "Cory Booker Says the U.S. Needs to 'Reexamine' Its
'Entire Relationship' with Saudi Arabia," Yahoo, October 18, 2018, https://
news.yahoo.com/cory-booker-says-u-s-needs-re-examine-entire-relation
ship-saudi-arabia-211344667.html.

136. Derek Seidman, "The Power Behind the Pipelines: PennEast Pipeline," Public Accountability Initiative, February 6, 2018, https://public-accountability
.org/report/the-power-behind-the-pipelines-penneast-pipeline/.

137. Opensecrets.org, "PennEast Pipeline: Report Images," 2015, https://
www.opensecrets.org/lobby/client_reports.php?id=F198799%20%20%20
&year=2015.

138. "The PennEast Pipeline Cuts Through Hunterdon County," Stoppenneast
.org, March 3, 2017, https://www.stoppenneast.org/index.php/county-pages
/hunterdon-county.

139. Mike Spille, "The Dense Web of Financial Interests," The Cost of the Pipeline, September 3, 2016, https://thecostofthepipeline.com/2016/09/03/the
-dense-web-of-financial-interests/; "Sen. Booker 'Extremely Concerned'
About PennEast in Letter to FERC," Insider NJ, press release, April 2, 2018,
https://www.insidernj.com/press-release/sen-booker-extremely-concerned
-penneast-letter-ferc/.

140. Laura Nahmias, "Lobbyists Prepare for Medical Marijuana Boomlet,"
Politico, January 6, 2015, https://www.politico.com/states/new-york/albany
/story/2015/01/lobbyists-prepare-for-medical-marijuana-boomlet-018639.

141. Josefa Velasquez, "Lobbying Strategy for Medical Marijuana Runners-up
May Be Paying Off," Politico, April 21, 2017, https://www.politico.com

/states/new-york/albany/story/2017/04/21/despite-losing-medical-marijua
na-runner-ups-maintain-lobbying-presence-in-albany-111402.

142,. Ted Sherman, "Here Are the High-Powered Influencers, Many Close to
Gov. Murphy and Lawmakers, Pushing for Legal Weed in N.J.," NJ.com,
March 22, 2019, https://www.nj.com/marijuana/2019/03/here-are-the
-high-powered-influencers-many-close-to-gov-murphy-and-lawmakers
-pushing-for-legal-weed-in-nj.html.

143. Carmin Chappell, "Cory Booker Introduces Bill to Legalize Marijuana Nationwide, with Support from Fellow 2020 Candidates," CNBC, February 28,
2019; Marijuana Justice Act of 2019, S. 597, 116th Cong. (2019), https://
www.cnbc.com/2019/02/28/cory-booker-introduces-bill-to-legalize-mar
ijuana-nationwide.html; https://www.congress.gov/bill/116th-congress
/senate-bill/597/text.

CHAPTER 5: ELIZABETH WARREN

1. Suzanna Andrews, "The Woman Who Knew Too Much," *Vanity Fair,* November 2011, https://www.vanityfair.com/news/2011/11/elizabeth-warren
-201111.

2. John Cassidy, "Elizabeth Warren's Moment," *New York Review of Books,*
May 22, 2014, https://www.nybooks.com/articles/2014/05/22/elizabeth
-warrens-moment/.

3. Elizabeth Warren, *A Fighting Chance* (New York: Metropolitan Books, 2014),
https://books.google.com/books/about/A_Fighting_Chance.html?id=rN
S4AwAAQBAJ; "A Fighting Chance," Amazon.com, as quoted in a comment
from *New York Review of Books.*

4. Warren, *A Fighting Chance.*

5. Jonathan M. Hanen, "The Elizabeth Warren Cheering Squad," Capital Research Center, May 1, 2015, http://capitalresearch.org/app/uploads/OT0515
.pdf.

6. Ibid.

7. Andrews, "The Woman Who Knew Too Much."

8. Susan Bordo, *The Destruction of Hillary Clinton* (Brooklyn: Melville House,
2017) p. 54.

9. Andrews, "The Woman Who Knew Too Much."

10. " 'Occupy Wall Street' Protests Turn Violent When Demonstrators Clash
With Police," Fox News, November 21, 2015, https://www.foxnews.com
/us/occupy-wall-street-protests-turn-violent-when-demonstrators-clash
-with-police.

11. Antonia Felix, *Elizabeth Warren: Her Fight. Her Work. Her Life* (Naperville, IL:
Sourcebooks, 2018), p. 196; Samuel P. Jacobs, "Elizabeth Warren: 'I Created
Occupy Wall Street,' " Daily Beast, July 13, 2017, https://www.thedailybeast
.com/elizabeth-warren-i-created-occupy-wall-street.

12. Felix, *Elizabeth Warren*, p. 187; Warren, *A Fighting Chance*, p. 2.
13. Cassidy, "Elizabeth Warren's Moment."
14. Andrews, "The Woman Who Knew Too Much."
15. Jeffrey Toobin, "The Professor," *New Yorker*, September 10, 2012, https:// www.newyorker.com/magazine/2012/09/17/the-professor-jeffrey-too bin; Stephanie McCrummen, "Elizabeth Warren: What Kind of Senator Will She Be?," *Washington Post*, November 9, 2012, https://www.washingtonpost .com/politics/elizabeth-warren-what-kind-of-senator-will-she-be/2012/11 /09/081a6fbc-2a8a-11e2-b4e0-346287b7e56c_story.html.
16. Ylan Q. Mui, "Democrat's Control of Senate Could Hinge on Warren Campaign," *Washington Post*, September 19, https://www.washingtonpost.com /business/economy/democrats-control-of-senate-could-hinge-on-warren -campaign/2011/09/16/gIQA1HUYfK_story.html.
17. "Elizabeth Warren Fast Facts," CNN, July 3, 2019, https://www.cnn.com /2015/01/09/us/elizabeth-warren-fast-facts/index.html.
18. Sabrina Tavernise, "How Elizabeth Warren Learned to Fight," *New York Times*, June 24, 2019, https://www.nytimes.com/2019/06/24/us/politics /elizabeth-warren-republican-conservative-democrat.html; Warren, *A Fighting Chance*, p. 6.
19. Warren, *A Fighting Chance*, pp. 11–17.
20. Nancy Moffit, "The Two Income Trap," *Wharton Alumni Magazine*, Fall 2003, p. 9, http://whartonmagazine.com/issues/fall-2003/the-two-income -trap/.
21. Warren, *A Fighting Chance*, pp. 23–27, 38; "Elizabeth Warren Fast Facts."
22. Stephanie Ebbert, "Directories Identified Warren as Minority," *Boston Globe*, April 30, 2012, http://archive.boston.com/news/local/massachusetts/articles /2012/04/30/elizabeth_warren_was_listed_as_a_minority_professor_in _law_directories_in_the_80s_and_90s/.
23. Gregory Krieg, "Here's the Deal with Elizabeth Warren's Native American Heritage," CNN, October 15, 2018, https://www.cnn.com/2016/06/29 /politics/elizabeth-warren-native-american-pocahontas/index.html.
24. William Cummings, "In Response to Trump's 'Pocahontas' Jibes, Warren Releases Results of DNA Test," *USA Today*, October 15, 2018, https://www .usatoday.com/story/news/politics/2018/10/15/elizabeth-warren-dna-test /1645840002/.
25. Elizabeth Hartfield, "Elizabeth Warren Says She Used Native American Heritage to Meet Friends," ABC News, May 2, 2012, https://abcnews.go.com /blogs/politics/2012/05/elizabeth-warren-says-she-used-native-american -heritage-to-meet-friends/.
26. Mary Carmichael and Stephanie Ebbert, "Warren says she told schools of heritage," *Boston Globe*, May 31, 2012, http://archive.boston.com/news /local/massachusetts/articles/2012/05/31/elizabeth_warren_acknowledges _telling_harvard_penn_of_native_american_status/?page=full.

27. Ibid.

28. Aaron Blake, "University of Pennsylvania also listed Elizabeth Warren as a minority," *Washington Post,* May 10, 2012.

29. Felix, *Elizabeth Warren,* pp. 101, 103.

30. Carmichael and Ebbert, "Warren says she told schools of heritage."

31. Jennifer Levitz, "Law Review Called Senate Candidate Warren 'Woman of Color,' " *Wall Street Journal,* May 15, 2012.

32. "Welcome Guinier," *Harvard Crimson,* February 4, 1998, https://www.the crimson.com/article/1998/2/4/welcome-guinier-pwe-welcome-the -announcement/; Hartfield, "Elizabeth Warren Says She Used Native American Heritage to Meet Friends."

33. Idil Tuysuzoglu, "Tensions and Tenure: Elizabeth Warren at the Law School," *Harvard Crimson,* May 22, 2018, https://www.thecrimson.com /article/2018/5/22/warren-tenure/; Ebbert, "Directories Identified Warren as Minority."

34. Kevin D. Williamson, "Elizabeth Warren's Wall Street Money Machine," *National Review,* April 18, 2012, https://www.nationalreview.com/2012/04 /elizabeth-warrens-wall-street-money-machine-kevin-d-williamson/; Homepage, Cleary Gottlieb, accessed April 3, 2019, https://www.clearygottlieb.com/; "Cleary Gottlieb Steen & Hamilton LLP," Vault, accessed June 20, 2019, https:// www.vault.com/company-profiles/law/cleary-gottlieb-steen-hamilton-llp.

35. Teresa A. Sullivan, Elizabeth Warren, and Jay Lawrence Westbrook, *The Fragile Middle Class: Americans in Debt* (New Haven: Yale University Press, 2000).

36. Felix, *Elizabeth Warren,* p. 107.

37. Larkin Warner, *The Encyclopedia of Oklahoma History and Culture,* s.v. "Oklahoma Economy," n.d., https://www.okhistory.org/publications/enc/entry .php?entryname=OKLAHOMA%20ECONOMY.

38. Felix, *Elizabeth Warren,* pp. 145–47.

39. "Elizabeth Warren Bought Foreclosed Homes to Make a Quick Profit," *National Review,* May 27, 2015, https://www.nationalreview.com/2015/05 /elizabeth-warren-real-estate-profiteer-jillian-kay-melchior-eliana-johnson/.

40. Jerry Kronenberg, "Records: Prof profited by buying, selling homes," *Boston Herald,* June 2, 2012 (updated November 17, 2018), https://www.boston herald.com/2012/06/02/records-prof-profited-by-buying-selling-homes/; Melchior and Johnson, "Elizabeth Warren Bought Foreclosed Homes to Make a Quick Profit."

41. Search done at the Oklahoma County Clerk website. Select ROD, and search for "Warren Elizabeth." Amounts are on individual documents; http://okcc .online/

42. Andrews, "The Woman Who Knew Too Much."

43. Verified Statement of Professor Elizabeth Warren in Accordance with Section 1103 of the Bankruptcy Code and Rule 2014 of the Federal Rules of Bank-

ruptcy Procedure, In the United States Bankruptcy Court for the District of Delaware, Kaiser Aluminum, et al. Chapter 11 proceedings, Case No. 02–10429 (JFK), Section 18, https://www.scribd.com/document/291507147/In-Re-Kaiser-Elizabeth-Warren-Verified-Statement.

44. Jonathan D. Glater: "Management; For Armstrong, Bankruptcy Is Lesser of Two Evils," *New York Times*, December 20, 2000, https://www.nytimes.com/2000/12/20/business/management-for-armstrong-bankruptcy-is-lesser-of-two-evils.html; Annie Linskey, "Dow Breast Implant Case Spotlights Elizabeth Warren's Work Helping Big Corporations Navigate Bankruptcies," *Washington Post*, July 15, 2019, https://www.washingtonpost.com/politics/dow-breast-implant-case-spotlights-elizabeth-warrens-work-helping-big-corporations-navigate-bankruptcies/2019/07/15/06b0d676–82fc-11e9–95a9-e2c830afe24f_story.html.

45. Ibid.

46. Linskey, "Dow Breast Implant Case Spotlights Elizabeth Warren's Work."

47. Matthew Sturdevant, "Travelers Asbestos Case Remains at Center of U.S. Senate Race Between Scott Brown, Elizabeth Warren," *Hartford Courant*, October 12, 2012, https://www.courant.com/business/hc-xpm-2012–10–12-hc-travelers-scott-brown-elizabeth-warren-20121012-story.html.

48. "Elizabeth Warren's Legal Work," ElizabethWarren.com, accessed June 26, 2019, https://elizabethwarren.com/legal-work/.

49. Verified Statement of Professor Elizabeth Warren, Case No. 02–10429 (JFK); Inflation Calculator, $700 in 2002 —> $998.33 in 2019, n.d., http://www.in2013dollars.com/us/inflation/2002?amount=700.

50. Hillary Chabot, "Miner: Elizabeth Warren's biz 'hypocritical,'" *Boston Herald,* September 25, 2012, 2018, https://www.bostonherald.com/2012/09/25/miner-elizabeth-warrens-biz-hypocritical/; "Coal Act," United Mine Workers of America, accessed June 27, 2019, http://umwa.org/for-members/pensions-retiree-info/coal-act/.

51. Chabot, "Miner: Elizabeth Warren's biz 'hypocritical.'"

52. Ibid.

53. "Interview Elizabeth Warren," *Frontline*, May 16, 2006, https://www.pbs.org/wgbh/pages/frontline/retirement/interviews/warren.html.

54. Chabot, "Miner: Elizabeth Warren's biz 'hypocritical.'"

55. "Interview Elizabeth Warren"; "Elizabeth Warren's Legal Work."

56. In Re Fairchild Aircraft Corp., 184 B.R. 910 (W.D. Tex. 1995), https://law.justia.com/cases/federal/district-courts/BR/184/910/1870056/; William A. Jacobson, "Documenting another Elizabeth Warren Fib—Fairchild Aircraft case," Legal Insurrection, November 3, 2012, https://legalinsurrection.com/2012/11/documenting-another-elizabeth-warren-fib-fairchild-aircraft-case/.

57. Jacobson, "Documenting."

58. "Prior to Debate, Warren Releases Information on Her Cases," *Boston Globe,*

October 1, 2012, https://www.boston.com/uncategorized/noprimary tagmatch/2012/10/01/prior-to-debate-warren-releases-information -on-her-cases; William A. Jacobson, "Elizabeth Warren Represented Large Utility Seeking to Liquidate Rural Electric Cooperative," Legal Insurrection, October 9, 2012, https://legalinsurrection.com/2012/10/elizabeth-warren -represented-large-utility-seeking-to-liquidate-rural-electric-cooperative/.

59. William Jacobson, "Elizabeth Warren's Implausible Dow Chemical Claim," Legal Insurrection, October 10, 2012, https://legalinsurrection.com/2012 /10/elizabeth-warrens-implausible-dow-chemical-claim/.

60. Linskey, "Dow Breast Implant Case Spotlights Elizabeth Warren's Work."

61. Ibid.

62. William Jacobson, "Elizabeth Warren held asbestos workers hostage to inter-corporate fight," Legal Insurrection, October 21, 2012, https://legal insurrection.com/2012/10/elizabeth-warren-held-asbestos-workers-hos tage-to-inter-corporate-fight/.

63. "Tax Returns," ElizabethWarren.com, n.d., https://elizabethwarren.com /tax-returns/; Elizabeth Warren, Personal Financial Disclosure, 2009.

64. Homepage, Armstrong World Industries Asbestos Personal Injury Settlement Trust, accessed April 8, 2019, http://www.armstrongworldasbestostrust. com/; "Elizabeth Warren's Legal Work."

65. Armstrong Holdings, Inc., 2004, form 10-Q, quarter 3 (filed with the Securities and Exchange Commission for the quarterly period ended September 30, 2004), https://www.sec.gov/Archives/edgar/data/7431/000119312504186 232/d10q.htm. Verified Statement of Professor Elizabeth Warren, Case No. 02–10429 (JFK), Section 18, pp. 3, 5.

66. Verified Statement of Professor Elizabeth Warren, Case No. 02–10429 (JFK).

67. "Elizabeth Warren," Harvard University, last updated June 25, 2008, http:// www.law.harvard.edu/faculty/ewarren/Warren%20CV%20062508.pdf; "Elizabeth Warren's Legal Work."

68. "Prior to Debate, Warren Releases Information on Her Cases"; Elizabeth Warren, Personal Financial Disclosures, 2008 and 2009.

69. Moffit, "The Two-Income Trap," p. 8; "Elizabeth Warren," Harvard University.

70. Libby Nelson, "Elizabeth Warren Wants to Kill the Neighborhood School," Vox, April 16, 2014, https://www.vox.com/2014/4/16/5621630/elizabeth -warren-wants-to-kill-the-neighborhood-school; Felix, Elizabeth Warren, pp. 134–35.

71. "Elizabeth Warren Suggests She's Not in the 1%," BuzzFeed News, January 27, 2012, https://www.buzzfeednews.com/article/buzzfeedpolitics/eliz abeth-warren-says-shes-not-in-the-1; Elizabeth Warren, Personal Financial Disclosures, 2008 and 2009.

72. Elizabeth Warren, Personal Financial Disclosures, 2008 and 2009.

73. "Harvard Layoffs Update, and More 'Reshaping' to Come," Harvard Maga-

zine, September 2009, https://harvardmagazine.com/2009/06/harvard-lay offs-update-more-reshaping-come; William A. Jacobson, "Another Item for *The Elizabeth Warren File*," Legal Insurrection, November 27, 2012, https://legalinsurrection.com/2012/11/another-item-for-the-elizabeth-warren-file/; Mary Carmichael, "Harvard Link Could Aid, Hinder Warren," *Boston Globe,* September 20, 2011, https://www.bostonglobe.com/metro/2011/09/19/har vard-connection-could-aid-hinder-warren/2a5aK3CYrMOwxQ67jL0EjM /story.html.

74. Carmichael, "Harvard Link Could Aid, Hinder Warren"; Internal Revenue Service, Elizabeth Warren Form 1040, 2008 and 2009.

75. Kat Stoeffel, "Elizabeth Warren has a sidekick in Daughter Amelia," The Cut, September 10, 2012, https://www.thecut.com/2012/09/elizabeth -warrens-daughter-is-her-sidekick.html.

76. Felix, *Elizabeth Warren,* pp. 139, 140, 149–50; Bob Irvy, Bradley Keoun, and Phil Kuntz, "Secret Fed Loans Gave Banks $13 Billion Undisclosed to Congress," Bloomberg, November 27, 2011, https://www.bloomberg.com/news /articles/2011-11-28/secret-fed-loans-undisclosed-to-congress-gave-banks -13-billion-in-income; Robert Chess and Ryan Kissick, "Business Talent Group: Growing the Market for Independent Business Talent," Case No. E621, "Entrepreneurship," May 11, 2017, https://www.gsb.stanford.edu /faculty-research/case-studies/business-talent-group-growing-market -independent-business-talent.

77. Michael Scherer, "The New Sheriffs of Wall Street," *Time,* May 13, 2010, http://content.time.com/time/magazine/article/0,9171,1989144,00.html.

78. Andrews, "The Woman Who Knew Too Much."

79. "Leadership," Business Talent Group, accessed June 24, 2019, https://business talentgroup.com/leadership/.

80. Jessica Pressler, "Morgan Stanley Exec Changes License Plate After No One Finds Joke That Funny," Intelligencer, December 9, 2009, http://nymag.com /intelligencer/2009/12/morgan_stanley_exec_changes_li.html.

81. "Bailed Out Banks," CNN Money, n.d., https://money.cnn.com/news/spe cials/storysupplement/bankbailout/.

82. "Leadership," Business Talent Group, accessed June 24, 2019, https://business talentgroup.com/leadership/.

83. "Geithner Is the Greatest (Possibly a Genius) . . . ," *Economic Policy Journal,* November 24, 2008, https://www.economicpolicyjournal.com/2008/11 /geithner-is-greatest-possibly-genius.html; "Bailed Out Banks"; "Portfolio Company Highlights: Boston Private Financial Holdings, Inc.," The Carlyle Group, accessed June 27, 2019, https://www.carlyle.com/our-business/port folio-of-investments/boston-private-financial-holdings-inc.

84. "Leadership," Business Talent Group, on Internet Archive, n.d., https://web .archive.org/web/20081225151047/http://www.businesstalentgroup.com /who_we_are/advisors.php (captured December 25, 2008).

85. Felix, *Elizabeth Warren,* pp. 139–40; Jody Greenstone Miller, "Temporary Workers and the 21st Century Economy," *Wall Street Journal,* November 30, 2009, https://www.wsj.com/articles/SB100014240527487039394045745679 42566170348.

86. George Zornick, "Elizabeth Warren Takes on the 'Gig Economy,'" *Nation,* May 20, 2016, https://www.thenation.com/article/elizabeth-warren-takes -on-the-gig-economy/.

87. Chess and Kissick, "Growing the Market for Independent Business Talent," p. 7.

88. Clare Malone, "Get Elected, Get Your Kids Rich: Washington Is Spoiled Rotten," Daily Beast, February 27, 2014, https://www.thedailybeast.com /get-elected-get-your-kids-rich-washington-is-spoiled-rotten.

89. Chess and Kissick, "Growing the Market for Independent Business Talent," p. 7.

90. Ellen Malcolm with Craig Unger, *When Women Win: Emily's List and the Rise of Women in American Politics* (New York: Houghton Mifflin Harcourt, 2016), pp. 280–81, https://books.google.com/books?id=q2YpCgAAQBAJ&print sec=frontcover&dq=When+Women+Win:+Emily%E2%80%99s+List+and +the+Rise+of+Women+in+American+Politics&hl=en&sa=X&ved=0ah UKEwjoy_j-2oLjAhUrT98KHWOGDOEQ6AEIKjAA#v=onepage&q =Elizabeth%20Warren&f=false.

91. David Corn, "Elizabeth Warren: Passed over for CFPB Post, But . . . ," *Mother Jones,* July 18, 2011, https://www.motherjones.com/politics/2011/07 /obama-elizabeth-warren-cfpb-cordray-senate/.

92. Julie Vorman, "Reform Bill Gives Birth to $550-Million Consumer Bureau," Center for Public Integrity, July 15, 2010, https://publicintegrity.org/busi ness/reform-bill-gives-birth-to-550-million-consumer-bureau/.

93. Felix, *Elizabeth Warren,* p. 168; Timothy F. Geithner, *Stress Test: Reflections on the Financial Crisis* (New York: Broadway Books, 2014), p. 427.

94. Felix, *Elizabeth Warren,* p. 169.

95. Peter Schroeder and Megan R. Wilson, "Warren showed softer side to Wall Street behind the scenes as Obama aide," The Hill, October 4, 2012, https:// thehill.com/business-a-lobbying/260111-warren-showed-softer-side-to -wall-street-as-obama-aide.

96. Ibid.

97. Emily Jashinsky, "Elizabeth Warren Is Hypocritically Meeting with Wall Street CEOs," *Washington Examiner,* September 20, 2017, https://www .washingtonexaminer.com/elizabeth-warren-is-hypocritically-meeting -with-wall-street-ceos.

98. Jonathan Martin, "As Warren and Sanders Jockey for Support, One Takes a Road More Traveled," *New York Times,* September 19, 2017, https://www .nytimes.com/2017/09/19/us/politics/bernie-sanders-elizabeth-warren -democrats-presidential-election.html.

99. C. Thompson, "Elizabeth Warren Calls for Dimon to Resign from New York Fed," Bloomberg, May 13, 2012, https://www.bloomberg.com/news /articles/2012–05–13/elizabeth-warren-calls-for-dimon-to-resign-from -new-york-fed.

100. Felix, *Elizabeth Warren,* p. 132; "Sushil Tyagi," LinkedIn profile, accessed January 15, 2019, https://www.linkedin.com/in/sushil-tyagi/.

101. Elizabeth Warren and Amelia Warren Tyagi, *All Your Worth: The Ultimate Lifetime Money Plan* (New York: Free Press, 2005), p. 276, https://books. google.com/books/about/All_Your_Worth.html?id=IfGaD4FKm04C; "Elizabeth Warren Opens Up to INDIA New England," India New England News, December 31, 2012, https://indianewengland.com/2012/12/elizabeth -warren-opens-up-to-india-new-england/.

102. Specific Power of Attorney, Los Angeles, California, Kali Gori Private Limited, December 18, 2009.

103. "TriColor Films—Los Angeles, CA," Tricolorfilms.com, on Internet Archive, accessed July 1, 2019, https://web.archive.org/web/20021129195220 /http://www.tricolorfilms.com/ (captured November 29, 2002).

104. Shilpa Rohatgi, "Bharat Bala Hopes to Create a Buzz at Cannes with His English-French Film 'Hari Om,' " *India Today,* December 8, 2003, https:// www.indiatoday.in/magazine/society-the-arts/story/20031208-bharat -bala-hopes-to-create-a-buzz-at-cannes-with-his-english-french-film -hari-om-791384–2003–12–08; "Nadeem, Taurani Gave Contract Money to Kill Gulshan: Witness," Rediff.com, September 25, 2001, http://m.rediff .com/news/2001/sep/25gul.htm; "Gulshan Kumar Murder Case: Mumbai Police Arrest Tips Audio Owner Ramesh Taurani," *India Today,* October 20, 1997, https://www.indiatoday.in/magazine/indiascope/story/19971020 -gulshan-kumar-murder-case-mumbai-police-arrests-tips-audio-owner -ramesh-taurani-832352–1997–10–20.

105. "The Song of Sparrows," *New York Times,* on Internet Archive, accessed June 26, 2019, https://web.archive.org/web/20080311071208/http://movies .nytimes.com/movie/452648/The-Song-of-Sparrows/details (captured March 11, 2008); "Persian Films," Ohio State University, accessed July 25, 2019, https://library.osu.edu/documents/middle-eastern-studies/Middle East Films/Persian Films at OSU.pdf.

106. Stephen Holden, "Losing His Soul, Then Finding It Again, After a Season in Hell," *New York Times,* April 2, 2009, https://www.nytimes.com/2009/04/03 /movies/03spar.html?rref=collection%2Fcollection%2Fmovie-guide&action =click&contentCollection=undefined&region=stream&module=stream _unit&version=latest-stories&contentPlacement=1&pgtype=collection.

107. "The Song of Sparrows (2008)," *New York Times,* on Internet Archive, accessed June 27, 2019, https://web.archive.org/web/20101012090309/http:// movies.nytimes.com:80/movie/452648/The-Song-of-Sparrows/details (captured October 12, 2010).

108. "The Song of Sparrows," Thesongofsparrows.com/fa, on Internet Archive, n.d., translated, https://web.archive.org/web/20130103002223/http:/www .thesongofsparrows.com/fa/ (captured January 8, 2013).

109. "About Us," Cultural and Art Organization of Municipality of Tehran, accessed July 1, 2019, https://int.farhangsara.ir/about-us.

110. "Schoolchildren's Masters Are Honored in the Special Program the Seal of Hostages," farhangsara.ir, accessed on June 24, 2019, translated, https://far hangsara.ir/tabid/4166/ArticleId/79121/ (translated).

111. "Qods Cultural Center Hosts Marchers of Qods Day," farhangsara.ir, accessed on June 17, 2019, translated, https://farhangsara.ir/tabid/4166/Arti cleId/79050/ (translated); Amir Vahdat, "Protestors in Iran, Iraq Burn Israel, US Flags on 'Quds Day,' " Associated Press, May 31, 2019, https://www .apnews.com/fe7f04ea375d4ff0b194c63ea22cc61e.

112. "Marching on the Day of the Saint of Tehran (translated)," Wikipedia, n.d., photograph, https://en.wikipedia.org/wiki/File:%D8%B1%D8 %A7%D9%87%D9%BE%DB%8C%D9%85%D8%A7%DB%8C%DB%8C _%D8%B1%D9%88%D8%B2_%D9%82%D8%AF%D8%B3_%D8%AF%D 8%B1_%D8%AA%D9%87%D8%B1%D8%A7%D9%86_-_%DB%B6–%DB %B2%DB%B8.jpg; https://www.apnews.com/fe7f04ea375d4ff0b194c63ea 22cc61e.

113. "Agents and Actors," Thesongofsparrows.com/fa/عوامل-و-بازیگران, on Internet Archive, n.d., translated, https://web.archive.org/web/20130103002223 /http:/www.thesongofsparrows.com/fa/%D8%B9%D9%88%D8%A7%D9 %85%D9%84–%D9%88–%D8%A8%D8%A7%D8%B2%DB%8C%DA%AF %D8%B1%D8%A7%D9%86.

114. John F. Burns and Michael R. Gordon, "U.S. Says Iran Helped Iraqis Kill Five G.I.'s," *New York Times*, July 3, 2007, https://www.nytimes.com /2007/07/03/world/middleeast/03iraq.html.

115. Hossein Jaseb and Fredrik Dahl, "Ahmadinejad Says Israel Will 'Disappear,' " Reuters, June 2, 2008, https://www.reuters.com/article/us-iran-israel-usa /ahmadinejad-says-israel-will-disappear-idUSL0261250620080603.

116. "Najva Ashorai," IMDb, n.d., https://www.imdb.com/title/tt1179449/refer ence.

117. "TriColor Films—Los Angeles, CA," Tricolorfilms.com, on Internet Archive, accessed September 3, 2019, https://web.archive.org/web/20021209175900 /http:/www.tajmahalfilm.com/partners.htm (captured June 22, 2003).

118. Elizabeth Warren (U.S. Senator Elizabeth Warren), Facebook post, April 10, 2017, https://www.facebook.com/senatorelizabethwarren /posts/759883547507474; George Zornick, "Elizabeth Warren's 'Big Fight' Against Monopolies," *Nation*, February 15, 2018, https://www.thenation .com/article/elizabeth-warrens-big-fight-against-monopolies/; Haley Sweet- land Edwards, "The Bubbling Concern over Two Beer Giants' Blockbuster

Merger," *Time*, July 26, 2016, http://time.com/4422937/beer-merger-bud weiser-miller-coors/.

119. Arthur Delaney, "Elizabeth Warren: Beer Lover," Huffington Post, October 25, 2012, https://www.huffpost.com/entry/elizabeth-warren-beer _n_2016621.

120. "Kali Gori Breweries Private Limited," *Economic Times*, accessed August 12, 2019, https://economictimes.indiatimes.com/company/kali-gori-breweries -private-limited-/U15541UR2011PTC033447.

121. "Kali Gori Breweries Private Limited," Zauba Corp, accessed August 12, 2019, https://www.zaubacorp.com/company/Kali-Gori-Breweries-Private -Limited/U15541UR2011PTC033447; "Kali Gori Breweries Private Limited," OpenCorporates, accessed August 12, 2019, https://opencorporates .com/companies/in/U15541UR2011PTC033447.

122. Specific Power of Attorney, Los Angeles, California, Kali Gori Private Limited, December 18, 2009.

123. Search under the name Craftbev International Amalgamated at Delaware's Division of Corporations: https://icis.corp.delaware.gov/Ecorp/Entity Search/NameSearch.aspx.

124. Steven R. Reed, "Michigan Brewing Co. Auction Sells out, Falls Short," *Lansing State Journal*, June 21, 2012.

125. William Blair, "Food For Thought, Overview, Analysis, and Trends in the Food and Food Retailing Industries," Calendar 2013, p. 5, https://www .williamblair.com/Research-and-Insights/Insights/~/media/Downloads /Emarketing/2014/IB/Food_For_Thought_2014_01.pdf; "Total Beverage Solution Acquires Celis Beers," PR Newswire, December 10, 2013, https:// www.prnewswire.com/news-releases/total-beverage-solution-acquires -celis-beers-235240051.html; "Dave Pardus," LinkedIn profile, accessed July 30, 2019, https://www.linkedin.com/in/dave-pardus-2249a411/; "Celis Brewery, Austin's First Craft Brewery Is Set to Reopen," PR Newswire, February 21, 2017, https://www.prnewswire.com/news-releases/celis -brewery-austins-first-craft-brewery-is-set-to-reopen-300410461.html.

126. Elizabeth Warren, "Unsafe at Any Rate," *Democracy Journal*, no. 5 (Summer 2007), https://democracyjournal.org/magazine/5/unsafe-at-any-rate/.

127. Opensecrets.org, "Cleary, Gottlieb et al.: 2010," accessed June 25, 2019, https://Opensecrets.org/lobby/firmbills.php?id=D000032662&year=2010; Gary Rivlin, "How Wall Street Defanged Dodd-Frank," *Nation*, April 30, 2013, https://www.thenation.com/article/how-wall-street-defanged-dodd -frank/; Robert Schmidt and Jesse Hamilton, "When Washington's Revolving Door Spins," *Washington Post*, September 8, 2012, https://www.washing tonpost.com/business/when-washingtons-revolving-door-spins/2012/09/07 /af2906b6-f79e-11e1-8398-0327ab83ab91_story.html.

128. Sarah N. Lynch, "SEC Chief's Leadership 'Extremely Disappointing': Sena-

tor Warren," Reuters, June 2, 2015, https://www.reuters.com/article/us
-sec-warren-white/sec-chiefs-leadership-extremely-disappointing-senator
-warren-idUSKBN0OI2CW20150602.

129. Linette Lopez, "Uncovered Emails Show the Cozy Relationship Between the
SEC and Wall Street Lawyers," *Business Insider*, September 5, 2012, http://
Businessinsider.com/finally-we-have-details-on-the-cozy-relationship-be
tween-the-sec-and-its-former-officials-turned-wall-street-lawyers-2012-9.

130. Andrews, "Elizabeth Warren."

131. Michael McAuliff, "Progressive Change Campaign Committee Pats Self on
Back for Elizabeth Warren's Campaign," Huffington Post, September 18,
2012, https://www.huffingtonpost.ca/2012/07/19/progressive-change
-campaign-committee_n_1687275.html.

132. Abby Goodnough, "Senator, a Guardsman, Seeks Afghanistan Stint," *New
York Times*, May 2, 2011, https://www.nytimes.com/2011/05/03/us/politics
/03brown.html; Patrick Howley, "The Warren Tribe," *Washington Free Beacon*, May 16, 2012, https://freebeacon.com/national-security/the-warren
-tribe/; "Demos Supports Elizabeth Warren to Head New Consumer Protection Bureau," Demos, July 20, 2010, https://news.cision.com/demos
—a-network-for-ideas-and-action-ltd/r/demos-supports-elizabeth-warren
-to-head-new-consumer-protection-bureau,g504196.

133. Howley, "The Warren Tribe."

134. Chess and Kissick, "Growing the Market for Independent Business Talent,"
p. 8.

135. Rich Barlow, "Elizabeth Warren Calls for More Federal Research Money,"
BU Today, April 16, 2014, http://www.bu.edu/today/2014/elizabeth
-warren-calls-for-more-federal-research-money/; Foundation for the National Institutes of Health, Inc., Internal Revenue Service, Form 990, 2015,
p. 8, https://fnih.org/sites/default/files/final/pdf/FNIH%202015%20990
.pdf; Foundation for the National Institutes of Health, Inc., Internal Revenue
Service, Form 990, 2016, https://fnih.org/sites/default/files/final/pdf/FNIH
_2016_990_for_public_inspection.pdf.

136. "APTS Commends the U.S. Senate Health, Education, Labor and Pensions
(HELP) Committee for Their Support of Ready to Learn in the Every Child
Achieves Act of 2015," America's Public Television Stations (APTS), press
release, April 15, 2015, https://apts.org/news/press-releases/apts-com
mends-us-senate-health-education-labor-and-pensions-help-committee
-their-support-ready-learn; Homepage, Business Talent Group, on Internet
Archive, accessed August 12, 2019, https://web.archive.org/web/201508
12170719/http://businesstalentgroup.com/ (the screenshot of the site was
captured on August 12, 2015); "#77 Business Talent Group," *Forbes*, accessed
June 25, 2019, https://www.forbes.com/companies/business-talent-group
/#933944670d69.

137. Massimo Calabresi, "Elizabeth Warren Goes to Bat for Medical Device In-

dustry," *Time*, February 5, 2015, http://Time.com/3695581/Elizabeth
-warren-medical-device-lobbyists-obamacare/; Ballotpedia, s.v. "Elizabeth
Warren/Committees," n.d., https://ballotpedia.org/Elizabeth_Warren
/Committees.

138. Calabresi, "Elizabeth Warren Goes to Bat for Medical Device Industry."

139. "J&J's Ortho Clinical Diagnostics Business Snapped Up by Carlyle Group for
$4.15 Billion in a Sale That Will Impact OCD's Clinical Laboratory Custom-
ers," Dark Daily, January 20, 2014, https://www.darkdaily.com/jjs-ortho
-clinical-diagnostics-business-snapped-up-by-carlyle-group-for-4–15-bil
lion-in-a-sale-that-will-impact-ocds-clinical-laboratory-customers/; Homepage, Business Talent Group, on Internet Archive, accessed August 12, 2019,
https://web.archive.org/web/20181025074740/https://businesstalentgroup
.com/ (captured October 25, 2018).

140. Opensecrets.org, "Elizabeth Warren Action Fund: Donors, 2018," accessed
August 12, 2019, https://www.opensecrets.org/jfc/donors.php?id=C006
31861&cycle=2018; Opensecrets.org, "PAC for a Level Playing Field: Donors, 2018," n.d., https://www.opensecrets.org/pacs/pacgave.php?cmte
=C00540195&cycle=2018; Opensecrets.org, "Sen. Elizabeth Warren—
Massachusetts: Contributors, 2020," accessed August 12, 2019, https://www
.opensecrets.org/members-of-congress/contributors?cid=N00033492&
cycle=2020; Opensecrets.org, "Massachusetts Senate Race: Contributors,
2012," accessed August 12, 2019, https://www.opensecrets.org/races/con
tributors?cycle=2012&id=MAS1&spec=N.

141. As quoted in Felix, *Elizabeth Warren,* p. 161.

142. "AFL-CIO: Spending Detail: Contributions Gifts Grants," Unionfacts.com,
accessed July 26, 2019, https://www.unionfacts.com/spending/AFL-CIO
/Contributions_Gifts_Grants.

143. Mashpee Wampanoag Tribe Reservation Reaffirmation Act, S. 2628, 115th
Cong. (2018), https://www.congress.gov/bill/115th-congress/senate-bill
/2628/text; "U.S. Senate Joins House in Filing Bill to Preserve Mashpee
Wampanoag Land into Trust," Cape Cod, March 27, 2018, https://www
.capecod.com/newscenter/u-s-senate-joins-house-in-filing-bill-to-preserve
-mashpee-wampanoag-land-into-trust/.

144. Valerie Richardson, "Elizabeth Warren doubles down on bid to make way
for controversial tribal casino," *Washington Times,* May 31, 2018, https://
www.washingtontimes.com/news/2018/may/31/elizabeth-warren-doubles
-down-bid-make-way-casino/; Michael Graham, "Elizabeth Warren Takes
Gamble on Wampanoag Casino," *Boston Herald*, May 31, 2018, https://www
.bostonherald.com/2018/05/31/elizabeth-warren-takes-gamble-on-wampa
noag-casino/.

145. Philip Marcelo, "US Sen. Warren Supports Repealing State Casino Law,"
Sun Chronicle, September 2, 2014, https://www.thesunchronicle.com/news
/local_news/us-sen-warren-supports-repealing-state-casino-law/article

_84d4e36c-32ac-11e4-a47b-001a4bcf887a.html; "Sen. Warren Plans to Vote for Repeal of Massachusetts Casino Law," Indianz.com, September 5, 2014, http://www.indianz.com/IndianGaming/2014/028209.asp.

146. Natwar M. Gandhi, Associate Director, Tax Policy and Administration Issues, letter to The Honorable Bill Archer, Chairman, Committee on Ways and Means, House of Representatives, August 20, 1996, https://www.gao .gov/assets/90/85897.pdf; Milton J. Valencia, "Judge Deals Setback for Tribe's Casino Plan," *Boston Globe*, July 28, 2016, https://www.bostonglobe .com/metro/2016/07/28/federal-judge-deals-setback-mashpee-wampanoag -billion-dollar-casino-plan/Bsor5BOAVqnv6ILtuVF4RK/story.html.

147. Valerie Richardson, "Warren Blasted for Backing Cape Cod Tribe over Blue-Collar Burg for Casino Jobs," *Washington Times*, July 18, 2018, https:// www.washingtontimes.com/news/2018/jul/18/elizabeth-warren-bill-back ing-masphee-wampanoag-tr/; Graham, "Elizabeth Warren Takes Gamble on Wampanoag Casino."

148. Graham, "Elizabeth Warren Takes Gamble on Wampanoag Casino"; Philip Conneller, "Genting Deliberating Recovery of $400 Million Investment in Massachusetts Casino After DOI Leaves Tribe High and Dry," Casino.org, September 18, 2018, https://www.casino.org/news/genting-considering -recovery-of-400-million-mashpee-casino-loan.

149. "Real Estate," Cleary Gottlieb, accessed January 28, 2019, https://www.cleary gottlieb.com/practice-landing/real-estate (see Investment and Financing).

CHAPTER 6: SHERROD BROWN

1. Suzanne Goldsmith, "Columbus City Council member Elizabeth Brown is making the personal political," *Columbus Monthly*, July 26, 2017, https:// www.columbusmonthly.com/lifestyle/20170724/columbus-city-council -member-elizabeth-brown-is-making-personal-political/1.

2. Joshua Jamerson, "Sherrod Brown Casts Himself as Progressive Before It Was Cool," *Wall Street Journal*, February 1, 2019, https://www.wsj.com/articles /sherrod-brown-casts-himself-as-progressive-before-it-was-cool-11549 017000.

3. Benjamin Wallace-Wells, "Sherrod Brown Wants to Bring a Working-Class Ethos Back to the Democratic Party," *New Yorker*, December 13, 2018, https://www.newyorker.com/news/the-political-scene/sherrod-brown -wants-to-bring-a-working-class-ethos-back-to-the-democratic-party; George Packer, "The Throwback Democrat," *Atlantic*, February 7, 2019, https://www.theatlantic.com/ideas/archive/2019/02/sherrod-brown -just-what-democrats-need-2020/582208/; "Brown Delivers Remarks at Na-tional Action Network Legislative and Policy Conference," Sherrod Brown's Senate page, press release, November 14, 2018, https://www.brown .senate.gov/newsroom/press/release/brown-delivers-remarks-at-national

-action-network-legislative-and-policy-conference; Anthony Gockowski, "Sherrod Brown Cites Bible to Attack Trump's 'Inhumane' Immigration Policies," *Ohio Star,* July 21, 2019, https://theohiostar.com/2019/07/21/sher rod-brown-cites-bible-to-attack-trumps-inhumane-immigration-policies/.

4. Nina Burleigh, "Working-Class Hero: Does Sherrod Brown have the recipe to beat Donald Trump in 2020?," *Newsweek,* December 13, 2018, https:// www.newsweek.com/2018/12/21/2020-elections-sherrod-brown-demo crats-trump-1255743.html; Henry J. Gomez, "How Sherrod Brown Turned His Rumpled Authenticity into a Brand—and Gave Himself a Good Story to Tell in 2020," December 20, 2018, Sherrodbrown.com (blog), https://www .sherrodbrown.com/blog/2018/sherrod-brown-rumpled-authenticity/.

5. Packer, "The Throwback Democrat."

6. Christopher Hayes, "Who Is Sherrod Brown?," *In These Times,* November 21, 2005, http://inthesetimes.com/article/2406/who_is_sherrod_brown.

7. Connie Schulz, "Now What?" in *And His Lovely Wife: A Memoir from the Woman Beside the Man* (New York: Random House, 2008), pp. 31–32.

8. Packer, "The Throwback Democrat"; "You Wouldn't Want to Have Sherrod Brown's Shoes," *News Journal* (Mansfield, OH), October 23, 1978, https:// www.newspapers.com/image/295549370/.

9. "Fellow Democrats roast secretary of state hopeful till he's a golden Brown," *News Journal* (Mansfield, Ohio), May 7, 1982, https://www.newspapers.com /image/295912324/.

10. Wallace-Wells, "Sherrod Brown Wants to Bring a Working-Class Ethos Back to the Democratic Party."

11. Hayes, "Who Is Sherrod Brown?"

12. Packer, "The Throwback Democrat."

13. "Sherrod Brown: State Rep.—61st District," *News Journal* (Mansfield, OH), November 3, 1974, https://www.newspapers.com/image/296778268/; Hayes, "Who Is Sherrod Brown?"

14. Hayes, "Who is Sherrod Brown?"

15. Packer, "The Throwback Democrat."

16. "Fellow Democrats roast secretary of state hopeful till he's a golden Brown."

17. "Down to business," *News Journal* (Mansfield, Ohio), November 17, 1978, https://www.newspapers.com/image/295856160/.

18. "You Wouldn't Want to Have Sherrod Brown's Shoes."

19. "Overcrowded conditions at dog pound alleviated," *News Journal* (Mansfield, Ohio), February 26, 1981, https://www.newspapers.com/image/296304 309/; "How area legislators voted on key Ohio issues," *News Journal* (Mans-field, Ohio), November 25, 1981, https://www.newspapers.com/image /296016323/.

20. "2 Brown victories tempered by formal protest," *News Journal* (Mansfield, Ohio), May 25, 1982, https://www.newspapers.com/image/295855894/.

21. Hayes, "Who Is Sherrod Brown?"

22. Ibid.
23. "What makes the difference?" *Mansfield News Journal*, October 30, 1983, https://www.newspapers.com/image/296118174/.
24. Randolph Smith, "A tale of murder enmeshed with politics," *Akron Beacon Journal*, January 22, 1984, pp. A1, A12, A13, https://www.newspapers.com /image/153861216/; Peter Phipps, "State aide's murder leaves a scary puzzle," *Akron Beacon Journal*, September 4, 1983, https://www.newspapers.com /image/145389397/; Colleen Shaughnessy, Homicide file, report date August 1, 1985, Complaint No. 83052047, pp. 97, 99.
25. Phipps, "State aide's murder leaves a scary puzzle."
26. Smith, "A tale of murder enmeshed with politics."
27. Phipps, "State aide's murder leaves a scary puzzle."
28. Colleen Shaughnessy, Homicide file, pp. 106, 313.
29. Ibid., p. 132.
30. Ibid., p. 104.
31. Ibid., p. 341.
32. Smith, "A tale of murder enmeshed with politics."
33. Associated Press, "Student, 18, arrested in slaying of state aide in Cleveland office," *Akron Beacon Journal*, February 22, 1985, https://www.newspapers .com/clip/15067773/homicide_investigation_of_colleen/.
34. Associated Press, "Jury finds teen-ager innocent in Cleveland stabbing death," *Journal Herald* (Dayton, Ohio), November 22, 1985, https://www .newspapers.com/image/394964847/.
35. "Sherrod Brown closing quarters in office building at Cleveland," *News-Journal* (Mansfield, Ohio), February 1, 1984 https://www.newspapers.com /image/295428944/.
36. "Colleen Mary Shaughnessy," Find A Grave, accessed July 16, 2019, https:// www.findagrave.com/memorial/5898684/colleen-mary-shaughnessy.
37. Jessica Wehrman, Laura A. Bischoff, and William Hershey, "DeWine, Brown clash over 20-year-old drug deal allegations," *Dayton Daily News*, November 6, 2006, https://www.newspapers.com/image/411069880/.
38. Ibid.; Jim Geraghty, "Twenty Things You Didn't Know About Sherrod Brown," *National Review*, March 4, 2019, https://www.nationalreview.com /2019/03/sherrod-brown-twenty-facts-about-ohio-senator/.
39. Associated Press, "Drug probe covered up, says former patrolman," *Cincinnati Enquirer*, July 5, 1990, https://www.newspapers.com/image/101955964/.
40. Hayes, "Who Is Sherrod Brown?"
41. Sabrina Eaton, "Over Time, Sen. Sherrod Brown Reversed His Stance on Term Limits," Cleveland.com, July 12, https://www.cleveland.com/metro /index.ssf/2018/07/sherrod_brown_on_term_limits.html.
42. Ibid.
43. Sherrod Brown, "Election 1992: Getting There," in *Congress from the Inside:*

Observations from the Majority and the Minority (Kent, OH: Kent State University Press, 2004), pp. 7, 12.

44. "Annual Picnic," Montgomery County Democratic Party, September 7, 2017, http://www.montgomerydems.org/event/annual-picnic (observed on June 27, 2019), https://www.facebook.com/events/greene-county-ohio-democratic-party/meet-charlie-brown-brother-of-sen-sherrod-brown/103983733572622/.

45. "Brothers hold posts in adjoining states," *New York Times,* January 15, 1985, https://www.nytimes.com/1985/01/15/us/brothers-hold-posts-in-adjoining-states.html.

46. "West Virginia attorney general indicted," *Orlando Sentinel,* February 11, 1986, https://www.orlandosentinel.com/news/os-xpm-1986-02-11-02000 60246-story.html.

47. Fred Grimm, "Scandal Becomes Growth Industry in W. Virginia," *Miami Herald,* May 20, 1990, https://www.nytimes.com/1989/08/23/us/state-s-attorney-in-a-deal-resigns.html.

48. "Sherrod Brown on Government Reform," Ontheissues.org, accessed June 28, 2019, http://www.ontheissues.org/economic/Sherrod_Brown_Government_Reform.htm.

49. Opensecrets.org, "Lawyers/Law Firms: Top Contributors," 2019–2020, accessed July 26, 2019, https://www.opensecrets.org/industries/indus.php?ind=k\$1; Timothy P. Carney, "Trial Lawyer Industry Tries to Buy a Democratic Majority," *Washington Examiner,* October 22, 2014, https://www.washingtonexaminer.com/trial-lawyer-industry-tries-to-buy-a-democratic-majority.

50. "Charles G. Brown," Swankinturner.com, on Internet Archive, n.d., https://web.archive.org/web/19981205234832/http://www.swankin-turner.com/charlie.html (captured December 5, 1998); "Charles G. Brown," Organic & Natural Health Association, n.d., https://organicandnatural.org/staff-board/charles-g-brown/; "Consumers for Dental Choice," Swankin & Turner, July 1, 2019, http://www.swankin-turner.com/projects.html; "James S. Turner," Swankin & Turner, accessed June 28, 2019, https://www.swankin-turner.com/jim.html.

51. Genetic Literacy Project, "Citizens for Health: James Turner Founded Advocacy Group Lobbies for Supplement Industry, Funds Jeffrey Smith," July 17, 2018, https://geneticliteracyproject.org/glp-facts/citizens-for-health/.

52. James Gormley, "Introducing the Transpartisan Review Project," Citizens for Health (blog), July 4, 2016, https://www.citizens.org/5675-2/; FEC data.

53. The Following Informal Admonition Was Issued by Bar Counsel on November 1, 2007, RE: In re Charles G. Brown, Esquire, Bar Docket No. 2005-D303.

54. Genetic Literacy Project, "Citizens for Health Lobbies for Suspect Alternative

Meds, Supplements (and Free Love?)," April 29, 2014, https://geneticliteracy project.org/2014/04/29/citizens-for-health-lobbies-for-questionable -alternative-meds-supplements-free-love/; Colby Vorland, "When Quackery Masquerades as 'Free Choice': Comment on Nutritional Counseling Licensure Debate in Forbes," Nutsci.org (blog), May 23, 2012, http://nutsci .org/2012/05/23/when-quackery-masquerades-as-free-choice-comment -on-nutritional-counseling-licensure-debate-in-forbes/; "Consumers for Dental Choice," Swankin & Turner; Institute for Nutritional Dentistry, "Our Faculty," on Internet Archive, accessed July 27, 2019, https://web .archive.org/web/20131101073615/http://www.naturaldentistry.org/faculty _list_natural_dentistry.htm.

55. Genetic Literacy Project, "Citizens for Health Lobbies for Suspect Alternative Meds, Supplements (and Free Love?)."

56. Holly Yeager, "Brown Awaits Decision on Committee Assignment, Gillmor Gets GOP Leadership Post," *States News Service*, December 7, 1992.

57. Holly Yeager, "Brown Gets Subcommittee Assignments," States News Service, January 7, 1993.

58. Sabrina Eaton, "Brown Gains Clout, Friends in Capitol," *Plain Dealer,* May 26, 1997.

59. "Would You Use a Substance That Is Banned in Animals?," William P. Glaros, DDS, Inc., September 6, 2011, https://www.biologicaldentist.com /635/would-you-use-a-substance-that-is-banned-in-animals/.

60. "Consumers for Dental Choice," Swankin & Turner.

61. Report on the Activity of the Committee on Commerce for the 104th Cong., H.R. Rep. No. 104–882, 104th Cong. (1997), https://www.congress .gov/congressional-report/104th-congress/house-report/882/1?q=%7B%22 search%22%3A%5B%22%5C%22sherrod+brown%5C%22+%5C%22dental +amalgam%5C%22%22%5D%7D&s=2&r=1; Environmental Health Policy Committee, "Dental Amalgam and Alternative Restorative Materials: UHPHS Risk Management Strategy: A Status Update," accessed July 28, 2019, https://health.gov/environment/amalgam2/USPHS.html.

62. Consumers for Dental Choice, "Major Breakthrough—Assoc. of Trial Lawyers of America Conduct Seminar: 'Mercury Silver Dental Fillings was the Next Mass Tort,' " toxicteeth.org, on Internet Archive, March 9, 2004, https://web.archive.org/web/20100629110813/http://www.toxicteeth.org /natCamp_LegalAct_triallawyers.cfm (captured June 29, 2010); Tom Harrigan, "Attorney on other end of dental lawsuit," Associated Press, on Internet Archive, n.d., https://web.archive.org/web/20030429072814/http://www .testfoundation.org/hglawsuits.htm.

63. "About Us," Campaign for Mercury Free Dentistry, n.d., http://www.toxic teeth.org/about_Us.aspx.

64. American Dental Association, "Dental Amalgam: What Others Say," last

updated March 2019, https://www.ada.org/en/press-room/press-kits/dental
-fillings-press-kit/dental-amalgam-what-others-say.

65. "Major Breakthrough—Assoc. of Trial Lawyers of America Conduct
Seminar: 'Mercury Silver Dental Fillings was the Next Mass Tort' "; Class
Action Complaint, *Anita Tibau, an individual; Cindy Blake, an individual; on
behalf of themselves, and all those similarly situated v. American Dental Association, a
corporation; California Dental Association, a corporation; and Does 1 through 2000,
inclusive*, June 12, 2001, www.cfsn.com/toxicteeth/Class.PDF.

66. Julia Marsh, "Law Firm Behind $2.5B in Verdicts, Settlements 'on Verge of
Collapse,' " *New York Post*, March 25, https://nypost.com/2015/03/25/law
-firm-behind-2-5b-in-verdicts-settlements-on-verge-of-collapse/.

67. The State Bar of California, "Attorney Licensee Profile: Shahin F. Khorrami," accessed July 31, 2019, http://members.calbar.ca.gov/fal/Licensee
/Detail/180411; Matt Hamilton, "L.A.-Based Trial Attorney Accused of
Misappropriating Clients' Money," *Los Angeles Times*, September 3, 2015,
https://www.latimes.com/local/lanow/la-me-ln-shawn-khorrami-attorney
-state-bar-accused-20150903-story.html; Beth Winegarner, "Calif. Plaintiffs'
Firm Held in Contempt; Creditor Wins $7M," Law 360, October 28, 2015,
https://www.law360.com/articles/719841/calif-plaintiffs-firm-held-in-con
tempt-creditor-wins-7m.

68. "Charles Brown," Law Offices of Shawn Khorrami, on Internet Archive,
n.d., https://web.archive.org/web/20041117105011/http://63.199.49.133
/Attorney%20Web/Brown.htm; "Charles Gailey Brown," prabook.com,
accessed February 15, 2019, https://prabook.com/web/charles_gailey
.brown/886373.

69. Consumers for Dental Choice, "Legal Action," on Internet Archive, n.d.,
https://web.archive.org/web/20100629100900/http:/www.toxicteeth.org
/natCamp_legalAction.cfm (captured June 29, 2010).

70. Consumers for Dental Choice, "Major Breakthrough—Assoc. of Trial Lawyers of America Conduct Seminar: 'Mercury Silver Dental Fillings was the
Next Mass Tort.' "

71. Medical Advertising Reform Act, H.R. 3696, 109th Cong. (2005), https://
www.congress.gov/bill/109th-congress/house-bill/3696.

72. "Rep. Brown Introduces DTC Legislation," US Fed News, September 9,
2005.

73. In Re Bextra and Celebrex Marketing, Sales Practices and Products Liability
Litigation, Case No. 3:05-md-01699, https://www.plainsite.org/dockets
/mwx5f9g7/california-northern-district-court/in-re-bextra-and-celebrex
-marketing-sales-practices-and-products-liability-litigation/, https://www
.courtlistener.com/docket/5729397/1/in-re-bextra-and-celebrex-marke
ting-sales-practices-and-products-liability/, https://www.law360.com
/cases/4d2b88485bab5c0bb4000001.

74. Attorney Shawn Khorrami Releases Commentary in Response to Government Inquiries into Off-Label Drug Use Marketing by Pharmaceutical Companies, Market Wire, March 28, 2007; Sens. Dodd, Kennedy, Reps. Waxman, Dingell, Brown Call on Administration to Stop FDA Provision Undercutting State Laws That Protect Patients, US Fed News, February 24, 2006.

75. Associated Press, "Congress Demands Info on Vioxx Whistleblower," Fox News, December 10, 2004, https://www.foxnews.com/story/congress-de mands-info-on-vioxx-whistleblower ; Congressional Record—House, Con-gress.gov, June 8, 2005, https://www.congress.gov/crec/2005/06/08 /CREC-2005–06–08-pt1-PgH4251–2.pdf.

76. "Vioxx Class Action," Law Offices of Shawn Khorrami, on Internet Archive, August 21, 2004, https://web.archive.org/web/20041206102838 /http://63.199.49.133/Cases%20Web/Vioxx/Intro.HTM (captured December 6, 2004).

77. "Charles Brown," Law Offices of Shawn Khorrami.

78. Class Action Fairness Act of 2005, 109th Cong. (2005), *Congressional Record* 151, no. 18, https://www.congress.gov/congressional-record/2005/02/17 /house-section/article/H723–1; Class Action Fairness Act of 2005, S.5, 109th Cong. (2005), https://www.congress.gov/bill/109th-congress/senate -bill/5/all-actions.

79. "Class Action Fairness Act of 2005 (CAFA): Overview," Practical Law Com-pany, 2013, https://www.weil.com/~/media/files/pdfs/cafa_overview.pdf; "Sherrod Brown on Government Reform."

80. Congressional Debate between Bob Goodlatte, Sherrod Brown, and Mike Ross, regarding S. 5: The Class Action Fairness Act, n.d., https://www .c-span.org/congress/bills/billAction/?991164.

81. Final Vote Results for Roll Call 38, Class Action Fairness Act, house.gov, February 17, 2005, http://clerk.house.gov/evs/2005/roll038.xml; Anthony J. Sebok, "The Class Action Fairness Act of 2005: A Reasonable Law, but One that Should Not Be a Wedge for Wide Tort Reform," Find Law, February 21, 2005, https://supreme.findlaw.com/legal-commentary/the-class-action-fair ness-act-of-2005.html.

82. U.S. Food and Drug Administration, "FDA Investigates Animal Illnesses Linked to Jerky Pet Treats," last updated August 21, 2018, https://www .fda.gov/animal-veterinary/news-events/fda-investigates-animal-illnesses -linked-jerky-pet-treats.

83. "With Tainted Pet Treats from China Leading to Illness and Death in Ohio Family's Pets, Brown Urges Swift Action from FDA to Protect Consumers," Sherrod Brown's Senate page, press release, February 19, 2012, https://www .brown.senate.gov/newsroom/press/release/with-tainted-pet-treats-from -china-leading-to-illness-and-death-in-ohio-familys-pets-brown-urges -swift-action-from-fda-to-protect-consumers; Jonel Aleccia, "3 Big Brands

May Be Tied to Chicken Jerky Illness in Dogs, FDA Records Show," NBC News, March 13, 2012, https://www.nbcnews.com/healthmain/3-big -brands-may-be-tied-chicken-jerky-illness-dogs-420251; Cindy Galli, "Toxic Treats from China Killing US Dogs, Say Pet Owners," ABC News, March 16, 2012, https://abcnews.go.com/Blotter/toxic-treats-china-killing -us-dogs-pet-owners/story?id=15927579.

84. *Jennifer Holt v. Globalinx Pet LLC, et al.*, Case no. 8:13-cv-00041, terminated May 2, 2013, https://www.law360.com/cases/50f6e631227d204cf40043d7.

85. Opensecrets.org, "Sen. Sherrod Brown—Ohio: Summary," n.d., https:// www.opensecrets.org/members-of-congress/summary?cid=N00003535 &cycle=2020&type=C.

86. Peter S. Lublin and Patrick Austermuehle, "Congress Considers Two New Bills Limiting Arbitration and Class Action Waivers in Consumer Contracts —Chicago Class Action Defense Attorneys Near Oak Brook and Naperville," Chicago Business Litigation Lawyer Blog, May 8, 2019, https://www.chicagobusinesslitigationlawyerblog.com/congress-considers -two-new-bills-limiting-arbitration-and-class-action-waivers-in-consumer -contracts-chicago-class-action-defense-attorneys-near-oak-brook-and -naperville/.

87. Anita Waters, "Labor Launches Biggest Campaign Ever in Ohio Midterm Elec- tions," People's World, September 24, 2018, https://www.peoplesworld.org /article/labor-launches-biggest-campaign-ever-in-ohio-midterm-elections/.

88. "Sherrod Brown: Contributions from Unions," Unionfacts.com, accessed July 19, 2018, https://www.unionfacts.com/pol/Sherrod_Brown_D/N000 03535.

89. Clare Malone, "Ohio's Democratic Revolution?" Salon, November 4, 2012, https://www.salon.com/2012/11/04/ohios_democratic_revolution/.

90. Dan La Botz, *A Vision from the Heartland: Socialism for the 21st Century,* p. 49, https://www.scribd.com/document/39288031/A-Vision-From-the -Heartland-By-Dan-La-Botz; Andrew Romano, "Want to Beat Trump in 2020? Look at Sherrod Brown's Big Win in Ohio," Huffington Post, Novem- ber 10, 2018, https://www.huffpost.com/entry/yahoo-news-sherrod -brown-beat-trump-2020_n_5be6ebcbe4b0dbe871ab811b.

91. "Your Vote Is Not Enough," *IATSE Official Bulletin*, Third Quarter, no. 613 (2006), p. 54, https://www.scribd.com/document/88917783/613.

92. Opensecrets.org, "Rep. Sherrod Brown—Ohio District 13," n.d., https:// www.opensecrets.org/members-of-congress/summary?cid=N00003535 &cycle=1998&type=I.

93. Office of Labor-Management Standards, LM-2 Labor Organization Annual Report for the Ohio Education Association, filed on November 26, 2013, http://rishawnbiddle.org/outsidereports/ohio_nea_dol_filing_2013.htm.

94. Hayes, "Who Is Sherrod Brown?"

95. "John Ryan," LinkedIn profile, accessed July 29, 2019, https://www.linked

in.com/in/john-ryan-071a159; Gomez, "How Sherrod Brown Turned His Rumpled Authenticity into a Brand."

96. U.S. Department of Labor, Office of Labor-Management Standards, "Labor-Management Reporting and Disclosure Act of 1959, As Amended," accessed May 21, 2019, https://www.dol.gov/olms/regs/statutes/lmrda-act.htm.

97. U.S. Chamber of Commerce, "Bearing Down on Employers: The New Labor and Immigration Landscape," September 1, 2010, https://www.uschamber.com/report/bearing-down-employers-new-labor-and-immigration-landscape.

98. Hearing of the Committee on Health, Education, Labor, and Pensions, Nomination of Gregory Jacob, of New Jersey, to be Solicitor of Labor, U.S. Department of Labor; and Howard Radzely, of Maryland, to be Deputy Secretary of Labor, U.S. Department of Labor, 110th Cong. (2007), https://www.congress.gov/110/chrg/shrg38876/CHRG-110shrg38876.htm.

99. "United Food & Commercial Workers, Local 75," Unionfacts.com, accessed July 30, 2019, https://www.unionfacts.com/local/employees/544266/UFCW/75/.

100. "UFCW Endorses Brunner," Business Wire, March 27, 2009, https://www.businesswire.com/news/home/20090327005529/en/UFCW-Endorses-Brunner (note: For reference to above salaries, Locals 911 and 1099 mentioned here merged to form Local 75).

101. Brown Named Co-Chair of Bipartisan House-Senate Committee to Solve Pension Crisis," Sherrod Brown's Senate page, press release, February 26, 2018, https://www.brown.senate.gov/newsroom/press/release/brown-named-co-chair-of-bipartisan-house-senate-committee-to-solve-pension-crisis.

102. Tahman Bradley, "Is Detroit Dig Latest Search for Jimmy Hoffa's Body?," ABC News, September 15, 2009, https://abcnews.go.com/US/fbi-confirm-dig-search-jimmy-hoffa-body/story?id=8583134.

103. Carl F. Horowitz, "James Hoffa (Both of Them) and the 'Central States' Crackup," Capital Research Center, February 2016, https://capitalresearch.org/app/uploads/LW1602-final-draft-160202.pdf; "About Us," Central States Pension Fund, accessed August 5, 2019, https://mycentralstatespension.org/about-us; Elizabeth Bauer, "Understanding the Central States Pension Plans Tale of Woe," Forbes, December 3, 2018, https://www.forbes.com/sites/ebauer/2018/12/03/understanding-the-central-states-pension-plans-tale-of-woe/#1882f5f76c10.

104. Lesley Clark, "Coal Miners Appeal to McConnell to Back a Rescue of Their Pensions," McClatchy DC Bureau, May 8, 2019, https://www.mcclatchydc.com/news/politics-government/congress/article230129654.html; "Brown Named Co-Chair of Bipartisan House-Senate Committee to Solve Pension Crisis."

105. Rachel Greszler, "Not Your Grandfather's Pension: Why Defined Benefit

Pensions Are Failing," The Heritage Foundation, May 4, 2017, https://www.heritage.org/node/249512/.

106. Rachel Greszler, " 'Protecting' Private Union Pensions with Bottomless Bailouts Is a Recipe for Disaster," The Heritage Foundation, December 4, 2017, https://www.heritage.org/budget-and-spending/report/protecting-private-union-pensions-bottomless-bailouts-recipe-disaster.

107. "Brown Named Co-Chair of Bipartisan House-Senate Committee to Solve Pension Crisis"; "Brown Stands with Ohio Retirees to Call for Action on Plan to Protect Ohio Pensions, Keep Promises to Ohio Workers," Sherrod Brown's Senate page, December 18, 2017, https://www.brown.senate.gov/newsroom/press/release/brown-stands-with-ohio-retirees-to-call-for-action-on-plan-to-protect-ohio-pensions-keep-promises-to-ohio-workers.

108. Ibid.

109. Greszler, " 'Protecting' Private Union Pensions with Bottomless Bailouts Is a Recipe for Disaster."

110. Hearing Before the Subcommittee on Oversight and Investigations of the Committee on Energy and Commerce, U.S. House of Representatives, 109th Cong. (2005), https://www.govinfo.gov/content/pkg/CHRG-109hhrg24255/html/CHRG-109hhrg24255.htm.

111. Mallory Factor, "Union-Label President," in *Shadowbosses, Government Unions Control America and Rob Taxpayers Blind* (New York: Center Street, 2012), pp. 93–94; James Shark, "Workers Reject Card Checks, Favor Private Ballots in Union Organizing," The Heritage Foundation, February 16, 2007, https://www.heritage.org/jobs-and-labor/report/workers-reject-card-checks-favor-private-ballots-unionorganizing.

112. "Dorm Flight," Cleveland Scene, April 20, 2005, https://www.clevescene.com/cleveland/dorm-fight/Content?oid=1490378.

113. Sabrina Eaton, "Lobbyists, clergy, among the diverse groups that give their top campaign dollars to Sherrod Brown," Cleveland.com, September 14, 2018, https://expo.cleveland.com/news/erry-2018/09/ee7e208a3a5392/lobbyists-clergy-among-the-div.html.

CHAPTER 7: BERNIE SANDERS

1. Dan Bolles, "When Irish Eyes Are Smiling," *Seven Days*, March 12, 2008, https://www.sevendaysvt.com/vermont/when-irish-eyes-are-smiling/Content?oid=2132999; VenomousNewfie, "The Unicorn song—The Irish Rovers—Lyrics," YouTube video, posted on April 23, 2010, https://www.youtube.com/watch?v=h4bc9UwZsYs.

2. Peter Freyne, "Senatorial Matters," *Seven Days*, September 29, 1999, https://www.sevendaysvt.com/vermont/senatorial-matters/Content?oid=2431504.

3. Terri Hallenbeck, "Fifty years, 13,450 students and 5,000 interviews: UVM's Garrison Nelson Calls It a Career," *Seven Days*, October 18, 2017, https://

www.sevendaysvt.com/vermont/fifty-years-13450-students-and-5000-inter
views-uvms-garrison-nelson-calls-it-a-career/Content?oid=9191443.

4. Kim Phillips-Fein, Charles Postel, Robert Greene II, and Michael Kazin, "Who Is the Real Progressive: Hillary Clinton or Bernie Sanders?," *Nation,* February 24, 2016, https://www.thenation.com/article/who-is-the-real -progressive-hillary-clinton-or-bernie-sanders/; Stephanie McCrummen, "His Most Radical Move," *Washington Post,* February 5, 2016, https://www .washingtonpost.com/sf/national/2016/02/05/his-most-radical-move/.

5. Darcy G. Richardson, *Bernie: A Lifelong Crusade Against Wall Street & Wealth* (Sevierville Publishing, 2015), pp. 35, 37.

6. Pat Bradley, "Spider Species Named After Sanders," WAMC Northeast Public Radio, September 26, 2017, https://www.wamc.org/post/spider-species -named-after-sanders.

7. Jannay Valdez, *Bernie Sanders, He Would Have Been Elected President 2016: Brilliant Study on Bernie, The Clintons and the Kennedy Assassination* (North Carolina: Lulu Publishing Services, 2019).

8. Richardson, *Bernie,* pp. 21–22; Sam Frizell, "The Radical Education of Bernie Sanders," *Time,* May 26, 2015, https://time.com/3896500/bernie-sand ers-vermont-campaign-radical/.

9. Ofer Aderet, "Mystery Solved: Haaretz Archive Reveals Which Kibbutz Bernie Sanders Volunteered On," *Haaretz,* February 4, 2016, https://www .haaretz.com/israel-news/.premium-haaretz-reveals-which-kibbutz-bernie -sanders-volunteered-on-1.5400356; Ben Sales, "50 years on, Bernie Sanders still champions values of his Israeli kibbutz," *Times of Israel,* February 9, 2016, https://www.timesofisrael.com/50-years-on-bernie-sanders-still-champions -values-of-his-israeli-kibbutz/; "Found! Bernie's Kibbutz During His Lost Months as Volunteer; But at Sha'ar HaAmakim, no one recalls the young socialist; Sanders stays mum," *Forward,* February 19, 2016.

10. Ben Sales, "50 Years."

11. Tamara Keith, "Leaving Brooklyn, Bernie Sanders Found Home in Vermont," NPR, June 20, 2015, https://www.npr.org/sections/itsallpolitics/2015/06/20 /415747576/leaving-brooklyn-bernie-sanders-found-home-in-vermont.

12. Richardson, *Bernie,* p. 29.

13. Nina Burleigh, "Socialism, Syrup and Fighter Jets: Bernie Sanders on the Campaign Trail," *Newsweek,* October 2, 2015, https://www.newsweek .com/2015/10/02/bernie-sanders-campaigns-2016-presidential-campaign -democratic-party-374897.html.

14. Tim Murphy, "How Bernie Sanders Learned to Be a Real Politician," *Mother Jones,* May 26, 2015, https://www.motherjones.com/politics/2015/05 /young-bernie-sanders-liberty-union-vermont/; Richardson, *Bernie,* p. 30; Michael Kruse, "Bernie Sanders Has a Secret," Politico, July 9, 2015, https://www.politico.com/magazine/story/2015/07/bernie-sanders-vermont -119927_Page3.html.

15. Judy Kutulas, *After Aquarius Dawned: How the Revolutions of the Sixties Became the Popular Culture of the Seventies* (Chapel Hill: University of North Carolina Press, 2017), p. 81; Murphy, "How Bernie Sanders Learned to Be a Real Politician."

16. Murphy, "How Bernie Sanders Learned to Be a Real Politician."

17. Ibid.; Richardson, *Bernie,* pp. 186, 189; Greg Guma, *The People's Republic: Vermont and the Sanders Revolution* (South Burlington, VT: New England Press, 1989), pp. 31, 42.

18. John Nichols, "Go Knock on Some Doors; Bernie Sanders Sounds Off," *Progressive,* May 1, 1996.

19. Dudley Clendinen, "It's New Politics vs. Old in Vermont as Mayor Strives to Oust Alderman," *New York Times,* February 28, 1982, https://www.nytimes .com/1982/02/28/us/it-s-new-politics-vs-old-in-vermont-as-mayor-strives -to-oust-alderman.html.

20. Lisa Belkin, "Being married to Bernie," Yahoo, November 3, 2015, https:// www.yahoo.com/news/being-married-to-bernie-1291469214744630.html.

21. Catherine Lucey and Ken Thomas, "Jane Sanders Is Central in Her Husband's Surging Campaign," Associated Press, February 18, 2016, https:// apnews.com/d604bf0a489e4363a8869c7b8d558441.

22. Lisa Belkin, "Being married to Bernie," November 3, 2015, https://www .yahoo.com/news/being-married-to-bernie-1291469214744630.html.

23. Steven Soifer, *The Socialist Mayor: Bernard Sanders in Burlington, Vermont* (New York: Bergin & Garvey, 1991), pp. 180–81, 186–87; "Role of Youth Office Aide Merited Closer Examination," *Burlington Free Press,* June 28, 1983, https://www.newspapers.com/image/203386739/; Mark Johnson, "Sparks Fly at City Hall," *Seven Days,* June 16, 1988, https://www.sevendaysvt.com /vermont/-at-city-hall/Content?oid=2434429.

24. Johnson, "Sparks Fly at City Hall."

25. Soifer, *The Socialist Mayor,* p. 68.

26. Guma, *The People's Republic,* p. 107.

27. Ibid., p. 135.

28. John Walters, "Walters: Advocate for the Homeless to Challenge Sanders for Senate Seat," *Seven Days,* July 7, 2017, https://www.sevendaysvt.com/Off Message/archives/2017/07/07/walters-advocate-for-the-homeless-to-chal lenge-sanders-for-senate-seat.

29. Peter Freyne and Amy Schegel, "City vs. MCHV: Charity on the Line," *Seven Days,* August 6, 1987, https://www.sevendaysvt.com/vermont/city-vs -mchv-charity-on-the-line/Content?oid=2434371; Mark Johnson, "Medical Center Beats Bernie," *Seven Days,* September 24, 1987, https://www.seven daysvt.com/vermont/medical-center-beats-bernie/Content?oid=2434374.

30. Peter Freyne, "El Cheapo!," *Seven Days,* October 16, 1996, https://m.seven daysvt.com/vermont/el-cheapo/Content?oid=2433883.

31. Guma, *The People's Republic,* p. 59.

32. Ibid., pp. 41, 109; "Antonio 'Tony' Pomerleau," *Burlington Free Press*, accessed July 15, 2019, https://www.legacy.com/obituaries/burlingtonfreepress/obit uary.aspx?n=antonio-pomerleau-tony&pid=188141527.

33. Soifer, *The Socialist Mayor,* pp. 84, 181, 187; Candace Page, "Tony Pomerleau, Vermont Developer and Philanthropist, Dies at 100," *Burlington Free Press,* https://www.burlingtonfreepress.com/story/news/2018/02/09/antonio -pomerleau-vermont-developer-and-philanthropist-dies-100/322621002/; Mitch Wertlieb, "Antonio Pomerleau, Vermont Philanthropist, Dies at 100," VPR, February 9, 2018, https://www.vpr.org/post/antonio-pomerleau -vermont-philanthropist-dies-100#stream/0.

34. Guma, *The People's Republic,* p. 93.

35. Ibid., pp. 109–10.

36. Ibid., pp. 110, 113, 121.

37. Soifer, *The Socialist Mayor,* p. 78.

38. Guma, *The People's Republic,* p. 113.

39. Richardson, *Bernie,* pp. 227, 231, 232; Guma, *The People's Republic,* p. 90.

40. Mike Davis, Steven Hiatt, et al., *Fire in the Hearth: The Radical Politics of Place in America* (Brooklyn, NY: Verso, 1990), p. 143.

41. Richardson, *Bernie,* p. 227.

42. Guma, *The People's Republic,* p. 90.

43. Richardson, *Bernie,* p. 227.

44. Ibid., pp. 34–35.

45. Tim Mak, "Bernie Sanders Loves This $1 Trillion War Machine," Daily Beast, February 9, 2016, https://www.thedailybeast.com/bernie-sanders -loves-this-dollar1-trillion-war-machine?ref=scroll.

46. Richardson, *Bernie,* pp. 201, 303.

47. Nataly Pak and Sruthi Palaniappan, "Who Is Bernie Sanders? Everything You Need to Know About the Senator from Vermont," ABC News, July 30, 2019, https://abcnews.go.com/Politics/bernie-sanders-senator-vermont /story?id=61058675; Guma, 158; FEC data; Columbia University Irving Medical Center, "Newly Established Phyllis Mailman Professorship Will Advance the Research and Development of Lifesaving Vaccines," Newswise, June 24, 2019, https://www.newswise.com/articles/newly -established-phyllis-mailman-professorship-will-advance-the-research -and-development-of-lifesaving-vaccines; Glenna Whitley, "Vision Quest: Jim and Christine's Quasi-Mystical Adventure," *D Magazine*, June 1995, https://www.dmagazine.com/publications/d-magazine/1995/june/vision -quest-jim-and-christines-quasi-mystical-adventure/; "James Gollin," Influ- ence Watch, accessed June 25, 2019, https://www.influencewatch.org /person/james-gollin/; "Reed Rubin," Wellsfargoadvisors.com, accessed June 25, 2019, https://home.wellsfargoadvisors.com/reed.rubin.

48. Gloria L. Cronin and Lee Trepanier, *A Political Companion to Saul Bellow* (Lexington: University of Kentucky Press, 2013) pp. 211, 215.

49. Richardson, *Bernie,* pp. 300–302.

50. Belkin, "Being Married to Bernie."

51. Vermont Secretary of State Corporations Division, "Sanders & Driscoll, L.L.C.," accessed June 19, 2019, https://www.vtsosonline.com/online /BusinessInquire/TradeNameInformation?businessID=11218; Belkin, "Being Married to Bernie."

52. Richardson, *Bernie, p.* 38; Jasper Craven, "Special Report: Sanders Campaign Millions Go to Mystery Firm," VTDigger, July 15, 2016, https://vtdigger .org/2016/07/15/sanders-campaign-millions-go-to-mystery-firm/.

53. Bernard Sanders, Personal Financial Disclosure, 2013, http://pfds.open secrets.org/N00000528_2013.pdf; Vermont Secretary of State Corporations Division, "Business Search Result," n.d., https://www.vtsosonline.com /online/BusinessInquire/BusinessSearch.

54. David Gram, "Sanders Admits Campaign Paid Family Members," *Rutland Herald*, April 14, 2005, https://www.rutlandherald.com/news/sanders -admits-campaign-paid-family-members/article_287658f4-732a-57a5-8ab1 -be235bf5c33f.html.

55. "Recording Disbursements," Federal Election Commission, n.d., https:// www.fec.gov/help-candidates-and-committees/keeping-records/records -disbursements/.

56. Eli Clifton and Joshua Holland, "Bernie's Fundraising Was Revolutionary. How He Spent His Money Was Not," Slate, July 13, 2016, https://slate.com /news-and-politics/2016/07/how-bernie-spent-his-millions-was-anything -but-revolutionary.html.

57. Gram, "Sanders Admits Campaign Paid Family Members."

58. Ryan Grim, "The Reluctance of Bernie Sanders to Release His Damn Tax Returns Is Part of a Bigger Issue," Intercept, April 5, 2019, https://theinter cept.com/2019/04/05/bernie-sanders-tax-returns/; Ken Thomas and Richard Rubin, "Bernie Sanders Releases Tax Returns," *Wall Street Journal,* April 15, 2019, https://www.wsj.com/articles/bernie-sanders-releases-tax -returns-11555365600.

59. Alice B. Lloyd, "Jane Sanders's Little College That Couldn't," *Washington Examiner,* July 31, 2017, https://www.washingtonexaminer.com/weekly -standard/jane-sanderss-little-college-that-couldnt.

60. Charlotte Hallé, "Burlington Boss 'Clueless' About Fake Degrees," *Haaretz,* January 18, 2002, https://www.haaretz.com/1.5276580.

61. Paul Heintz, "Jane Says: Sanders' Secret Weapon or a Political Liability?," *Seven Days,* June 17, 2015, https://www.sevendaysvt.com/vermont/jane -says-sanders-secret-weapon-or-a-political-liability/Content?oid=267 0992.

62. Associated Press, "Burlington College to send students to Cuba," *Brattleboro Reformer,* July 26, 2007, https://www.reformer.com/stories/burlington-col lege-to-send-students-to-cuba,272017.

63. "Burlington College sets program in Cuba," Rutland Herald Online, July 21, 2007, https://www.rutlandherald.com/news/burlington-college-sets-pro gram-in-cuba/article_c3c600d1-d5a1-51e4-9294-7c706ea9d4c6.html.

64. Ken Picard, "Havana Dreams Deferred," *Seven Days*, March 5, 2008, https://www.sevendaysvt.com/vermont/havana-dreams-deferred/Content ?oid=2132940.

65. Alex Seitz-Wald, "The 25 best things we learned from Bernie Sanders' book," MSNBC, May 28, 2015, http://www.msnbc.com/msnbc/the-25 -best-things-we-learned-bernie-sanders-book; Marc Frank, *Cuba Looks to the Year 2000* (New York: International Publishers, 1993), p. 84.

66. Bruce Edwards, "School solidifies ties to Cuba," *Rutland Herald,* March 10, 2013, https://www.rutlandherald.com/news/business_vermont/school-solid ifies-ties-to-cuba/article_fedce925-6b08-59c7-bab6-8d0c8d4b63a9.html.

67. "Study Abroad: Cuba Cuban Studies," StudyAbroad.com, https://www .studyabroad.com/institutions/burlington-college/study-abroad-cuba -cuban-studies-276267.

68. Associated Press, "Burlington College to send students to Cuba."

69. Tim Johnson, "Financial questions dog Burlington College," *Burlington Free Press,* August 16, 2014, https://www.burlingtonfreepress.com/story/news /education/2014/08/15/financial-questions-dog-burlington-college /14117505/.

70. "Spending by Prime Award," USASpending.gov, accessed November 28, 2018, https://www.usaspending.gov/#/search/92ff650c19a891f13badd42f0 80847fe.

71. Leon J. Thompson, "She's Nailed It," *Business People-Vermont*, November 2015, http://www.vermontguides.com/2015/vtwoodwork1115.html; Jasper Craven, "One family, two schools: Questions raised about another Sanders deal," VTDigger, June 13, 2017, https://vtdigger.org/2017/06/13/one-family -two-schools-questions-swirl-around-another-sanders-deal/

72. Brady C. Toensing, letter to Eric S. Miller (U.S. attorney for the District of Vermont) and Fred W. Gibson, Jr. (Acting Inspector General, FDIC), January 10, 2016; M. Ferrer, "Nepotism at Burlington College," Medium, February 13, 2017, https://medium.com/@m.ferrer/nepotism-at-burlington -college-1a9af167ae9b.

73. Craven, "One family, two schools."

74. Ibid.

75. "Vermont Woodworking School Expansion Project Receives USDA Grant for Bio-Mass Furnace," Vermontbiz.com, September 10, 2008, https://ver montbiz.com/news/september/vermont-woodworking-school-expansion -project-receives-usda-grant-bio-mass-furnace; "Woodworking school meets in old barn," *Sun Community News & Printing,* February 10, 2009; https:// www.suncommunitynews.com/articles/the-sun/woodworking-school -meets-in-old-barn/.

76. David J. Tinsley, "Committee and Subcommittee Assignments," S. Pub. 110–16, 110th Cong., December 1, 2007, https://www.govinfo.gov/content /pkg/GPO-CPUB-110spub16/pdf/GPO-CPUB-110spub16.pdf.

77. Harry Jaffe, *Why Bernie Sanders Matters* (New York: Regan Arts, 2012), p. 112.

78. Craven, "One family, two schools."

79. Johnson, "Financial questions dog Burlington College."

80. Ken Picard, "Burlington College Students Press for Changes after Prof's Dismissal," *Seven Days*, November 25, 2008, https://www.sevendaysvt.com /vermont/burlington-college-students-press-for-changes-after-profs-dis missal/Content?oid=2135730.

81. Burlington College, Internal Revenue Service, Form 990, 2009, https:// www.citizenaudit.org/2011_06_EO/03–0229504_990_201006.pdf/.

82. Opensecrets.org, "Bernie Sanders: Assets," 2012, https://www.opensecrets. org/personal-finances/assets/Bernie-Sanders?cid=N00000528&year=2012.

83. Opensecrets.org, "Bernie Sanders: Assets," 2014, https://www.opensecrets .org/personal-finances/assets/Bernie-Sanders?cid=N00000528&year=2014.

84. Burlington College, Internal Revenue Service, Form 990, 2007, Statement 9, p. 29.

85. Johnson, "Financial questions dog Burlington College."

86. Alicia Freese, "Pass or Fail: What Happens If Burlington College Drops Out?," *Seven Days*, August 20, 2014, https://www.sevendaysvt.com/vermont /pass-or-fail-what-happens-if-burlington-college-drops-out/Content?oid =2420094; Morgan True, "Pomerleau advised Sanders on college land deal he also saved," VTDigger, August 6, 2017, https://vtdigger.org/2017/08/06 /pomerleau-advised-sanders-college-land-deal-also-saved/.

87. John Walters, "Ho-Ho Pomerleau: Vermont Pols Kiss the Ring," *Seven Days*, December 13, 2017, https://www.sevendaysvt.com/vermont/ho-ho-pomer leau-vermont-pols-kiss-the-ring/Content?oid=11038207.

88. Greg Guma, "Campus Paradise Lost: The Fall of Burlington College," June 26, 2017, http://gregguma.blogspot.com/2016/05/campus-paradise -lost-fall-of-burlington.html.

89. Laura Krantz, "Burlington College to sell 25 acres to real estate developer," *Vermont Business Magazine*, October 25, 2014, https://vermontbiz.com/news /october/burlington-college-sell-25-acres-real-estate-developer; http:// vehbfa.org/wp-content/uploads/2010-VEHBFA-Annual-Report.pdf.

90. VEHBFA *2010 Annual Report*, http://vehbfa.org/wp-content/uploads /2010-VEHBFA-Annual-Report.pdf; Morgan True, "Jane Sanders overstated donation amounts in loan application for Burlington College," VTDigger, September 13, 2015, https://vtdigger.org/2015/09/13/jane-sanders-over stated-donation-amounts-in-loan-application-for-burlington-college/.

91. Lloyd, "Jane Sanders's Little College That Couldn't."

92. Maggie Severns, "What Happened at Sanders U," Politico, February 11,

2016, https://www.politico.com/story/2016/02/bernie-sanders-jane-vermont
-burlington-college-219114.

93. Mark Johnson and Elizabeth Hewitt, "Philanthropist: Burlington College Could Have Survived," VTDigger, August 4, 2017, https://vtdigger
.org/2017/08/04/philanthropist-burlington-college-survived/.

94. Danny Hakim, "Jane Sanders and the Messy Demise of a Vermont College,"
New York Times, June 21, 2019, https://www.nytimes.com/2019/06/21/us
/politics/jane-omeara-sanders-burlington-college.html?.

95. Morgan True, "Emails reveal FBI, Justice probe of Burlington College,"
VTDigger, April 27, 2017, https://vtdigger.org/2017/04/27/emails-reveal
-fbi-justice-probe-burlington-college/.

96. Aidan Quigley, "Trustee denies impropriety in Burlington College land
deal," VTDigger, June 26, 2019, https://vtdigger.org/2019/06/26/trustee
-denies-impropriety-in-burlington-college-land-deal/.

97. "Dr. Carol Moore named president of Burlington College," *Vermont Business
Magazine,* December 5, 2014, https://vermontbiz.com/news/december/dr
-carol-moore-named-president-burlington-college.

98. Alicia Freese, "Former Burlington College President Unloads on Board, Jane
Sanders," *Seven Days,* September 6, 2016, https://www.sevendaysvt.com
/OffMessage/archives/2016/09/06/former-burlington-college-president
-unloads-on-board-jane-sanders.

99. Paul Heintz, "Sanders Nemesis to Air TV Ad Bashing Wife's 'Golden Para-
chute,' " *Seven Days,* September 17, 2014, https://www.sevendaysvt.com
/OffMessage/archives/2014/09/17/sanders-nemesis-to-air-tv-ad-bashing
-wifes-golden-parachute; Burlington College, Internal Revenue Service,
Form 990, 2012; Bernard Sanders, Personal Financial Disclosure, 2013.

100. True, "Emails Reveal FBI, Justice Probe of Burlington College"; Morgan
True, "Fox News Says FBI's Burlington College Probe Ongoing," VTDigger, December 8, 2017, https://vtdigger.org/2017/12/08/fox-news-says-fbis
-burlington-college-probe-ongoing/.

101. Morgan True, "Case closed, no charges for Burlington College burglary
suspect," VTDigger, May 5, 2017, https://vtdigger.org/2017/05/05/case
-closed-no-charges-burlington-college-burglary-suspect/

102. Ibid.

103. Ibid.

104. Ibid.

105. Ibid.

106. True, "Emails reveal FBI, Justice probe of Burlington College."

107. Ida A. Brudnick, "Congressional Salaries and Allowances: In Brief," last
updated April 11, 2018, p. 2, https://www.senate.gov/CRSpubs/9c14ec69
-c4e4–4bd8–8953-f73daa1640e4.pdf, p. 2.

108. Chase Peterson-Withorn, "How Bernie Sanders, the Socialist Senator,
Amassed a $2.5 Million Fortune," *Forbes,* April 12, 2019, https://www

.forbes.com/sites/chasewithorn/2019/04/12/how-bernie-sanders-the-social ist-senator-amassed-a-25-million-fortune/#46a9cc0736bf.

109. United States Senate, "Books Written by Sitting Senators," n.d., https:// www.senate.gov/senators/BooksWrittenbySittingSenators.htm; Open secrets.org, Personal Finances Search, "McCain," n.d., https://www .opensecrets.org/personal-finances/search?q=mccain&type=person; John S. McCain, Personal Financial Disclosure, 2007, http://pfds.opensecrets.org /N00006424_2007.pdf; John S. McCain, Personal Financial Disclosure, 2013, http://pfds.opensecrets.org/N00006424_2013.pdf; John S. McCain, Personal Financial Disclosure, 2014, http://pfds.opensecrets.org/N00006424_2014.pdf; Hillary Hoffower, "A Look at the Life and Fortune of John McCain, Who Had a Sprawling Real Estate Portfolio and Donated $1.7 Million in Book Sales to Charity," Business Insider, August 25, 2019, https://www.businessinsider.com /john-mccain-net-worth-real-estate-charity-2018–5.

110. "Advanced Search for Legislation," Bills Sponsored by Bernard Sanders, Gov-track.us, n.d.,https://www.govtrack.us/congress/bills/browse?sponsor=400 357#enacted_ex=on.

111. Jennifer Calfas, "Bernie Sanders Made More than $1 Million in 2016," Money, June 5, 2017, http://money.com/money/4805379/bernie-sanders -2016-income/; "Bernie Sanders Criticizes Democrats and Republicans in 'Where We Go From Here,' " NPR, November 27, 2018, https://www.npr .org/2018/11/27/670800149/bernie-sanders-criticizes-democrats-and -republicans-in-where-we-go-from-here.

112. Jill Lepore, "Bernie Sanders's Long Run," New Yorker, July 9, 2015, https:// www.newyorker.com/news/daily-comment/bernie-sanderss-long-run; FEC data; Opensecrets.org, "Vendor/Recipient: Perseus Books," 2012, accessed July 18, 2019, https://www.opensecrets.org/expends/vendor.php?year=2012 &vendor=Perseus%20Books; Bernie Sanders, The Speech: On Corporate Greed and the Decline of Our Middle Class (New York: Perseus Books, 2015), https:// www.amazon.com/Speech-Corporate-Greed-Decline-Middle/dp/15685855 35#reader_1568585535.

113. "Bernie Sanders," Verso Books, n.d., https://www.versobooks.com/authors /1242-bernie-sanders; FEC data.

114. Calfas, "Bernie Sanders made more than $1 million in 2016."

115. Kevin O'Connor, "Is Bernie Sanders' new book sign of a 2020 bid?," VT Digger, June 17, 2018, https://vtdigger.org/2018/06/17/bernie-sanders-new -book-sign-2020-bid/.

116. Andrew Bast, "Bernie Sanders releases 10 years of tax returns detailing mil-lions in earnings," CBS News, April 16, 2019, https://www.msn.com/en-us /news/politics/bernie-sanders-releases-10-years-of-tax-returns-detailing -millions-in-earnings/ar-BBVYb8B.

117. Howie Carr, "Carr: FBI Trailing 'Socialist' Bernie Sanders and Wife over Bank Loan Deal," BostonHerald.com, July 5, 2017, https://www.boston

herald.com/2017/07/05/carr-fbi-trailing-socialist-bernie-sanders-and-wife
-over-bank-loan-deal/.

118. Philip Bump, "Bernie Sanders Is the 19th Poorest Member of the United
States Senate," *Washington Post*, April 14, 2016, https://www.washingtonpost
.com/news/the-fix/wp/2016/04/14/bernie-sanders-is-the-19th-poorest
-member-of-the-united-states-senate/?utm_term=.0bc440b37c85.

119. John Walters, "Bernie Sanders Made More than $1 Million in 2016," *Seven
Days*, June 4, 2017, https://www.sevendaysvt.com/OffMessage/archives
/2017/06/04/walters-bernie-sanders-made-more-than-1-million-in-2016;
Jasper Craven and Mark Johnson, "UPDATED: Sanders Lake Home Purchase Leaves Questions Unanswered," VTDigger, August 18, 2016, https://
vtdigger.org/2016/08/18/sanders-lake-home-purchase-leaves-questions
-unanswered/.

120. Carr, "FBI Trailing 'Socialist' Bernie Sanders and Wife."

121. John Walters, "Bernie Sanders Made More than $1 Million in 2016"; Tim
Marcin, "Bernie Sanders Mocks Greedy Rich People, Is Also Rich," *Newsweek*, April 21, 2017, https://www.newsweek.com/bernie-sanders-criticized
-twitter-users-having-three-houses-587721.

122. Craven and Johnson, "Sanders Lake Home Purchase Leaves Questions Unanswered."

123. Walters, "Bernie Sanders Made More Than $1 Million in 2016"; Dave Levin-
thal, "How Bernie Sanders Beat the Clock—and Avoided Disclosure," Center
for Public Integrity, August 18, 2016, https://publicintegrity.org/federal-pol
itics/how-bernie-sanders-beat-the-clock-and-avoided-disclosure/.

124. Eric Levitz, "We're All 'Socialists' Now," Intelligencer, June 13, 2019, http://
nymag.com/intelligencer/2019/06/bernie-sanders-socialism-speech-gwu.html.

125. Eric Bradner, "Bernie Sanders: Prolific Democratic Party fundraiser," CNN,
February 8, 2016, https://www.cnn.com/2016/02/05/politics/sanders-dem
ocratic-fundraisers/index.html.

126. Greg Guma, "Lockheed Martin in Vermont: Senator Bernie Sanders' Corporate Conundrum," Global Research, May 28, 2015, https://www.global
research.ca/lockheed-martin-in-vermont-senator-bernie-sanders-corporate
-conundrum/5452106.

127. Bradner, "Bernie Sanders: Prolific Democratic Party fundraiser."

128. "The AllEarth Renewables Leadership Team," AllEarth Solar, accessed January 31, 2019, https://www.allearthrenewables.com/our-leadership-team.

129. "7,000 Jobs: Stimulating the Vermont Economy," Bernie Sanders's Senate
page, July 28, 2010, https://www.sanders.senate.gov/newsroom/must
-read/7–000-jobs-stimulating-the-vermont-economy.

130. "Sanders visits solar regional testing center," Bernie Sanders's Senate page,
press release, October 12, 2017, https://www.sanders.senate.gov/newsroom
/press-releases/sanders-visits-solar-regional-testing-center; "David Blitters-

dorf," Davidblittersdorf.com, accessed January 2, 2019, https://www
.davidblittersdorf.com/hubfs/David%20Blittersdorf/Docs/David_Blitters
dorf_VT_biography.pdf?t=1484930216324&hsLang=en-us; "The AllEarth
Renewables Leadership Team."

131. Andrew Stein, "Sanders Opposes State Wind Moratorium Proposal," VT
Digger, January 28, 2013, https://vtdigger.org/2013/01/28/sanders/.

132. Robin Smith, "State Seeks $20,000 Fine Over Kidder Hill Wind Mills,"
Caledonian Record, July 1, 2017, https://www.caledonianrecord.com/news
/state-seeks-fine-over-kidder-hill-wind-mills/article_f83c474e-2be5-595b
-9ea0-43d366414967.html; Energizevermont.org, "Wind Developer Blittersdorf Sues Project Neighbors," National Wind Watch, press release, August
21, 2012, https://www.wind-watch.org/news/2012/08/21/wind-developer
-blittersdorf-sues-project-neighbors/.

133. "David Blittersdorf, President and CEO of AllEarth Renewables, Plans
to Shift Renewable Development Resources Out of State," Green Energy
Times, March 12, 2018, http://www.greenenergytimes.org/2018/03/12
/david-blittersdorf-president-and-ceo-of-allearth-renewables-plans-to-shift
-renewable-development-resources-out-of-state/.

134. Erin Mansfield, "Special Report: Tax Breaks Drive Vermont's Solar Gold Rush,"
VTDigger, 2015, https://vtdigger.org/fullimagestory/solar-is-everywhere/.

135. Ibid.

136. Stein, "Sanders Opposes State Wind Moratorium Proposal."

137. April McCullum, "Scott Turns to Regulators for Wind Moratorium," *Burlington Free Press*, May 31, 2017, https://www.burlingtonfreepress.com/story
/news/politics/government/2017/05/31/phil-scott-new-vermont-rules-lead
-less-industrial-wind/354072001/.

138. Garret Keizer, "Bernie Betrayed Us," National Wind Watch, March 31, 2013,
https://www.wind-watch.org/news/2013/03/31/bernie-dont-betray-us/;
"Sanders visits solar regional testing center"; "Senate Passes Sanders Amendment to Fund Williston Solar Regional Testing Center," Bernie Sanders's
Senate page, press release, June 25, 2018, https://www.sanders.senate.gov
/newsroom/press-releases/senate-passes-sanders-amendment-to-fund-willis
ton-solar-regional-testing-center.

139. "Week in Review," Bernie Sanders's Senate page, press release, September
28, 2007, https://Sanders.senate.gov/newsroom/press-releases/2007/09/28
/week-in-review.

140. "Endorsements," Environmentalists For Bernie, accessed January 2, 2019,
http://environmentalistsforbernie.org/endorsements/.

141. Greg Guma, "How Lockheed and Sandia Came to Vermont," Maverick Media, November 4, 2013, http://muckraker-gg.blogspot.com/2013/11/how
-lockheed-and-sandia-came-to-vermont.html.

142. Alexander Cohen, "Defense Contractor Employees Give the Most Money to

Hillary Clinton," Center for Public Integrity, April 1, 2016, https://public
integrity.org/national-security/defense-contractor-employees-give-the
-most-money-to-hillary-clinton/.

143. Mak, "Bernie Sanders Loves This $1 Trillion War Machine."

144. Nick Zazulia, "F-35: How the Trillion-Dollar Program Got Here and Where
It's Going," Avionics International, September 4, 2018, https://www.aviation
today.com/2018/09/04/f-35-program-update/.

145. Adam Silverman, "Pentagon F-35 Review Unlikely to Affect Vermont,"
Burlington Free Press, February 5, 2017, https://www.burlingtonfreepress
.com/story/news/2017/02/05/pentagon-f-35-review-unlikely-affect-ver
mont/97373894/.

146. Mak, "Bernie Sanders Loves This $1 Trillion War Machine"; Paul Barrett,
"Is the F-35 a Trillion-Dollar Mistake?," *Bloomberg Businessweek,* April 4,
2017, https://www.bloomberg.com/news/features/2017-04-04/is-the-f-35
-a-trillion-dollar-mistake.

147. Greg Guma, "How Lockheed and Sandia Came to Vermont."

148. Russell Berman, "How One Donor Is Profiting Off the Trump and Sanders
Campaigns," *Atlantic,* August 26, 2016, https://www.theatlantic.com/poli
tics/archive/2016/08/how-one-donor-is-profiting-off-the-trump-and
-sanders-campaigns/497501/; Russell Berman, "The Donors Who Love
Bernie Sanders a Little Too Much," *Atlantic,* May 13, 2016, https://www
.theatlantic.com/politics/archive/2016/05/the-bernie-sanders-donors-who
-are-giving-too-much/482418/.

149. Ibid.; *Brad Woodhouse, American Democracy Legal Fund, Before the Federal Election Commission v. Senator Bernard Sanders and Bernie 2016 and Susan Jackson,
Treasurer,* complaint, February 29, 2016, p. 2, https://www.fec.gov/files/legal
/murs/current/118426.pdf.

150. Larry Noble quoted in Berman, "How One Donor Is Profiting Off the
Trump and Sanders Campaigns."

151. Emma Baccellieri, "Clinton's California Lead—in Donations," Opensecrets
.org, June 6, 2016, https://www.opensecrets.org/news/2016/06/clintons
-california-lead-in-donations/.

152. Federal Election Commission, "Excessive, Prohibited, and Impermissible Contributions: BERNIE 2016," May 10, 2016, https://docquery.fec.gov/pdf/847/2
01605100300045847/201605100300045847.pdf; Federal Election Commission,
"Excessive, Prohibited, and Impermissible Contributions: BERNIE 2016,"
February 11, 2016, https://docquery.fec.gov/pdf/988/201602110300034988/20
1602110300034988.pdf; Jasper Craven, "FEC Threatens Audit of Sanders Campaign Donations," VTDigger, May 14, 2016, https://vtdigger.org/2016/05/14
/fec-threatens-audit-of-sanders-campaign-donations/; Scott Blackburn, "The
Story of Stupid Campaign Finance Laws: A Tale of Sanders' Donors," Institute
for Free Speech (blog), February 25, 2016, https://www.ifs.org/blog/the-story
-of-stupid-campaign-finance-laws-a-tale-of-sanders-donors/.

153. Alex Lubben, "Bernie Sanders Colluded—with the Australian Labor Party," Vice, February 28, 2018, https://news.vice.com/en_us/article /437pbg/bernie-sanders-campaign-colluded-with-russia-federal-election -commission-finds; Heather McNab, "Young Sydneysiders Call US Citizens in Support of Presidential Hopeful Bernie Sanders," *Daily Telegraph*, June 21, 2016, https://www.dailytelegraph.com.au/newslocal/city -east/feeling-the-bern-young-sydneysiders-call-us-citizens-in-support -of-presidential-hopeful-bernie-sanders/news-story/a4d72a4a47370d02c3 dbf91d81b715a3.

154. Craven, "Special report: Sanders campaign millions go to mystery firm."

155. Ibid.

156. Dennis B. Murphy, "Old Towne Media Received over $83 Million from the Sanders Campaign," Medium, February 9, 2018, https://medium.com /@dennisbmurphy/old-towne-media-received-over-83million-from-the -sanders-campaign-a76873c0aef0; Jonathan Topaz and Kristen East, "Bernie Sanders' Wife Accounts for All His Reported Assets," Politico, July 16, 2015, https://www.politico.com/story/2015/07/bernie-sanders-wife-accounts -for-reported-assets-120261.

157. "Editorials from around New England," Associated Press, January 12, 2018, https://apnews.com/013c4681d38e431b95ce0a9fa2be7349; "Editorial: Railing Against the 1 Percent," *Caledonian Record*, July 19, 2016, https://www .caledonianrecord.com/opinion/editorial/editorial-railing-against-the-per cent/article_c2c15872-de8e-5b9b-b314-83ed0be9a547.html.

158. N.J. Eberle, "Old Towne Media, LLC: Buying a Political Revolution," Medium, April 23, 2016, https://medium.com/@VonEbsy/old-towne-media-llc -buying-a-political-revolution-40cbac5cb4c3.

159. Eliza Newlin Carney, "Nonprofit Structure Backfires on 'Our Revolution,'" *American Prospect,* September 1, 2016, https://prospect.org/article/nonprofit -structure-backfires-our-revolution; Jasper Craven, "Sanders launches think tank," VTDigger, June 9, 2017, https://vtdigger.org/2017/06/09/sanders -launches-think-tank/.

160. Vermont Secretary of State Corporations Division, "American People's Historical Society," accessed November 30, 2018, https://www.vtsosonline.com /online/BusinessInquire/BusinessInformation?businessID=41079.

161. "Vermont Patent & Trademark Depository Library," GuideStar, accessed November 30, 2018, https://www.guidestar.org/profile/03-0350831; "Re: Agenda for Thursday Meeting—Sanders Research," Wikileaks, November 5, 2015, https://wikileaks.org/podesta-emails/emailid/21823.

162. Jasper Craven, "Sanders Institute has little to show for first year and $500K," VTDigger, July 29, 2018, https://vtdigger.org/2018/07/29/sanders-institute -little-show-first-year-500k/.

163. Danny Hakim, "Sanders Institute Suspends Operations as Senator Runs for President," *New York Times,* March 14, 2019, https://www.nytimes

.com/2019/03/14/us/politics/bernie-sanders-public-policy-group.html
?action=click&module=RelatedCoverage&pgtype=Article&region=Footer.

164. Vermont Secretary of State Corporations Division, "The Sanders Institute INC," accessed November 30, 2018, https://www.vtsosonline.com/online /BusinessInquire/BusinessInformation?businessID=333112; The Sanders Institute, Internal Revenue Service, Form 990, 2017, https://pdf.guidestar.org /PDF_Images/2017/813/250/2017–813250230–0f86c804–9.pdf.

165. Lenny Ben-David, "Lenny Ben David on *The Arab Lobby* by Mitchell Bard," Jerusalem Center for Public Affairs, April 5, 2012, http://jcpa.org/article /lenny-ben-david-on-the-arab-lobby-by-mitchell-bard-2/; Anne Gearan, "Sanders Wins Greater Say in Democratic Platform; Names Pro-Palestinian Activist," *Washington Post*, May 23, 2016, https://www.washingtonpost .com/politics/sanders-scores-platform-concessions-from-democratic-national -committee/2016/05/23/e9ee8330–20fc-11e6-aa84–42391ba52c91_story .html?utm_term=.17c72c2489d2.

166. "Clients," Zogby Research Services, accessed July 22, 2019, http://www .zogbyresearchservices.com/clients.

167. Hussain Abdul-Hussain, "Broken Washington: The Cases of Zogby and the Brookings Institute," Huffington Post, October 21, 2010, https://www.huff post.com/entry/broken-washington-the-cas_b_771238.

168. Carney, "Nonprofit Structure Backfires on 'Our Revolution.'"

169. Ibid.

170. Ibid.

CHAPTER 8: AMY KLOBUCHAR

1. David Choi, "2020 Presidential Contender Amy Klobuchar Doesn't Deny 'Throwing' a Binder Amid Reports of Anger Issues Among Staffers," Business Insider, February 12, 2019, https://www.businessinsider.com/amy -klobuchar-throwing-binder-office-staffers-minnesota-2019–2.

2. Matt Stieb, "Senator Klobuchar's Staff Mistreatment Reportedly Goes Back a Decade, Includes Throwing Binders," Intelligencer, February 8, 2019, http:// nymag.com/intelligencer/2019/02/report-klobuchars-staff-mistreatment -goes-back-a-decade.html.

3. Jeremy Stahl, "A *Veep* Joke About Leg-Shaving Was Inspired by a Rumor About Amy Klobuchar," Slate, February 12, 2019, https://slate.com /news-and-politics/2019/02/veep-amy-klobuchar-leg-shaving-rumor.html

4. Nolan D. McCaskill, "The 'Worst Bosses' in Congress?," Politico, March 22, 2018, https://www.politico.com/story/2018/03/21/worst-bosses-congress -476729

5. James Appleby, President, Local 2938, letter to Michael Buseing, RE: Request for ASFCME endorsement by Amy Klobuchar, February 8, 2006, https://www.scribd.com/document/399214761/AFSCME-Letter-on

-Amy-Klobuchar-2006; Matt DeLong, "Eight Things to Know About Amy Klobuchar," *Star Tribune*, February 10, 2019, http://www.startribune.com /eight-things-to-know-about-amy-klobuchar/505579901/.

6. Molly Redden and Amanda Terkel, "Harry Reid Rebuked Amy Klobuchar for Mistreatment of Staff," Huffington Post, February 8, 2019, https://www .huffpost.com/entry/amy-klobuchar-mistreat-staff-harry-reid_n_5c5db1ec e4b03afe8d674530 (Note: see letter linked from the article); "Union Urges Minn. Senate Candidate Be Denied Endorsement," *Congress Daily,* February 22, 2006.

7. Tina Nguyen, "Terrified Aides Say Amy Klobuchar Is Just Like Trump," *Vanity Fair,* February 8, 2019, https://www.vanityfair.com/news/2019/02 /senator-klobuchar-temper-rumors.

8. "Top 10 Minnesota Daily Newspapers by Circulation," Agility PR Solutions, Data as of August, 2019, https://www.agilitypr.com/resources/top-media -outlets/top-10-Minnesota-daily-newspapers-by-circulation/.

9. Amy Klobuchar, *The Senator Next Door: A Memoir from the Heartland* (New York: Henry Holt and Company, 2015), pp. 24–28; Ben Terris, "Amy Klobuchar's Complicated Political Inheritance," *Washington Post*, May 7, 2019, https://www.washingtonpost.com/news/style/wp/2019/05/07/feature/amy -klobuchars-complicated-relationship-with-her-father-has-defined-her-as-a -person-and-a-candidate/?utm_term=.32a7c3ab0d5f.

10. "Klobuchar, Amy, (1960–)," Biographical Directory of the United States Congress, accessed June 14, 2019, http://bioguide.congress.gov/scripts/bio display.pl?index=k$00367; Klobuchar, *The Senator Next Door,* pp. 61, 67, 76.

11. Klobuchar, *The Senator Next Door,* pp. 77, 80.

12. Josephine Marcotty, "Painful times with dad helped Klobuchar create drive to succeed," *Star Tribune*, October 8, 2006, http://www.startribune.com /painful-times-with-dad-helped-klobuchar-create-drive-to-succeed/5055 76691/.

13. "Walter Mondale Fast Facts," CNN Library, December 19, 2018, https:// www.cnn.com/2013/08/30/us/walter-mondale-fast-facts/; Klobuchar, *The Senator Next Door,* p. 81.

14. Klobuchar, *The Senator Next Door,* p. 84.

15. "John Bessler—Amy Klobuchar's Husband," Superbhub, March 17, 2019, http://superbhub.com/biography/john-bessler-net-worth-wife/.

16. Marcotty, "Painful times with dad helped Klobuchar create drive to succeed."

17. Klobuchar, *The Senator Next Door,* pp. 111, 115, 127, and 134.

18. Ibid., pp. 139, 171, and 173.

19. Amy Sherman, "Burnsville, Minn. Contractor Charged in Major Swindle," *St. Paul Pioneer Press,* January 31, 2003; Amy Sherman, "St. Paul, Minn.-Area Contractor Gets Two Years in Major Swindle," *St. Paul Pioneer Press,* January 16, 2004.

20. "Tax probe now includes 42 Northwest Airlines employees," *Post Bulletin,* January 29, 2003, https://www.postbulletin.com/tax-probe-now-includes -northwest-airlines-employees/article_ce5a3069-c4aa-54e6-9565 -049d4b48c2a1.html; Klobuchar, *The Senator Next Door,* pp. 171–73; Associated Press, "More Northwest Pilots Accused of Tax Evasion," *Post Bulletin,* March 30, 2002, https://www.postbulletin.com/more-northwest-pilots -accused-of-tax-evasion/article_4350c38d-aeb4-5dea-bef4-c88d2720e7d2 .html.

21. Annalyn Censky, "Tom Petters gets 50 years for Ponzi scheme," CNN Money, April 8, 2010, https://money.cnn.com/2010/04/08/news/economy /Tom_Petters/; Alexandra Sifferlin, "Top 10 Swindlers—Schemers and Swindlers—Tom Petters," *Time,* March 7, 2012, http://content.time.com /time/specials/packages/article/0,28804,2104982_2104983_2104984,00 .html.

22. "Bill Mondale," LinkedIn profile, n.d., https://www.linkedin.com/in/bill -mondale-2231871/.

23. David Phelps and Jon Tevlin, "Part 1: The collapse of the Petters empire," *Star Tribune,* March 24, 2011, http://www.startribune.com/part-1-the-col lapse-of-the-petters-empire/33287804/; David Phelps, "Ted Mondale to pay $50,000 clawback to Petters receiver," *Star Tribune,* April 23, 2013, http:// www.startribune.com/ted-mondale-to-pay-50-000-clawback-to-petters -receiver/204203021/; "Mondale, Ted A.," Minnesota Legislative Reference Library, accessed August 1, 2019, https://www.leg.state.mn.us/legdb/full detail?id=10436.

24. Phelps, "Ted Mondale to pay $50,000 clawback to Petters receiver."

25. Kevin Diaz, "Donor Loyalties Are Clear in U.S. Senate Race; Kennedy's donations come from political action committees and corporations; many of Klobuchar's financial backers are lawyers," *Star Tribune,* October 28, 2006; Matthew Boyle, "Documents: Sen. Klobuchar Took Ponzi Schemer's Campaign Contributions, Didn't Prosecute," Daily Caller, October 19, 2012, https://dailycaller.com/2012/10/19/documents-sen-klobuchar-took -ponzi-schemers-campaign-contributions-didnt-prosecute/; FEC data.

26. Boyle, "Documents: Sen. Klobuchar Took Ponzi Schemer's Campaign Contributions, Didn't Prosecute."

27. Ibid.

28. Ibid.

29. Tom Scheck, "Klobuchar Calls Daily Caller Story 'Inaccurate,' " Minnesota Public Radio, October 22, 2012, https://blogs.mprnews.org/capitol-view /2012/10/klobuchar_calls_2/.

30. Associated Press, "Minn. Businessman Tom Petters Rose Quickly, Fell Faster," *Post Bulletin,* November 15, 2008, https://www.postbulletin.com /minn-businessman-tom-petters-rose-quickly-fell-faster/article_bb5cf23b -d016-5dba-b72d-f25d91a7e802.html.

31. Nicole Garrison-Sprenger and John Welbes, "Early Signs of Petters Debacle Unheeded," Twincities.com, October 15, 2008, https://www.twincities .com/2008/10/15/early-signs-of-petters-debacle-unheeded/.

32. Mariah Blake, "The Turnaround Men," *New Republic,* October 26, 2011, https://newrepublic.com/article/96713/petters-ponzi-scheme; FEC data.

33. Garrison-Sprenger and Welbes, "Early Signs of Petters Debacle Unheeded"; Daily Caller, "Klobuchar Petters Documents the Daily Caller," Scribd, October 19, 2012, https://www.scribd.com/doc/110532291/Klobuchar-Petters -Documents-the-Daily-Caller.

34. Blake, "The Turnaround Men"; Government Exhibit 353-A, FBI phone call between Tom Petters and Bob White, October 1, 2008.

35. "Introduction to My Forthcoming Book: Ponzi-Dot-Gov: How the Government Defrauds Innocent Citizens," James L. Merriner's website, accessed on April 16, 2019, http://www.jamesmerriner.com/ponzi-dot-gov_intro.html; "Author & Freelance Editor/Writer," James L. Merriner's website, n.d., http://www.jamesmerriner.com/bio.html; Jim Klobuchar, *Minstrel: My Adventures in Newspapering* (Minneapolis: University of Minnesota Press, 1997), pp. 218–19.

36. Brian Lambert, "Five More Questions: Doug Kelley's high-stakes, high-profile, high-altitude adventures," *Minnesota Post,* June 23, 2014, https:// www.minnpost.com/politics-policy/2014/06/five-more-questions-doug -kelleys-high-stakes-high-profile-high-altitude-adve/.

37. Boyle, "Documents: Sen. Klobuchar Took Ponzi Schemer's Campaign Contributions, Didn't Prosecute."

38. Ibid.

39. Blake, "The Turnaround Men."

40. "Polaroid and Petters Group Worldwide Sign Definitive Merger Agreement," Exhibit 99.1, January 7, 2005, https://www.sec.gov/Archives/edgar/data /1227728/000110465905000847/a05–1214_1ex99d1.htm; http://www .startribune.com/bankruptcy-jurors-award-petters-co-victims-3–5-million -in-clawback-money/502211391/.

41. "Update 2—Tom Petters found guilty of Ponzi scheme fraud," Reuters, December 2, 2009, https://www.reuters.com/article/petters-verdict/update-2 -tom-petters-found-guilty-of-ponzi-scheme-fraud-idUSN024978920091202; Associated Press, "50-Year Term for Minnesota Man in $3.7 Billion Ponzi Fraud," *New York Times,* April 8, 2010, https://www.nytimes.com/2010/04 /09/business/09ponzi.html.

42. David Phelps, "Petters largesse follows politicians," *Star Tribune,* January 27, 2012, http://www.startribune.com/petters-largesse-follows-politicians /138241909/.

43. Brian Friel, "The Utility Man," *National Journal,* June 2, 2007.

44. Philip Klein, "Amy Klobuchar is actually quite liberal," *Washington Examiner,* February 28, 2019, https://www.washingtonexaminer.com/opinion/col

umnists/amy-klobuchar-is-actually-quite-liberal; "Head to Head: Compare Voting Records—Bernard Sanders and Amy Klobuchar," ProPublica, voting records as of August 3, 2019, https://projects.propublica.org/represent /members/S000033-bernard-sanders/compare-votes/K000367-amy-klobu char/116.

45. Kevin Diaz, "Klobuchar: Aiming for the middle ground," *Star Tribune,* March 29, 2010.

46. Lisa Lerer, "Calling Herself 'Progressive,' Klobuchar Tries to Widen Appeal on Fox," *New York Times,* May 9, 2019; Lisa Lerer, "On Fox News, Amy Klobuchar Makes Her Case to the Left and the Right," *New York Times,* May 8, 2019, https://www.nytimes.com/2019/05/08/us/politics/klobuchar -town-hall.html.

47. Jim Geraghty, "Twenty Things You Probably Didn't Know about Amy Klo-buchar," *National Review,* January 23, 2019, https://www.nationalreview .com/2019/01/twenty-things-you-probably-didnt-know-about-amy-klobu char/.

48. Opensecrets.org, "Sen. Amy Klobuchar—Minnesota," n.d., https://www .opensecrets.org/members-of-congress/earmarks?cid=N00027500&cycle =2018&fy=FY08. Earmarks of note: 2008, Northstar Commuter Rail $53.9 million, Central Corridor Light Rail $10.2 million. In 2009 Central Corridor Light Rail Transit Project $20 million. In 2010, Northstar Com-muter Rail extension $3 million, Central Corridor Light Rail $2 million.

49. Ibid.

50. "Northstar Commuter Rail Line," Metro Transit, accessed June 12, 2019, https://www.metrotransit.org/northstar.

51. "Jocelyn Knoll," Dorsey & Whitney LLP, n.d., https://www.dorsey.com /people/k/knoll-jocelyn (see "Experience"); Opensecrets.org, "Sen. Amy Klobuchar—Minnesota: Contributors," 2005–2020, n.d., https://www .opensecrets.org/members-of-congress/contributors?cid=N00027500 &cycle=CAREER&type=C.

52. Metro Transit, "Northstar Commuter Rail Line," https://www.metrotransit .org/northstar.

53. La Velle E. Neal III, "Family will continue to run Twins," *Star Tribune,* Janu-ary 5, 2009, http://www.startribune.com/family-will-continue-to-run -twins/37125144/.

54. Brandt Williams, "Pohlad: Contribution to Twins Ballpark 'Fair, Substan-tial,'" Minnesota Public Radio, April 25, 2005, http://news.minnesota .publicradio.org/features/2005/04/25_williamsb_twins/.

55. Stuart Lavietes, "Carl R. Pohlad, Owner of Minnesota Twins, Dies at 93," *New York Times,* January 5, 2009, https://www.nytimes.com/2009/01/06 /sports/baseball/06pohlad.html; "Minnesota Twins awarded the 2014 All-Star Game," MLB News, August 29, 2012, https://www.mlb.com/news /minnesota-twins-awarded-the-2014-all-star-game/c-37546072.

56. J. Patrick Coolican, "Big Donors Propelled the DFL to Victory," *Star Tribune*, February 2, 2019, http://www.startribune.com/big-donors-propelled-the -dfl-to-victory/505253002/; Bob Collins, "Carl Pohlad, 1915–2009," MPR News, January 5, 2009, https://blogs.mprnews.org/newscut/2009/01/carl _pohlad_1915–2009/.

57. FEC data.

58. Clare Kennedy, "Pohlad grandson joins United Properties," Finance & Commerce, December 1, 2017, https://finance-commerce.com/2017/12 /pohlad-grandson-joins-united-properties/; Brandt Williams, "Target Field: A hit with the fans, but has it been an economic success?," *MPR News,* April 8, 2011, https://www.mprnews.org/story/2011/04/07/target-field-second-year.

59. Kennedy, "Pohlad grandson joins United Properties."

60. To Amend the Criminal Penalty Provision for Criminal Infringement of a Copyright, and for Other Purposes, S. 978, 112th Cong. (2011), https:// www.govinfo.gov/content/pkg/BILLS-112s978rs/pdf/BILLS-112s978rs.pdf; Chloe Albanesius, "Senate Panel OKs Bill That Makes Streaming Pirated Content a Felony," *PC Magazine*, June 17, 2001, https://www.pcmag.com /news/265860/senate-panel-oks-bill-that-makes-streaming-pirated-con tent-a.

61. Ted Johnson, "Justin Bieber: Sen. Amy Klobuchar Should be 'Locked Up' for Anti-Piracy Bill," *Variety,* October 28, 2011, https://variety.com/2011/biz /opinion/justin-bieber-sen-amy-klobuchar-should-be-locked-up-for-anti -piracy-bill-37185/.

62. FEC data.

63. OpenSecrets.org, "Minnesota Senate Race: Contributors," 2012, accessed June 12, 2019, http://www.opensecrets.org/races/contributors?cycle=2012 &id=MNS2.

64. John Eggerton, "Senate Bill Gets Tough on Pirates," Multichannel News, May 16, 2011; https://www.multichannel.com/news/senate-bill-gets-tough -pirates-264986.

65. FEC data.

66. A Bill to Amend the Internal Revenue Code of 1986 to Provide a Renew- able Electricity Integration Credit for a Utility That Purchases or Produces Renewable Power, S. 1291, 112th Cong. (2011), https://www.congress.gov /bill/112th-congress/senate-bill/1291?s=3&r=67.

67. Lobbying relationship, Lobbying by XCEL ENERGY, INC., n.d., https:// projects.propublica.org/represent/lobbying/300986187.

68. See Klobuchar's speech on the Senate floor, October 9, 2018: "Floor Speech on Climate Change," Amy Klobuchar's Senate page, October 9, 2018, https://www.klobuchar.senate.gov/public/index.cfm/mobile/events-speech es-and-floor-statements?ID=610EE17B-7C40–4DDA-A190-D16CABD B1AB1. She specifically mentions Xcel Energy. "Xcel Energy is another example of a company that appears to be ahead of the Federal Government.

They supported the Obama administration's Clean Power Plan. . . ." In March of the year before (2017), Xcel Energy announced a $1.6 billion project in New Mexico and Texas incorporating a 2.5 cents per kilowatt-hour federal tax credit; see: "New Xcel Energy Wind Facilities Offer $2.8 Billion in Customer Savings over 30 Years," Xcel Energy, March 21, 2017, https://www.xcelenergy.com/company/media_room/news_releases/new_xcel_energy_wind_facilities_offer_$2.8_billion_in_customer_savings_over_30_years. Seven weeks later she cosponsored the Clean Energy for America Act of 2017. Title I of that act incorporates a per-kilowatt-hour tax credit directly into Chapter 1 of the U.S. tax code.

69. FEC data.
70. Clean Energy for America Act, S. 1068, 115th Cong. (2017), https://www.congress.gov/bill/115th-congress/senate-bill/1068; "This bill amends the Internal Revenue Code to modify or replace several existing energy-related tax incentives to provide consolidated tax deductions and credits for the production of or investment in clean electricity. . . ."
71. "Head to Head: Compare Voting Records, Compare the Voting Records of Bernard Sanders and Amy Klobuchar in 2017–18," ProPublica, accessed June 14, 2019, https://projects.propublica.org/represent/members/S000033-bernard-sanders/compare-votes/K000367-amy-klobuchar/115; Opensecrets.org, "Sen. Bernie Sanders—Vermont: PACs," n.d., https://www.opensecrets.org/members-of-congress/pacs?cid=N00000528&cycle=CAREER; Opensecrets.org, "Sen. Amy Klobuchar—Minnesota: PACs," n.d., https://www.opensecrets.org/members-of-congress/pacs?cid=N00027500&cycle=CAREER&type=I.
72. Anna Yukhananov, "Senators propose relaxing FDA conflict rules," Reuters, October 13, 2011, https://www.reuters.com/article/us-fda-devices-bill/senators-propose-relaxing-fda-conflict-rules-idUSTRE79C7HY20111013.
73. Sloane Martin, "FULL SPEECH: Senator Amy Klobuchar Says She'll 'Lead from the Heart' as She Announces Run for President," WCCO, February 10, 2019, https://wccoradio.radio.com/articles/senator-amy-klobuchars-full-speech-she-announces-her-run-president-20.
74. Improving Medical Device Innovation Act, S. 2737, 114th Cong. (2016), https://www.congress.gov/bill/114th-congress/senate-bill/2737/text; FEC data.
75. "Klobuchar Invites CEO of Medtronic to SOTU," Amy Klobuchar's Senate page, January 22, 2011, https://www.klobuchar.senate.gov/public/index.cfm/amy-in-the-news?ID=098108C0-F7D9-4DDE-BA9B-61ED1B7B6211.
76. Opensecrets.org, "Medical Supplies: Recipients," 2012, n.d., https://www.opensecrets.org/industries/recips.php?ind=H4100&cycle=2012&recipdetail=S&Mem=Y&sortorder=U.
77. Ashley Balcerzak, "9 Things to Know about Amy Klobuchar," *Minnesota Post*, February 10, 2019, https://www.minnpost.com/national/2019/02/9-things-to-know-about-amy-klobuchar/.

78. "Sen. Amy Klobuchar," Political Party Time, n.d., http://politicalpartytime
.org/pol/N00027500/.

79. Brian Schwartz, "Democratic Sen. Amy Klobuchar will reject corporate PAC
money in 2020 bid," CNBC, February 11, 2019, https://www.cnbc.com
/2019/02/11/democratic-sen-amy-klobuchar-will-reject-corporate-pac
-money-in-2020-bid—.html.

80. "Senate Committee on the Judiciary: Subcommittee on Antitrust, Competition Policy and Consumer Rights," GovTrack.us, n.d., https://www.govtrack
.us/congress/committees/SSJU/01.

81. Liz Fedor, "Klobuchar airs concern over airline merger talk," *Star Tribune,*
January 15, 2008, http://www.startribune.com/klobuchar-airs-concern
-over-merger-talk/13783666/.

82. Joseph Simonson, "Klobuchar Slams Corporate Goliaths but Takes Their
Money Anyway," *Washington Examiner,* March 13, 2019, https://www.wash
ingtonexaminer.com/news/amy-klobuchar-slams-corporate-goliaths-but
-takes-their-money-anyway.

83. Ibid.

84. Ibid.

85. Ibid.

86. Kevin Diaz, "Wall Street cash flows to politicians: Minnesotans' share,
though relatively modest, shows how high the stakes are," *Star Tribune,*
April 27, 2010, http://www.startribune.com/wall-street-cash-flows-to
-politicians/92265234/.

87. Amy Klobuchar, "Senator Klobuchar Calls for National Innovation Agenda,"
Vote Smart, January 18, 2011, https://votesmart.org/public-statement/579
306/senator-klobuchar-calls-for-national-innovation-agenda.

CHAPTER 9: ERIC GARCETTI

1. Garcetti For Mayor 2013, "Salma Hayek Endorses Eric Garcetti for Mayor of
Los Angeles," YouTube video, posted on January 26, 2013, https://www
.youtube.com/watch?v=l0V4jGCpzUk.

2. Ted Johnson, "Local Pols Get the Business," *Variety,* February 4–February 1,
2013, https://variety.com/2013/more/news/local-pols-get-the-business-111
8065537/.

3. Nathan Taylor Pemberton, "Mr. Mayor, What Are Your Thoughts on Good
Charlotte and Charcoal Water?" *Interview,* June 12, 2019, https://www.inter
viewmagazine.com/culture/eric-garcetti-los-angeles-mayor-rorschach-test.

4. Chanan Tigay, "Eric Garcetti Is the Anti-Trump, Pro–*Star Wars* Man We
Need," *GQ,* June 12, 2018, https://www.gq.com/story/los-angeles-eric
-garcetti-presidential-run; Jake Blumgart, "Philly's New Mayor: How Many
Progressive Changes Can Jim Kenney Bring to an Old-Style City with an
Antique Political Culture?" *American Prospect,* Summer 2016.

5. Dakota Smith, "LA Mayor Eric Garcetti as VP Pick? Odds Are Slim, Political Experts Say," *Los Angeles Daily News,* June 16, 2016, https://www.dailynews.com/2016/06/16/la-mayor-eric-garcetti-as-vp-pick-odds-are-slim-political-experts-say/.

6. Gabriel Kahn, "Who Is the Real Eric Garcetti?" *Los Angeles Magazine,* July 2016, https://www.lamag.com/citythinkblog/real-eric-garcetti/.

7. Dakota Smith, "Mayor Eric Garcetti Touts LA as Model City in DNC Speech," *Los Angeles Daily News,* July 28, 2016, https://www.dailynews.com/2016/07/28/mayor-eric-garcetti-touts-la-as-model-city-in-dnc-speech/.

8. Dakota Smith, David Zahniser, Alene Tchekmedyiian, and Laura J. Nelson, "FBI Raids at DWP, L.A. City Hall Related to Fallout from Billing Debacle," *Los Angeles Times,* July 22, 2019, https://www.latimes.com/california/story/2019-07-22/fbi-searches-dwp-headquarters-in-downtown-l-a.

9. Tom Tugend, "I'm a Kosher Burrito, Says Mixed-Race LA Mayor," *Jewish Chronicle,* May 30, 2013, https://www.thejc.com/news/world/i-m-a-kosher-burrito-says-new-mixed-race-la-mayor-1.45411.

10. Kahn, "Who Is the Real Eric Garcetti?"

11. Tigay, "Eric Garcetti Is the Anti-Trump, Pro–*Star Wars* Man We Need."

12. Gabriel Kahn, "Who Is the Real Eric Garcetti?"

13. Tigay, "Eric Garcetti Is the Anti-Trump, Pro–*Star Wars* Man We Need."

14. Michael Finnegan and James Rainey, "The Mayor-Elect's Partner in Life," *Los Angeles Times,* May 25 2013, https://www.latimes.com/local/la-xpm-2013-may-25-la-me-amy-wakeland-20130526-story.html.

15. Kahn, "Who Is the Real Eric Garcetti?"

16. Tigay, "Eric Garcetti Is the Anti-Trump, Pro–*Star Wars* Man We Need"; Daniel Guss, "Garcetti's Malignant Corruption and Dishonesty," CityWatch, June 17, 2019, https://www.citywatchla.com/index.php/2016-01-01-13-17-00/los-angeles/17871-garcetti-s-malignant-corruption-and-dishonesty.

17. Kahn "Who Is the Real Eric Garcetti?"; Dakota Smith and Ben Poston, "When Developers Want to Build More Than Zoning Allows, L.A. Planning Commissioners Almost Always Say Yes, Times Analysis Finds," *Los Angeles Times,* February 10, 2017, https://www.latimes.com/local/lanow/la-me-ln-planning-commission-zoning-changes-20170210-story.html.

18. Matt Welch, " 'Like Undermining Motherhood and Apple Pie': Why Are California Dems in Local Government Embracing Eminent Domain Abuse?" *Reason,* November 2005, .

19. Tigay, "Eric Garcetti Is the Anti-Trump, Pro–*Star Wars* Man We Need."

20. Daniel B. Wood, "In Los Angeles Mayor's Race, a Big Win for Eric Garcetti," *Christian Science Monitor,* May 22, 2013, https://www.csmonitor.com/USA/Elections/2013/0522/In-Los-Angeles-mayor-s-race-a-big-win-for-Eric-Garcetti.

21. Sarah Rothbard, "Experts Probe Political Apathy Among Angelenos," UCLA

Newsroom, December 6, 2013, http://newsroom.ucla.edu/stories/experts
-probe-political-apathy-249635.

22. Tom Manzo, "Eric Garcetti Is Mayor of Los Angeles, Not the President—He
Should Act Like It," *Pasadena Star-News,* October 21, 2017, https://www
.dailynews.com/2017/10/20/eric-garcetti-is-mayor-of-los-angeles-not-the
-president-he-should-act-like-it/.

23. Smith and Poston, "When Developers Want to Build More Than Zoning
Allows."

24. "Editorial: Don't Bend California's Environmental Rules for Billionaire
Sports Owners or the Olympics," *Los Angeles Times,* September 8, 2017,
https://www.latimes.com/opinion/editorials/la-ed-clippers-ceqa-20170908
-story.html.

25. Michael Finnegan, "Garcetti Names Top Fundraiser as a Senior Advisor," *Los
Angeles Times,* August 6, 2013, https://www.latimes.com/local/lanow/la
-xpm-2013-aug-06-la-me-ln-garcetti-jacobs-advisor-20130806-story.html.

26. "Board of Directors," Mayor's Fund for Los Angeles, accessed September 6,
2019, https://mayorsfundla.org/about-us/board-of-directors/; "Occidental
Petroleum Corporation," Funding Universe, accessed July 20, 2019, http://
www.fundinguniverse.com/company-histories/occidental-petroleum-corpo
ration-history/.

27. Bill Boyarsky, "A Virtual Spy: *Dossier: The Secret History of Armand Hammer.*
by Edward J. Epstein," *Los Angeles Times,* October 27, 1996, https://www
.latimes.com/archives/la-xpm-1996-10-27-bk-58288-story.html.

28. "Board of Directors," Mayor's Fund for Los Angeles; Gene Maddaus,
"Garcetti Aide Gives Himself Grandiose New Title," *LA Weekly,* January 14,
2016, https://www.laweekly.com/garcetti-aide-gives-himself-grandiose-new
-title/.

29. "Leadership," Accelerator for America, n.d., http://www.acceleratorforam
erica.com/leadership; David Zahniser and Michael Finnegan, "L.A. Mayor
Garcetti Sets Up a Nonprofit to Aide City Initiatives," *Los Angeles Times,*
June 27, 2014, https://www.latimes.com/local/cityhall/la-me-mayor-non
profit-20140628-story.html; Peter Jamison, Doug Smith, and David Zahniser,
"Eric Garcetti's Mayor's Fund Lets Companies Give Big," *Los Angeles Times,*
March 3, 2015, https://www.latimes.com/local/cityhall/la-me-0303-garcetti
-fund-20150303-story.html; "Statement: Mayor Garcetti on Deputy Chief of
Staff Taking Leave of Absence," Mayor Eric Garcetti's website, July 20, 2016,
https://www.lamayor.org/statement-mayor-garcetti-deputy-chief-staff-tak
ing-leave-absence; "Transportation," Mayor Eric Garcetti's website, accessed
September 7, 2019, https://www.lamayor.org/transportation.

30. Receipt Committee Campaign Statement, California 2001/02 Form
460, Committee Name: Yes on Measure M—a Coalition of Mayor Eric
Garcetti, concerned citizens, labor organizations, businesses and non-profits,

September 24, 2016, https://apps1.lavote.net/Camp/Schedules/4298.pdf;
Laura J. Nelson, "Campaigns Supporting Metro's Transportation Tax Bring
in More Than $4.5 Million," *Los Angeles Times*, October 6, 2016, https://
www.latimes.com/local/lanow/la-me-ln-metro-sales-tax-fundraising
-20161006-snap-story.html; Homepage, HNTB, n.d., http://www.hntb
.com/; "How to Pass a Mega Transportation Measure: LA County's Measure M Lessons Learned," Los Angeles County Metropolitan Transportation
Authority, May 24, 2018, 44, http://libraryarchives.metro.net/DPGTL
/MeasureM/20180524-how-pass-mega-transportation-measure-lacounty
-measure-m-lessons-learned.pdf; HNTB, "Optimizing Infrastructure,"
Think, Infrastructure Solutions, no. 15, 2016, p. 13, http://hntb.com/HNTB
/media/HNTBMediaLibrary/Project/RelatedContent/HNTB_THINK_
OptimizingInfrastructure.pdf.

31. Laura Bliss, "Los Angeles Passed a Historic Transit Tax. Why Isn't It
Working?," CityLab, January 17, 2019, https://www.citylab.com/trans
portation/2019/01/los-angeles-public-transportation-tax-measure-m
-metro/580609/.

32. Edward-Isaac Dovere, "Garcetti, Possible 2020 Hopeful, Launches Innovation Group," Politico, October 30, 2017, https://www.politico.com/story
/2017/10/30/garcetti-possible-2020-hopeful-launches-innovation-group
-244242.

33. Aaron Mendelson, "Garcetti's PAC Raises $120,000 in First Few Weeks,"
scpr.org, February 2, 2018, https://www.scpr.org/news/2018/02/02/80386
/garcetti-s-pac-raises-120–000-in-first-few-weeks/; Opensecrets.org, "Democratic Midterm Victory Fund: Summary," 2018, n.d., https://www.open
secrets.org/pacs/lookup2.php?cycle=2018&strID=C00660985; Opensecrets
.org, "Democratic Midterm Victory Fund: Expenditures," 2018, n.d., https://
www.opensecrets.org/pacs/expenditures.php?cycle=2018&cmte=C00660985.

34. Tasia Wells, "Oppose That Schools Tax and You'll Be Sorry? Garcetti Aide
Says That's Not What Happened," *Los Angeles Times*, April 12, 2019, https://
www.latimes.com/local/lanow/la-me-ln-garcetti-rick-jacobs-threat-accusa
tion-20190412-story.html.

35. Aaron Mendelson and Mary Plummer, " 'A Tricky Area of Philanthropy': LA
Mayor Solicits Millions for His Favored Causes," scpr.org, August 23, 2017,
https://www.scpr.org/news/2017/08/23/74917/la-mayor-garcetti-behested
-payments/.

36. Ibid.

37. Ibid.

38. Ibid.

39. Ibid.

40. Ibid.

41. "CBS2 Investigates L.A. Mayor's Campaign Donations Tied to Landscaping
Company," CBS Los Angeles, November 9, 2015, https://losangeles.cbslocal

.com/2015/11/09/only-on-2-cbs2-investigates-l-a-mayors-campaign-dona
tions-tied-to-landscaping-company/.

42. Ibid.

43. Mendelson and Plummer, " 'A Tricky Area of Philanthropy.' "

44. Ibid.

45. Ibid.

46. Ibid.

47. David Zahniser and Emily Alpert Reyes, "A $72-Million Apartment Project.
Top Politicans. Unlikely Donors," *Los Angeles Times*, October 30, 2016,
https://www.latimes.com/projects/la-me-seabreeze/.

48. Ibid.; Susan Shelley, "As the City of Angels begins to look like the City of Ca-
pone," *Los Angeles Daily News,* January 15, 2019, https://www.dailynews
.com/2019/01/15/as-the-city-of-angels-begins-to-look-like-city-of-capone/.

49. Zahniser and Reyes, "A $72-Million Apartment Project. Top Politicans. Un-
likely Donors"; "Dana Boldt," LinkedIn profile, accessed September 7, 2019,
https://www.linkedin.com/in/danagarcettiboldt.

50. Emily Alpert Reyes and David Zahniser, "L.A. Developer Pleads Not Guilty
in Campaign Money Laundering Case," *Los Angeles Times*, June 4, 2018,
https://www.latimes.com/local/lanow/la-me-ln-leung-hearing-20180604
-story.html; Alene Tchekmedyian, "Former Congressional Aide Convicted
in Shakedown of Compton Marijuana Dispensary," *Los Angeles Times*,
March 1, 2018, https://www.latimes.com/local/lanow/la-me-ln-compton
-conviction-20180301-story.html.

51. *The People of the State of California v. Samuel Leung, et al.,* case no. BA465764,
http://da.lacounty.gov/sites/default/files/press/022318_Pair_Charged
_with_Money_Laundering_Offering_Bribes_to_LA_Elected_Officials.pdf;
"Developer Arraigned on Bribery Charges Tied to Sea Breeze Resi Project,"
Real Deal, June 4, 2018, https://therealdeal.com/la/2018/06/04/developer
-arraigned-on-bribery-charges-tied-to-failed-sea-breeze-project/.

52. Matt Tinoco, "The FBI Is Shaking up LA City Hall. They May Be Looking
for Chinese Money," LAist.com, January 14, 2019, https://laist.com/2019/01
/14/fbi_city_hall_corruption_huizar.php.

53. David Zahniser and Adam Elmahrek, "Garcetti Appointee Named in FBI
Warrant Quits His Post," *Los Angeles Times*, January 18, 2019, https://www
.latimes.com/local/lanow/la-me-ln-fbi-investigation-jacinto-20190118
-story.html.

54. Richard Fausset, Monica Davey, and Tim Arango, " 'It's the Human Way':
Corruption Scandals Play Out in Big Cities Across U.S.," *New York Times*,
February 5, 2019, https://www.nytimes.com/2019/02/05/us/fbi-corruption
-investigations.html.

55. Ileana Wachtel, "Garcetti, Clean Up the Corruption," Preserve LA, February 3, 2019, https://www.2preservela.org/garcetti-clean-up-corruption/.

56. Elijah Chiland, "Ethics Commission Delays Vote on Banning Devel-

oper Contributions to LA Politicians," *Curbed*, August 21, 2018, https://
la.curbed.com/2018/8/21/17765452/developer-contributions-ban-ethics
-commission.

57. Barbara Hernandez, "Chinese Investors Buying Troubled West Coast Hotels,
Cheap," CBS News, March 29, 2010, https://www.cbsnews.com/news/chi
nese-investors-buying-troubled-west-coast-hotels-cheap/; Roger Vincent,
"Shenzhen New World Group Buys Sheraton Universal Hotel," *Los Angeles
Times*, January 6, 2011, https://www.latimes.com/archives/la-xpm-2011-jan
-06-la-fi-sheraton-20110106-story.html.

58. Tinoco, "The FBI Is Shaking up LA City Hall. They May Be Looking for
Chinese Money."

59. "Hampton Inn & Suites & Courtyard by Marriott Santa Monica," Zinner
Consultants, accessed September 8, 2019, https://www.zinnerconsultants.
com/hampton-inn-suites-courtyard-by-marriott-santa-monica; "Our
Team," Zinner Consultants, accessed September 8, 2019, https://www.zinner
consultants.com/people.

60. "Metropolis Phase 1," Zinner Consultants, accessed July 24, 2019, https://
www.zinnerconsultants.com/projects#/oceanwide-plaza.

61. "2.5 Billion Century Plaza Development to Get Underway in March 2016,"
Business Wire, December 8, 2015, https://www.businesswire.com/news
/home/20151208006767/en/2.5-Billion-Century-Plaza-Development
-Underway-March.

62. John Zinner, "Mitigation Monitoring in Process," Zinner Consultants,
July 30, 2018, https://www.zinnerconsultants.com/blog/2018/7/30/mitiga
tion-monitoring-in-process.

63. "Inn at Playa Del Rey Joins Four Sisters Inns Collection; Los Angeles Hide-
away Borders Ballona Wetlands," Hotel Business Week, March 22, 2019,
https://www.hotelbusinessweekly.com/2019/03/22/inn-at-playa-del-rey
-joins-four-sisters-inns-collection-los-angeles-hideaway-borders-ballona
-wetlands/; Fair Political Practices Commission, California Form 700, Office
of the Mayor, City of Los Angeles, April 4, 2016, http://www.disclosures
.org/wp-content/uploads/2017/08/Mayor-Eric-Garcetti-2015–1.pdf; "Ipdr
Associatges, Lp," corporationwiki, n.d., https://www.corporationwiki.com
/California/Los-Angeles/ipdr-associates-lp/45805352.aspx; Note: Garcetti's
co-ownership is based upon the shared address of the hotel and his "partnership" in a hotel as shown in his disclosure form.

64. Apartment search, Horizon Buildings, Inc., n.d., https://www.horizonbuild
ings.com/searchlisting.aspx?ftst=&txtCity=CA&txtState=CA&Location
GeoId=29&LocationChanged=true&renewpg=1&LatLng=(36.778261,
-119.41793239999998)&; "LAX Northside Plan Update," Draft EIR, May
2014, https://www.lawa.org/-/media/lawa-web/lawa-our-lax/gdz/2–0
-lax-northside-plan-update-deir-project-description.ashx?la=en&hash
=E65507378805DD18ED7236C6145D3E4520F9329B; "LAX Northside Plan

Update to Provide Blueprint for 340-Acre Vacant Property," Gateway Los Angeles, June 15, 2016, https://www.gatewayla.org/gateway-la-lax-busi ness-district-news/2017/6/26/lax-northside-plan-update-to-provide-blue print-for-340-acre-vacant-property; Hannah Miet, "Horizon Buildings Buys Santa Monica Office for $28M," Real Deal, June 6, 2016, https://the realdeal.com/la/2016/06/06/horizon-buildings-buys-santa-monica -office-for-28m/.

65. David Zanhiser, "Political Donations Flow as Rick Caruso Seeks Approval for a 20-Story Tower Near the Beverly Center," *Los Angeles Times*, November 15, 2016, https://www.latimes.com/local/lanow/la-me-ln-caruso-de veloper-donations-20161115-story.html; David Zanhiser, "Developer Rick Caruso Agrees to Shave Height of Apartment Tower," *Los Angeles Times*, July 24, 2019, https://www.latimes.com/local/lanow/la-me-ln-caruso -apartment-project-20170118-story.html.

66. Daniel Guss, "Garcetti Turns (Remains?) Wimpy on Corruption," Front Page, October 24, 2016, http://www.thefrontpageonline.com/op-ed/garcetti -turns-remains-wimpy-on-corruption.

67. Ibid.; Dakota Smith, "Union Pressured Mayor Garcetti's Office to Oust Top Fire Official, Court Records Show," *Los Angeles Times*, February 1, 2019, https://www.latimes.com/local/lanow/la-me-ln-garcetti-deposition-fire -20190201-story.html.

68. Guss, "Garcetti Turns (Remains?) Wimpy on Corruption."

69. Smith, "Union Pressured Mayor Garcetti's Office to Oust Top Fire Official, Court Records Show."

70. Dakota Smith, "L.A. City Council OKs $800,000 settlement in lawsuit over fire marshal's dismissal," *Los Angeles Times,* February 20, 2019, https://www .latimes.com/local/lanow/la-me-ln-vidovich-settlement-20190220-story .html.

71. Steve Lopez, "L.A. is still a contender—for corruption crown," *Los Angeles Times,* February 10, 2019, https://enewspaper.latimes.com/infinity/article _share.aspx?guid=d20e50d1–8f1d–460b–8f76–5e1375013df8.

72. Joel Kotkin, "Eric Garcetti for President? Really?" *Pasadena Star-News,* December 3, 2017, https://www.pasadenastarnews.com/2017/12/02/eric -garcetti-for-president-really.

73. Kahn, "Who is the Real Eric Garcetti?"

74. Ibid.

CHAPTER 10: CONCLUSION

1. Rob Nikolewski, "Milton Friedman's 7 Most Notable Quotes," Daily Signal, July 31, 2014, https://www.dailysignal.com/2014/07/31/milton-friedmans -7-notable-quotes/.

2. Letter from George Washington to Major General Robert Howe, Founders

Online, August 17, 1779, https://founders.archives.gov/documents/Washington/03–22–02–0139.

3. Chris McGreal, "Robert Caro: A Life with LBJ and the Pursuit of Power," *Guardian*, interview, June 9, 2012, https://www.theguardian.com/world/2012/jun/10/lyndon-b-johnson-robert-caro-biography.

4. Nina Godlewski, "George Orwell Quotes: Famous Sayings on Author's 115th Birthday," *Newsweek*, June 25, 2018, https://www.newsweek.com/george-orwell-quote-birthday-life-author-animal-farm-1984–993960.

INDEX